*Feminist Sociology*

# Feminist Sociology
## Life Histories of a Movement

Barbara Laslett and
Barrie Thorne, editors

R Rutgers University Press
New Brunswick, New Jersey, and London

Library of Congress Cataloging-in-Publication Data

Feminist sociology : life  histories of a movement / Barbara Laslett
    and Barrie Thorne, editors.
        p.  cm.
    Includes bibliographical references and index.
    ISBN 0-8135-2428-8 (cloth : alk. paper). — ISBN 0-8135-2429-6
(pbk. : alk. paper)
        1. Women sociologists—Biography.    2. Feminists—Biography.
    3. Feminist theory.    I. Laslett, Barbara.    II Thorne, Barrie.
    HM19.F35  1997
    301'.0823—dc21                                                              97-1778
                                                                                            CIP

British Cataloging-in-Publication information available

Manufactured in the United States of America

# Contents

*Feminist Sociology*

Barbara Laslett and Barrie Thorne

# Life Histories of a Movement: An Introduction

*Feminism helped me to begin to make some order in my theoretical thinking and to understand why sociology had been alienating and confusing to me.*

—Joan Acker

*But, I confess, there is anger. . . . My anger may be somewhat inexplicable to colleagues who, despite the best intentions, have difficulty understanding at a gut level the injuries inflicted through large and small acts of arrogance by white men as they go about their business.*

—Evelyn Nakano Glenn

*Homophobia has a hidden nature because it is a fear. Acts that stimulate that fear are interrelated. They are also, I think, disabling. I have found the repeated job rejections I have experienced to be disabling, not only externally, but internally, in terms of my self-confidence and ability to do my work.*

—Susan Krieger

This book is a collection of life stories by participants in the movement to bring feminist insights into the field of sociology. The authors reflect on personal experiences—some extending to childhood and many encompassing friendships and intimate relations, as well as schooling, work, politics, and intellectual life—that illuminate two decades of convergence between a political movement and an academic discipline. This volume is organized around life histories. In addition to the life stories of thirteen individuals, each detailing a different biographical trajectory through a shared historical moment, the book conveys the life history of a movement that generated a new area of knowledge. And the book calls attention to life histories themselves as a resource for social theory and for the sociology of knowledge.

We open with a discussion of life history as a genre that is especially useful in examining the contextual nature of social life, tracing nuanced connections between social structure and human agency, and investigating the relationship of gender to the social construction of knowledge. We then focus more specifically on the case at hand, which is anchored in the auto-biographical essays: the creation of feminist sociology as a field of inquiry.

## Life Histories as Genre

In 1959 C. Wright Mills wrote that "the sociological imagination enables us to grasp history and biography and the relations between the two within society."[1] Sociologists have long worked with narratives of individual lives, but since the early 1980s there has been renewed interest in the uses of biographies, autobiographies, and life histories in the social sciences, in-cluding among sociologists.[2] This approach resonates with feminist perspec-tives in a number of ways.

Life histories bring forth "experience" and "voice"; they link the per-sonal and the political, the private and the public. Like consciousness-raising, they can bridge from individual experience to the development of more general and codified knowledge. They can also illuminate the dual aspects of experience as event, happening, occasion, and as subjectivity and inter-pretation.[3] Life histories draw attention to the specificities of historical con-texts and the ways in which they are implicated in social action. For example, from the end of World War II onward, women's increasing presence in public life—in the labor force, in institutions of higher learning, and in the social movements of the 1960s and 1970s—provided a context of possibilities for the creation of feminist scholarship. One focus of this scholarship has been an important and neglected theme in the sociology of knowledge: the rela-tionship of gender to the social construction of knowledge. Life stories pro-vide a way to understand how this happened.

Life histories can reveal categories of meaning that have been sub-merged in the prevailing social science language of "interests." Illness, sports, marriage, politics, summer camps, relocation camps—all parts of the sto-ries told here—lose meaning when translated into a single metric. The es-says in this volume point to complex constructions of self, motivation, and meaning. They show how childhood and family relationships, personal ex-periences of inequality and identity, visions of alternative possibilities—and feelings associated with all of these dimensions—have shaped research agen-das, teaching, and the creation of new kinds of relationships in homes, in communities, and in paid labor. These narratives also reveal the retrospec-tive shaping of meanings over time not only through the inevitable effect of the present on stories of the past, but also through conscious reconsideration of past events and actions.

Life histories draw sociological attention to temporality in other ways. They articulate life course transitions as they occur in particular historical contexts, as well as contingency, contradiction, and ambivalences, as Bob Connell's experiences in both Australian and U.S. sociology exemplify. Although varying by cohort, all of the people whose essays are included in this collection grew up as sociologists within a relatively narrow historical time frame and were affected by the reigning paradigms of American-brand structural functionalism, quantitative analysis, and positivism.[4] All were influenced by their graduate training programs and by the institutional hierarchies of prestige and resources that are part of contemporary American sociology. These intellectual and institutional contexts created the terrain on which each of us was professionally socialized into the discipline of sociology. They provided the frameworks within which contemporary U.S. feminist sociology came into being.[5]

Life histories expand the narrative and discursive repertoire of sociology. Conventional sociological writings are associated with specific styles of prose;[6] they call forth and create particular forms of writing, as does the writing of autobiography. Most of the authors in this volume found writing their essays to be an illuminating experience. For Joan Acker, it was a time for articulating the importance of "getting the man out of her head." Marjorie DeVault, who deliberately created space for experimentation in one of her classrooms, experienced surprise and embarrassment when she found herself worrying, "But is it sociology?" For Barbara Laslett, there was the gradual realization that the norms of a "cool" culture that defined professionalism and into which she had been socialized masked complex emotions and inhibited the rich possibilities of the sociological imagination.

The reading, as well as writing, of autobiography deserves consideration—for example, the ways in which readers enter the personal narratives of others by reading between the lines and using empathy and identification.[7] Life histories have an open quality; they present the author's understanding of her experiences, but with enough texture and detail to support other interpretations as well. Additionally, many people find life stories pleasurable to read; the narrative, plot, and action can engage readers, whereas other kinds of texts, such as tables and path models, and other languages, such as mathematical symbols and equations, are enjoyed by a more limited audience. Reading (and writing) life stories can also include pleasures of discovery, of reading accounts that one wishes to claim as one's own, as in Desley Deacon's fascination with the life of Elsie Clews Parsons.

Writing one's own life against the stories of others can also be a pro-vocative experience. Carolyn Heilbrun tells us that writing a woman's life may require different plots than those that have been most common in male life writing.[8] The essays in this collection are not stories that foreground only individual achievement; instead they recognize and celebrate connec-tions with others—family members and friends, graduate student support networks and women's groups, political comrades and intellectual men-tors. There is a pleasure in naming names, of those who helped and those who hindered the building of individual careers and the feminist sociology that was part of them. Some of the names are surprising—for example, of people, mostly men, who have subsequently become known for their hos-tility to feminist scholarship and feminists but who were, within the life stories told here, supportive of individual women. However, proponents of feminism are there in even greater numbers.

Life histories can broaden the literary conventions of sociology by helping to construct a "blurred genre" of sociological writing, one in which personal narratives and social theory come together. But life histories also have certain limitations as a resource for sociological inquiry. Autobiographi-cal writing involves the uncertain realm of memory and the construction of narratives in the present about the past, as many of the authors included in this volume discuss. It is not simply a problem of the accuracy of memory; emotions, images, and representations are also involved. As Luisa Passerini, who has used and written extensively about the life history method, ob-serves, autobiographical narration "is not static and given once and for all, but moves and changes according to the strength of feelings as they are influenced and formed by ongoing processes."[9] Thinking about this dy-namic is important to how we understand sociological "data" of all kinds. It also raises questions about reader interpretation of life stories and the limits of author control over them. Although these issues resonate with femi-nist approaches to scholarship, they are not gendered in any simple way. Nancy Miller points out that men's autobiographical or confessional writ-ing shares many of the characteristics associated with women's life writing, especially self-portrayal through relations with others.[10] However, these simi-larities have often gone unrecognized in favor of a rhetoric of individualism or gender difference.

Mary Jo Maynes argues that autobiographical texts are shaped by lit-erary conventions and by the contexts in which they are written.[11] They reflect the purposes of their writing and the audiences for whom they are intended, which raises issues of disclosure—what life writers say and do not say. Individual writers are differentially able and willing to be self-revealing. We have written these stories not for an audience of intimates but primarily for an audience of professional peers who may or may not be friendly to our stories and to the reasons for telling them here; the stories have thus been edited in their very telling. Supporters and positive influences are readily acknowledged, detractors less so, and these considerations have certainly affected the material presented in this collection.

Several conventions for writing life stories recur in this volume. Some of the authors tell "before and after" stories; others tell stories of "becoming." Although not necessarily experienced as such, these are primarily "success stories"—tales of overcoming adversity to achieve a professional status that rarely was a taken-for-granted, or even an anticipated, outcome. Many of the essays in this collection describe parallel becomings: becoming a sociologist, becoming a feminist, becoming politically aware and active (for some before, for others through feminism), becoming friends, colleagues, lovers, partners, parents. Losses, of husbands, colleagues, friends, are also part of these stories.[12] The authors describe tensions and convergences between these events and the shaping of identities. Bob Connell reminded us that because biographical and autobiographical narratives put the actor at the center of the story, they may exaggerate the importance of human agency and underestimate the constraints of social structures. Marjorie DeVault offers another useful reminder: life histories should be read not as straightforward accounts of agency but as a genre that puts more on the table and therefore provides more food for analysis.

Although written as individual narratives, the autobiographies also refer to collective experiences, including some of the formative moments of feminist sociology in the United States as an organized effort: the convening of a women's caucus during the 1969 annual meetings of the American Sociological Association (ASA) in San Francisco, the creation of the Sex Roles Section of the ASA, and, in 1971, the founding of Sociologists for Women in Society (SWS), an independent organization dedicated to professional development of and political advocacy for women within and outside of sociology. The essays recall moments of high energy, even epiphany, when local and national networks of women academics constituted themselves as gender-conscious collectivities.[13]

These life stories by no means encompass all, or even a substantial number, of the actors, actions, and institutions that have been significant in the growth of feminist sociology since the early 1970s. Desley Deacon and Bob Connell call attention to one other site of this development, Australia, but it is certainly not the only one. Although primarily raised and trained in the United States, the authors vary to some degree along lines of class origin, race, ethnicity, nationality, gender, sexual orientation, cohort, and institution. Each of these dimensions gives a somewhat different angle on feminist sociology as an intellectual and social movement.

Finally, we believe that life stories can contribute to contemporary theoretical debates in the social sciences. Life histories of intellectuals can provide insights into the social processes through which knowledge is created, transmitted, and changed. In so doing, life histories can demonstrate intersections of social structure and human agency in ways that are more empirically rich and theoretically nuanced than other techniques more commonly used by sociologists. In making these substantive linkages, however, we also want to draw attention to the peculiarly abstract character of much sociological theory in the United States, especially since World War II. The essays to follow demonstrate that narratives can provide alternative ways of "doing social theory" and have a useful place among the practices in which sociologists are engaged.

## The Theoretical Agenda

Feminist scholars have raised new theoretical questions about gender relations as one key dimension of social organization, and they have examined the gendered nature of institutions such as the state, economies, families, schools, politics, and sexuality. Feminists have also raised innovative questions about the epistemologies and methodologies of research. How did these innovations develop? How have they changed? And how are we to understand their still uneven institutionalization?

To consider these questions theoretically, we begin from Philip Abrams's concept of "structuring," a process in which "history and society are made by constant and more or less purposeful individual action and that individual action, however purposeful, is made by history and society."[14] If, as Abrams argues, the goal of sociological explanation is to understand the "'two-sidedness' of the social world," then life histories and autobiographies can make a particular contribution by allowing us to see, within concrete historical cases, how people use available cultural, material, and political resources to shape their own lives and the social institutions within which they live.[15] Life histories provide an especially insightful route to observe social actors over time, life course time and historical time, and to theorize human agency as it intersects with social structure.

Our interest in understanding "agency" as a sociological concept has both autobiographical and intellectual roots. The life stories in this book clearly demonstrate that in building feminist sociology, the authors, along with many others, were conscious agents of social change. It was not an innovation that could have been predicted by the structures of opportunity available to us as we entered the profession of sociology. Nor was it simply the outcome of the élan or the lessons we gained from activist lives in social and political movements, including the women's movement. Much of our inspiration came from those sources, but they did not determine the outcomes. Our efforts, with all their limitations and flaws, reflected purposeful action, inspired by values of social justice and equality, infused with powerful feelings (some of which may have had little or nothing to do with social justice), and enacted through conscious activity. Our actions may have reflected motivations that were more personal than institutional, intellectual, or political—for example, the search for independence, security, acceptance, success—but these, too, were energizing.

This belief in the possibilities of shaping our worlds, and not just being shaped by them, has also posed key theoretical questions that in some ways contradict the structuralism that is central to sociological theories ranging from structural functionalism to Marxism, symbolic interactionism, and linguistic analysis. Our experiences as feminists in sociology reflected what Dorothy Smith has called "bifurcated consciousness": sociological explanations did not accord with many of our lived experiences.[16] Explanations that saw us as determined by social structure, institutions, cultures, and even personalities did not accord with what we were doing as we helped to build feminist sociology or, for that matter, lives outside the normative social order. The essays describe not only serious commitment to professional lives and careers but also struggles to create equitable personal relationships, develop noncompetitive and caring contexts for work, raise nonsexist and nonracist children, and value ties to women. Of course, we were not always successful, and at times the personal costs of these efforts were high. Nonetheless, we were agents of change in sociology, in our lives, and beyond.

The social contexts in which we had been raised and were living were both enabling and constraining. Indeed, institutional, structural, cultural, and emotional constraints made consciousness-raising and support necessary. Agency, in the sense of getting things done and changing social circumstances, sometimes took the form of conceptual and practical obsessions, even when given other names, such as planning, strategizing, organizing, sharing ideas. Life histories, we believe, help us understand agency in both concrete and theoretical ways.

Life stories, especially contemporary ones, tend to highlight the personal—for example, early relationships and childhood experiences, partnering and parenting. The feminist tenet "The personal is the political" has strengthened this tendency, challenging the normative separation of private and public life. Feminist reflections on the construction of knowledge are more likely than other accounts to attend to gender, sexuality, and emotions, as well as to political, economic, and educational contexts. And here lies a major contribution of feminism to social theory and the sociology of knowledge.

Gender is relevant to the production of knowledge because the gendered nature of social life, of families, workplaces, politics, and cultures, establishes material and symbolic bases that help shape individual behavior and identity. Gender relations affect how and why people act as they do, including why they are attracted to some forms of intellectual work more than others.[17] There is a gendered component to the structures and cultures that shape sociological knowledge.[18]

Personal life, sexual meanings, and emotions—each shaped by gendered structures of possibilities, as well as their cultural meanings—can provide powerful motives for human action. In second-wave U.S. feminism, the technique of consciousness-raising generated insights into the importance of personal life for understanding social action. And as these essays make clear, the explicit integration of personal with intellectual and professional concern has been central to the ideology and practices of feminist sociology. This is evident, for example, in Evelyn Nakano Glenn's discussion of the Women and Work group; in the principles of collaboration that inform the University of Memphis Center for Research on Women as described by Lynn Weber, Elizabeth Higginbotham, and Bonnie Thornton Dill; and in networks of support in graduate school or early careers—for instance, the sharing of lecture materials that Barrie Thorne discusses and the Red Wednesday meetings for food, gossip, and intellectual critique in which Barbara Laslett participated.[19]

There is another way in which gender has entered into the construction of sociological knowledge: through the attachment of gendered meanings to institutional cultures and to the emotional dimensions of professional life and relationships. Laslett's biographical research on William Fielding Ogburn, a prominent American sociologist earlier in the twentieth century, reveals his preference for a "cool" professional environment, his belief that science is antithetical to emotion, and his wish to control emotions as a means to achieving "scientific" objectivity.[20] Professional cultures such as Ogburn and others espoused do not, however, emerge accidentally, nor do they follow from an inner logic of institutional forms or intellectual interests. They are fostered through conscious and unconscious action. And the

contestation of this professional culture by feminist sociologists in the contemporary period has been purposeful. The life stories in this volume document an important moment of change in the history of American sociology.
They mark "decisive conjunctions of action and structure; . . . moments of
structuring at which human agency encounters social possibility and can
be seen most clearly as simultaneously determined and determining."[21]

Emotions, of course, take many forms—anger and love, passion and
passivity, jealousy and concern. They vary over time and situation, are contradictory, and can often derail our best efforts to change the hierarchy of
sociological practices and the ideas we have inherited. But the life stories in
this volume show that emotions are more than internal psychological states.
As all the authors in this collection make clear, emotions are social phenomena shaped by the inequalities, cultures, and institutions (including
families) in which we live our lives. Emotions are also implicated in social
action. They are a source of energy, a reason for resistance and for cooperation, and a subject for sociological analysis.

Gender relations—relations to mothers and fathers, husbands and
lovers, sons and daughters, "sisters" and "brothers," and to mentors, colleagues, and friends as gendered beings—are complex, varied and changing. They often involve inequalities of power and resources, competition
and contestation, as well as companionship, comfort, and desire. Gender
relations, historically variable and constructed through interaction and
through culture, are also central to personal identity. Sexuality, as identity
and as desire, and the contexts within which sexual feelings emerge (often,
in these stories, in liberatory political situations) need to be included in
theoretical accounts of human agency and social action. Contemporary feminist theorizing of the fluid and constructed dimensions of sexuality is especially useful for this work.[22] And again, power is central to this process; as
Susan Krieger so movingly recounts, there is a cost in saying "no" to a man.

Emotions, sexuality, and gender relations need to be considered, then,
as we examine the development of feminist sociology. Life stories can, we
believe, help in this process; essays like those in this volume provide access
to the personal and gendered dimensions of our professional history in ways
less easily seen using other research strategies. Examining the relationship
of gender to the recent history of American sociology through the prism of
life histories also reveals the complexities of the structuring process.

The authors of these essays do not all agree on which dimensions of
their individual social positions, personalities, or values and beliefs—gender,
race, ethnicity, class background, sexuality, political commitments and professional socialization, psychological security and insecurities, alienation or

fears—are relevant to their participation in the building of contemporary feminist sociology. Such variation is, in fact, one of the contributions that individual life stories can make to the sociology of knowledge. With minimal instructions (we asked contributors to consider the development of feminist sociology through their own autobiographies, with attention to the theoretical underpinnings of their narratives), the authors went about constructing personal meanings out of social experiences in somewhat different ways. All of the authors consider individual, institutional, and historical dimensions of their involvement with feminist sociology, but some focus more than others on the subjective dimensions of their experiences. Each essay reveals working theories of the intersection of life histories with social action and institutional forms. By tracing connections among personal meanings, institutional locations, political opportunities, and possibilities for organization, we can see numerous pathways from personal location to social action and institutional change.[23]

## Contemporary U.S. Feminist Sociology: A Brief History

All of the life stories included in this collection intersect with the emergence of the women's liberation movement in the United States and Australia in the late 1960s and early 1970s. At that time, issues of gender were relatively invisible in sociological knowledge. When survey researchers and demographers were attentive at all, they used gender as an untheorized variable, and there was some attention to women's lives and experiences in the study of family and communities, arenas ideologically defined as "women's place." Structural functionalism, which was gradually losing theoretical hegemony in U.S. sociology, continued to be well entrenched in the study of families. Talcott Parsons theorized gender, but under the rubric of male and female "sex roles," a static and complementary notion that reified 1950s family ideology by assuming it was "dysfunctional" for marriage, family, and society for women to enter public life.[24] The sociological literature on work, organizations, stratification, social psychology, deviance and criminology, education, religion, research methodology, and theory included issues of gender and women's distinctive experiences, at best, as a footnote. The steady entry of women into graduate programs in the context of the second-wave feminist movement began to change that pattern.[25]

In the early 1970s feminists began to build networks across disciplines, often in women's studies programs, which sociologists helped create on many college and university campuses. An array of activist groups—some locally based, others more national, some focused within and others outside of academic disciplines—set out to enhance the presence of women in higher education. One goal was to alter the composition of college and university faculties by challenging patterns of discrimination and pressing for affirmative action. Women's caucuses and committees on the status of women sprang up throughout the social sciences and humanities; the essays here provide numerous examples of this process.

This demographic shift created a critical mass of women sociologists, many of whose lives and outlooks were shaped by the civil rights, student, and anti–Vietnam War movements and by the women's liberation movement as it emerged in that activist milieu. Lively feminist communities coalesced among mostly younger women, many of them students in cities such as Berkeley, East Lansing, Chicago, Gainesville, New York, Minneapolis, and Cambridge. Several of the authors describe early convergence between ` feminist activism and academic sociology in various local contexts, such as Eugene, Oregon (Acker); Boston-Cambridge, Massachusetts (Glenn, Thorne); Evanston-Chicago, Illinois (Sarah Fenstermaker), and Los Angeles (Laslett). They describe a new gender consciousness that began to develop out of structural contradictions that weighed on women who were educated much like men of their stratum but were expected to divert their energies to becoming wives and mothers and, at best, marginally employed professionals.[26]

Feminist groups and networks altered the contours of colleagueship for many women academics. SWS and the ASA Section on Sex Roles (in 1976 the name was changed to the Sex and Gender Section) altered the professional culture of sociology for many women who attended the national meetings, giving those who had felt isolated a sense of expanded presence and support.[27] In the early 1970s women predominated as presenters and audience in sessions organized by the Sex Roles Section at the ASA meetings. SWS set up a hospitality room and a parallel program with panels on subjects such as "how to write a dissertation" or "mentoring junior faculty," as well as substantive sessions of interest to sociologists of gender. These new networks of self-conscious colleagueship and support, which brought the ideas and activist energy of the women's movement into higher education, provided social contexts in which knowledge was produced and shared.

The ideas of the early years of the second wave of the women's movement—a critique of the "feminine mystique" embedded in 1950s gender ideology, an understanding of women as an oppressed "class" analogous to the proletariat in Marxism,[28] a revaluing of women and their experiences condensed in such slogans as "The personal is political"—at first consolidated in small consciousness-raising groups and umbrella organizations such as the Chicago Women's Liberation Union (described by Fenstermaker) and Bread and Roses in Boston (described by Thorne). The ideas spread through women's networks, the popular media, books, pamphlets, demonstrations, conferences, and other publicized events.[29] The movement raised questions about women's subordination in politics, work, religion, sexuality, and personal and family relationships. Sociologists had studied all of these institutional arenas, but they had rarely focused on gender relations and women's oppression. The question "Where are the women?" animated fresh lines of inquiry across the social sciences and humanities.

The feminist sociological literature of the early 1970s reflects these concerns. It includes critiques of the androcentrism of the field, calls for the development of a sociology that would value and accord more closely with women's lives and experiences, and empirical studies that picked up that call, for example, in the study of work and organizations, families, and mothering.[30] However, the movement to develop a sociology for women set out to do much more than add new topics of study. It also set out to critique the foundations of mainstream sociological knowledge itself, to recognize that power relations in the academy have conceptual, as well as material, consequences, as Dorothy Smith has made clear.[31] Feminists argued that sociological knowledge is deeply androcentric, as in notions of social class that define women only with reference to fathers or husbands (in her essay, Acker describes the development of this critique) and frameworks that use gender to explain women's patterns of work but not those of men (which Glenn discusses).

Another challenge to conventional sociology was spurred by analyses that focused on, as Sandra Harding phrases it, "the science question in feminism."[32] Feminist theorists, many from outside of sociology, criticized positivist epistemologies for neglecting the experiences of women and the relevance of social contexts, including gender, for processes of knowing. These critiques appealed to feminist sociologists who were dissatisfied with the hegemony of positivist epistemology and quantitative methods within the discipline; many feminists found these approaches inadequate or inappropriate for answering the questions that interested them. Feminist writings on epistemology, some blending into postmodern perspectives, continue to reverberate through the disciplines.[33]

The essays by Glenn and by Weber, Higginbotham, and Dill detail a critique that became influential in the 1980s as African-American, Latina, Asian-American, and lesbian feminists asked, "*Which* women's experiences?" They recognized the problematic nature of "woman" as a category, and they

provided insight into complex relationships among gender, social class, race/
ethnicity, and sexuality.[34] In a movement that linked the political and the
intellectual, and that bridged to activism around issues of race, ethnicity,
and sexuality, scholars within and outside of sociology laid out the ambitious goals of transforming the conceptual foundations of knowledge.[35]
Many of the essays in this volume discuss the development of that vision.

### The Process of Institutionalization

It is now over two decades since the women's liberation movement began
mobilizing in U.S. universities and within and across academic disciplines.
What have been the results in the field of sociology? By some measures, the
movement has been extremely successful, both spurred by and contributing to the increasing number of women sociologists. In 1970 women received 18 percent of Ph.D.s awarded in sociology in the United States. Over
the ensuing decades the proportion of women receiving sociology Ph.D.s
steadily increased, to a high of 53 percent in 1988; since then, there has
been some decline, to 47 percent in 1993.[36] In 1988, 69 percent of sociology bachelor's degrees were awarded to women.[37] The representation of
women in tenure-line faculty positions has increased, although less dra-
matically. In 1991 women made up 29 percent of all tenured and
tenure-track sociology faculty in the United States (46 percent were assistant professors; 30 percent associate professors; and 20 percent, full professors). Women continue to be underrepresented in more secure, well-paid,
and prestigious positions.[38] Unprecedented numbers of women now hold
offices in sociological societies, occasionally, if still rarely, achieving the highest positions.

In fact, there are many more women sociologists than ever before,
and Sex and Gender is now the largest research section in the ASA. In 1995
the Sex and Gender Section had 87 percent women members and a larger
proportion of graduate students than any other section. In contrast, revealing some occupational segregation by subfield, 28 percent of the members
of the ASA Theory Section were women.[39] Some sociologists believe that
the field is feminizing, and, knowing the iron law of patriarchy, they fear
that as the proportion of women increases, an occupation's prestige and
pay decline.[40] Others, who feel threatened by changes in professional culture and new sources of competition, also view this trend with alarm. There
is some indication of backlash in the discipline of sociology, especially against
women organizing as women and as self-proclaimed feminists.

What about the goal of transforming sociological knowledge? Two
decades of mobilization have turned the sociology of gender into a large

and flourishing specialty with the trappings of disciplinary legitimacy: listing in directories and job postings, the topic of Ph.D.-qualifying exams and specialized journals, structures of evaluation and rewards, and a network of scholars with "national reputations" in the sociology of gender who are called on for peer review. As Weber, Higginbotham, and Dill discuss, there has been substantial progress in transforming curricula to include issues of race, class, and gender. Indeed, the University of Memphis Center for Research on Women is a major story of institutional success. As several of the authors in this collection observe with a kind of surprised recognition, feminist sociology has become institutionalized, and some of its practitioners are now in positions of prestige and power in their universities and professional associations, as journal editors, and on committees that review grant proposals.

But has all of this effort gone any further than the effort that went into building other specialties, such as medical sociology or criminology? Has feminist sociology, with its political critique, become just another specialization in the ongoing division of labor of a large and fragmented discipline? What about the 1970s claims that starting with women's experiences and gender as a category of analysis would transform the orienting frameworks of the entire discipline, altering conceptions of institutions, organizations, the social, the self, social class, work, culture, families, and even methodologies of inquiry? Have these claims been realized?

In 1985 Judith Stacey and Thorne expressed disappointment that such a "feminist revolution" of sociological knowledge had in many ways been coopted and contained—for example, by functionalist conceptions of gender and by the use of gender only as a variable rather than a conceptually complex category of analysis.[41] This disappointment partly came from high expectations; compared with other social sciences (with the notable exception of anthropology), sociology seemed especially ripe for feminist transformation. The discipline's subject matter covers the whole of social life rather than one institutional domain, as does political science or economics. Sociology's fragmentation into many subfields and competing paradigms, compared with disciplines such as economics in which one paradigm is hegemonic, opens space for new ideas and knowledge-creating networks to take hold.

A decade after this lament over "the missing feminist revolution in sociology," there has been significant progress in challenging and reworking sociological frameworks. For example, feminist critiques of the gendered division between "public" and "private" social spheres have reconstructed basic paradigms in the study of families, sexuality, work, organizations, and the state.[42] Because of the equation of women with the "private" and with gender itself (as members of the unmarked category, men claimed both individual and generic status), it took longer to theorize the gendered nature of public institutions such as the state and organizations.[43] But this is well under way, along with theorizing of intersections of gender, class, race, sexuality, and age; attention to the historical, social, and discursive dynamics of gender relations; and a reexamination of men and masculinities.[44]

These transformative insights appear unevenly in the research and teaching of sociologists not directly engaged with feminist work. Many sociologists either ignore or regard feminist ideas with suspicion; many continue to treat gender, at best, as a variable or as just another specialized topic of study and therefore not one to which they need to be attentive. As Smith has recently written, "The curricula of sociology departments preserve the problematics of the past like DNA of flies preserved in amber."[45] This is especially true for courses, textbooks, and specialized journals in sociological theory. The theory canon (Durkheim, Weber, and Marx), which is often used to symbolically evoke coherence in a fragmented discipline, embeds "problematics of the past." Joan Alway has documented and analyzed the indifference and resistance of sociological theorists to feminist theory.[46] Alway traces this resistance not only to feminism's political origins and suspect source of authority (women's experiences), but also to feminists' questioning of dichotomies, such as public and private, nature and culture, that define the boundaries and identity of the field of sociology.

Feminism emerged from outside of the academy, and its originating purpose—to understand and end women's subordination—cuts across disciplines. In Stacey's essay in this collection, she argues that the most significant feminist breakthroughs in knowledge may take place in the "borderlands" between disciplines, with the potential, along with related critical movements, to transform the very mapping of knowledge.[47] The organization of sociology assumes the very divisions, such as between families and the state, that feminists have helped critique. Disciplines are not only intellectual communities; they also regulate their members and defend existing interests, using "boundary work" to sustain their differentiation.[48] Feminist sociologists encounter moments of boundary work when sociology colleagues tell them that their work is "not sociology."

Feminist sociologists often have strong personal and collegial ties to scholars and literatures outside the field; they teach in women's studies programs, and they read and publish in interdisciplinary journals. All of this has given them perspective on the conventions of the discipline; but as these essays make clear, interdisciplinarity is also a source of difficulty, especially for feminists seeking tenure in sociology departments. The authors vary in their degree of attachment to and alienation from conventional sociology;[49] some have found interdisciplinary women's studies programs to be a more congenial academic location.

*Convergences and Tensions Between the Women's Movement*
*and the Discipline and Profession of Sociology*
Sociological knowledge is sometimes depicted as freestanding and pristine, the product of objective and cumulative scientific inquiry. But the content and shifting contours of knowledge, including what comes to be "counted" as sociology, are influenced by the social and historical contexts within which knowledge is produced and disseminated. New schools of thought enter disciplines, and disciplines themselves become constituted and reconfigured through processes of mobilization and persuasion. Collective bids to alter disciplinary knowledge and practices have taken varied forms. For example, medical sociology and the new, more specialized ASA Section on Drugs and Alcohol emerged as specialties in part because of the opening of jobs for sociologists in medical schools and applied settings and the availability of funding for research on the social dimensions of health.

Other areas of sociological inquiry have been catalyzed by political movements, going back to social reformers, some of them feminists, in the early part of this century.[50] The civil rights, student, anti–Vietnam War, women's liberation, and gay and lesbian movements that emerged in the 1960s and 1970s left a strong imprint on knowledge and on patterns of specialization and conflict within U.S. sociology. Critical perspectives linked to questions of justice and emancipation spread from movements into universities, and new scholarly networks emerged. Several ASA sections—Marxist Sociology, Race and Ethnic Relations, and Sex and Gender—have overt political origins and commitments. Long-standing debates about whether value-free knowledge is possible or desirable and about whether taking an overt political stance contaminates or enriches the creation of knowledge have surrounded the struggles of feminist sociologists for resources and legitimation. Through what processes have feminist sociologists developed new knowledge, claimed authority, and sought to make their knowledge count within the discipline and profession? Like other groups with such aspirations, feminists mobilized networks, in this case drawing on the anger, elation, and bonding unleashed by the women's movement, consciousness-raising, and political commitments to social justice.

The authors describe their attraction to sociology as a mode of understanding: Fenstermaker initially was drawn to the investigative mode, Laslett to structural approaches to social inequality, Acker to Marxist frameworks and their concerns with justice. The authors also describe feelings of estrangement and alienation from a field that excluded them from full participation. The essays reveal the patriarchal and racist layering of academic institutions—for example, admissions and hiring practices that favored white men and were especially dismissive of married women with children and that expected patterns of deference. Smith has theorized this process, drawing on her experiences in an early consciousness-raising group when she was a sociology graduate student in Berkeley.[51] She describes the bifurcated consciousness of women who encountered sociological knowledge that did not fit their experiences as women. By trusting and sharing their experiences, for example, of housework and mothering, they could explore fault lines in conventional knowledge (which serves the interests of ruling) and create an oppositional sociology "for women."

These essays show this process at work in the emergence, sense of collective agency, knowledge claims, and rhetoric of feminist sociology. The authors describe the process of attending to and revaluing their own and other women's experiences as they helped open up topics such as housework (Fenstermaker), caring work (DeVault), paid domestic labor (Glenn), and relations of gender, race, and class (Glenn; Weber, Higginbotham, Dill). They also detail the rethinking of mainstream sociological topics such as work and organizations (Acker, Glenn), families (Laslett, Stacey, Thorne), and persistent taboos against fully exploring the more public implications of sexuality (Krieger, Deacon).

The autobiographies reveal mixed patterns of opportunity, constraint, and possibility. The sheer number of women who are undergraduate and graduate students, readers, and book buyers, and the practical demand for knowledge about rape, sexual harassment, wage gaps, and the feminization of poverty, among other subjects, have opened opportunities for feminist sociologists. The essays point to other resources that have enhanced some women sociologist's opportunities (and sometimes confronted them with double binds)—for example, prodding from the state in the form of affirmative action regulations, heterosexual and daughterlike ties to powerful men, class privileges and elite educations that muted gender disadvantage. The essays also describe experiences of disenchantment when utopian notions of sisterhood came up against the realities of competition, hierarchy, and unacknowledged practices of exclusion among women and when female solidarity felt at odds with other loyalties and interests (Acker).

Finally, the essays raise questions about the price of conventional success. Feminist sociologists who came out of the more radical wings of the movement articulated a vision of democratized teaching and learning that would replace "power over" with "empowerment" and develop knowledge that is socially, politically, and emotionally engaged. But, as Connell describes, the forces of disciplinary and institutional structures are strong, propelled by individual and collective desires for recognition and resources. Thriving in the conventional ways of the discipline—measured by numbers of practitioners, student enrollments, job openings, tenurings, outlets for publication, presence in positions of power and prestige—also means that feminist sociology has developed its own systems of ranking and control and even a canon of knowledge. The authors discuss the process of institutionalization with a mix of pride, irony, and criticism; they are concerned by the increasing detachment of academic feminism from political practice.[52] They also observe that the bureaucratization and absorption of feminism into the hierarchical structures of universities and the profession are far from complete. Life histories can make these emotional and political complexities visible and available for discussion without the polarizing effects of more polemical statements.[53]

Many feminist sociologists have sustained a commitment to political activism and collective modes of work. They describe themselves as "outsiders within" (Weber, Higginbotham, and Dill) and "marginal insiders" (DeVault) and as experiencing tensions between the heated-up mode of movement activism and the more detached mode of the academic profession (Thorne). Connell reflects upon the contradictory position of men who have feminist politics and intellectual commitments. Glenn and Weber, Higginbotham, and Dill describe practices of feminist, as well as more mainstream, sociologists that excluded women of color, and Krieger describes overt and subtle structures of heterosexual privilege in the shaping of careers. Critical perspectives of this kind have challenged the 1970s emphasis on commonality among women and led to efforts to understand differences. They have also been accompanied by forms of political action that take account of multiple differences and complex structures of power. These intersections have yet to be fully theorized, a challenge that partly involves constructing alternatives to the statistical model of causation so common in contemporary American sociological analysis. Narrative forms, including personal narratives, may provide one avenue for building such alternatives.

## Conclusion

The life stories that follow describe historical conditions that contributed to the rise of a feminist sociology in the United States at the beginning of the 1970s. And as reflections by participants who helped create this new area of knowledge, these essays offer insight into individual and collective agency working within and reshaping those conditions. This introduction has called attention to the theoretical contributions of autobiographical writing to the sociology of knowledge and to social theory, including the contributions of feminism to the crafting and use of life histories as a genre. We have also argued that personal narratives can illuminate relationships between social structure and human agency, between social circumstances and the changing construction of knowledge. Feminist sociology, the case of knowledge change that we have set out to understand, has provided useful new tools for understanding its own history and dynamics. By making gender a central category of analysis and exploring connections between the "personal" (e.g., sexuality and emotions) and the "public" (e.g., political and material resources and cultural capital), feminists have enriched sociologists' usual, more limited focus on economic, political, and cultural dimensions of knowledge creation.

In view of these contributions, why has feminist work remained a voluntary, rather than an integral, part of contemporary sociological theory? Why have theorists interested in the sociology of knowledge kept their distance from feminist sociology? As discussed earlier, there are structural and organizational answers to this question. In addition, because feminist scholarship is interdisciplinary and often entails questioning the ruling intellectual paradigms within the discipline, it has the potential to threaten established boundaries around and relations of dominance and deference within sociology. But if our analysis of the rise of contemporary feminist sociology has more general implications, it suggests that social structure provides a necessary but not sufficient explanation for the uneven integration of academic feminism in the field, particularly among sociological theorists.

New intellectual movements, especially successful ones, do not go uncontested. They touch on and can threaten the interests, identities, and self-regard of those who work and take comfort from existing intellectual paradigms and professional norms and practices. These movements threaten relations of dominance and subordination within which both social and intellectual interests are defined. Especially when there are fewer resources to go around, respectful appreciation of alternatives seems at a minimum.[54]

The boundary work by which sociology has established its identity and legitimacy in the past comes once more into play. But boundary work does not happen automatically; it requires human agency. Our analysis and those in the life histories that follow suggest some of the dynamics involved in this process. Both the emergence of a feminist sociology and the resistance to it reflect encounters between social possibilities and human agency.

There are several truths to be gathered from the materials presented in this collection. We believe that women's capacities for self-organization in higher education go a considerable way toward explaining how and when feminist sociology emerged in the United States. But the actions that developed from and with these organizational resources have not eliminated the still existing and *gendered* distribution of power within institutions of higher learning. Just as feminist self-organization led to the development and spread of feminist scholarship in sociology, so, too, those who feel threatened—socially and perhaps personally—by that development are still in organizationally powerful positions to undermine and/or halt the gains that have been made.

But why, we might ask, would that occur? Why, rather than join, do those in dominant positions resist?[55] Here, too, we think lessons for the sociology of knowledge can be learned from the life stories included in this collection. The emergence of feminist sociology in the United States can be explained, at least in part, by changes in the organization, power, and meanings of gender relations, particularly women's increasing economic and cultural resources for resisting patriarchal authority throughout this century. The emotions and energies associated with those changes and—of particular importance in relation to the feminist movement—the challenges to heterosexuality associated with women's increasing capacity (and desire) "to say no to a man" are involved. In addition, we suggest that the incomplete institutionalization of these changes can help explain why feminist theory and sociological theory continue to travel along different intellectual and organizational trajectories. Women's presence and power in the academy have, without doubt, increased since 1970 but are not yet on a par with those of the mostly white, mostly middle-class men who established the norms, practices, and paradigms within institutions of higher learning.

Yet as the life stories presented here also suggest, power alone—its presence or absence or its institutional successes and failures—cannot account for the emergence of and resistance to the intellectual approach of which feminist sociology is one manifestation. Emotions, gender relations, and sexuality are also involved in the acceptance of or resistance to feminist sociology and feminist theory. The historical possibilities for women opened by economic changes and political events intersected with the energies, emotions, and analyses that the women's movement and consciousness-raising provided in the late 1960s and early 1970s in the United States. Out of this intersection and the lessons learned from earlier social movements—especially the civil rights and antiwar movements—the second-wave feminist movement in the United States grew. New ideas, lessened power differentials in gender relations and divisions of labor, and changes in understandings of masculinities, femininities, and sexualities were all part of the historical conditions that energized women's self-organization in second-wave feminism and in sociology.[56]

Social theory and the sociology of knowledge are, like other subjects of intellectual inquiry, the outcomes of particular historical circumstances and organizational forms, as well as individual and collective actions. Power, resources for organization, identity, *and feelings about them* are key dimensions of the intellectual and social processes from which new forms of scholarship emerge, sometimes succeed, and sometimes fail. This is not an intellectual process alone. It is a social one. And as this analysis of feminist sociology suggests, gender relations, emotion, and sexuality are part of these social processes. They join access to individual and collective power and organizational, material, and symbolic resources as analytically important elements of the intersections of social structure and human agency from which new intellectual movements emerge. Feminist sociology is a reality within contemporary scholarly discourse in the United States, and it is also a case from which we have much to learn about the sociology of knowledge and social theory.

## Notes

We wish to acknowledge, with thanks, the original encouragement and involvement of Charles Lemert in the work that resulted in this volume. Martha Heller, Marjorie DeVault, and Sarah Fenstermaker offered helpful comments on an earlier draft of this essay. Although unable to submit essays for this volume, Dorothy Smith and Arlene Daniels have inspired and supported many of the people whose essays are included.

1. C. Wright Mills, *The Sociological Imagination* (New York: Oxford University Press, 1959), p. 241.
2. For historical examples, see John Dollard, *Criteria for the Life History, with Analysis of Six Notable Documents* (New York: Peter Smith, 1949); and W. I. Thomas and Florian Znaniecki, *The Polish Peasant in Europe and America* (New York: Knopf, 1927). For recent examples, see Charles C. Lemert, "Whole Life Social Theory," *Theory and Society* 15 (1986): 431–442, Norman K. Denzin, *Interpretive Biography* (Newbury

Park, Calif., Sage, 1989); "Biography and Autobiography in Sociology," special issue of *Sociology: The Journal of the British Sociological Association* 27, no. 1 (1995); Barbara Laslett, "Unfeeling Knowledge: Emotion and Objectivity in the History of Sociology," *Sociological Forum* 5 (1990): 413–433; Barbara Laslett, "Biography as Historical Sociology: The Case of William Fielding Ogburn," *Theory and Society* 20 (1991): 511–538; Daniel Bertaux, ed., *Biography and Society* (Beverly Hills, Calif.: Sage, 1981); Daniel Bertaux and Martin Kohli, "The Life Story Approach: A Continental View," *Annual Review of Sociology* 10 (1984): 215–237; Bennett M. Berger, ed., *Authors of Their Own Lives: Intellectual Autobiographies by Twenty American Sociologists* (Berkeley and Los Angeles: University of California Press, 1990); Ann Goetting and Sarah Fenstermaker, eds., *Individual Voices, Collective Visions: Fifty Years of Women in Sociology* (Philadelphia: Temple University Press, 1995); Judith Long, *Telling Women's Lives: Subject/Narrator/Reader/Text* (forthcoming); Kathryn P. Meadow Orlans and Ruth A. Wallace, eds., *Gender and the Academic Experience: Berkeley Women Sociologists* (Lincoln: University of Nebraska Press, 1994); Personal Narratives Group, ed., *Interpreting Women's Lives: Feminist Theory and Personal Narratives* (Bloomington: Indiana University Press, 1989); Mary Jo Maynes, *Taking the Hard Road: Life Course in French and German Workers' Autobiographies in the Era of Industrialization* (Chapel Hill: University of North Carolina Press, 1995); John H. Stanfield II, ed., *A History of Race Relations Research: First-Generation Recollections* (Newbury Park, Calif.: Sage, 1993); and Luisa Passerini, *Autobiography of a Generation: Italy, 1968* (Hanover, N.H.: Wesleyan University Press/University Press of New England, 1996). For a review essay on some recent autobiographical works, see Robert Zussman, "Autobiographical Occasions," *Contemporary Sociology* 25 (1996): 143–148.

3. For debates among feminists about "experience" as a category of analysis, see Dorothy E. Smith, *The Everyday World as Problematic: A Feminist Sociology* (Boston: Northeastern University Press, 1987); Joan W. Scott, "Experience," in Judith Butler and Joan W. Scott, eds. *Feminists Theorize the Political* (New York: Routledge), pp. 22–40; and Judith Grant, *Fundamental Feminism: Contesting the Core Concepts of Feminist Theory* (New York: Routledge, 1993).

4. For a historical account of the development of scientism, objectification, and quantification in American sociology at the end of the nineteenth and early twentieth centuries, see Robert Bannister, *Sociology and Scientism: The American Quest for Objectivity* (Chapel Hill: University of North Carolina Press, 1987); and Laslett, "Unfeeling Knowledge."

5. Our focus on the United States, plus essays by two Australians, sets aside an array of fascinating cross-country comparisons of feminist sociology and feminism. We offer here a few brief comparative ideas, enriched by suggestions from Bob Connell. In the early 1970s in the United States, feminists encountered Parsonian "sex roles" as a reigning sociological paradigm, but in Britain and France, Marxism and structuralist psychoanalysis were more influential intellectual frameworks and had a strong initial shaping influence on feminist work in sociology. The U.S. women's movement moved to issues of racism and the problematic of diversity more quickly than did feminisms in Europe. Academic sociology is much larger and more institutionalized in the United States compared with Australia or Canada, which meant larger aggregate resources for U.S. feminists but a longer struggle to establish a major presence in the discipline. Finally, the dominant position of the United States in

global intellectual networks, for example, and the fact that sociologists in many other countries read and seek to publish in U.S. journals but not vice versa have made U.S. feminist sociology more inward turning than elsewhere.

6. See Albert Hunter, ed., *The Rhetoric of Social Research Understood and Believed* (New Brunswick, N.J.: Rutgers University Press, 1990), esp. Kai Erikson, "On Sociological Prose," pp. 23–34; Joseph R. Gusfield, "Two Genres of Sociology: A Literary Analysis of *The American Occupational Structure* and *Tally's Corner*," pp. 62–96; and Marjorie L. DeVault, "Women Write Sociology: Rhetorical Strategies," pp. 97–110.

7. For a relevant examination of reading, see Minrose Gwinn, "Space Travels: The Connective Politics of Feminist Reading," *Signs* 21 (1996): 870–905. See also Ann Goetting, "Fictions of the Self," in Goetting and Fenstermaker, eds., *Individual Voices. Collective Visions*, pp. 3–10.

8. Carolyn G. Heilbrun, *Writing a Woman's Life* (New York: Ballantine Books, 1988).

9. Luisa Passerini, "Women's Personal Narratives: Myths, Experiences, and Emotions," in *Personal Narratives Group*, ed., *Interpreting Women's Lives*, p. 196; Luisa Passerini, "A Memory for Women's History: Problems of Method and Interpretation," *Social Science History* 16 (1992): 669–692. See also Mary Jo Maynes, "Autobiography and Class Formation in Nineteenth-century Europe: Methodological Considerations," *Social Science History* 16 (1992): 517–537; and Gayle Greene, "Feminist Fiction and the Uses of Memory," *Signs* 16 (1991): 290–321.

10. Nancy K. Miller, "Representing Others: Gender and the Subjects of Autobiography," *Differences* 6 (1994): 1–27.

11. Maynes, *Taking the Hard Road.*

12. Indeed, tales of loss are likely to be underrepresented because they are too painful to document and to make public.

13. For additional information on and experiences of this history, see Orlans and Wallace, eds., *Gender and the Academic Experience;* Goetting and Fenstermaker, eds., *Individual Voices; Collective Visions*; Martin Oppenheimer, Martin J. Murray, and Rhonda F. Levine, eds., *Radical Sociologists and the Movement: Experiences, Lessons, and Legacies* (Philadelphia: Temple University Press, 1991); and Alice S. Rossi and Ann Calderwood, eds., *Academic Women on the Move* (New York: Russell Sage Foundation, 1973).

14. Philip Abrams, *Historical Sociology* (Ithaca, N.Y.: Cornell University Press, 1981), p. xiii. Abrams, of course, has not been alone in discussing these issues; other theorists have done so in important ways. See, for instance, Giddens' concept of structuration in Anthony Giddens, *Central Problems in Social Theory: Action, Structure, and Contradiction in Social Analysis* (Berkeley and Los Angeles: University of California Press, 1979); and Anthony Giddens, *The Constitution of Society: Outline of the Theory of Structuration* (Berkeley and Los Angeles: University of California Press, 1984). See also Bourdieu's concept of social reproduction in Pierre Bourdieu, *Outline of a Theory of Practice* (Cambridge: Cambridge University Press, 1977). We identify Abrams in particular because he was the original influence on Laslett's formulation of these problems. See Laslett, "Biography as Historical Sociology."

15. Abrams, *Historical Sociology*, p. 2.

16. Smith, *The Everyday World as Problematic.*

17. As the autobiographical essays included in this collection make clear, these choices

are not unconstrained. They reflect the opportunities available and those withheld, as well as reigning intellectual paradigms.

18. See Barbara Laslett, "Gender in/and Social Science History," *Social Science History* 16 (1992): 177–195, for further elaboration of this argument.

19. The absence of such networks, as described by Acker, is also relevant to the making of intellectual choices. In these cases, occasional male professors or colleagues provided some support and intellectual validation. Many others didn't.

20. Laslett, "Biography as Historical Sociology."

21. Abrams, *Historical Sociology*, p. 199; see also chapter 7.

22. Many feminist theorists have addressed these issues. See, for instance, Judith Butler, *Gender Trouble: Feminism and the Subversion of Identity* (New York: Routledge, 1990); and Judith Butler, *Bodies That Matter: On the Discursive Limits of "Sex"* (New York: Routledge, 1993).

23. See Nancy J. Chodorow, "Gender as a Personal and Cultural Construction," *Signs* 20 (1995): 516–544.

24. Talcott Parsons, "The Social Structure of the Family," in Ruth Anshen, ed., *The Family: Its Function and Destiny* (New York: Harper and Row, 1959). For an overview of feminist critiques of the functionalist view of the family, see Barrie Thorne, "Feminist Rethinking of the Family: An Overview," in Barrie Thorne, with Marilyn Yalom, eds., *Rethinking the Family: Some Feminist Questions* (New York: Longman, 1982), pp. 1–24.

25. In 1970, 18 percent of new Ph.D.s in sociology were awarded to women; by 1980 the figure was 38 percent; Data are from Patricia A. Roos, "Occupational Feminization, Occupational Decline? Sociology's Changing Sex Composition," *American Sociologist* (forthcoming).

26. Wini Breines, *Young, White, and Miserable: Growing up Female in the Fifties* (Boston: Beacon, 1992); Grant, *Fundamental Feminism*.

27. A detailed description of these changes can be found in Pamela Roby, "Women and the ASA: Degendering Organizational Structures and Processes, 1964–1974," *American Sociologist* 23 (1992): 18–48.

28. This argument, as we can now see, reflected the unnuanced state of theories about women's oppression, which ignored *differences* among women along lines of race, class, sexuality, generation, and historical context. And it rarely considered women as subjected to colonialism, imperialism, and the global expansion of world capitalism. Women of color have been particularly central in making white, middle-class, and western feminists aware of the importance of these differences.

29. See Jo Freeman, *The Politics of Women's Liberation* (New York: Mackay, 1975).

30. Among the influential feminist sociological writings of the 1970s: Joan Huber, ed., *Changing Women in a Changing Society* (Chicago: University of Chicago Press, 1973); Marcia Millman and Rosabeth Moss Kanter, eds., *Another Voice: Feminist Perspectives on Social Life and Social Science* (Garden City, N.Y.: Anchor Press, 1975); Nancy J. Chodorow, *The Reproduction of Mothering* (Berkeley and Los Angeles: University of California Press, 1978); Rosabeth Moss Kanter, *Men and Women of the Corporation* (New York: Basic Books, 1977).

31. Dorothy E. Smith, *The Conceptual Practices of Power: A Feminist Sociology of Knowledge* (Boston: Northeastern University Press, 1990).

32. Sandra Harding, *The Science Question in Feminism* (Ithaca, N.Y.: Cornell University Press, 1986).

33. Harding, ibid., reviews several lines of feminist epistemological critique ("feminist empiricism," "standpoint theory," and "postmodern" feminist positions). See also Sandra Harding and Merrill Hintikka, eds., *Discovering Reality: Feminist Perspectives on Epistemology, Metaphysics, Methodology, and Philosophy of Science* (Dordrecht: Reidel, 1983); Sandra Harding, ed., *Feminism and Methodology: Social Science Issues* (Bloomington: Indiana University Press, 1987); Helen Longino, *Science as Social Knowledge: Values and Objectivity in Scientific Inquiry* (Princeton, N.J.: Princeton University Press, 1990); Shulamit Reinharz, *Feminist Methods in Social Research* (New York: Oxford University Press, 1992); and Smith, *The Everyday World as Problematic*. For a recent review of these issues and debates in relationship to sociology, see Marjorie L. DeVault, "Talking Back to Sociology: Distinctive Contributions of Feminist Methodology," *Annual Review of Sociology* 22 (1996): 29–50.

34. Early and influential examples of this critique include the Combahee River Collective, "A Black Feminist Statement," in Zillah R. Eisenstein, ed., *Capitalist Patriarchy and the Case for Socialist Feminism* (New York: Monthly Review Press, 1979), pp. 362–372; Angela Davis, *Women, Race, and Class* (New York: Random House, 1981); Bonnie Thornton Dill, "Race, Class, and Gender: Prospects for an All-inclusive Sisterhood," *Feminist Studies* 9 (1983): 131–150; Cherríe Moraga and Gloria Anzaldúa, eds., *This Bridge Called My Back: Writings by Radical Women of Color* (Watertown, Mass.: Persephone Press, 1981); Patricia Hill Collins, *Black Feminist Thought: Knowledge, Consciousness, and the Politics of Empowerment* (Boston: Unwin Hyman, 1990); and Adrienne Rich, "Compulsory Heterosexuality and Lesbian Existence," *Signs* 5 (1980): 631–660.

35. Millman and Kanter, eds., *Another Voice*; Elizabeth Minnich, *Transforming Knowledge* (Philadelphia: Temple University Press, 1990); Smith, *The Everyday World as Problematic*; Smith, *The Conceptual Practices of Power*, and Dorothy E. Smith, *Texts, Facts, and Femininity* (New York: Routledge, 1990).

36. Roos, "Occupational Feminization," Table 1.

37. U.S. Department of Education, National Center for Education Statistics, *Digest of Education Statistics, 1992* (Washington, D.C.: GPO, 1992).

38. Roos, "Occupational Feminization," Table 4.

39. Ibid., Table 9.

40. Barbara Reskin and Patricia Roos, *Job Queues, Gender Queues* (Philadelphia: Temple University Press, 1990); Roos, "Occupational Feminization."

41. Judith Stacey and Barrie Thorne, "The Missing Feminist Revolution in Sociology," *Social Problems* 32 (1985): 301–316.

42. On this point, see also Judith Stacey and Barrie Thorne, "Is Sociology Still Missing Its Feminist Revolution?" *A.S.A. Theory Section Newsletter* 18 (summer 1996): 1–3. Examples of feminist reconstruction of basic frameworks include Evelyn Nakano Glenn, *Issei, Nisei, Warbride: Three Generations of Japanese-American Women in Domestic Service* (Philadelphia: Temple University Press, 1986); Barbara Laslett and Johanna Brenner, "Gender and Social Reproduction: Historical Perspectives," *Annual Review of Sociology* 15 (1989): 381–404; Judith Stacey, *Brave New Families: Stories of Domestic Upheaval in Late Twentieth Century America* (New York: Basic Books, 1990); Jeff Hearn and Wendy Parkin, *"Sex" at "Work": The Power and Paradox of Organization Sexuality* (New York: St. Martin's Press, 1987); and R. W. Connell, *Gender*

*and Power: Society, the Person, and Sexual Politics* (Stanford, Calif.: Stanford University Press, 1987).

43. Examples of such theorizing include Joan Acker, "Hierarchies, Jobs, and Bodies: A Theory of Gendered Organizations," *Gender & Society* 4 (1990): 139–158; Jennifer Pierce, *Gender Trials: Emotional Lives in Contemporary Law Firms* (Berkeley and Los Angeles: University of California Press, 1995); and R. W. Connell, "The State, Gender, and Sexual Politics: Theory and Appraisal," *Theory and Society* 19 (1990): 507–544.

44. Examples of these lines of work include Collins, *Black Feminist Thought;* Margaret L. Andersen and Patricia Hill Collins, eds., *Race, Class, and Gender: An Anthology* (Belmont, Calif.: Wadsworth, 1992); Judith Lorber, *Paradoxes of Gender* (New Haven, Conn.: Yale University Press, 1994); Barrie Thorne, *Gender Play: Girls and Boys in School* (New Brunswick, N.J.: Rutgers University Press, 1993); and R. W. Connell, *Masculinities,* (Berkeley and Los Angeles: University of California Press, 1995). Sociologists have drawn many transformative ideas from the interdisciplinary terrain of feminist theory.

45. Dorothy E. Smith, "Response to Judith Stacey's and Barrie Thorne's Essay," *A.S.A. Theory Section Newsletter* 18 (summer 1996): 4.

46. Joan Alway, "The Trouble with Gender: Tales of the Still-missing Feminist Revolution in Sociological Theory," *Sociological Theory* 13 (1995): 209–228.

47. See also Stacey and Thorne, "Is Sociology Still Missing Its Feminist Revolution?" including comments on the essay by Dorothy Smith, Michael Burawoy, Kum-Kum Bhavnani, and Chris Ingraham. Our vantage point comes from within sociology; other issues emerge if one starts, instead, from women's studies as a self-consciously interdisciplinary field. For example, Stanton and Stewart discuss the "dialogic interaction" and "permeable and changing" relation between women's studies and the disciplines. Even though women's studies is idealized as "interdisciplinary," they argue that it is more a "pluridisciplinary landscape." See Donna C. Stanton and Abigail J. Stewart, "Remodeling Relations: Women's Studies and the Disciplines," in Donna C. Stanton and Abigail J. Stewart, eds., *Feminisms in the Academy* (Ann Arbor: University of Michigan Press, 1995), pp. 1–16. Burawoy cautions that it is "in the disciplines that power resides, so it is in the disciplines it has to be contested." See Michael Burawoy, "The Power of Feminism," *A.S.A. Theory Section Newsletter* 18 (summer 1996): 5.

48. On boundary work in the construction of academic disciplines, see Thomas F. Gieryn, "Boundary Work and the Demarcation of Science from Non-science: Strains and Interests in Professional Ideologies of Scientists," *American Sociological Review* 48 (1983): 781–795; and Ellen Messer-Davidow, David R. Shumway, and David J. Sylvan, eds., *Knowledges: Historical and Critical Studies in Disciplinarity* (Charlottesville: University Press of Virginia, 1993).

49. See Barbara Laslett, "How *Signs* Ruined Me for Sociology: Or, Feminist Scholarship, Interdisciplinarity, and Boundary Maintenance in Sociology" (Paper presented at the 1996 meetings of the Pacific Sociological Association, Seattle, Washington, March).

50. See Desley Deacon's essay in this volume on Elsie Clews Parsons; Laslett, "Gender-in/and Social Science History"; Ellen Fitzgerald, *Endless Crusade: Women Social Scientists and Progressive Reform* (New York: Oxford University Press, 1990); and Mary

Jo Deegan, *Jane Addams and the Men of the Chicago School. 1892–1918* (New Brunswick, N.J.: Transaction Books, 1988).

51. Dorothy E. Smith, "A Berkeley Education," in Orlans and Wallace, eds., *Gender and the Academic Experience*, pp. 45–56; Smith, *The Everyday World as Problematic*. Smith continues to affirm "starting from experience" as a foundation of inquiry, as in "Sociology from Women's Experience: A Reaffirmation," *Sociological Theory* 10 (1992): 88–98. For a critique of experience as a basis for theorizing, see Scott, "The Evidence of Experience"; and Grant, *Fundamental Feminism*.

52. For an insightful discussion of the deteriorating relationship between feminist theory and practice, see Heidi Hartmann, Ellen Bravo, Charlotte Bunch, Nancy Hartsock, Roberta Spalter-Roth, Linda Williams, and Maria Blanco, "Bringing Together Feminist Theory and Practice: A Collective Interview," *Signs* 21 (1996): 917–951. See also Stacey and Thorne, "Is Sociology Still Missing Its Feminist Revolution?" and commentaries.

53. Marjorie DeVault offered this insight.

54. See Joan Huber, "Institutional Perspectives on Sociology," *American Journal of Sociology* 101 (1995): 194–216.

55. For a relevant analysis, see William Goode, "Why Men Resist," in Thorne with Yalom, eds., *Rethinking the Family*, pp. 131–150.

56. For an expansion of the argument about successes and failures in women's self-organization, see Johanna Brenner and Barbara Laslett, "Gender, Social Reproduction, and Women's Self-organization in the Development of the U.S. Welfare State," *Gender & Society* 5 (1991): 311–333; and Johanna Brenner, "The Best of Times, the Worst of Times: Feminism in the United States," in Monica Threlfall, ed., *Mapping the Women's Movement: Feminist Politics and Social Transformation in the North* (London: Verso, 1996), pp. 17–72.

*Joan Acker*

# My Life as a Feminist Sociologist; or, Getting the Man out of My Head

*I* never intended to become an academic or a sociologist. But by now I have spent over thirty years as both. This is one account of how I came to do what I had not intended and of how being a woman and a feminist has shaped my experiences of academia and sociology and the work that I do. I am aware of the ambiguities of autobiography so much discussed today, but I will ignore them. This is a chronological tale, more or less the truth, or the truth for today.

As a teenager, I wanted a life of adventure, preferably as a foreign correspondent, traveling to strange places, doing daring deeds to get the news. I was probably patterning my future on a dream of what my father should have been. He was a writer, but not an adventurer. My mother was a college graduate who came from an impoverished upper-middle-class intellectual family. She always worked and was a political activist: I saw both as what women normally did. We did not suffer during the Depression because my father had a good job with the American Legion. Both of my parents clearly thought I was smart and encouraged me to become anything I wanted to be.

Although I was an editor of my high school newspaper in Indianapolis and my college literary magazine in New York, I recognized before I was twenty that a life of exciting journalistic travel did not fit with my other aspiration—to be a wife and mother. Logistically, those goals did not mesh. Moreover, I had already learned from the other girls in the second grade that being an assertive and enterprising person reduced a girl's attractiveness to boys. Since assertiveness and enterprise were some of the qualities required for becoming a world-class journalist, what would be my chances of finding the right man if I was successful? I did not see this dilemma as any evidence of inequality between women and men and took it for granted as indicating only difference, not disadvantage, the clear evidence of gender discrimination around me.

I was aware of, and concerned about, race and class early in my life. I began to question racism as a young teenager in Indianapolis, where I grew up, when I was puzzled and hurt that the African-American woman who took care of me, my sister, and our house would not sit next to me on the streetcar. But I could not interpret this until, at the age of nineteen, I moved to New York, entered Hunter College, and began my political education. I had a new stepfather who was a radical, and my mother agreed with him. In addition, I met the most amazing radical people among my peers. In my philosophy courses we studied dialectical and historical materialism. Psychology courses were taught by people on the Left who related individual experience to class and race. I supported labor unions, went on demonstrations, and decided that whatever work I might do, it should not contribute to capitalist domination. I still feel that way but understand much better than I did then the ambiguities and difficulties in attaining that laudable goal.

Thus, at Hunter I chose a combined major in sociology and social work, which was preparatory for graduate education in social work. My decision to become a social worker was determined both by my wish to do something that could be done in most communities, enhancing my ability to combine marriage and work, and by my political commitment that I not pursue a career that would exploit other people. My course was more sociology than social work, and I must have been developing some awareness of "the woman question": in one sociology course I wrote a paper comparing the explanations of women's positions in the work of Thorsten Veblen and Robert Park. I did an honor's thesis on the family court in Manhattan, giving me a taste of the pleasures of research, and I graduated Phi Beta Kappa, cum laude with honors in sociology.

In spite of the evidence to the contrary, I did not think of myself as an intellectual. That was for the men in my groups of radical friends. The men took care of the finer points of Marxist theory, while we women concerned ourselves with such things as organizing fund-raising events and door-to-door canvassing for the American Labor Party. I recognize now that refusing to see myself as a "thinker" was self-protective: the objects of my affection now were Left intellectual/activist men, and one thing that made them attractive was their intellectual exploits. I would not compete with them on that ground and risk revealing myself either as stupid or more competent than they. Either way I might be rejected. I believe, as I look back, that I was perfectly happy with this resolution of my dilemma and totally unaware that such a resolution might be problematic.

Immediately after college graduation, I went off to the University of Chicago to get a master's in the School of Social Service Administration (SSA). Those were exciting times. World War II had recently ended. The university was flooded with returning veterans, and there was optimism about individual prospects and the possibilities of solving the social problems of the Depression era. SSA presented a progressive/liberal understanding of society and social problems, not unlike a Scandinavian social democratic approach. The Social Security Act was only ten years old, and the energy and enthusiasm that had gone into shaping it were still around. Edith Abbott and Sophenisba P. Breckenridge, founders of the school when the social welfare teachers had been eased out of the Department of Sociology at Chicago, were still alive, and Abbott did some lecturing at the school. Our understanding of the impact of poverty was informed by Charlotte Towle's *Common Human Needs*, which emphasized respect and empathy. I studied psychiatric social work, getting a thorough grounding in the work of Freud. My friends and I spent a lot of time discussing how to combine Marxism and psychoanalytic theory, with little success. These intense encounters with Freud left me highly suspicious of the value of a psychoanalytic perspective for most of the issues in which I was interested, and I have never been convinced that I should change this critical view.

Outside of class, I was active in founding, and the first chairperson of, a student chapter of the United Office and Professional Workers Union, which was later destroyed by McCarthy-era anticommunism. We gathered signatures for Henry Wallace, wrote and performed skits opposing the Taft-Hartley Act, and supported antiracism efforts and community organizers such as Saul Alinsky. Women's issues were nowhere to be seen. Since I was often a vocal participant in both political and theory discussions, I was beginning to see myself as a thinker, as well as a doer.

I received my M.A. from the University of Chicago in 1948, got married, and soon got pregnant. I married an intellectual, New York radical, graduate student in sociology, and we moved to Manhattan, where we started confronting together the problems of family and work. Our solutions were the only ones that seemed possible at the time. He worked full-time and continued to a doctorate in psychology, studying at night. I worked part-time as a social worker and took care of the kids (soon there were three). Although my husband was supportive, that did not change the structural facts. Over the years, our solution became more and more impossible for me. In the late 1950s Simone de Beauvoir's *The Second Sex* was translated into English, and I used it as I used Dr. Spock—when some new problem came up, I looked it up in de Beauvoir.

Combining work, politics, and family life was difficult but possible in New York City, but not in Mountain View, California, where we moved with my husband's career. There I spent a year or two out of the labor force in a suburban tract house. I had a few part-time jobs, but most of the time I was doing the laundry or gardening in rubber thongs, jeans, and my husband's old shirts. It was there that I fully faced what had happened to the superstudent, superorganizer I had been. I had lost much of my self-confidence. This was clear to me when I panicked after I had agreed to put out the two-page PTA newsletter. I had no sense that I could do it. Then one day I found myself in Sears, my youngest child in a stroller, staring at the fabric counter for ten minutes, trying to decide what to buy for my current sewing project, and realizing that whatever I bought, I would have no place to wear the dress I would make.

I decided that I had to do something. I knew that my male colleagues from graduate school were moving into important administrative and policy jobs, while I was always starting over at the bottom. In addition, I wanted to get out of social work because the work I had done seemed to be hopeless battling against impossible problems. Trying to help solve, individual by individual, problems created by the maldistribution of economic and social power became, for me, too depressing. The only way I knew to make up the gap of twelve years of sporadic and part-time work, and to do something in which I could feel some hope, was to get more education. I had worked on a research project located in the Stanford Department of Sociology; my background was in sociology; this was the obvious answer. When I talked to the head of the Stanford Sociology Department, however, he was decidedly cool to the idea that I might apply there, indicating that I was the wrong age and the wrong sex. At about that time, my husband had a chance at a job at the University of Oregon, and when I applied, I was immediately accepted as a doctoral student in the Department of Sociology there.

So with my greatly reduced sense of intellectual efficacy, at the age of thirty-seven I returned to academia, an instrumental move to try to circumvent social structure. I and my husband and our three children moved to Eugene in 1961, a decision made for both of us. In that small town, combining work or school with parenthood was much easier than in the other cities in which we had lived. Our house was two blocks from campus, and the public schools were almost as close. I never again had to drive the children anywhere. It was easy to hire students to take care of the kids when necessary. Altogether a good solution.

The Department of Sociology was both welcoming and not welcoming. Two of the all-male faculty were particularly supportive, Herb Bisno and Robert Ellis. Others, such as Robert Dubin, seemed to have a dim view of women as graduate students and sociologists. Dubin, as I recall, openly expressed his disapproval in the classroom. I think that these attitudes were one of the reasons that, although there were several women in my cohort, I was the only one who survived. I tried to ignore these verbal attacks on women and on the surface was successful, probably because I had a very supportive husband and because I saw no alternative to persevering. In addition, I was older than most of the other women, with a certain success as a professional to bolster me. Moreover, I had men friends among the students, including John McCarthy and Scott McNall, who, as I saw it, accepted me as one of them, their equal.

The intellectual world of the university and the Department of Sociology at the University of Oregon was very different from the world in which I had first experienced higher education. There was no talk of Marx or of Freud. This was the era of Talcott Parsons, Robert Merton, functionalism, and quantitative analysis. I had to learn a new vocabulary and a new way of thinking. I knew nothing about roles, statuses, and institutions or about consensus, a totally new word for me. When Miriam Johnson asked me if I, too, was interested in socialization, I didn't know what she was talking about. Approaches to class that we had scornfully rejected as bourgeois at Hunter were the only approaches discussed. Most courses were rigorously nonhistorical, except for the "history of social thought" in which students regularly fell asleep.

I still did not think of myself as really an intellectual. Although I did very well in all my courses, I experienced a disconcerting distance, even alienation, from the theoretical material. This I interpreted as a lack of fit between my earlier Marxist perspective and the Parsonian functionalism that was substantially the only doctrine taught at that time. Now I would interpret at least part of my disquiet in terms of what Dorothy Smith has called a bifurcated consciousness. I had to insert myself into a way of thinking in which I could not recognize myself. I did it, but the fit was superficial; I never became a believer.

I continued during my graduate student years to be politically active; I had no feelings of alienation in that arena. I was among the faculty and students who organized one of the first teach-ins in the United States to oppose the Vietnam War. The civil rights movement was also expanding, and my husband and I were active there. With the War on Poverty emerging after the assassination of John Kennedy, great possibilities for reform seemed to be suddenly present. I was by that time teaching courses on social welfare as a graduate student, and I did a good bit to involve women in the welfare rights movement in my courses and to support them as I could. We did not at that time see welfare rights as a woman's movement, but in retrospect it was clearly that.

As I approached the dissertation, I was unclear about what I wanted to do. Dubin offered me dissertation support through a Ford Foundation grant he had for research on organizations, and I accepted. He made a few good suggestions about methods and theory, but mostly he left me on my own, and I wrote an acceptable thesis on the Department of Welfare's relationships with business firms. I got a great deal of help in finishing my thesis—one of my male colleagues took over my classes, and my husband took over child care and housework so that I could work without interruption. I finished the Ph.D. in 1967. With all this accomplished, I still felt like an outsider, not a real sociologist, whatever that might have been.

With my degree in hand, I had nowhere to go, committed as I was to being with my family in Eugene. Happily for me, the Department of Sociology offered me a job, a tenure-track position. The late 1960s were still a period of expansion in higher education, and I was one of the many who benefited. I think that I was hired partly because I could teach the social welfare courses. I was the first woman to have a regular, tenure-track position in the Department of Sociology at Oregon. In spite of some new supportive male colleagues, also recently hired and on the Left politically, I did not feel myself a part of the group. Moreover, I still felt estranged from the discipline. Its problems were only peripherally interesting to me; its ways of thinking were still foreign.

In retrospect I can also see that I was intimidated by "science." Although structural functionalism did not really sink into my brain, the idea that we were building a science did. I soaked up notions that science was built through hypothesis testing and the use of rigorous standards of evidence that could be met by a researcher following carefully set procedures and quantitative analysis. This rigor was paralyzingly extreme, but also mysterious, I see in looking back. It was so extreme that I never even considered publishing anything from my first independent research, a study of doctor-patient contact based on meticulously recorded observational data. Somewhere in my thinking was a sociologist-judge (a distillation of all the old boys who had been my teachers, perhaps) who would find me lacking in precision, having too small a sample, or showing some other defect.

The beginning of the women's movement and my divorce in the late

1960s changed my life and my thinking. Feminism had been creeping into my consciousness since the late 1950s, and by 1969 I was ready for the explosion of the movement in Oregon. I think it was in 1969 that there was a large feminist conference on the University of Oregon campus, carefully monitored by the FBI, we later learned. The same year I taught my first course on women, a seminar with graduate students. This was very exciting, and the next term I followed it with a large course in the sociology of women, with the graduate students as discussion leaders. That was the best course I ever taught. There was practically no literature, certainly little critical feminist literature. I scoured the library and made up the course content as I went along. Both the students and I were charged with energy and interest. Often there was standing room only in the classroom. It was an evening class, and sometimes we had to be evicted by the cleaning crew that came in at 11:00 P.M.

I began to do critiques of mainstream theory as I taught this first course. Since I had been teaching courses on class and stratification and on organizations, these were the areas in which I began to see inconsistencies, contradictions, and absences of women. Women, it was perfectly obvious, were absent or were treated inconsistently in all class and stratification studies, including those by Marxists. Almost all mobility studies were done with samples of men. In other kinds of studies, women were presumed to take the class positions of their husbands, but if women had no husbands and were employed, they had their own class positions. A woman's class position could change for no other reason than that she had married, but marital status was not a primary determinant of class in any theoretical tradition. Class theories could not account for the subordination of married women to their husbands' class positions or for women's secondary status in the labor force. Class and stratification analyses were blind to one of the most pervasive and systematic inequalities, that based on sex. How, then, could these theories pretend to conceptualize societywide economic and status structuring?

In spite of excitement about such new feminist ideas and feminist organizing, I still felt uneasy in academia, an odd person, still the only woman in the department. I seriously considered leaving the university world and took a year away, working in a large mental health agency, to see what it would be like. I made a lot more money as a management person, but sociology had spoiled me for the world of those who deal only with individual troubles. I returned to Oregon, with assurances from one of the male faculty that it was great to have me back because I had the best-looking legs in the department. Commitment to feminist work prevailed over such reassurances, and I stayed in the discipline, finally thinking that I might yet be a real sociologist.

The women's movement made the difference, led me to decide to stay. Feminism helped me to begin to make some order in my theoretical thinking and to understand why sociology had been so alienating and confusing to me. As for so many of us, the effort to understand why I felt like an outsider, perpetually uncomfortable, perhaps just not getting it, was extremely stimulating. Finally I was asking myself questions that made sense to me, that were interesting. They were my questions, not questions dredged from some "body of literature" and couched in the concepts of some bodiless "theorist." These questions were about the discipline (why was sociology so unreceptive to questions about women?) and about particular theoretical issues (what was it about the internal structures of theories of class or formal organization, for example, that either marginalized women or made them invisible?).

The 1970s were exhilarating. When I returned to Eugene, many things started to happen. I and some of my friends on the faculty began a research group on women. The first project was a study of the status of women at the University of Oregon, a process going on at many universities. We found, of course, few women either tenured or in tenure-track positions and a large gender wage gap. With this as ammunition, some of us started a campaign for affirmative action by the university. After an investigation by the federal Department of Health, Education, and Welfare, the university was forced to move on the issue, and the battleground turned to the department.

Richard Hill was by that time, 1972, the department head. He opposed affirmative action on the grounds that he was against quotas of any kind. However, after late hours of argument, he changed his mind and became the strongest male supporter of women and of feminist research on the campus.

Dick's support was critical in the establishment of our women's research center as a recognized part of the institution. With his help, I and two others put together a proposal to the graduate school for such an interdisciplinary center. When all other department heads could see no sense in the proposal and it was turned down, Dick suggested that we establish it in the Department of Sociology. This proposal was approved, and we got a small amount of money per year, enough to pay a graduate assistant to do some research and keep things going. This Center for the Sociological Study of Women was the reason that a man named William Harris decided in 1975 to make the University of Oregon the sole beneficiary of his estate. The rest of that story comes later.

Also in the early 1970s, another woman, Miriam Johnson, joined the faculty, and we began to have Ph.D. students doing dissertations on women. These were heady days of sisterhood and cooperation, at least in my perception. We began to hire more women, and the feminist presence in the department became obvious. Sociology was the first department to reach its affirmative action goals. Some of us cooperated on research proposals. We developed a feminism scale and carried out another study of the status of women at the university. This time a human subjects review was required, and we had difficulty getting approval on the grounds that findings might embarrass the university. We also developed a series of new courses about women and revised other courses, such as the family course, to reflect the new feminist research and theory. These courses were an important part of the women's studies program we were also developing. In all of this, there was nothing but support from the male members of the sociology faculty. Even so, there were rumors that the men were worried and possibly envious and thought that we were plotting and acting as a bloc in the department. This was true, of course.

During the same years, the early 1970s, I began to publish and to get rid of some of the inner prohibitions that said that my work was never perfect or scientific enough. I submitted my first article, on women and stratification, in 1970 to the *American Journal of Sociology,* thanks to the urging of my colleague Steven Deutsch.[1] I argued that invisibility of women in class analyses could be rectified by scholars taking the individual, not the family, as the unit. In this way, women could be seen as having their own class positions, which might or might not be the same as those of the men, if any, in their lives. The article was published in 1973, but I soon saw that the problem could not be so easily solved by the assigning of women to their own class positions, that only a fundamental rethinking of the conceptualization of class could produce theories that would include both women and men. I have worked sporadically on this problem, now called gender and class, ever since.

My second article, a feminist critique of the Hawthorne Studies and of Michael Crozier's work published in the *Administrative Science Quarterly* in 1974, was coauthored with Don Van Houten, one of the most congenial coauthors I have ever had.[2] I cotaught a seminar on race and sex—we weren't talking about gender then—with David Wellman. I participated in student-initiated seminars on the Frankfurt School and went dancing on Saturday nights with other Left faculty and graduate students. I was never close to the doctrinaire Marxists in the department because they seemed to be full of their own brilliance and I couldn't be just a listener to their pontifications.

However, other male colleagues who were progressive but critical of ortho-doxy were closer to my emerging perspective than were my women col-leagues. I did not see this at the time, in the euphoric days of "early" academic feminism.

My intellectual interests joined those who were working to reclaim Marxist theory for the feminist project. I joined them primarily through journals and books, as I had no colleagues, other than some very good graduate students, at Oregon with this perspective. Somewhat later I found Nona Glazer in Portland, and still later Sally Hacker in Corvallis, Oregon, both of whom shared my point of view. Marxist theory was very difficult to reclaim when it came to class analysis. Marxist feminist arguments that do-mestic labor produces value broke new ground but finally were not suc-cessful in producing a gendered theory of class. I thought that other efforts were also unsatisfactory.

Socialist feminism, in contrast to Marxist feminism, seemed by the early 1970s to offer a feminist critical stance toward Marxism, while not rejecting the overall critique of capitalism or the commitment to emancipa-tion and democracy. Theories of capitalism and patriarchy seemed a solu-tion but also had limitations. Those were pre-postmodernist times, so the criticisms did not attack patriarchy/capitalism theories as totalizing grand narratives that silence the voices of numerous others. However, to my mind the criticisms were serious. Dual systems theories were flawed, as Iris Young pointed out, in the way that they constructed a theory of women's oppres-sion as a corrective to the theory of class oppression, leaving class theory, which had already been analyzed as sorely deficient, essentially unaltered.[3] This was the fundamental defect that made me reject this solution to the problem. Yet I still wanted, intellectually and politically needed, a theoreti-cal approach that would allow me to think about myself and other women as located within large, historical processes that had something to do with our different fates.

Getting articles accepted by the *American Journal of Sociology* and the *Administrative Science Quarterly* and having the support of men and women colleagues were not enough to give me complete confidence in my ideas and my capacities. I had contraindications. For one thing, I could never get my research funded; eventually I gave up writing research proposals.

Another problem was that I, along with many others, was in uncharted territory. The critique of knowledge both from the Frankfurt School perspec-tive and emerging feminist work was most persuasive, but there was still a huge distance between those critiques and a feminist sociology grounded in women's experiences. Dorothy Smith's theoretical and methodological work on a sociology *for* women opened new ways of thinking for me.[4] Dorothy came to Eugene in 1972 or 1973 to present a paper at the western meetings of the American Association for the Advancement of Science. Dorothy's analysis gave clarity and form to the estrangement, even disassociation, I felt as a woman in a still almost totally male academic world. The idea of a bifurcated consciousness—that women going into an academic discipline have to learn to think in ways that have already erased their presence, that there are no words in the conceptual vocabularies of the academic disciplines that accurately express the experiences of women—rang absolutely true for me. And the implications were daunting: everything had to be rethought; nothing, no work, no theory, could simply be uncritically accepted. Dorothy also proposed an approach, a place to begin—in the everyday experiences of women. Our explorations should only start there, she said; our aims should be to comprehend how those experiences come about, how they are, in practice, tied into the social relations that constitute the larger society. Applying these ideas in actual research was not easy, as two of my then-graduate students, Kate Barry and Joke Esseveld, and I found out in research on the lives of middle-aged women that we started in 1976. The process of trying to do nonexploitative, possibly emancipatory research was fraught with contradictions. Analysis of masses of interview material on individual lives was even more difficult. The construction of categories or types based on some sort of conceptual scheme was a common strategy at that time. This we rejected on the ground that it violated the complexities of the women's lives—to force them into categories meant stripping away content that was essential to understanding lives as experience extending through time. Moreover, we had rejected all conceptual frameworks, such as role or socialization theory, that seemed to be available. At the same time, we did not want to present unanalyzed life histories, for we had theoretical interests and the women with whom we were working wanted and expected interpretations. The result of our endless discussions about how to do feminist analysis was that we published only two articles from this research.[5] Perhaps another reason that we never produced a book from this research was that I had not completely escaped from my doubts about being a scholar.

In retrospect, I see a review article I published in *Current Sociology* in 1980 as the culminating example of my inhibiting inner strictures.[6] I worked on that ten-page article for a year, reading, analyzing, and assessing everything that could possibly relate to theoretical and empirical issues about women and class/stratification. I believe that the article was good but that the amount of work involved could have produced a book instead of an article in which every sentence was a tightly packed condensation of days and weeks of work.

My interpretation of what was going on in my thinking has developed as I have thought about another incident that occurred somewhat later. This was known in my department as the Sex and Work Discussion. In the Sociology Department there were, most of us believed, several male faculty members who regularly had affairs with women graduate students. Not just once or twice, but in succession. The women so favored often benefited, or appeared to benefit, from the relationships, with easy teaching assistant assignments from their lovers, and even, some said, with special consideration in evaluations. Some of the women students who were not so entangled came to me with the complaint that such benefits were not fair. I agreed to take the matter up in the department and put "sex and work" on the next agenda. My intention was just to get the department to affirm the same policies for such couples that we had for married couples on the faculty. For example, Ben Johnson would never sit on a committee deciding on the promotion of his wife, Miriam Johnson.

However, the discussion immediately took off into indignant charges that I was trying to police the private lives of faculty and students and was interfering with their civil rights. I and others retorted that it was not a matter of civil rights but fairness—people should not get special favors because of their intimate ties. One woman graduate student talked about the devastating consequences to her self-esteem after she broke off a relationship with a faculty member at another university. She, who had been the intellectual star of her cohort, was suddenly attacked by her rejected lover as academically incompetent. Suddenly, I found myself quoting Jessie Bernard to the effect that if a woman wants to become a productive scholar, "you've got to get the man out of your head." And, I went on, "you've got to get the man out of your bed." This, of course, did nothing to dampen the controversy or endear me to those with such relationships. Most of the men involved, including leading Marxists in the department, and the women who were their followers were decidedly cool toward me for a number of years.

However, we did go on to establish a policy about faculty serving on committees evaluating students with whom they have an intimate relationship and suggesting that they not ask that such students be assigned to them as teaching or research assistants. Later, such a policy was established for the university as a whole.

But the point of this story is in the insight about the importance of the man in your head and the man in your bed. I think that remnants of the man in my head—in my case the guardians of science and the representatives of theoretical sophistication—lasted much longer than I had thought. The work of many feminists, Dorothy Smith in particular, helped me to unclutter my brain and start thinking differently. Ultimately, I had to confront the problem on my own because part of the solution for me was to be willing to take chances, to commit myself fully to my own position, unconstrained by any lingering questions about what "they" might think. That came slowly, but, on the whole, it happened.

As to the man in your bed—fortunately I never had an enduring relationship with a sociologist (my ex-husband began transforming himself into a psychologist soon after we married). I think that my problems might have been more difficult had this been the case because the man in my head and the man in my bed might have been the same person, multiplying the negative effects of relative powerlessness. Although I am talking about heterosexual relationships, I think it is possible that similar processes operate in nonheterosexual situations. I was lucky (or wise) enough to never live with anyone after my divorce. I love to live alone, and I doubt that I could have done what I have done in the last twenty-five years if my living arrangements had been different. I have sometimes lived with one or more of my children, all of them male, but they were never a problem.

The era of feminist togetherness was drawing to a close in my department by the last years of the 1970s. Our collaboration on research had been precariously held together by enthusiasm. However, there were deep divisions among us. I was a socialist feminist concerned with transforming Marxism and developing research from women's perspectives. The others were functionalists and/or committed to positivist models of science that, to my mind, were marred most severely by their faith that the researcher occupies a space outside the phenomenon under investigation. I had no direct disagreements with my women colleagues that I can remember, but we slowly stopped our collaboration; we were interested in different issues. I was also much more an activist, and more radical in my activism, than they were.

These differences developed into open conflict when the benefactor of our research center died and we found out that the center would get more than $3 million. The issues were about whether the center should be exclusively devoted to research or should have some connection to women's studies and some ties to feminist activism in the community. We arrived at a truce, the reorganized center began to function in fall 1983, and I became the director. Unfortunately, disagreements about the direction of the center continued, and it became evident to all of us that the two sides could not come together. I and a number of others did not want to replicate a traditional university research center; on the other side there was a refusal to involve the center in anything but traditional academic research. There were other differences. I was convinced about the feminist critique of science and was working on various criticisms of sociology that went far beyond the positions of those who disagreed with me. I worked on reform efforts—such as the comparable worth task force in Oregon and saw this as the opportunity for research, as well as action. Some of those on the other side couldn't see this, believing that such research was, at best, only applied work.

The conflict was resolved for me when in late 1986 I left to work in Stockholm. In a long-term perspective, the center conflict had a most positive outcome for me as a scholar and a person. I was invited to work at the Swedish Center for Working Life, where I spent three years. At this Swedish Center I had the most supportive work environment I had ever had, including a marvelous library, great colleagues, and plenty of time. As an outsider, I was free from the organizational conflict in which I had always been enmeshed. I had the time and the emotional space to develop my ideas rapidly and to do, for me, a lot of writing. Living in a new country where I was not controversial, I was able to finally become the arbiter of my own work. This made me much more comfortable with outside criticism. Now, most of the time, I welcome, rather than dread, it. And I have benefited tremendously from criticisms and suggestions from many colleagues, including Nona Glazer, Dorothy Smith, Harriet Holter, Sally Hacker, Don Van Houten, Ronnie Steinberg, Arlene Daniels, Judith Lorber, Joke Esseveld, Kate Barry, Annika Baude, Wuokko Knocke, Lena Gonäs, Hildur Ve, Arnlaug Leira, and Cynthia Cockburn.

In Sweden I completed yet another paper on gender and class, which had its beginnings in my efforts to interpret in class terms the experiences of the middle-aged women in our study of the late 1970s.[7] Instead of trying to locate them in a preordered class scheme, I tried to start from what was most problematic for them and to ask how that came about, as Dorothy Smith suggests. For many of the women, economic, social, and emotional dependence was most problematic. Interpreting dependence as an aspect of the way they were situated in the social relations of our society, I argued that their locations within relations of distribution, which include the wage, personal or family relations, and welfare, produced their dependence. To understand capitalist societies, it was necessary, I thought, to theorize distribution as well as production—that women, children, and men not gainfully employed participate in capitalist societies and that failure to include all of these people in understandings of class structure constitutes a failure of adequate comprehension.

I also began to argue, along with others, that social relations are gendered, that relations that constitute class also constitute gender and race/ethnicity as well. Thus, we have to talk about one system, or complex of relations, not dual or multiple systems. I also began to see that to avoid the dangers of dual or multiple systems theories, we would have to study social relations as concrete practices and processes occurring under specific historical conditions. In other words, the highest-level abstractions were useless, except perhaps as general, orienting guides. I argued with friends who were still structural Marxists about level of analysis—mode of production, social formation, conjuncture—and I worried (but not much) about what happened to Marxism if we totally abandoned the labor theory of value. I finally concluded that Marxism as usually interpreted could not be pushed or pulled into a feminist version because it was constructed with abstractions within which gender could not appear. I think that Dorothy Smith is right when she argues that women and gender cannot be satisfactorily brought into Marxist political economy because "the very presuppositions of discourse have already denied them presence."[8] Political economy, she suggests, takes its topics, relevances, and boundaries from "the main business," the organization, management, planning, and ruling of the capitalist economy, arenas in which women are absent and gender is present but invisible.

In trying to set down this chronology, I realize that I cannot remember exactly when I began to think in certain ways. I am also not sure whose work I have appropriated, so I have probably come to believe that ideas that came from others were somehow mine. In any case, by the time of publication, I had decided that my article on class, gender, and the relations of distribution had not satisfactorily solved the problem of women and class and that I would stop ruminating about Marxism. Perhaps my way of putting the issue—women and class—only revealed that I was still caught in a paradigm I was trying to reject. Moreover, women of color were showing that white feminist theory reproduced relations of power and domination among women. Postmodern feminist criticism was making similar charges, and socialist feminist theorizing seemed to have few openings toward solutions.

Still in my Swedish period of peace and productivity, I dealt with this conceptual impasse by turning to empirical work to try to figure out what I meant when I said that all social relations are gendered. I started with class and gender in the concrete practices of doing comparable worth in Oregon, writing a book about gender/class processes that became visible in the process of organizational change.[9] Comparable worth projects attempted to achieve pay equity between women's and men's jobs by first evaluating those jobs on the same criteria, then by comparing the salaries of women's and men's jobs with similar evaluation scores, and finally by adjusting pay levels so that jobs with comparable scores would have comparable pay. Most projects used the services of job evaluation consultants with experience and methods to sell. In my research on the Oregon project, I was able to observe the Hay Associates method of job evaluation. Analyzing the data from that project, I realized that I had seen, as Hay Associates consultants explained job evaluation, the discursive creation of ostensibly gender-neutral categories whose gendered nature is hidden by the denial of the existence of human bodies in the categories. The consultants told us emphatically that in order to evaluate jobs, we had to think of them as abstract, hierarchically ordered sets of "job demands," unconnected to actual people, thus containing no bodies and no gender. These were "gender–neutral" concepts, positions, and hierarchies, central to notions of structure, that make it so difficult to insert women into most theoretical discourse, and they were being actively produced as a real organization was being reconstructed. This recognition led me to try to think more about bodies and sexuality, their absence in organizational theory, and how all this might be linked to women's relative subordination in organizations. Of course, my reading Michel Foucault and feminist discussions of bodies and sexuality must have had a lot to do with this line of thinking.[10]

Another attempt to deal with the conceptual dead end of socialist feminism through empirical work was a study of Swedish banks. I tried to help women in the bank workers' union discover why the gender wage gap was increasing after having shrank for ten years. The answer to the question was that the trend toward equality halted when individually set wage increases became more frequent; managers saw men as more deserving than women of extra increases. Small decisions made possible by particular economic and political conditions—deregulation of banks, a booming economy, a tight labor market, and wage restraint on the part of unions—resulted in a growing gender wage gap.[11]

In this study I learned again how unstable is the reality underlying such a simple concept as a job. In Swedish banks, as well as in the state of Oregon, a "job" is something that is in a constant process of definition and redefinition, a process sometimes manipulated to preserve sex segregation. Macrostructural and quantitative analyses reify jobs as things that exist independently of the (gendered) processes of their construction, as well as independently of the sex of incumbents. This reification hides the ongoing structuring of gender.

The study of banks also took me back to questions about power and high finance and away from abstractions of class and gender. I could not understand what was happening to bank tellers without understanding Swedish banks' situations in a changing world of finance capital. For a long time, having rejected "levels of analysis" in some of its meanings, I had also been uneasy with notions of micro and macro and with the way that sociologists in general think "structure." People, all men in this case, made decisions about Swedish banks as a whole in response to ideology and to decisions other people made in Sweden and other countries. The effects of their decisions could, if one wanted to tag them so, be seen as macrostructures or macroforces, but that is mystifying, erasing gender, bodies and sexuality. Sally Hacker, before she died in 1988, had started to explore connections among technology, forms of masculinity, sexuality, and power, suggesting that working with technology is pleasurable, even erotically pleasurable, and that these pleasures may be linked to pleasures of power.[12] I think that Sally's work should be extended, although I am not suggesting a return to Freud or even a rereading of Herbert Marcuse. She was onto something different, I think, grounded in her own bodily experiences and her empirical research.

I had, and still have, another, continuing project in Sweden—to understand the contradiction between the Swedes' belief that theirs is a sex-equal society and the most evident, to me and my Swedish feminist friends, subordination of women. How is this contradiction maintained and made invisible to so many? How is it that Sweden has made so much and so little progress toward gender equality? One way or another, I have been working on this question since I began spending considerable time in Sweden in 1981. This is another way of looking at gender and class, but this time in the context of debates about the welfare state. I have been influenced by feminist discussions of culture and language and have been interested by the ways that women's issues have been phrased to fit into male-defined political agendas. Now my question is changing as the Swedish welfare state is threatened in this era of the renaissance of predatory capitalism. Since 1992 I have been studying how politically active women in Sweden are responding to threats to the welfare state and how the discourses of reform are changing in Sweden.[13]

So where am I now, in 1996? The man in my head is, I hope, dead, and I have not replaced him with a feminist authority. I cannot find a label for my theoretical position. Socialist feminism no longer exactly fits; but it never had an exact meaning. Marxism can't be made over, yet we still need it in these days of a totalizing and globalizing capitalism. Perhaps feminists will still find a way to transform it. Adequate theory, for me, must attend to the criticisms from women of color, women from postcolonial countries, and from at least some of the postmodernist and poststructuralist feminists. Language, images, identity, texts, are important, but they are not everything; capitalism is still there, and its effects become more, not less, alarming.

I think there is a pressing need for a new feminist analysis of economy that breaks out of the boundaries of "the economic" as represented by both neoclassical and Marxist political economy. (Rational choice theory frightens me.) I understood that a new feminist economics is a practical, political necessity when I interviewed activist Swedish women who were talking about a women's party. They realized that they could not successfully engage in the political process unless they could present an economic program that would make possible their other policy goals. Such an economics would privilege people over profits and encompass environmental issues; its standpoints would be located outside the "main business," in the daily struggles of women around the world. Of course, such efforts are being made by some feminist scholars already. Perhaps the new Marx of the twenty-first century will be a feminist collective.

To prepare the ground for that collective, there is still a lot of deconstruction and reconstruction to do. Our ways of conceptualizing are deeply implicated in the relations of ruling. As a consequence, we may be reproducing the ideological forms of the relations we oppose even as we are criticizing them. But there is no easy solution. For example, I recently was asked to write a short piece on gendered institutions and did so.[14] However, I should have questioned the concept of institution, which is firmly rooted in a theoretical tradition of which I have been critical. Instead, I used the concept because it does stand for something we can recognize. Many of the concepts that enter into the objectifying, mystifying practices of theory, contributing to the invisibility of women and gender, represent the organization of social relations that still exists and that feminists often oppose. To the extent that institution implies a universal normative form, it obscures or renders deviant many different ways that people construct their lives. The use of such a concept is part of the process of embedding it and its normative assumptions in the taken-for-granted of sociological talk. Yet sometimes not to use this concept as a convenient shorthand is awkward, even distorting. Similar dilemmas exist in many other efforts to move beyond the conceptual practices we have criticized.

All of this is interesting, even exciting, but in the absence of a vibrant social movement, I miss the 1970s. I also feel insulated now by age and, possibly, retirement from teaching, from the sorts of exhilarating battles that used to take a lot of my time and energy. I have received some awards for my work, which are affirmations for me but also signal that critical feminist sociology now has a legitimate place in the discipline in the United States. This is due to the work of many, many feminist scholars. I only hope that we don't lose our critical edge as we start to get such mainstream rewards. The attenuation of the links between academic feminism and the women's movement means that our primary source of creativity and vitality is much weaker, making it easier to forget that critical edge has to do with feminist action, as well as academic politics.

I feel satisfied, even though theoretical problems seem more difficult now than twenty-five years ago. My work has evidently had some impact. I think I am a better, more productive scholar today than I ever was. I am doing new research on gender and organizational restructuring with Don Van Houten. I return frequently for long periods of time to Sweden, Finland, and Norway, where I have many coworkers and friends. I do research in Scandinavia, and my work is sometimes published in Nordic languages. My political commitments have not changed, and I still think it is possible to do research that has both theoretical and practical implications. Feminist sociology has been an adventure worth doing.

## Notes

1. Joan Acker, "Women and Social Stratification: A Case of Intellectual Sexism," *American Journal of Sociology* 78 (1973): 174–183.
2. Joan Acker and Donald Van Houten, "Differential Recruitment and Control: The Sex Structuring of Organizations," *Administrative Science Quarterly* 19 (June 1974):152–163.
3. Iris Young, "Beyond the Unhappy Marriage: A Critique of the Dual Systems Theory," in Heidi Hartmann et al., *Women and Revolution* (London: Pluto Press, 1981).
4. Dorothy E. Smith, *The Everyday World as Problematic: A Feminist Sociology* (Boston: Northeastern University Press, 1987).
5. Joan Acker, Kate Barry, and Joke Esseveld, "Feminism, Female Friends, and the Reconstruction of Intimacy," in Helena Lopata, ed., *The Interweave of Social Roles: Men and Women*, vol. 2 (Greenwich, Conn.: JAI Press, 1981); Joan Acker, Joke Esseveld, and Kate Barry, "Objectivity and Truth: Problems in Doing Feminist Research," *Women's Studies International Forum* 6 (1983): 423–435.
6. Joan Acker, "Women and Stratification: A Review of Recent Literature," *Contemporary Sociology* 9 (1980): 25–34.
7. Joan Acker, "Gender, Class, and the Relations of Distribution," *Signs* 13 (1988):473–497.

8. Dorothy E. Smith, "Feminist Reflections on Political Economy," *Studies in Political Economy* 30 (1989): 52.

9. Joan Acker, *Doing Comparable Worth: Gender, Class, and Pay Equity* (Philadelphia: Temple University Press, 1989).

10. Joan Acker, "Hierarchies, Jobs, and Bodies: A Theory of Gendered Organizations," *Gender and Society* 4 (1990): 139–158; Joan Acker, "Gendering Organizational Theory," in Albert J. Mills and Peta Tancred, ed., *Gendering Organizational Analysis* (London: Sage, 1992).

11. Joan Acker, "Thinking About Wages: The Gendered Wage Gap in Swedish Banks," *Gender and Society* 5 (1991): 390–407; Joan Acker, "The Gender Regime of Swedish Banks," *Scandinavian Journal of Management* 10 (June 1994): 117–130.

12. Sally Hacker, *Pleasure, Power, and Technology* (Boston: Unwin Hyman, 1989); Sally Hacker, "Doing It the Hard Way" (Boston: Unwin Hyman, 1990).

13. Joan Acker, "Reformer och kvinnor i den framtida valfardstaten" (Reforms and women in the future welfare state), in Joan Acker et al., *Kvinnors och mans liv och arbete* (*Women's and men's life and work*) (Stockholm: SNS Forlag, 1992).

14. Joan Acker, "From Sex Roles to Gendered Institutions," *Contemporary Sociology* 21 (1992): 565–569.

*Barbara Laslett*

# On Finding a Feminist Voice: Emotion in a Sociological Life Story

*E*motions. This is a life story about emotions. About doubts and uncertainties, passions and commitments, risk-taking and resistance. For me, as for many intellectuals, confronting feelings has been especially marked in the context of my work. Emotions have shaped my intellectual choices and fueled the energy with which I have pursued them. This story is about that process—about how feelings affected my professional life, about how I came to recognize their sociological importance, and about how I have come to think about them theoretically. The various experiences that make up this personal narrative describe the journey that got me from where I started to where I am now—and the voice I found along the way. My narrative also provides a theoretical argument about the importance of emotions in the development of feminist sociology.

In 1965 I entered the doctoral program in sociology at the University of Chicago. I was thirty-two years old, the mother of a one-year-old daughter and a three-year-old son, and a faculty wife. I hadn't been a student since 1959, when I had received an interdisciplinary master's degree in social science from the University of Chicago. I was very nervous and very uncertain about my abilities. My undergraduate career had not been a distinguished one, and I wasn't at all sure about how I would fare in the highly competitive atmosphere into which I was entering, especially given my family responsibilities. Would I be able to do it? As it turns out, I wasn't the only one who was uncertain. From stories that reached me after the fact, the department had been resistant to admitting me. (A faculty wife! A mother! Surely not a good investment!) And throughout my graduate student career, whenever I met a certain eminent sociologist in the hallways of the social sciences building, he would look at me with a puzzled expression on his face and say, "Oh, yes, you're Mrs. Laslett. Your husband teaches in the History Department. Are you really serious about this?"

I didn't really need other people's doubts; I had quite enough of my own. In 1950 I had entered the College at the University of Chicago as an undergraduate. My parents had supported an expectation that I would go to college but surprised me by saying that I could go out of town. I had just assumed that I would go to one of the city colleges in New York City, where I had grown up. To the extent that I had thought about my future at all, it was to do a fine arts degree at Brooklyn College.[1] My choice of the University of Chicago was based on very little knowledge. I had a friend who was there, and I didn't really know about many other places. At the time I chose Chicago, I had no idea that a radical experiment in undergraduate education was in place or that Chicago was a great university.

Both of my parents were raised in poor, Orthodox Jewish families, and to my knowledge neither of them had finished more than about a tenth-grade education. During my lifetime, my father was a self-employed salesman of commercial refrigeration; he had immigrated to the United States from what was then part of the Austro-Hungarian Empire just before World War I. My mother, who had been born in the United States, achieved a relatively high-level job for a woman in the 1920s. She had managed to get to and through secretarial school and had ended up as private secretary to the chief lawyer at Paramount Films when its offices were located in New York. I had one brother, five years older than myself, and although the story is a bit murky, I think my mother returned to work after my brother's birth. She did the office work in my father's business from the time I was five years old until they both retired in the late 1950s. I grew up in a mainly lower-middle-class environment in the Bronx, where I went to quite ordinary public schools.

After two not very lustrous years in the undergraduate program at the University of Chicago, I dropped out of college—not quite knowing why I was there or where I was going. Although I had done well as a high school student, I wasn't that outstanding that I could tell whether my poor performance as an undergraduate was because I wasn't smart enough or because I spent too much time fooling around and singing folk songs. I worked at various clerical jobs in New York for the next four years and, after a romance gone awry, returned to Chicago in 1956 to finish my undergraduate degree. I continued on for an M.A. in social science (finally, my college grades began to indicate that I might have some intellectual ability), although I didn't have any clearly formulated career plans at the time. I thought vaguely about being a left-wing political journalist—an odd goal given that I suffered quite badly from writer's block. But I didn't have to figure out that future quite yet.

I was married in 1959 and emigrated to England with my husband at the beginning of 1960; there I had a variety of jobs (including some teaching and research at the University of Liverpool) until we moved back to Chicago in August 1962, where my husband had a faculty appointment. Our son, Michael, was born in October of that year. After one year of full-time motherhood, I began looking around for a job and was fortunate enough to find part-time work as research assistant to Alice S. Rossi. I worked for her between 1963 and 1965. As part of the job interview, Alice asked what I thought I would be doing in ten years. I answered that I expected to be working at a job but I had no clearly formed professional ambitions. That was to change substantially over the next two years.

What was not to change for a very long time was the question about my intellectual abilities. I carried those doubts with me for most of my career. Only within the past few years have I found a voice in which I have some confidence. Without the women's movement, I don't think it would have been possible. I especially don't think I could have come to understand, honor, and celebrate the pleasures and commitments that fuel and foster the voice I have found. Without the energy and directions that my feelings encouraged, I also would not have been as likely to participate in the political and intellectual work that has fostered feminist scholarship in sociology and within the academy in general. Those actions are part of the story that follows.

## William Fielding . . . Who?

Like many stories, however, I have to begin closer to the end of my narrative than the beginning—with a research project I started to work on in the early 1980s. It was a study of the life and work of the Chicago/Columbia sociologist William Fielding Ogburn (1886–1959), a major figure in the history of American sociology. Throughout most of his career—from 1919, when he joined the faculty at Barnard College/Columbia University until 1951, when he retired from the University of Chicago, where he had moved in 1927—Ogburn was an outspoken advocate of objectivism and quantification in sociology. For him, the goal of sociology was to become more scientific, and it was this goal, as well as his definition of science, that I wanted to understand sociologically. But why did I choose this topic? Why did I choose this man's life to study? Why did I choose a life history approach at all? In one way, I didn't know the answer to these questions when

I began this work. In another way, however, like any family tree, there are traceable connections.

Although I never met Ogburn, I was socialized into the discipline of sociology at the University of Chicago, where he spent many years of his career and where he left his imprint on the faculty and on the graduate training program. My thesis supervisor, the late Robert W. Hodge, was trained by one of Ogburn's most prominent students, Otis Dudley Duncan. Hodge was therefore an Ogburn "grandchild," and I was a "great-grandchild"; the language of kinship was actually used to describe relations between the generations of Duncan and Hodge progeny. The women's movement and an emerging feminist discourse within the academy affected how I thought about the work I had been trained to do. I began to question the positivist tenets that had been so central to my graduate education. Given the family connections, it is not too surprising that Ogburn should come to my mind as one of the founding fathers of scientism in American sociology. Given his often outspoken beliefs on the proper conduct of sociology, however, my choice was based on more than the fictive kinship between us.

William Fielding Ogburn is perhaps best known in sociology for his theory of social change and the place of "cultural lag"—a concept he created—in that process. Equally important, however (perhaps even more so), were Ogburn's articulation and advocacy of sociology as a science. He believed that the social sciences had to be radically differentiated from social philosophy and from social action, each of which had been part of the discipline's history. For Ogburn, sociology as a science should be concerned only with the discovery of new knowledge, generating empirical facts that are reliable, precise, and enduring. But he also believed there are psychological barriers to obtaining exact scientific knowledge.

Throughout his career, Ogburn was concerned about the impact of emotion on science. As a young man, he had read widely in psychoanalytic theory; the theory of the unconscious particularly impressed him. The unconscious nature of our desires, he thought, posed problems for the objective, scientific sociologist. For Ogburn, emotion was an enemy of science because it selected some factors for attention while blinding us to others. Statistics, however, offered a solution, he believed, because of the attention given to selection and representativeness and because techniques such as partial correlation (which he was among the first to use in social research) could, he thought, control the distorting effects of emotion.[2]

But Ogburn's views about science and emotion only became clear to me once my research was well advanced. When I began, I thought the answer to my question of how and why scientism in U.S. sociology had developed as it had would lie in the political arena. I expected the explanation to be found in the increasing demand for social scientists in government from World War I onward, particularly during the New Deal, which served the social interests of the mostly white, mostly middle-class men who responded to this demand. After working on the project for some time, however, I realized that the biographical research design to which I was committed could not adequately address the interest-based theory of social action that had shaped my early expectations. Yet, I did not want to abandon the design I was using. I didn't really have a good reason for my stubbornness. I hadn't yet figured out how to make sociological use of what biographical research could provide. I was certainly pressed to justify my choice as sociological (versus psychological, individual, and/or just plain perverse) many times over the years to follow. It was an intellectual challenge that engaged my thoughts and feelings for a long time. But despite my inability to respond in a satisfying way to the challenges that even the friendliest of my critics raised, I wouldn't give up the study. Somehow, it just *felt* right, although it took me a very long time to figure out why. And the answer—about the importance of emotions to a life story—came from Ogburn himself.

## A Political Past, Sort of . . .

I came to sociology with a strong commitment to progressive politics, although not much in the way either of political knowledge or political sophistication. My politics was a loose leftism that reflected post-World War II progressivism in the United States and was closer to the Old Left of the 1930s than the New Left of the 1960s; central to my politics were antiracism and folk music. My parents were liberal Democrats, and although there were some radicals in my family—one uncle was a union organizer; a couple of aunts and uncles were socialists—my immediate family environment was not very political at all. But my parents made a decision that, like sending me to the University of Chicago, was fateful for my future: they sent me to an interracial summer camp in upstate New York in 1946, when I was thirteen years old, and I went there through summer 1948 as well.[3] I think my parents' decision was an unselfconscious one—the camp fees were affordable for a lower-middle-class family, the camp has been advertised in the *New York Times Magazine* and therefore had to be respectable, and they had some vague ideas, I am sure, about racial discrimination and social inequality as wrong. For me, however, the experience was of enormous emotional importance because it connected antiracism with personal freedom and autonomy—and with being able to get away from my family. (My lifelong love of folk and political music began there as well.) From that point on, opposition to racism and opposition to social injustice were central parts of my identity. Indeed, in an important way they gave me an identity. They made me different from most of the people I knew. And they were infused with powerful feelings. I now had justifiable grounds to rebel against the conventional lower-middle-class environment in which I lived. My political activism (as well as numerous confrontations with the more conservative members of my family) was a very satisfying part of that rebellion.

In the late 1940s and early 1950s, having antiracist commitments automatically connected me to left-wing political groups and projects. My sense that these projects were important, and that being left wing was special, was reinforced during the postwar Red scare and the McCarthy period. Although usually characterized as a time of political quiescence and social conformity, this was a politically active period for me, sometimes as a folk music advocate, sometimes in more directly political ways.[4] Friends were being investigated by the FBI about their politics as they were drafted into the army during the Korean War. My sense of the importance and value of being a leftist in American society was again reinforced.

These political commitments had attracted me to sociology in the first place, but in the course of professional socialization and a personal trajectory shaped by Ogburnian standards, I had begun to be uncertain about their legitimacy as a basis for my work. It was only with the intellectual developments that grew out of the political movements of the 1960s and 1970s, especially the growth of Marxist and feminist sociologies, that I began to recover a sense that it was appropriate to try to connect my intellectual interests and my political commitments. But a tension between them still existed for me. How could I combine the powerful feelings associated with my politics with the highly rationalist practice of sociology that I was learning? I think the discomfort that tension produced, and a rebelliousness that somehow seemed like a precious aspect of myself, partly explains why I chose to study Ogburn's life and why I kept at it despite my difficulty in articulating the project in recognizably sociological terms. But it was in the confrontation with Ogburn's life, work, and ideas that I began to develop my own voice.

## Chicago Sociology—My Version

Now I can start my story closer to the beginning of my life as a sociologist—with an account of the sociological heritage to which I was exposed as a graduate student at the University of Chicago in the mid-1960s. When I speak here of "Chicago sociology," I do not mean what has come to be called the Chicago School—particularly the case study and fieldwork methods associated with Robert Park, Ernest Burgess, and Everett Hughes or the symbolic interactionism of George Herbert Mead and Anselm Strauss.[5] For me, Chicago sociology was social demography and survey research; it was these "factions" that had begun to dominate the department in, I think, the late 1950s and early 1960s.

When I had returned to college in 1956 to complete my B.A., I took my first course in sociology; it was on research methods and was taught jointly by Peter Blau and Otis Dudley Duncan. Duncan was soon to leave Chicago, but he returned (I think it was in 1966 or 1967) when I was a doctoral student taking a course with Peter Blau on social stratification. Duncan's guest lecture was on the status attainment model, which was to dominate so much sociological discourse about social stratification, a field that had a natural attraction for me, in the years to follow. The lecture was also about the uses of path analysis in sociology. It was very heady stuff—I was impressed by the analytic possibilities that this statistical technique seemed to offer, but I was also thrilled at having a glimpse of the "cutting edge" in sociology by the men who were honing it.[6]

Less directly Ogburnian, Peter Blau, Peter Rossi, and Jim (James A.) Davis were also important intellectual influences on me. These were the people who encouraged me to think I might actually become a sociologist, and given discouragements from other departmental quarters, I have always been grateful for their support. Their ideas strongly influenced me.[7] I was particularly attracted to the kind of structuralist thinking that was being developed at Chicago by people such as Peter Blau and Jim Davis. The attraction lay, in part, I think, in the capacity of structural analysis to explain people's behavior independent of their wills and intentions. And their feelings. To me, that was the lure and power of a sociological imagination—to see structural problems in place of personal troubles. This would, in time, be one major reason that I found Marxism intellectually attractive.

But there is a particular hindsight to storytelling—when you know the end before you start—that makes this account a great deal more linear and focused than I experienced it. I was also having my share of personal troubles—kids' ear infections, strep throats, and sleeping problems; my constantly interrupted sleep and studies; worries about child care; an intellectual insecurity that got worse, rather than better, over time; the juggling of my roles as mother, faculty wife and hostess, and a graduate student; and a marriage that was beginning to unravel. So mainly I spent my time studying and just trying to keep it all together. There were, of course, important events that punctuated my graduate student career. After my first year, Pete Rossi offered me a National Opinion Research Center (NORC) training fellowship. His good opinion of me boosted my confidence and paid for child care as well. But the fellowship was not renewed for the following year, and I had to go begging for financial support from men who neither encouraged my studies nor thought my fellowship request legitimate.[8] (After all, I had a husband to support me, didn't I?) I was given another fellowship,[9] grudgingly, but my minimal confidence had been badly shaken. I felt a little better about myself, however, when, a couple of months after I was turned down for the NORC fellowship, I was the only one in my cohort to get honors in our Ph.D. written examinations.[10] That was a high, a sense of achievement, of validation, right up there with having babies!!!

Two aspects of my Chicago heritage are, I think, important to my story: (1) the strong empirical emphasis of Chicago sociology and, with it, a focus on research methodology, especially, in my experience, statistics—which I found attractive but embarrassingly difficult. And (2) a superrationalism, a positioning of one's self in the world of sociology based on a belief in the power of the intellect alone to uncover sociological truths. Part of this belief, although not explicitly articulated as such, was the Ogburnian idea that to be truly objective, one had to maintain an emotional distance from one's intellectual work. I carried these influences with me as I began my career as a sociologist. What I didn't see at the time was how much this position denied the connection between feelings and intellect and that such a connection fosters one's sociological imagination. It was only later still that I realized that this denial was part of the legacy that I had inherited at Chicago.

Nevertheless, it seems reasonable to ask why these parts of the Chicago heritage affected me so strongly—because there were others that I did not adopt: Morris Janowitz's concern with civic responsibility, Peter Blau's concern with theory building. I think now that the inattention to emotions—or, more accurately, an ideological and rhetorical commitment to such inattention—helped me concentrate on work under very difficult personal circumstances. Had I dared open myself to the feelings that were so much a part of those years—worries about my children, about my marriage, about my intellectual abilities—I think I would have been sunk. Of course, given the distorting effects of my efforts at emotional control (unsuccessful, I am sure, as often as they were successful), I was sunk anyway. Fortunately, feminism and William Fielding Ogburn came along to help me out of my dilemma.

## The Beginning of My Life as a Feminist

I had not thought much about feminism one way or the other until I began working as a research assistant for Alice Rossi in 1963. In my political circles in the late 1940s and early 1950s, "male chauvinism" certainly was not politically correct, but I don't remember anything happening because of it.[11] Nor was much thought given to what feminism might mean for our politics or for our personal lives. But when I began to work for Alice, she gave me a manuscript copy of her soon to be published *Daedalus* article "Equality Between the Sexes: An Immodest Proposal," and I was very inspired by it—intellectually and personally.[12] Even so, I didn't realize that feminism was a response to women's oppression or that it had anything to do with me. I was to do so soon enough.

My first full-time job as a sociologist was as a lecturer in the Department of Sociology at UCLA.[13] I didn't fully understand that to be a lecturer meant that I could not work up through the academic ranks from this non-tenure-track position. I found out quickly enough, however, that of the six or seven young faculty members hired by the UCLA department in 1968, I was the only woman and the only lecturer. All the rest were men. All of them had tenure-track appointments. Even if I didn't yet have a feminist consciousness fully available to me, I knew there was something wrong with that situation!

I went to my first professional meetings in 1969 in San Francisco. That was quite a time. Ralph Turner, one of the luminaries in the UCLA department, was president of the American Sociological Association; it was the formal beginning of radical sociology, with its separate sessions at Glide Memorial Church; and there were disruptions at several regular sessions at the San Francisco Hilton. I did not identify as part of the sociological liberation movement that was being built then.[14] Indeed, I did not see myself as a radical sociologist at all. I was a radical person but definitely a conventional sociologist.

For me, however, those meetings were important for other reasons. First, the oral defense of my dissertation (a secondary analysis of survey data on work satisfaction among a sample of American men) was, for reasons of convenience, held at the convention hotel. In attendance were Bill Hodge, Morris Janowitz, Peter Blau, David Street, and Robert K. Merton. I felt that I was really traveling in the big time. The previous evening at a session in which Bill had been on a panel, he and a group of his students, including myself, left the meeting room together. On the way out, Bill stopped to say hello to Robert Merton, introduced me as one of his students, and invited Merton to the oral. I was thrilled and petrified. Out of sheer nervousness, I carried myself with characteristic Chicago arrogance during the oral, and my dissertation was approved without changes. Second, and immediately afterward, I went down to the meeting of the first ASA Women's Caucus session, which had been organized by Alice Rossi. The room was bursting at the seams.

Alice had organized the panel from a life course perspective, asking women who were at different points in their sociology careers to make presentations. I was to speak as a graduate student/junior faculty person. I had told Alice when she invited me to be on the panel that I wasn't sure I could make it because my oral was scheduled for the immediately preceding time slot and I didn't know how long it would last. I got there in time, however. Alice greeted me, asked how the exam had gone, and when my turn came to speak, introduced me as the newest Ph.D. in the room.

It is perhaps not surprising that I can remember the feelings I had at the event but not much else. I was so dazed that I don't even remember who else was on the panel, except for Marlene Dixon (a leading figure among radical sociologists), who came up to me at some point and offered congratulations for getting my union card. At any rate, when I got up to the microphone I began to speak about the sexist way—I had learned the language by then—I had been treated at UCLA: the only woman, the only lecturer. And I remember ending my presentation with a rousing cry that went something like "And I'm not going to let them get away with it!" God, did I feel powerful!

Feeling powerful and being powerful, however, are two different things, and after two years as a lecturer at UCLA, I accepted a tenure-track position at San Fernando Valley State College (now California State University, Northridge). While I was there, my first *American Journal of Sociology* paper was published and my first historical paper on the family was accepted for publication in the *Journal of Marriage and the Family*.[15] About a year after I moved out to Valley State, I heard that a tenure-track job was open in the Department of Sociology at the University of Southern California. I applied for and got it.

Sometime in there, I became involved with the political action part of feminism in sociology. (Of course, I joined Sociologists for Women in Society as soon as it was founded.) I don't recall why I was approached, but in the early 1970s I was asked by Gertrude Seiznick, then president of the Pacific Sociological Association, to serve on a committee, with Arlene Daniels and Sol Kobrin (a colleague at USC), to investigate a sex discrimination case in the region. It was a fascinating experience—as well as providing me with the first opportunity to meet and work with Arlene Daniels, who has remained a sociological colleague and personal friend.[16] Arlene and I spent some time serving on the Committee on Discrimination Against Women in the Pacific Sociological Association, and soon after I also served on the American Sociological Association's Committee on Freedom of Research and Teaching. Both of these appointments gave me opportunities to participate in investigations of discrimination charges, and I learned much about university governance and grievance procedures. Unfortunately, I soon had personal reasons to appreciate the knowledge that these investigations had provided.

I became an assistant professor at the University of Southern California in 1972. In the 1973–1974 academic year, my husband had a visiting appointment at the University of Warwick in England, and we spent the year living in London. In fall 1973, after I got back to Los Angeles, I was told by the chairman of my department, Malcolm Klein, that my contract would not be renewed. I was astounded. My publication record was quite respectable and seemed likely to continue that way. So the action wasn't professional. It wasn't even personal. It was just, I was told, that the Department of Sociology had a budgetary problem. Mac explained the problem and informed me of his decision not to renew my contract.[17] To my knowledge, he made the decision without having my work evaluated and without consulting other department members. I appealed the decision through the university grievance system. And won. I then immediately went up for my tenure review.

Those were hard times. For two and a half years, I didn't know where my future lay or if I had one in sociology. At first I went on the national job market and began to think seriously about what it would mean to be part of a commuter family. But when I won my appeal, I decided that if I didn't get tenure, I would find a nonacademic job in Los Angeles. Fortunately, I didn't have to put that decision to the test. I was promoted in 1975, and I thought that I could relax a bit, that the rest of my career in sociology would run along the familiar lines that I had developed at the University of Southern California. Of course, I was wrong!

## An Important Move—into Marxism

Early in my time at USC, I began working on a quantitative study of family structure in nineteenth-century Los Angeles using data from the individual federal census schedules. This was a trendy thing to do in historical scholarship if one worked on the family and had quantitative skills. Both were true of me. Intellectually, I was moving away from the fields I had focused on as a graduate student: the sociology of work and social stratification. I had quantitative skills, and I wasn't quite ready to give up the professional legitimation they gave me. There was little support in my department for the historical family project I was working on. Nevertheless, the fact that I tried to get grants—and sometimes was successful—seemed to satisfy some of my senior colleagues that I really was a sociologist.

Nevertheless, I had tenure, and I was ready to branch out intellectually. I knew that I needed more training in statistics. But I had come to realize that I needed more training in social theory as well, especially Marxist theory. I knew I would not have time to study both statistics and Marxism while teaching, doing research and writing, being active in professional and feminist organizations, and, of course, being a mother and a wife.[18] I chose Marxism and spent the following two years taking courses on Marxist theory with Robert Brenner in the Department of History at UCLA.

My story is still in the mid-1970s, when Marxism had begun to gain some academic respectability in the United States. For me, it was the first time that I was able to connect my political and intellectual identities. To be a Chicago-trained, quantitative sociologist no longer required that I disassociate myself from my politics. That hope was encouraged by Erik Olin Wright's quantitative work on class structure, which was just beginning to appear in print.[19] But I still wasn't clear about how to apply the broader conceptions of historical materialism to my research on nineteenth-century families in Los Angeles. I tried to do so in my first *American Sociological Review* article and was quite embarrassed to be told afterward that I had incorrectly understood Marx's ideas about "The So-Called Primitive Accumulation" in *Capital*.[20] But, it was a first step in trying to bring together my intellectual and political interests.

The rise of Marxist sociology gave me something to identify with that legitimated a connection between my intellectual interests in structural analysis and my feelings about social justice. Although by then I had a feminist personal and political identity firmly in place, I hadn't yet figured out how to combine all these parts of myself intellectually. William Fielding Ogburn was to help me do so.

## Back to Ogburn . . . and Emotion

I spent most of the 1980–1981 academic year as a Fellow at the Center for Advanced Study in the Behavioral Sciences in Stanford, California. It was the best of times and the worst of times. I loved the intellectual stimulation and companionship, the marvelous working conditions, the sense of having been chosen, the new people I was meeting, the (mostly illusory) sense of community and common enterprise. My son, who began as an undergraduate at Berkeley that same year, seemed to be doing fine; the same could not be said either of my daughter or of my marriage. I was living alone for the first time in many years; my husband and Sarah, who was in her junior year of high school, remained in Los Angeles. I traveled back— or they came up to me—about every other weekend. It was a reasonable arrangement theoretically; in practice it was a disaster.

I was beside myself with worry and guilt. I could no longer ignore my emotions. They were blocking everything else out. So early in that year I turned to Nancy Chodorow, who was also a fellow at the Center. I did not know Nancy well then. We had met only once, briefly, at the 1980 American Sociological Association meetings a few weeks before our Center year began, at a dinner celebrating the tenth anniversary of the founding of Sociologists for Women in Society. But I remember walking into her office at the Center one day early in fall, bursting into tears, and saying that feminism had made us sisters and I needed her help. She was wonderfully supportive throughout the year, and we have been close friends ever since. But she was *not* supportive of what I was doing intellectually.

One of the rituals at the Center is the Wednesday night seminar at which fellows make presentations from the work they are doing. Nancy was the commentator on my paper (on changes in nineteenth-century Los Angeles family structure), and although appreciative of some of the things I was trying to do, she criticized me for not being enough of a feminist sociologist, for not incorporating gender relations into my analysis. I was shocked. How could I not be a feminist sociologist when I had devoted so much time and energy to women's issues in the profession? Wasn't my insistence on the importance of the family for understanding social change feminist enough? I didn't really understand the criticism, but it stayed with me. It wouldn't be until I moved to the University of Minnesota and was among a group of wonderful women's historians and other feminist scholars that I began to understand what it might mean to do a gendered historical analysis of the family.

I don't remember exactly when different things happened after my Center year was over. My life got pretty chaotic. My marriage ended; I got a visiting teaching appointment at the University of Chicago that allowed me to do archival work on Ogburn; my daughter graduated from high school, started college at the University of California, Berkeley, quickly dropped out, and moved to Arco Santi in Arizona to raise herbs and live a communal life; and my son went off for a junior year in France. I was offered the editorship of *Contemporary Sociology,* which I accepted. I had enjoyed a similar, if smaller, job as book review editor for *Sociology and Social Research,* the sociological journal published out of USC. But in addition, I knew that I would probably be unable to concentrate on my intellectual concerns given the chaos of my life at the time and that the editorship might give me some cover for not publishing much.[21] I got a job offer from the University of Minnesota in spring 1983 and moved myself and *Contemporary Sociology* there that summer.

## The Warming Breeze of Feminism in the Upper Midwest

The focus of my intellectual interests began to change again as I edited *Contemporary Sociology* during my first three years at Minnesota. The job made it possible for me to see and learn from broader intellectual developments in the social sciences, especially in historical and feminist scholarship. Of particular importance, I think, was that Minnesota provided an intellectual community in which biography and life histories were seen as a legitimate genre of social research.[22] Mary Jo Maynes, in the Department of History at Minnesota, who has become a treasured friend, as well as colleague, was particularly important to me in this regard. During this time, I began to write up the results of the Ogburn research, but I hadn't found the right voice yet. I was still making the political argument (expansion of the state, increased demand for social scientists in government, etc.), but the fit between the theory and the data was not comfortable for me; a single life history wasn't enough to sustain the argument. There's nothing like a little free time to concentrate, however, and that became available to me in 1986 after I had finished being editor of *Contemporary Sociology* and had a sabbatical leave from Minnesota.

I spent most of the 1986–1987 academic year as a visiting scholar at the Center for the Social Sciences at Columbia University. For much of that time, I read in feminist sociology/philosophy of science and in social studies of science. I was especially influenced by the writings of Evelyn Fox Keller and Susan Bordo, whose work I had become familiar with as part of my general reading in feminist scholarship and my reading of the debates in the sociology of scientific knowledge.[23] I came to see those fields as the appropriate frame for what I was learning from Ogburn's life story. I was finally able to see the *sociological* importance of emotion. William Fielding Ogburn gave me the insight, and the University of Minnesota gave me the time and money to pursue it.

At some point during my years working on the Ogburn project, I interviewed Ogburn's surviving son, Fielding. It wasn't an especially illuminating interview, but it was nevertheless a breakthrough for me because he gave me, among other personal documents that proved helpful, a copy of a single, undated page of typescript that his father had written. The relevant passage reads: "My father, planter and merchant, died in 1890 when I was four. Then began my long struggle to resist a dear mother's beautiful but excessive love. To the successful outcome, I attribute my strong devotion to objective reality, my antipathy to the distorting influence of emotion."

Ogburn had found a way to distance himself from "the distorting influence of emotion"—the creation of scientism in the culture and practice of academic sociology. He spent a great deal of time and energy creating the kind of intellectual standards and working conditions that he found emotionally comfortable. Of course, he was not alone in these preferences and activities. Despite opponents, Ogburn's views were shared by many academic men, and their collective energies helped institutionalize a positivist analytic vision in the world of American sociology. Ogburn told me that I had to locate his professional actions in his family relationships. As a historical sociologist, I realized that both the professional and the personal dimensions of that life had to be seen within their historically specific context.

But what had seemed to work for Ogburn wasn't working for me. I had, wisely or not, tried to follow his explicit dictum to "crush out emotion and . . . discipline the mind so strongly" that my beliefs and commitments, and my feelings, did not carry over into my sociological work.[24] It had been a mostly unconscious strategy for getting on with my work under difficult circumstances. Yet I had not been able to use my own, largely alienated, experience—as Dorothy Smith recommends we do—to understand the world of American sociology.[25] I now found myself able to do so and to make intellectual connections between the two fields in which I had done most of my work—the history of the American family and the history of American sociology—by recognizing the relationship of gender, sexuality, and emotion to them both.[26] The story goes like this.

Ogburn identified his early family relationships as key to understanding his "devotion to objective reality." Although he mentioned his relationship with his mother as particularly important and did not make much of his absent father, I saw them both as relevant, historically, as well as individually. Ogburn's family relationships were not just those of an individual life story; they reflected changes in the social organization of gender relations in nineteenth-century North America and their reorganization at the beginning of the twentieth, as well as changes in economic, political, and cultural life. I had finally come to see the theoretical importance of historical changes in the organization of social reproduction and of the gender relations that were central to it—if variable social reproduction and gender relations could have potential theoretical power in historical sociology.[27]

## Ogburn's Voice and Mine

As I've already said, the answer I expected when I began my Ogburn research was that scientism in American sociology reflected the expanded demand for social scientists by the government. In this context, which included the post–World War I Red scare and anticommunism in American politics and higher education in general, I thought that sociologists, whose early history was connected to social reform, might see the need to make claims about their objectivity. This was certainly true for Ogburn, who was conscious of the dangers of appearing too radical and, by the end of his career, called political action in academia, especially left-wing activism by professors, "unfair" to his academic employers because it could bring public criticism down on them.[28]

The growth of government interest in the social sciences, as well as faith in planning for social change, was part of the expansion of the state from World War I onward.[29] The demand for people to put this faith into practice was constructed, in part, by the very men who would be called on to satisfy it; men like Ogburn not only met the demand but also created it partly through the rhetoric of science they were constructing for the social sciences. In addition, the occupational opportunities available to American men—especially white, Protestant men whose family origins had led them to expect social deference and authority—were changing as the economy moved away from its more local and agrarian past and into a more national, urban, and international capitalist market economy.[30] The occupations and professions that had previously supported their social positions—farming, small business, law, medicine, the clergy—were changing. Salaried work was increasingly replacing self-employment, and some professions, such as the clergy, were declining in status, while others, medicine, for instance, were raising standards and limiting entry. The opportunities for middle-class men to ensure their social standing were in flux.[31]

In the course of my Ogburn work, however, I came to see that explanations that emphasized the traditional markers of social position—class, status, and power—were necessary but not sufficient. A focus on social structure and the individual's location within it—usually occupation, education, income, and the lifestyle to which the person was connected—neglected important and socially relevant social characteristics such as race and gender.[32] For instance, the increasing importance of men's labor market characteristics for the meaning of masculinity had not been considered important, even though gender relations were central elements of the social changes that were occurring.

For the most part, theories of action have been neglected in these accounts. Interest-based models are implicit in many historical studies of the social sciences in nineteenth- and twentieth-century America but are not often made explicit.[33] The master trope in much contemporary social theory for talking about action, rational choice models, often explains behavior as an unmediated and direct outcome of social position. To the extent that emotions enter into conceptions of rationality, they are transformed into a metric of calculation and/or are treated as sources of irrationality.[34]

The conclusion I drew about why scientism in American sociology emerged how and when it did was that however much political developments, professional aspirations, and social interests had affected the history of the discipline, gender relations, sexuality, and personal life were also important parts of that history. In my study of Ogburn's life, I had come to see that the growth and spread of scientism in the social sciences in the early decades of the twentieth century were connected to the gendered character of social organization in the nineteenth. Of particular importance was the organization of family, economic, and political life around the rhetoric and practice of separate spheres for women and men in the earlier time period and their reorganization during the later one. According to this model, emotion was part of women's sphere in the domestic setting, while rationality was masculine and a feature of the marketplace.[35] But I had also come see that the rhetoric of emotional specialization encoded in the doctrine of separate spheres needed to be viewed not as part of the natural order, as many nineteenth-century authors claimed, but as historical outcomes whose emergence and institutionalization could be known. Most important, perhaps, I came to see the sociological relevance of emotion, gender, and sexuality to theories of human agency and social action. Furthermore, I saw a need to move away from explanations that favored structural forces *or* human agency and to be more attentive to their intersections.[36]

If we are to examine human agency at particular historical intersections, we must have a better way to theorize agency, to understand why people do what they do under concrete historical conditions. My Ogburn research allowed me to begin that project and to see sex, gender, and emotions as central to the theoretical task. Family relationships, sexual identity, and cultures of sexuality can provide powerful motives for human actions, and gender relations are central to understanding them. Furthermore, sexual energy and meaning can be attached to social phenomena in ways that are not obviously related to sexuality or gender at all, as in the meaning of occupational activity and success for men's gendered sense of masculinity. Furthermore, the sexual nature of that energy gives some actions, but not others, a particular charge, a particular emotional power.

Ogburn's categories of emotion versus objectivity and his rhetorical insistence that the former be excluded from the realm of scientific sociology were not, in the final analysis, of much use to me. It would not, I think, have taken me so long to find a feminist voice, nor would it have been as much of a struggle if I hadn't accepted the categories of my Ogburnian heritage. Of course, Ogburn didn't create these categories; he, as I after him, had inherited them from our individual pasts and from the intellectual discourses that were part of them. But he was part of my past as someone who was influential in changing the meanings of science in twentieth-century sociology and in institutionalizing these new meanings in the academy. His successes were, perhaps, especially relevant to me given that I was trained to be a sociologist in the same department in which he (and his students) had been influential. I wonder if it would have taken me so long to find a feminist voice if the dichotomous thinking that Ogburn employed—emotion versus objectivity—had not been so widely accepted and perpetuated within the discipline.

Feminist scholars have documented historical variation in the meanings and organization of masculinity, femininity, and sexuality, but it is not sufficient to stop there. It is also important to ask how and why the gendered meanings of cultural forms and social institutions develop as they do. In the case of U.S. sociology, I have suggested that part of the answer is to be found in the changing economic and political life during the early history of sociology's growth, particularly in the period after World War I. But the answer is also to be found in changing family and gender relations and in the ideologies associated with them. One of the conclusions I drew from my research on William Fielding Ogburn was that, consciously or unconsciously, achieving a gendered identity—indeed, creating new meanings for masculinity—was part of the intellectual agendas of the mostly white, mostly middle-class male social scientists of the time. And creating "masculinized" settings in the colleges and universities, research centers and government agencies, in which these men worked was also part of the agenda. The development *and gendering* of ideas about hard and soft science, hard and soft methods, hard and soft fields of inquiry have charged these dichotomized categories of thought with an emotional power that can obscure their gendering power. The other conclusion was about the sociological significance of emotion—in Ogburn's life and in my own.

## Finding My Voice

The years between 1990 and 1995 were especially satisfying and demanding ones for me. As the editor (with Ruth-Ellen B. Joeres) of *Signs: Journal of Women in Culture and Society* during that time, I was able to bring together the two pieces of my identity—the political and the academic—that had so often been at war with each other. The stimulation and struggle of putting together a journal that satisfied standards from both realms of experience helped me find the theoretical voice that is now central to my intellectual work. In the process I also began to recognize that the efforts to separate my intellectual and political values that one part of me had, misguidedly, internalized from my graduate training had done more harm than good. And that recognition also helped me better understand the problems that the Ogburn and Los Angeles projects had posed for me.

There were emotional components, albeit contradictory ones, to the work I was doing—and the way I was doing it—that go some way toward explaining the tenacity with which I kept to my Chicago habits. My contradictory commitments—to objectivism, to social justice—and the intellectual and personal discomfort those contradictions aroused led me to a more conscious critique of positivism and ultimately helped me overcome what were, for me, limitations of the sociology I had learned as a graduate student and had practiced throughout the early years of my career. They also were part of what led me to the Ogburn project. Of particular importance was a recognition of the positive uses of emotion in my intellectual work.

Emotions—doubts, fears, commitments, identity, self-concept, anger, and pleasure—not only make particular subjects and methods interesting to us, but they also provide the energy to pursue them even when the way to do so is not clear. Feelings, including the ambivalences and contradictions that are often present, also help us make use of our own experience as a basis for questioning how particular social conditions might affect others. Through recognition of our own feelings, reflexivity—a key tenet of feminist research methodology—can become a powerful tool in our pursuit of knowledge. Reflexivity need not be simply (or simplistically) a form of self-referencing that results in thinking that others experience the world in the same ways that we do. But recognizing the role of feelings in our own lives can lead us to ask how they affect the lives of others.

Perhaps I can now say why I stuck with the Ogburn and the LA projects. Emotions that derived from my commitments and interests carried me along and fostered my continued work on these studies despite the intellectual troubles I was having with them. It was only when I understood the power of feelings in Ogburn's life that I became able to construct a theoretical account that made sociological sense of his life—and mine. Had I not incorporated the Ogburnian (and Chicago) dictum about the need to separate emotions from my sociological research and writing, perhaps it would not have taken me so long to recognize emotions' importance. Had I not had reasons of my own for sticking to the objectivist model of sociology, I might not have been so hesitant to acknowledge the relation of emotions to sociological practice and sociological theory.

Feelings are part of our professional norms and practices, however much they have been rhetorically proscribed. The coolness of tone, the definition of emotion as unprofessional and unscientific, the insistence that we eschew our feelings, limit our abilities to see and value the emotional components in our professional lives and the theoretical importance of emotion in the social life we study. Without further thought, emotions—and their gendered character—are assumed to be separable from our actions, capable of being "'eschewed." The recognition of emotions will not benefit the work we do, however—or the professional environment in which we do it—if such recognition is used only to establish better control over them. In exploring the positive values of engagement and commitment in this essay, I do not mean to suggest that analytic distance, and the skills and emotions that achieving such distance entail, cannot also be powerful tools in sociological analysis. But they cannot be the only ones.

## An Afterthought

I have learned many things—about myself and about social theory—in writing this essay. And the work I have done here has also led me to rethink some of the ideas I had when I began it. I have seen more clearly than at the outset the theoretical importance of emotion in debates about social structure, human agency, and their intersections. I have also learned more about the usefulness of personal narratives in sociological study and their contributions to social theory.[37] We need to consider further how social actors as thinking, feeling selves in relations with others can be most fruitfully integrated into sociological theory and practice and how the historical context, which includes such actors, as well as structures, institutions, and cultures, both constructs and is constructed by them. Ogburn wanted to control emotions so that they would not bias sociological observations and interpretations. In some ways, feminist methodology, with its emphasis on recognizing the researcher's place in the research process, has also called attention to how researchers create, rather than uncover, knowledge. There is, however, an important difference. Ogburn wanted to "crush out emotions," to control them statistically and normatively. For the most part, contemporary feminists in the social sciences do not. Rather, as scholars we want to study emotions and use them as a way to learn about the world, perhaps even to change it.

But I have also come to understand that having a good idea is no guarantee that anything will flow from it without advocacy and organization. I learned this from being a feminist in the academy and now am using that knowledge outside of it as well. So in my sixties, I have returned to the political activism of my younger years as a founding and active member of Progressive Minnesota, an affiliate of the New Party, a national political party dedicated to democratic politics and social justice. I have also returned to another love of my youth and have become a student of jewelry making at the Minneapolis Technical College.

A final word. My daughter, Sarah, pointed out after she read an early draft of this essay that in it I left her in Arizona and my son, Michael, in France. As I write this, however, Sarah is in graduate school and sings with a local jazz band, and Michael works in the reform wing of the U.S. trade union movement and continues our tradition of political music as well as political activism. And when we can, the three of us still sing together. As for myself, I am looking toward retiring and being able to focus on my intellectual interests more than the responsibilities of a university professor allow. I look forward to continuing the personal relationships that have so enriched my life, of course; to carrying on with my political activities; and to making jewelry. Maybe I'll even find new things to explore, new places to go, new people to know.

## Notes

I want to thank, as always, the personal and intellectual comradeship of Johanna Brenner and Mary Jo Maynes.

1. My fantasy was to have a little shop on West 4th Street in Greenwich Village where I would make and sell copper jewelry. Somehow I thought a fine arts degree was the way to get there.
2. For a more detailed account of Ogburn's views and life story, see my "Unfeeling

Knowledge: Emotion and Objectivity in the History of Sociology," *Sociological Forum* 5 (1990): 413–433; and my "Biography as Historical Sociology," *Theory and Society* 20 (1991): 511–538.

3. In contrast to some of the better known interracial summer camps in the Northeast, the one I attended was *not* part of the existing left-wing culture and institutions. The camp owner and director was an African-American doctor who was also a Republican, and when counselors arrived wearing Henry Wallace for President buttons in 1948, they were told to take them off. I had my first crush while at this camp and usually had a different one each year.

4. The music to which I was especially committed was connected to the labor movement and African-American blues. In the groups I was in, it was definitely political to support and be interested in these cultural forms.

5. For a discussion of the Chicago School, see Martin Bulmer, *The Chicago School of Sociology: Institutionalization, Diversity, and the Rise of Sociological Research* (Chicago: University of Chicago Press, 1984). When I entered the doctoral program in 1965, Hughes, Strauss, and David Reisman had all left Chicago, although I had taken courses with Hughes and Reisman in my earlier student days there. I became affiliated with the more quantitative and positivist segment of the department, largely because I was explicitly not welcomed by a faculty member who had organized another group to which my political values and intellectual interests drew me. In my experience, the "quants" were a lot more meritocratic than those who explicitly professed liberal values.

6. In my memory, I recall Duncan calling path analysis a "heuristic device," a phrase that I have always found helpful in thinking about sociological models—even if Duncan didn't say it.

7. Alice Rossi was not a faculty member in the Department of Sociology (or in any other department of the university—to the institution's impoverishment), and although our friendship continued after I began my doctoral training, she no longer played a mentoring role in my intellectual development. She had already done so, however, as a model of sociological excellence and intellectual passion during the two years I had worked for her.

8. A newly appointed young faculty person was in charge of the fellowship committee at NORC. He didn't think I was smart enough to merit a renewal of my fellowship and told me so when I inquired about the decision of nonrenewal. Maybe all "quants" are not so meritocratic after all.

9. Thanks to the efforts of Pete Rossi.

10. While the young faculty member who had denied the renewal of my fellowship never acknowledged that perhaps he had made a mistake about my abilities—an unrealistic hope on my part, I guess—my performance on these exams did bring me to the notice of Robert W. Hodge. He was a wonderful thesis supervisor and a highly supportive colleague after graduate school, even though my intellectual interests soon began to diverge from the quantitative analysis of survey data that had been the basis of my dissertation.

11. "Male chauvinist pig" was not a phrase available to us then; we did have the term "male chauvinism," however.

12. Alice S. Rossi, "Equality Between the Sexes: An Immodest Proposal," *Daedalus* 93 (1964): 607–652.

13. My husband had got a tenured job in the Department of History there in 1968; for neither of us were my career possibilities a prominent part of our decision to move to Los Angeles, nor did we consider job hunting as a couple.

14. For some accounts of the radical sociology movement and its activities at the 1969 ASA, see Martin Oppenheimer, Martin J. Murray, and Rhonda F. Levine, eds., *Radical Sociologists and the Movement* (Philadelphia: Temple University Press, 1991).

15. See Barbara Laslett, "Mobility and Work Satisfaction: A Discussion of the Use and Interpretation of Mobility Models," *American Journal of Sociology* 77 (1971): 19–35; and Barbara Laslett, "The Family as a Public and Private Institution: An Historical Perspective, *Journal of Marriage and the Family* 35 (1973): 480–492. As a graduate student, I had never taken a course in the sociology of the family. But when I began working at UCLA, a large undergraduate course on the subject was part of my teaching assignment. I found the field at that time not very interesting, and having a historian husband, John Laslett, undoubtedly influenced my move into the historical study of the family and later into historical sociology more generally.

16. See the wonderful essay by Arlene Kaplan Daniels, "When We Were All Boys Together: Graduate School in the Fifties and Beyond," in Kathryn P. Meadow Orlans and Ruth A. Wallace, eds., *Gender and the Academic Experience: Berkeley Women Sociologists* (Lincoln: University of Nebraska Press, 1994), pp. 27–43, for an autobiographical account of her place in the growth of feminist sociology, as well her importance to many of the authors in this volume.

17. A senior faculty member who for the preceding several years had been working in a different unit of the university decided that he wanted to return to the department—a right that he had been guaranteed. During his absence, I had been hired in a tenure-track position. When the senior member chose to exercise his "retreat rights," there were not sufficient funds to pay us both. That was the problem.

18. While in Los Angeles, I had been instrumental in founding a local chapter of SWS. In addition, I was part of a group—we called ourselves Red Wednesday (because sometimes we met on Wednesday)—of women Marxist sociologists that included Edna Bonacich, Johanna Brenner, Norma Chincilla, Nora Hamilton, and Julia Wrigley. Not everyone in this group would have self-identified as a "feminist," although gender inequality would be criticized by us all. We met monthly for supper, gossip, and critique of our writings in progress.

19. Erik Olin Wright and Lucca Perone, "Marxist Class Categories and Income Inequality," *American Sociological Review* 42 (1977): 32–55. Barbara Heyns, part of the group of Hodge students with me at Chicago, was a major influence in teaching Erik Wright the quantitative skills that have been central to his work. I guess that makes Erik my nephew.

20. Barbara Laslett, "Social Change and the Family: Los Angeles, California, 1850–1870," *American Sociological Review* 42 (1977): 268–291. That my error was not caught by the people who reviewed the paper for the *American Sociological Review* indicates that I was not alone in needing to understand Marx better.

21. I had ended my year at the Center without much to show for it in terms of published work. My feelings over that lack of productivity were so connected with the breakup of my marriage that it took me quite a few years to recognize that the problems were intellectual, as well as personal. I hadn't yet seen how to connect feminist theory and gender relations to the historical family work I was doing. I

was to do so in the context of a series of papers that Johanna Brenner and I wrote together from the mid-1980s onward. See Johanna Brenner and Barbara Laslett, "Social Reproduction and the Family," in Ulf Hismelstrand, ed., *The Social Reproduction of Organization and Culture* (London: Sage, 1986), pp. 116–131; Barbara Laslett and Johanna Brenner, "Gender and Social Reproduction," *Annual Review of Sociology* 15 (1989): 381–404; and Johanna Brenner and Barbara Laslett, "Gender, Social Reproduction, and Women's Political Self-organization in the Development of the U.S. Welfare State," *Gender and Society* 5 (1991): 311–333. But it was really in the context of the Ogburn research, which I was doing simultaneously, that these various lines of thought came together for me.

22. See Personal Narratives Group, ed., *Interpreting Women's Lives: Feminist Theory and Personal Narratives* (Bloomington: Indiana University Press, 1989), which emerged from a conference at the University of Minnesota in 1986.

23. Evelyn Fox Keller, *Reflections on Gender and Science* (New Haven, Conn.: Yale University Press, 1985); Susan Bordo, "The Cartesian Masculinization of Thought," *Signs* 11 (1986): 439–456.

24. William Fielding Ogburn, "The Folkways of a Scientific Sociology," *Scientific Monthly* 30 (1930): 300–306.

25. She does so brilliantly in, among other writings, Dorothy E. Smith, "A Berkeley Education," in Orlans and Wallace, eds., *Gender and the Academic Experience,* pp. 45–56. See also Dorothy E. Smith, *The Everyday World as Problematic: A Feminist Sociology* (Boston: Northeastern University Press, 1987); and Dorothy E. Smith, *The Conceptual Practices of Power: A Feminist Sociology of Knowledge* (Boston: Northeastern University Press, 1990).

26. Perhaps another one of the reasons it took me so long to recognize these connections was the state of macrohistorical sociology itself. Family history was treated primarily as a demographic subject and rarely connected to the growing field of historical sociology or women's history. I had to figure out how to make such connections in the absence of an existing intellectual debate or community.

27. See Laslett and Brenner, "Gender and Social Reproduction"; and Brenner and Laslett, "Gender, Social Reproduction."

28. He hadn't thought that way as a younger scholar. See William Fielding Ogburn, "A Few Words by Professor Ogburn" (Address to the annual Institute and Banquet of the Society for Social Research, University of Chicago, Chicago, Illinois, June 8–9, 1951).

29. See Barry Karl, "Presidential Planning and Social Research: Mr. Hoover's Experts," *Perspectives in American History* 3 (1969): 347–409. See also William A. Tobin, "Studying Society: The Making of *Recent Social Trends* in the United States, 1929–1933," *Theory and Society* 24 (1995): 537–565.

30. In relation to the social sciences, see Dorothy Ross, "Socialism and American Liberalism," *Perspectives in American History* 11 (1978): 7–79; Dorothy Ross, *The Origins of American Social Science* (New York: Cambridge University Press, 1991); Thomas Haskell, *The Emergence of Professional Social Science* (Urbana: University of Illinois Press, 1984); and Lewis A. Coser, "American Trends," in Tom Bottomore and Robert Nisbet, eds., *A History of Sociological Analysis* (New York: Basic Books, 1978), pp. 287–320.

31. I make this argument more fully in Barbara Laslett, "Gender in/and Social Science History," *Social Science History* 16 (1992): 177–195.

32. People who have studied the history of the social sciences have not often asked whether it made a difference that most of that history was constructed primarily by white males. For exceptions, see John H. Stanfield, *Philanthropy and Jim Crow in American Social Science* (Westport, Conn.: Greenwood Press, 1985); Alford A. Young Jr., "The 'Negro Problem' and the Character of the Black Community: Charles S. Johnson, E. Franklin Frazier, and the Constitution of a Black Sociological Tradition, 1920–1935," *National Journal of Sociology* 7 (1993): 95–133; and Charles Lemert, *Sociology After the Crisis* (Boulder, Colo.: Westview Press, 1995), esp. chaps. 6, 8. I seem to have fallen into the same trap in my work—especially problematic, perhaps, given Ogburn's southern roots. For an example of how the autobiographical mode can be used to capture this history, see John H. Stanfield II, ed., *A History of Race Relations Research: First-generation Recollections* (Newbury Park, Calif.: Sage, 1993).

33. For some exceptions, see Robert Bannister, *Sociology and Scientism: The American Quest for Objectivity* (Chapel Hill: University of North Carolina Press, 1987); Ross, "Socialism"; and Peter Novick, *That Noble Dream: The "Objectivity Question" and the American Historical Profession* (New York: Cambridge University Press, 1988). Although these authors do consider why the actors about whom they write behaved as they did, they do not engage explicitly with the relevant theoretical discourses.

34. For a critique of these limitations from within the discourse about these models, see Margaret Mooney Marini, "The Role of Purposive Action in Sociology," in James S. Coleman and Thomas J. Fararo, eds., *Rational Choice Theory: Advocacy and Critique* (Newbury Park, Calif.: Sage, 1992), pp. 21–48.

35. See, among others, Laslett and Brenner, "Gender and Social Reproduction"; Lenore Davidoff, "'Adam Spoke First and Named the Order of the World': Masculine and Feminine Domains in History and Sociology," in Helen Corr and Lynn Jamieson, eds., *Politics of Everday Life: Continuity and Change in World and Family* (New York: St. Martin's Press, 1990), pp. 229–255; and Linda K. Kerber, "Separate Spheres, Female Worlds, Women's Place: The Rhetoric of Women's History," *Journal of American History* 75 (1988): 9–39.

36. For a discussion of such intersections, see Philip Abrams, *Historical Sociology* (Ithaca, N.Y.: Cornell University Press, 1982).

37. And, indeed, these lessons have led to my newest research project—on the uses of personal narratives in the social sciences—on which I am collaborating with Mary Jo Maynes and my sociological colleague Jennifer Pierce.

*Evelyn Nakano Glenn*

# Looking Back in Anger?
# Re-remembering My
# Sociological Career

## Graduate Training and Its Irrelevance

I came into sociology without a past and without a memory. I obtained my first job in 1972 as an assistant professor of sociology having taken no sociology courses as an undergraduate and only a few as a graduate student. My intellectual journey in sociology began at a point when I had already been installed as a "sociologist." This odd situation came about because, after getting an undergraduate degree in experimental psychology at Berkeley, I did my doctoral work in the old Social Relations Department at Harvard. "Soc Rel" offered interdisciplinary training in social anthropology, clinical psychology, and social psychology, as well as sociology. Although I had a first-year proseminar with Talcott Parsons and took several seminars taught by other sociologists, most of my course work was in social and cognitive psychology, and my dissertation was in experimental social psychology.

My experience at Harvard in the 1960s was alienating, for reasons that I did not at the time understand. Only later did I label my feelings as anger. At the time I merely thought I felt out of place and isolated. I was aware that women were there on sufferance, for although we were admitted on an "equal basis" as men, we were not accorded equal treatment. An example: the readings for our courses were on reserve in two places, the Social Relations and Lamont libraries. The latter permitted entry only to men and was the only one open on Sundays. This was in the days before photocopying, so we had to spend large blocks of time taking notes from reserved readings. There was intense competition to get two-hour and overnight materials that were due to be discussed in class that week and before exams. In effect, the men students had twice as much opportunity during the week and an extra day on the weekend to do the reserve reading. Having no analysis, let alone a label to characterize sexist practices, none of the women students, myself included, directly challenged this arrangement. To cope, I adopted a strategy that has sometimes been used by groups that are denied rights of adult citizenship, which is to get around a restriction by enlisting a member of the privileged group to act as a proxy. Asian immigrants barred from owning land in California gained access to land by engaging white middlemen to purchase and hold it in their names. White women have always gained access to privileges through their relations with men rather than as independent actors. When everything I needed was checked out of the Social Relations library, my husband, Gary, would go to Lamont and, using my identification card (which had no picture), would check out reserve reading for me. On the one occasion he was challenged, he claimed his name was pronounced Eve-lin (as in Evelyn Waugh) and was allowed to take out the material. He also played in my stead on the (non-coed) social relations softball team and became "one of the boys." We socialized with other graduate student couples, all of whom were made up of a male student and his wife. I felt odd as the one crossing gender and student-spouse lines, though in fact Gary was in a more awkward position as the male spouse. Women were supposed to be in an adjunct position. However, he dealt well with the situation, showing an interest in school gossip, as well as discussing politics, sports, and other issues with everyone. I became friends with several of my classmates' wives, and over the years most of them have become professionals in their own right (sometimes after divorce). One of them recently lauded me and Gary for having been ahead of our time as a "liberated" couple. However, an incident a few years ago reminded me of the strength of "old-boy" ties in graduate school and the exclusion of women from them. The marriage of the daughter of one of our cohort became the occasion for a minireunion. Afterward when some of us looked at the wedding photographs, we noticed one taken of the old "Harvard Soc Rel gang." In the photo were my male classmates and my husband. The bride, Beth Ogilvie, her feminist sensibilities outraged, had a huge blowup of the photo reproduced with a superimposed picture of my face floating over the men's heads, which she gave me as a thank-you gift.

Out of forty or so first-year graduate students in Social Relations, I was one of only two people of color and in all the years of my graduate training, the only Asian American. Of eighteen or so seminars I took, none was taught by a person of color and only one was taught by a woman, an assistant professor who left after two years. This continued a pattern from my undergraduate days at Berkeley. In four years there I had only one female graduate student instructor in French and no teacher of color. Given the lack of "role models," it might seem unlikely that I would feel I could or should have an academic career.

I suspect my ambition was a form of rebellion against my family and the gender strictures of Japanese American culture. My parents were second-generation Japanese Americans who had grown up in working-class immigrant families in northern California. Married in 1939, they had their first child (me) in 1940. My father was the most ambitious in his family of eight siblings. He managed two years of business college after high school and moved up to a white-collar position as a manager in an "Oriental" import store in San Francisco's Chinatown. This promising start was cut short in 1942 with the commencement of World War II and the forced evacuation and imprisonment of 120,000 Japanese Americans in remote concentration camps. My parents, I, and all of our relatives were incarcerated. The three of us were sent to Gila, Arizona, and I later lived with relatives in the Heart Mountain, Wyoming, camp. I was in the concentration camps from ages one-and-a-half to five. My earliest memories are of playing with marbles in our barracks quarters, walking down to communal bathrooms, and eating meals at large tables in our block dining hall. Later, I recall playing with other children (depending on the season) in the dust or mud around our barracks. In 1944 my father was able to leave the Gila camp to take a factory job in Chicago. My mother and I remained incarcerated until the war was over. Because my mother was ill, we didn't leave until October 1945, when we departed to join my father.

The loss of my father's career just as he was getting established and beginning a family must have been devastating. Always quiet, he became completely uncommunicative and absorbed in working. My mother, unlike her two sisters and five sisters-in law, was never employed outside the home. She was never idle, however. She sewed most of her own clothes and mine (something I felt mortified by when I was a teenager), prepared elaborate meals, baked, kept house, and shopped for bargains. All major decisions were made by my father, and although my mother worried, she was happy to cede the responsibility to him. My mother has always been a "cheerful pessimist." She expects the worst but is sanguine about it. She took out her powerlessness by nagging. However, since my father seldom responded to anything she said, she confided her complaints to me. My reaction to this was resentment toward my father and a determination not to be in a position like my mother, which meant that I would have a job or career.[1]

The circumstances of my parents' life left little time or energy for contemplation or thinking about larger world events. They both kept busy every moment and seemed to be occupied with the quotidian.[2] The lesson of being uprooted from their homes and the trauma of the concentration camp experience—that you are not in control of your future—undoubtedly made thinking too deeply frightening. In all the time I was growing up, my parents took only one vacation, a four-day trip to Wisconsin. Neither explicitly stressed education or discussed vocational plans with me. Later on, they seemed to assume that my younger brother would go to college, but here, too, they never pushed him in any direction. My father remained indifferent about my going to college and graduate school. My mother was more supportive, but her concerns, understandably, were of a practical nature. The only advice I ever recall her giving me about college was a suggestion that I study dental hygiene because she had a Japanese American woman hygienist who made $7 an hour.

Before my junior year in high school, we left Chicago and moved to Oakland, California. My father bought a motel, using all of his savings and money from the sale of our six-plex in Chicago for the downpayment. We lived in the little owner's unit, and my parents did almost all of the labor, from maintenance to cleaning the rooms. They got up early to start cleaning, stayed up late, and got up in the middle of the night to register latecomers. They were tied to the business 365 days a year. Meals and conversations were constantly interrupted by calls on the switchboard or people coming into the office. Although I was sometimes recruited to clean rooms, my parents were often dissatisfied with the careless work I did and would redo the job. The first few years were touch and go financially. Several times my father had to hock his car to make the mortgage payment.

I was eager to get away to go to college, but I couldn't do so. Although I was accepted at Stanford, USC, UCLA, and Berkeley, I went to Berkeley, my last choice, for financial reasons: it was cheap and close to home, so I could commute. I liked the bigness and the anonymity, which made me feel free rather than alienated. I started out in premed (a good Asian American major) with the idea of going into psychiatry, but I switched to psychology after my sophomore year. I was converted by a large introductory class of eight hundred students taught by David Krech and Richard Crutchfield. I loved the class and was convinced that the best life in the world would be as a psychology professor like the two guys up on the stage, teaching and doing research. Luckily or unluckily, I managed to avoid thinking too much about a major obstacle: my shyness, manifested in utter fear of speaking in class, let alone standing up and talking in front of a group. I was also naively unaware of the significance of another big difference between me and those two guys on the stage. The first hint was given me by a professor in another class, who when I asked him to write a letter of recommendation for graduate school said, "I'm glad to write a letter, but you should know you'll have a hard time as a woman in the university." I was shocked since I knew his own wife was a professor. When I asked him what he meant by this, he gave me a rather vague response but noted that his wife had difficulty combining career and family.

Going as far away as possible to graduate school, all the way to New England, was a way to escape the parochialism of my family and the racism still experienced by Asians on the West Coast. In the early 1960s, Chinese and Japanese American students were still excluded from many aspects of student life, barred from many social organizations, and could expect to face severe restrictions in the job market. One reason I felt "free" as a Japanese American in Cambridge was because there weren't enough of us to discriminate against. The surrounding area of Boston and New England had no significant Asian American presence, except for a small run-down Chinatown in Boston. I found that my race/ethnicity made me hypervisible at times and invisible at other times. During my second summer at Harvard, my major professor invited a group of his students to stay at a house he rented in New Hampshire. Local residents would stop and stare at me—I was an exotic novelty in northern New England. In downtown Boston, where we sometimes went clubbing, I would be approached by servicemen who assumed I was a prostitute or bar girl. During these encounters, I felt angry and helpless at being unable to express my anger. Yet at other times, my ethnicity made me invisible. At Harvard, in particular, because I was not black, my ethnicity didn't count.[3]

I did not connect these experiences as a woman of color to my life in the university, nor did I relate my own life to what I studied or to my alienation. For the first time, I developed doubts about my intellectual ability. Once launched in graduate school, I soldiered on out of fear of failure—I was terrified of being annihilated if I did not complete the degree. My husband, who was not a student and had no desire to be one, was totally supportive and understood that I needed to get through somehow.

Nevertheless, despite the tribulations, the fact of having a Harvard degree has stood me in good stead. For someone with a devalued gender/race status, the imprimatur of a "first-class" institution provides potential employers and grant-givers with external confirmation of intellectual competence. The irony is that none of my Harvard connections—whether faculty or other students—has ever been even slightly useful professionally. I value the graduate school friendships I made and maintained over the years, but they simply are not professional relationships.

When I applied for my first academic jobs out of graduate school, my search was restricted to the Boston area. My husband was settled in a good job, and we had two children, the younger only a few months old. Having no mentor to advise me about the "proper" way to job-hunt, I simply mailed my résumé to all sociology and psychology departments within a one-hour radius of Cambridge. This was 1972, during the boom years in sociology. Despite my lack of qualifications, I was interviewed by seven schools and offered jobs at five of them. My decision to accept the offer from Boston University proved an unfortunate choice, one that eventually exacted a huge toll, personally and professionally. But that became evident only later.

I have sometimes joked that my lack of formal training in sociology probably saved me a lot of hassle; had I fully absorbed the structural functional paradigm then prevalent, I would have had to struggle to break out of that mind-set. Instead my brain was a tabula rasa. The disadvantages of not having gone through formal training were the lack of connection to senior sponsors and a circle of peers with whom I had gone to graduate school. I had to acquire a working knowledge of the field while also teaching and moving toward tenure. Because my dissertation was in a different field—experimental social psychology—I didn't have a dissertation to turn into articles or a book. I had to develop a research agenda from scratch. I was like my immigrant grandparents: having to make a living while learning a new language and culture.

## Gender and the Sociology of Work

My real training in sociology came through simply doing it, with support from feminist sociologists. Happily for me, my entrance as a faculty member coincided with two developments: the beginnings of the "feminist revolution" in sociology and the rise of Marxist studies of the labor process. I learned a lot by teaching courses on the family, on work, and on women. In 1973 Chandra Mukerjee and I designed the first "women's studies" course at Boston University. It had the quaint title "Changing Sex Roles." We used a few of the handful of books available (e.g, *The Second Sex, The Diary of Anais Nin*),[4] magazine articles, and mimeographed pieces from various women's liberation publications. Chandra was something of a prodigy—with a Ph.D. from Northwestern at age twenty-four—and much more sophisticated than me in analyzing and explicating the texts. I learned a lot from her. Barbara Melber, a lecturer in our department, cotaught the course with me the following year. Barbara had a strong comparative background, having written a dissertation at the University of Chicago on women in Sweden. We focused on the new feminist anthropology, using the now classic *Woman, Culture, and Society* as a text.[5] Barbara's lecture on the theory of how women's universal oppression stemmed from a public-private dichotomy stood out as a model of clarity.[6] I also helped design and cotaught "Women and Work" a number of times with Roz Feldberg, who joined the BU faculty at the same time I did. Roz introduced me to Marxist feminist thought and to the work of feminist historians. Our weekly meetings to discuss readings and topics before each class became miniseminars, from which we generated many research questions that we later pursued. In the mid-1970s, faculty and graduate students interested in feminist issues formed a gender task force in the department. For several years the task force was a beehive of activity, holding colloquia and workshops and designing new courses for a specialization in gender sociology.

Of many issues raised by feminist activists and scholars, the one that most intrigued me had to do with women's paid and unpaid labor: British and American Marxist analyses of housework were focusing attention on the extent of women's direct and indirect exploitation and on the relation of the "private" household to the larger political economy. Historians and social scientists were starting to focus again on women's paid employment, a topic neglected since the 1920s. Whereas in the 1950s and 1960s the existence of separate men's jobs and women's jobs was so taken for granted as to be invisible, by the 1970s some scholars were beginning to problematize occupational segregation by showing that the gender composition of occupations changed over time. My stint as a student-cum-housewife made "women's work" a natural interest. It was a topic outside the sociological mainstream and in that sense ripe for development.

Roz Feldberg had taught in Scotland for a year and was plugged into the network of Marxist feminists who were doing much of the writing on women's work. She was interested in doing research on clerical work, and I was interested in studying secretaries, so we began to collaborate by conducting interviews with thirty office workers in a variety of settings. The publication in 1974 of Harry Braverman's *Labor and Monopoly Capital* stimulated a spate of research on changes in the labor process and the use of technology to increase managerial control through deskilling.[7] Influenced by his approach, we began exploring the impacts of office automation, which was then just beginning to spread. Braverman overlooked the gendered aspects of labor degradation; we explicitly looked at how women's jobs were affected in distinct ways and at how the gender composition of particular jobs affected the way technology was applied.

Over the next few years, we wrote and obtained two major grants from the Center for the Study of Metropolitan Problems of the National Institute of Mental Health (NIMH) to study the impacts of office automation on clerical workers. The center, headed by Elliot Liebow, funded quite a few studies of work and workers in the 1970s. Under the grant we conducted extensive interviews in two large companies. We also published a number of articles on clerical work and on the sociology of work, which combined analysis of large-scale economic transformation and examination of workers' concrete day-to-day experiences in the workplace.[8]

During this time, I became increasingly plugged into feminist and Marxist circles in sociology through professional meetings and associations. This was important considering my lack of graduate school associations. Someone recruited me to join the Massachusetts Sociological Association (MSA) and run for office, which I won—I think unopposed; over the next few years I held other offices and became president in 1976. The biannual conferences of MSA initiated me into professional meetings. Pam Roby, a rising star at Brandeis and an energetic organizer, started the Boston Area Women Social Scientists. Through that organization, Helen MacGill Hughes, who lived down the street from me in Cambridge, recruited me to assist in editing the newsletter of the Sociologists for Women in Society. Helen, who was married to well-known sociologist Everett Hughes, was of that early generation of women sociologists who never had a full-time academic position. She worked on the periphery, managing the *American Journal of Sociology*, doing other editing work, and publishing some of her own research. During the 1970s, she was hired by several Boston area colleges to teach courses on women. I succeeded Helen as editor of the SWS Newsletter and in that way got involved in SWS. I admired and was inspired by the confidence, wit, and political savvy of the founding mothers and activists, such as Arlene, Pam, Joan Huber, Doris Wilkinson, and Nona Glazer, but truthfully I did not feel that I could be one of them. I pretty much stayed quiet and listened. Getting involved in SWS activities at the annual meetings of the Society for the Study of Social Problems (SSSP) and the American Sociological Association eased my entry into these larger organizations. I suspect my conspicuous status as one of the few Asian American women led to my being nominated to committees of both organizations almost from my first year of membership. I circulated through a succession of "status" committees having to do with the situation of women and racial minorities and eventually was elected to the Board of Directors of SSSP and to the Council of the ASA.

The research on clerical work connected Roz and me to a developing network of Marxist scholars in labor studies. This was the only primarily male network in which I developed ties. I recall prefacing my paper at the first Labor Process Conference at SUNY Binghamton by noting that I was the only woman speaker and criticizing the organizers for male bias. Jim Geschwender, the coorganizer with Phil Kraft, told me years later that this made a favorable impression on him; later he was instrumental, along with Joan Smith and other folks in sociology and women's studies, in getting a position for me at Binghamton. A second labor process conference at UC Santa Cruz had at least a handful of women participating.

Having a network of scholars reading and responding to our clerical work studies was gratifying. The most impressive aspect of the new labor studies was that researchers such as Michael Buroway and Louise Lamphere were observing and participating on the shop floor and centering their analyses on the actual experiences of workers. However, some of the theoretical debates seemed to reveal serious gaps and limitations in Marxist labor theory for understanding women's work and underlined for me the importance of remaining grounded in women's experiences. For example, listening to arguments about whether someone's analysis was consistent with Karl Marx's categories, my reaction was, "Who cares?" Prior to hearing these discussions, I had briefly immersed myself in the ongoing debate over how to determine women's class position. Hearing these debates led me to give up this project as a largely futile exercise that involved starting with accepted categories and trying to fit women into them.

A second, and at times overlapping, network that developed in the late 1970s was an interdisciplinary group of women doing studies of women and work. Made up for the most part of Marxist feminist anthropologists, historians, and sociologists, different groupings formed to hold working conferences and retreats. Karen Sacks was one of the "centerwomen" (to use her own term) in the network.[9] As director of research for the Business and Professional Women in Washington, D.C., and later director of women's studies at UCLA, she organized numerous conferences and panels. By including me in these activities, she was the instigator of several papers of mine that were later published.

One particular group within this network has been vitally important to me. In 1979 twelve of us formed a women and work group. Initially, we had a grant from the American Sociological Association, but we found our gatherings so fruitful that we continued to meet at our own expense, alternating spring meetings in New York and fall meetings in Cambridge. Several members taught at small non-research-oriented schools. Those of us at larger institutions usually were the only members of our departments doing research in this area. The group thus provided intellectual support that was unavailable in our institutions. We felt excited because our scholarship was breaking new ground. Subsequently, interest in "women and work" grew apace with the general rise in gender studies. By the late 1980s, it seemed that everybody was studying women and work. As the interest of some members shifted and others dropped out and new people joined, we redefined the group's focus to studies of gender and race.[10]

Prior to each meeting, those wanting feedback send copies of work in progress to the members. At the meeting, the group devotes two to three hours to discussing each paper. What makes the process effective is that we trust each other enough to present drafts that are still confused or disorganized. We have also developed group rituals involving bagels, Chinese food, and time for sharing personal news. Over the years we have contributed immensely to each other's work. Individual members have published numerous monographs and articles, drafts of which were discussed, vetted, and reread by the group. In 1987 we published a collection of our papers in a volume, *Hidden Aspects of Women's Work*.[11]

Sociology has turned out to be a better field for me than social psychology. Because it is open to virtually any topic and to a variety of methods, it allowed me to explore issues that were meaningful in terms of my own experiences and to develop a distinctive voice. Sociology has provided a way to apprehend the "big picture": I like being able to see the connections between what people experience in their daily lives and larger historical and contemporary developments. Sociology also allows me to be creative.

In graduate school, my knowledge seemed both fragmented and unconnected to my life. I was interested in materials taught in my courses, but I never constructed a picture of how the social world fit together. I enjoyed reading and critiquing social psychology studies, but I did not come up with clever experimental designs of my own. I mastered quantitative methods by working for two years as research assistant on a project that developed a computerized content analysis program and taking advanced quantitative methods. Experience with the programs did not inspire me to formulate interesting questions to explore through analysis of large data sets. The end result of all this training was that I doubted my ability to do innovative research. In contrast, though I never took a course in or received any systematic training in interviewing or ethnography, each came easily to me. Starting with the small concrete details of people's accounts, I spun out lines of inquiry into large-scale social structures and processes, such as the labor market, technological change, and geographic and social movements of populations. I delighted in immersing myself in archival research, poring over census data, and creating new tables. I enjoyed constructing a sociological story by piecing together bits of evidence. I have concluded that the most important thing about my choice of methods was that qualitative and historical methods engaged me and inspired creative uses of data. I wonder if other sociologists find a kind of "natural" fit between particular methods and creativity.[12]

While I was becoming increasingly comfortable and productive as a sociologist, the situation of my department at Boston University—and of the junior faculty in it—was deteriorating. The sociology boom of the 1960s and 1970s was rapidly receding in the wake of increasing political conservatism. Roz Feldberg and I submitted a third grant proposal to NIMH, which was approved but not funded because of a shift in government support away from "social" research (that is, research that focuses on institutional and social sources of difficulties) and toward "psychological" research (that is, research that focuses on individual adjustment and mental health.) Indeed, the Center for the Study of Metropolitan Problems, our first funding source, was eliminated. At Boston University, it was becoming apparent to us that sociology was viewed with hostility and suspicion by BU president John Silber and his administrators.[13] Our department chair advised junior faculty to delay tenure review as long as possible in order to build up our publications. However, the situation deteriorated to the point where our accomplishments were largely irrelevant. The administration frequently ignored the recommendation of departmental and faculty review committees. The increasingly hostile environment and the arbitrary and vindictive use of power by the Silber administration spurred the faculty to vote for collective representation by an American Association of University Professors–affiliated union in 1981. When the administration refused to negotiate a contract, the faculty elected to strike. The level of faculty support for the strike was remarkably high, including virtually all of Liberal Arts, the School of Management, and the Law School. Sociology faculty members, along with those in political science and psychology, were among the most visible on the picket line and as public spokespeople. The strike was successful. We got a contract. The bitterness continued, however, as the university administration pursued appeals in court and a policy of retribution. S. M. Miller, our former chair, and three other prominent faculty organized a movement to have John Silber removed as president. I signed a petition to the trustees demanding his dismissal, though I doubted its effectiveness. The movement failed, and sociology appeared to be targeted for reprisal. After the strike, virtually no one in sociology got tenure, regardless of positive department and college peer reviews. Terry Freiberg, a well-regarded young

Marxist theorist and a popular teacher, was denied renewal of his contract even before he reached the stage of tenure review. The department shrank as people were fired, took jobs elsewhere, or retired early to escape the hostile and demoralizing environment. In the peak years of the mid-1970s, the department had about twenty-seven members; by the late 1980s that number had shrunk to fifteen.[14]

While these events were unfolding, Roz and I managed to continue our clerical work study. Our NIMH grants allowed us to set up a small "island" of feminist teaching and research. For several years we had a project office with a secretary, Roz Geffen, and several graduate assistants. In our joint research we tried to work in a feminist way that involved sharing ideas and writing rather than parceling out individual credit. Our presence made some difference for women graduate students. Over the years I directed some wonderful graduate students working on feminist topics. But one of our research assistants left graduate school after two years, saying that she did not want to go through the kind of stress Roz and I were undergoing just to survive in academia.

Prophetically, my long and fruitful collaboration with Roz did not survive the stresses of the final stages of our troubles at Boston University. The end of our collaboration was as painful as the end of a marriage. Roz was and is a brilliant thinker, a gifted researcher, and an inspired teacher. She would easily have been granted tenure and achieved eminence in any normal university. After leaving BU, Roz began vital work as a researcher and administrator for the Massachusetts Nurse's Association. Nevertheless, the fact that she was driven out of the university was not only unjust but was also a loss for feminism in the academy. The attack on sociology at BU and other universities—and our inability to mobilize more support against such attacks—reflects the field's low prestige and exposes the illusory nature of faculty governance.[15] Protective legal mechanisms are ineffective in the face of arbitrary disregard of peer review. I am concerned about this and other recent attacks on sociology because since the mid-1970s white women and men and women of color have become better represented in sociology than in most other disciplines. Because of the recency of our entry, we make up a higher proportion of those "last hired." Cutting or eliminating sociology departments will therefore hurt us disproportionately. I am also concerned that the response of the more prestigious (or upwardly striving) sociology departments may be to try to shed the "low-status" image by emphasizing topics and approaches that are most comfortable and appealing to the white men who still dominate the academy and by turning away from the concerns of the marginal, oppressed, and powerless—by definition the "low status."

## Japanese American Women

During my early years at BU, I began a second stream of research that grew out of my family and personal roots. My study of Japanese American women domestic workers very much ties in with an emotional ambivalence in my life: Japanese American culture/community simultaneously draws me in (comfort, belonging, connectedness) and drives me away (stifling, limited, parochial). My relationship to the community has been cyclical. My earliest memories are from the concentration camp in Gila, Arizona, where my family and I were incarcerated during World War II. At first my father and mother were always around, and other extended kin were housed in nearby barracks. The communal bathrooms and mess hall led to an enforced closeness with the larger community. In 1944 after my father was allowed to leave the camp to work in the Midwest, my mother became ill with tuberculosis and was hospitalized for a year. After that I lived with my mother's parents, who were in the Heart Mountain, Wyoming, concentration camp. They were also raising my eldest cousin, Betty, so I suddenly had a sibling, an older sister, for the first time. Ba-chan (grandmother) was an amusing storyteller and somewhat of a scold. Ji-chan (grandfather) had been a tenant farmer and then a foreman at a fruit ranch in the Sacramento delta. I was afraid of him, for he was strict and upright. He did not, however, mind a bit of earthy peasant humor. We all must have communicated in Japanese since neither spoke much English.

In October 1945, four months after the war ended, my mother was released from the hospital, and we joined my father in Chicago. We lived in two rooms of a three-story tenement building that had been carved up into small apartments. My father's parents, my aunt and her husband, an uncle, his wife and kids, and assorted single aunts also lived in the building. Gradually all the uncles, aunts, and cousins left to go back to California, and my paternal grandparents died, leaving my parents and my new baby brother and me alone in Chicago. I lived a double life, one in public school and the neighborhood, which was largely Jewish, and another revolving around Buddhist church, Japanese school, and Japanese American basketball. I never spoke Japanese again, and when I visited my maternal grandparents or they visited us, I was unable to communicate much with them.

In my freshman year at Senn High School, the factory where my father worked moved downstate. My father commuted for about a year, but it was grueling. He decided that the time had come to pull up stakes. We moved back to the Bay Area. We rejoined the Alameda Buddhist temple that my father's father had helped found in 1915. I went to my two last years of high school in Oakland and spent four years at Berkeley. In 1962 I left for Cambridge with my husband-to-be and lived there for the next twenty-eight years. We returned to California for visits once or twice a year, and I retained an unresolved longing eventually to return, much as my parents had longed to return to California from Chicago. My husband once remarked that Japanese Americans have an "elephant's graveyard" instinct: we all have to go back to our homeland to deposit our bones with those of our ancestors.

In 1974 when I was coteaching the course "Women and Work," I found a little material on African American women, but none on Asian American women. On one of my summer visits to California, I interviewed a half-dozen immigrant (issei) and American born (nisei) women engaged in paid housework. I was aware that domestic service was a line of work in which many Japanese American women had engaged and that this experience had never been documented or even mentioned in histories of Japanese Americans. Like a lot of women's work, it was outside the formal economy and therefore overlooked. What I wanted to do was treat their work seriously as real work: I wanted to know how they got jobs, how they planned and carried out their work, how they managed relationships with employers, and what the work meant to them.

I located the women through my mother's friendship networks and family connections. My mother accompanied me on many of the interviews as go-between and translator. I really enjoyed the interviewing. I was enthralled especially by the older women's spunk and humor, moved by the stories of hardships and tragedies, and uplifted by these women's eventual triumph. A surgeon friend from Ellsworth, Maine, Eji Suyama, read my book and remarked, "You really liked those old ladies, didn't you?" I hadn't thought about it in those terms, but he was right.

As I tried to make sense of what the "old ladies" were telling me, many questions arose: Why did Japanese American women in the Bay Area get involved in domestic service? What did this have to do with immigration? What were the consequences of immigrant occupations for mobility in subsequent generations? How did the women's experiences compare with those of other immigrant women and of other women of color? How did social structure and personal agency intersect in shaping their experience?

What started out as a small project tangential to my main research grew larger and larger as it connected up to broader questions about the intersection of social history and individual lives and the dialectics of structural determinacy and human agency.[16] Seeking a larger context for the interview material, I began to read a wide array of literature, ranging from studies of Japanese Americans, domestic workers, and women workers, to economic models of the labor market, to the new family history.

I initially wrote two articles, one on immigrant labor markets and the other on pre–World War II issei women.[17] I soon realized that there was ample material for a book. The writing went quickly, and I finished the first draft of the book in about two months in 1981. I have detailed this sequence of events because there was a certain "seat of the pants" quality to my modus operandi. I started with the interviews and sought ways of making sense of the material. A reading of my book *Issei, Nisei, Warbride,* which begins with conceptual frameworks for looking at women, labor migration, and domestic service, gives a misleading impression of the analytic process.[18] In actuality, the theoretical framework came about after, not before, the data.

Between the first draft and the final manuscript, four years elapsed. An important source of intellectual support during the revision stage was my involvement with a group of women of color scholars, the Inter-University Group Studying the Intersection of Race and Gender. The members, Bonnie Dill, Elizabeth Higginbotham, Cheryl Gilkes, Ruth Zambrana, and I, each had done original research on a particular group. We were dissatisfied with "white feminist analysis," which ignored how race/ethnicity interacted with gender in shaping the lives of women of color. We felt that comparative analysis across groups would get at this interaction. Reading with this group fostered in me a better understanding of connections between the histories of African American, Latina, and Asian American women, an understanding that I tried to incorporate in the final draft of my book manuscript. The comentoring within this group and within the Women and Work Group provided continuity that was sorely lacking in my employment.

My intellectual work was disrupted by a series of personal and professional dislocations that eventuated from the nasty situation at BU. When I came up for tenure in 1981–1982, I was turned down after a grueling one-year process, despite the strong support of my department. Filing a grievance on the grounds of gross distortion of my record by a university committee, I won the right to a second review.[19] I took a visiting position in Hawaii in 1983 to recuperate and give birth to my third child. On my return, I went through a second tenure review, only to be denied again by the administration, despite positive reviews by all faculty committees. The administration's intent was telegraphed early in the process when, after several years of giving me merit raises, it refused to give me the raise recommended by a faculty merit committee for that year. Obviously the whole process was a sham and a waste of time and effort.[20]

Throughout this period my feminist and labor studies networks really came through for me. Over twenty senior women and men wrote detailed and thoughtful evaluations for the two rounds of my tenure review. Their succor buoyed me emotionally, even as their evaluations were being judged irrelevant by the Boston University administration. The support was the one positive aspect of this trying period. It is the one reason I am still in academia today. When I finally had to go on the job market, some of these same people, having read and vetted my entire oeuvre, were able to write lengthy letters of recommendation.

Having reached the end of the road at BU, I was faced with the crisis of whether I would take a job outside of Boston/New England in order to remain in academia. Was it fair to ask Gary and the children to pull up roots and disrupt their lives for the sake of my career? If I left academia, would I always feel that John Silber had driven me out? Perhaps it was another expression of the rebellious streak that had set me on a "nontraditional" path in the first place or perhaps it was the same fear of annihilation that had led me to soldier on in graduate school that caused me to continue. Gary always stressed the importance of my intellectual work and remained flexible and optimistic. He felt and continues to feel that we can do anything and make any arrangement work. He argued for relocating the whole family to wherever the best job for me appeared. He was running a small consulting business and felt he could move. By late fall of my last year at BU, I had an offer from Florida State University in Tallahassee, which I accepted. As spring approached, however, we reluctantly concluded that Gary should remain in Cambridge with our daughters, Sara and Antonia, so that they could finish high school there. I would move down to Tallahassee with one-year-old Patrick, and we would make regular visits back and forth.

We had been impressed by the humanity and empathy of the sociology faculty at FSU: I brought a six-month-old baby to the job interview, and Mike Armer, the chair, and other faculty and spouses provided child care help so that I could go to interviews and give a colloquium. The people at FSU were wonderful colleagues, and the pace of life in Tallahassee was relaxing. However, the lack of ethnic diversity was a shock. In a black-white society—Cubans were not in this part of the state—I was truly an anomaly. This was brought home to me when I went to the Department of Motor Vehicles to register my car. The young African American clerk who was filling out my form came to the section on race, glanced at me, and typed in "white." She knew for sure that I was not "black," and in her mind there was only one alternative. The two years I spent at Florida State helped me regain my perspective. I learned just how abnormal the situation at BU was and that life in academia was rewarding in a normal place. I discovered that the strain of commuting was less draining than the stress of working in a hostile environment. At the same time, however, Patrick missed his father and sisters and was always upset when Gary left Tallahassee or we left Cambridge. Long-distance commuting clearly was not viable as a long-term arrangement. Also, rather than preparing for relocation, my family seemed to be getting more entrenched in Cambridge. Gary had been able to use his connections to get a desirable position with the state; Sara and Annie planned to attend college in New England. I began looking for a job in the Northeast. Two good offers came through, and I accepted a position at the State University of New York, Binghamton. I respected the work of the sociologists there, and the women's studies group was active and supportive. Although I still had to commute, it was a much easier one that could be done on a weekly basis as a five-hour drive or a one-hour flight. I also loved the undergraduate and graduate students, who were bright and interested, unspoiled and appreciative of our efforts. The sociology department was extremely generous in accommodating my schedule.

*Issei, Nisei, Warbride* finally appeared in 1986, at the end of my second year at FSU.[21] It was two books really, one that told the women's stories in their own words and another that was a historical/structural analysis. This dual aspect reflected the fact that I had had two audiences in mind in writing the book: sociologists and members of the Japanese American community. I had tried to write as accessibly as possible, although the first three chapters, which were historical and analytic, were heavy going for nonspecialist readers. Nonetheless, many people in the community struggled through the difficult parts and read the whole book. I was invited to give talks and lectures in churches and community venues. The most gratifying part of these presentations was having people say that the book was true to their own experience or those of their sisters or mothers. Members of the audience frequently related incidents in their own lives that were as dramatic or telling as any told in the book.

Readers have told me they found the stories and voices of the women personally engaging. I know that writing the book was personally fulfilling.

It brought together in one project personal emotional issues and intellectual ones: the desire to connect and bond with my Japanese grandmothers in ways I couldn't when they were alive and my need to understand the workings of women's (and my own) oppression and resistance. I was able to creatively use the tension I mentioned earlier between wanting to merge my identity in the group and wanting to maintain independence and analytic distance.

## Comparative Work on Women of Color

Since the mid-1980s, my research has increasingly turned to comparative historical research on African American, Latina, and Asian American women's work. My initial interest in comparative study grew out of my writing and teaching about Asian Americans in the late 1970s. I became dissatisfied with the cultural frameworks that seemed to pervade the literature: Japanese and Chinese American family, economic practices, and community formation were explained as extensions or adaptations of Chinese/Japanese values and cultural forms, such as Confucianism and familialism. The cultural bias I felt stemmed from the Euro-American's conception of Asian Americans as "perpetual foreigners." Asian Americans and Asians were lumped together and (in current terminology) viewed as "other." Like the essentialized woman, Asians and Asian culture were seen as eternal and unchanging. Interpreting the social patterns of Japanese and Chinese Americans in cultural terms emphasized their "uniqueness," denied their commonalties with other people of color, and obscured the impacts of racist legal, political, and economic structures on their lives in the United States.

The usefulness of comparative analysis for getting at underlying structural factors that were obscured by cultural explanations first became clear to me when I worked on a paper on the Chinese American family in 1980. A dean at Boston University had asked me to give a public lecture on the Chinese American Family in a series addressed to various communities in Boston. Desperate to get a handle on something interesting to say, I talked to a number of people in the Chinese American community about their families. One of my students who had immigrated from Hong Kong as a ten-year-old and been caught up in school busing mentioned that she had attended a different school every year and then remarked that she had felt most comfortable in the schools that were predominately black. Startled, I asked her why, and she replied, "Oh, blacks are more similar to the Chinese. They both emphasize family a lot." This casual remark jolted a needle out of its track and got me thinking along new lines. I felt intuitively that she was right: there were important similarities between the black family and the Chinese family that were, however, obscured by the contrasting stereotypes of the former as pathological and disorganized and the latter as close-knit and cohesive. I began applying the institutional framework used for analyzing black families to Chinese Americans, looking at how family formation and strategies might have been affected by immigration restrictions, denial of citizenship, and color bars in employment. Working out an institutional analysis turned on three kinds of evidence: first, that Chinese Americans displayed different family formations in different historical periods marked by shifts in immigration law and other political/legal constraints; second, that Chinese immigrants in other societies, such as the Philippines, displayed dissimilar patterns of family formation; and third, that other groups with very different cultures displayed patterns similar to those of Chinese Americans under similar circumstances. I worked out these ideas in an article on the Chinese American family, and I have carried over this strategy of using comparative analysis to get at underlying structural factors to other projects.[22]

Similarly, my study of Japanese American domestic workers had led me to the realization that they were not unique. Relegation to domestic service and other "degraded" forms of women's work was something they shared with black women in the South and Mexican women in the Southwest. Studying these groups' involvement in domestic work showed the reasons for their concentration in domestic service to be similar, stemming from their position as women members of a subordinated racial caste within a dual-race labor system. Their relations with employers were also similar despite divergent cultural backgrounds. This is important because racial/ethnic women's subordination is often attributed to their personal or cultural characteristics. Because they do work that is degraded, that places them in positions of subordination, African American, Latina, and Japanese American women are seen as naturally subservient and in need of white guidance. In this way race and gender ideologies are created and affirmed in everyday life.

I began systematic comparisons of the labor histories of African American women in the South, Mexican American women in the Southwest, and Chinese American women in the West while working with the Inter-University Group on Race and Gender. The group had decided to prepare a monograph on the work, family, and community lives of African American, Latina, and Asian American women. Our central argument, based on the internal colonialism model, was that racial, ethnic women were subject to distinct forms of labor exploitation and political/legal restrictions that differentiated their experiences from those of European American women.[23] This focus reflected the politics of the era when African American, Latina, Asian American, and Native American women were attempting to forge alliances and to place the experience of women of color at the center of analyses of society and culture. Getting our ideas accepted proved difficult. Our draft manuscript was rejected by a university press editor. In retrospect, the criticism that accompanied the rejection was overly harsh. It became difficult to regroup, given everyone's busy schedule. Although we did not produce the hoped-for synthetic history, we did important intellectual groundwork. Concepts developed collectively influenced our individual research and the work of the Center for Research on Women at Memphis State, which was organized by Bonnie Dill, Elizabeth Higginbotham, and Lynn Cannon.[24] The center's summer institutes, working paper series, and social science bibliography were crucial elements in the flowering of social science scholarship on women of color in the 1980s.[25]

The center also fostered connections among scholars with similar interests. I met historian Elsa Barkley Brown through the institute. After I got to Binghamton, I recruited her there.[26] Elsa became an important sounding board and influence on me. In her study of the postbellum African American community of Richmond, Virginia, she explicates the multirhythmic, nonlinear, nondualistic nature of African American culture and shows how the African American community drew strength from economic, class, and gender diversity. She has frequently helped me sort out my thinking about interdependence and difference and encouraged my comparative work on women of color.[27]

My current research builds on the burgeoning literature in women's history and feminist sociology that documents the historical specificity and variability of womanhood among different groups. Women's history has become more inclusive, its narrative multistranded, multivoiced. Similarly, feminist sociology is paying attention to race/ethnicity/class differences among women. Yet I am troubled by the concept of "multiculturalism." This concept in women's history has taken the form of seeing all women as having fractured identities, as being oppressed in different ways, and as having partial and incomplete perspectives. It is an attempt to be inclusive without acknowledging the fact that differences among women are not random but systematically connected. I am attempting in my current work to unravel those connections. I am working out in a variety of ways how the racial division of labor among different groups of women creates hierarchical, interdependent relations among them, to show (paraphrasing Elsa

Barkley Brown) that white women lead the lives they do precisely because of the lives that women of color lead.

## Up and out of Sociology?

In 1990 I made an enormous change in my family's life and in my personal and professional life when I accepted a position at the University of California, Berkeley, with a joint appointment in the Ethnic Studies and Women's Studies Departments. I turned down an offer of a professorship in sociology and a center directorship at an Ivy League university to do so. My reasons were primarily personal: a desire to be closer to my aging parents and mother-in-law and perhaps also the pull of the Japanese American community. Happily, my two grown daughters, Sara and Annie, have opted to live in California, at least for now. My eleven-year-old son, Patrick, is playing basketball and baseball in a Japanese American league. This takes family history full circle: my father was the "Babe Ruth" of the Japanese American baseball league of the 1920s, according to a recent article in the vernacular press. My husband, who runs a nonprofit foundation in Boston, is bearing the brunt of the move by having to commute between coasts on a biweekly basis.

My main professional unease comes from not being part of a sociology department. Even though most of my interests in gender and race can be accommodated within the Ethnic Studies and Women's Studies Departments, I would like to have the broader disciplinary home: as long as I was in sociology, any substantive interest I might develop could be accommodated. It is not clear what will happen now if my interests shift. Although it is theoretically possible to interact with sociologists at Berkeley, practically it rarely occurs, given institutional arrangements and demands to be involved in departmental business. Once again I find supportive relationships with feminist sociologists occurring outside my employment, through professional meetings, informal groups, and long-distance phone calls.

When I taught in sociology departments, I was located at the margins and struggled to integrate the perspectives of women and people of color. Today I am housed in two interdisciplinary departments that center precisely on the perspectives and experiences of these groups. However, these departments are themselves marginalized within the academy. Furthermore, I have found that each department tends to emphasize commonalties among the groups it studies (e.g., Asian Americans, women) as the basis for shared identity and pushes to the periphery what the other sees as central. I find myself in the subgroup within ethnic studies that is struggling to bring gender in as a central analytic concept in understanding ethnic immigration, politics, and education. Similarly, I am in the subgroup within women's studies attempting to incorporate the perspectives of women of color into feminist theory building.

Being in a kind of straddling position, trying to integrate gender into the study of ethnic communities and race/ethnic diversity into women's studies, is contributing to my own efforts to develop a framework that incorporates race and gender not as additive but as interlocking systems. There seems to be an enrichment that takes place when ideas/concepts from one field are introduced into another field. Ethnic studies colleagues in literature are introducing me to developments in postmodern and postcolonial discourse theory; I have found particularly useful the notion of positionality and the questioning of oppositional categories. The racial formation model of my colleague Michael Omi has shown me how to problematize race in the same way that gender has been problematized by feminist sociologists. By examining race and gender as interlocking, historically variable, and contested constructions, I hope to move toward integrated theory.

Both departments are in the process of changing themselves. Ethnic Studies is working on revamping the curriculum to be more truly interdisciplinary and to draw on developments in cultural studies and postcolonial theory. Women's Studies was granted departmental status two years ago. Our faculty, who have all had joint appointments with a disciplinary "home," need to define themselves more centrally as women's studies scholars and teachers. We are beginning to recruit a younger generation of scholars who have interdisciplinary backgrounds and who are committed to transnational, transdisciplinary, and multicultural feminisms. By participating in these changes, perhaps I will transform myself once again. It occurs to me that this shift to ethnic studies and women's studies is not unlike the shift I experienced when I entered sociology from social psychology. I expect my transformation will come about by my doing whatever it is that needs doing and working with others on the process of change. Once again, I am an immigrant.

## Epilogue: A Response to a Query as to Whether I Am Still Angry

Some colleagues, including the editors of this volume, after reading an earlier draft of the present essay, asked me, now that I am a tenured full professor at the University of California, Berkeley, whether I am still angry. They say I need to acknowledge and appreciate my success. They are, of course, right. My career has turned out well after all, through some luck and the help of many, many people. I have also been fortunate in my personal life; my partner for thirty-two years has been unwavering in his love and support, and we have three healthy and accomplished children. I have little reason to be bitter. But, I confess, there is anger. I don't like feeling angry, but I have come to accept that it will probably always be there, simmering below the surface and easily inflamed by daily reminders of the continued injustices that women of color suffer in academia. My anger may be somewhat inexplicable to colleagues who, despite the best intentions, have difficulty understanding at a gut level the injuries inflicted through large and small acts of arrogance by white men as they go about their business.

Most of us "successful" women of color in academia have had to endure numerous assaults on our worth and dignity in the process of getting our professional training and in being hired, retained, and promoted. We've had to fight our colleagues to make space for people like us in "their" departments. In most places, once we get in, we remain tokens, suffering both invisibility and hypervisibility. My experience as a woman of color knocking at the door of predominately white male departments and as the sole Asian American within predominately white male departments has made me an eyewitness to how racism and sexism operate at the informal level to keep departments white male bastions. I have been on both sides of the fence, as a member of a department that purports to be recruiting minority women faculty, yet manages not to make an appointment, and as an applicant, usually having been invited to apply, who did not get the appointment. I am not talking about cases where someone else is appointed— someone who might be better or equally qualified. Rather, I am talking about cases where no one is appointed at all—which can only imply that they think we are so bad that they'd rather leave the position vacant than give it to any of us. Over the years I have seen some rather bizarre posturing by colleagues and potential colleagues to explain these outcomes.

I make two assumptions at the outset. First, I assume that I and the other minority women academics whose experiences I draw on for this account are qualified for the positions for which we were being considered. Most of us have managed to maintain careers, and some have gone on to success in institutions better than the ones that rejected us. Second, I assume that most of the white males who dominate departments do not see themselves as racist and sexist and would probably pass a lie detector test if questioned outright. Nonetheless, their worldviews, habits, and collective actions lead to outcomes that are racist and sexist.

The discrimination I am talking about is often difficult to pinpoint because it is cloaked within a complicated process of "peer evaluation" that too often magically produces rather predictable outcomes. The evaluation process for candidates for academic positions and for promotion to tenure is indeed rigorous. In addition to vitae, letters of recommendation, teaching evaluations, and extensive personal interviews with other faculty, students, deans, and administrators, the candidate is required to submit all scholarly publications and present a research-based colloquium. The plethora of material reviewed implies a grueling but fair process in which one's peers read and evaluate the material and then come together as a group to discuss the candidates and reach a group consensus. The actual process hardly ever resembles this ideal. Many of those making the judgment do not read much of anything in the candidate's file, least of all her writing. It is too time consuming and difficult to do so if the candidate's area is outside of their field of interest. Most white male academics are not familiar with or interested in scholarship on gender, race, or ethnicity, especially if it focuses on the experiences of men and women of color. Thus, in most cases the majority of those making decisions will either not have read all the material or, if they have read it, not appreciate its significance.

How, then, do those making up the majority, who have not read the material or are not expert in the subfield, form a judgment? Quite simply, they rely on the judgment of those who do have a firm opinion, and those with the firmest opinions are likely to be those most invested in excluding work that doesn't agree with their conceptions. They don't necessarily have to be experts in the subfield to have a firm opinion about it, but they have to care enough about excluding it. Thus, peer judgments turn out not to be all that independently arrived at. Rather, the group consensus coalesces around a few facile characterizations, generally of the ilk that the candidate's scholarship is "weak," methodologically "sloppy," and/or "lacks theoretical significance." These terms were used by some senior faculty members to derogate the scholarship of a minority candidate for an assistant professorship in one department. Surprised because I knew how influential this candidate's work was in the field of race and ethnicity, I asked an acquaintance in the department what had happened. He said he hadn't looked at the work himself, but he had heard that it wasn't very good, and besides the candidate had not published much. When I said, "What about his book?" which had been widely praised in scholarly reviews, my acquaintance obviously hadn't heard about the book but added triumphantly, "Besides, he took a long time to finish his degree." I am sure this acquaintance will continue to believe the rejection was justified because the candidate was unproductive, despite clear evidence in the file to the contrary. I was reminded of the technique of the "big lie" in the McCarthy era: a characterization repeated often and loudly enough takes on credibility. I was a member of a department where a minority candidate gave a talk based on work in progress; the research was dismissed as of limited significance by faculty opposed to the candidate. The full paper on which the talk was based was subsequently published in a major disciplinary journal. Disconfirmation of judgment never chastens those who participate in derogating a candidate's work. They develop a convenient amnesia.

The dynamics of peer evaluation also help explain why race exclusion and gender exclusion occur even when a majority of faculty favor "diversifying" and developing gender and/or race studies in the department. I used to be puzzled by this, having encountered situations where the majority of faculty in the department are in favor of an appointment, and yet it doesn't happen. It is not unlike the question of why the National Rifle Association can prevent the passage of gun control laws even though the majority of Americans favor control. In departmental politics, as in national-level politics, a small group can prevail over an unorganized majority by the vociferousness of its views and its willingness to put a lot of effort into carrying the day.

Even the most liberal and enlightened white men are not willing to stir up conflict and dissent or risk their relations with white male colleagues for the sake of race and gender justice. They are not unlike the personally tolerant "liberals" in the 1950s who, when confronted by intransigent white supremacists, would not support "forced" integration on the grounds that it would foment unrest. These "friends" are the most aggravating because they'll let you down when you most need their support. They rationalize and excuse their colleagues' behavior; they "understand" and have compassion for racist/sexist sentiments because they identify more with their colleagues than with those who are excluded. They are intellectually supportive, but they have no emotional stake in race and gender justice, and they are unwilling to give up their comfort—which includes getting along with their colleagues—for the excluded. They will never be there when the chips are down. It took a while for me to learn this. I once became furious at the chair of my department for undercutting our faculty's vote in favor of a black woman candidate—whom he had heartily endorsed—when he realized that a male colleague in another department was vehemently opposed to the candidate. It appeared that the chair was more concerned with avoiding conflict and enmity than with acting honorably in relation to the candidate. I didn't fully understand the logic of this behavior until another incident a while later when I was discussing with an acquaintance a controversy that had arisen when his department declined to even interview a minority candidate who had been recommended by the recruitment committee. Minority students and faculty had complained and demonstrated, drawing media attention to the issue. My acquaintance had been on the recruitment committee and was involved in choosing the short list but had gone on leave before the decision was made. He was seen by minority students as a white person supportive of their concerns, so I expected him to express regret about not having been there to advocate for at least interviewing the candidate. Instead, he said, "I'm glad I wasn't there; it was just as well not to be part of the conflict."

Another scenario that I have seen replayed over and over is one where a position has been created as a result of organized efforts by students, the administration, or sometimes a subgroup within the faculty to diversify the faculty or to develop minority or gender studies. Those opposed to targeted searches (usually in the name of maintaining "quality" and preventing "race-conscious" hiring), abetted by those who are indifferent, may reluctantly agree to go along with the recruitment effort but make it difficult to get any candidate approved. A common ploy is to anoint one particular person—preferably one who is not available—as the only worthy scholar of his or her ethnicity. (This is easy because usually only one black/Latino or Latina/Asian American is allowed to be prominent in an academic field at any one time; she or he therefore appears as the "exception.") Usually the person so designated will already have a better job or have multiple bidders. Since that person is not available, it is argued, it is better to make no appointment than to get someone "second rate." In most such cases the position eventually gets eliminated altogether.

When you are one of the candidates in this situation, it rapidly becomes apparent that those interviewing you are merely going through the motions and that they don't care whether the position is filled. At two different universities in different years, I interviewed for positions in Asian American sociology that had been created as a result of student protests. On both occasions someone interviewing me managed to work into the conversation his feeling that it was a shame that the department could not get X/Y, who was truly outstanding. Whether or not X or Y was, in fact, better qualified is not the point. I doubt that in any other academic job search, a faculty member or an administrator would blatantly insult a candidate by lamenting the unavailability of another scholar. At one of the schools, the chair of sociology blithely informed me that he did not think race and ethnic relations would ever be an important topic in his department. I found this statement astounding in light of the centrality of issues of race and ethnicity in the development of American sociology. Furthermore, the campus was located in an urban center experiencing large-scale racial conflict. Needless to say, no appointment was made, although a few years later the department appointed a white male scholar specializing in race/ethnicity. In another case told to me by a Chicana sociologist, a rather reluctant department did make her an offer, but at a salary below what she was currently earning. Although she wanted to be at the institution, she correctly interpreted this as a less than good faith offer and turned it down. Nevertheless, the department could claim that despite extensive efforts, no Chicano or Chicana sociologist would accept an offer.

For those of us caught in this particular scenario, "peer review" adds insult to injury. Not only do we not get the jobs because they really don't want us or like the type of research we do; we are also invited to apply, put through the wringer, and then informed that, through a fair and thorough process, we have been judged unworthy. If we don't accept this judgment or shrug our shoulders philosophically, and instead raise the possibility that racism or sexism colored the process, everyone in the department, even those who are usually at odds over various internal matters, draws together in common defense of departmental prerogatives, citing "confidentiality" of procedures.

So to respond to my colleagues: yes, I am still angry, partly because of my own experiences from years past, but also because I observe the same processes of exclusion, marginalization, and ghettoization at work. I do not wish to minimize the gains we have made. In my own university women of color have reached double digits if we include non-U.S.-born women. Some of us are tenured, so collectively we have some influence. But we are a tiny minority, concentrated in certain ghettos—Asian American, Chicano, Native American, African American, and Women's Studies; our presence relieves pressure on mainline departments to develop more inclusive faculty, curricula, and scholarship. These departments remain white male bastions. Scholarship in these departments can go on ignoring race and gender and continue to build theory that is partial. Moreover, wherever we are located, we have to be constantly vigilant against backsliding and attempts to roll back our gains.

## Notes

This essay was completed in July 1994 and has not been revised for this publication. I let it stand as a document that reflects my "memory" at that point. My thanks to all of the participants of the working meeting on "The Missing Feminist Revolution

Revisited: Gender, Life Histories, and Human Agency"—organized by Barbara Laslett and Barrie Thorne—for their feedback and encouragement. This essay is dedicated to Gary Glenn, a feminist before I was, for sharing the experiences described here and for understanding white male privilege.

1. My mother recalls my declaring as a young teenager that I never intended to have children. She took this declaration seriously, and it stabbed her in the heart. I don't remember ever saying this and believe that I always intended to have children.

2. I was wrong. I now realize that my father has always kept up with "current events" by reading the paper and now by watching hours of television news. However, he never discussed anything that he heard or watched with us, so none of us ever knew what he thought about issues.

3. Being the lone Asian American and/or lone Asian American woman became so usual that I became comfortable with it. In the three universities where I taught before my present job, I was the only Asian American woman in my college or division. At Boston University there was one other Japanese American in my department, Scott Miyakawa, who became a cherished colleague. His gentleness and caring drew many minority and international students to him. I felt we had a special kinship because of our shared heritage. Scottie passed away in 1981. Although my uniqueness might seem to make me stand out, most of the time, because I was "not black," my ethnicity was invisible. I recall sitting in a faculty meeting in which there was a discussion about the lack of minority on the faculty and someone remarked, "For example, all of us sitting here are white." My interjection of "not quite" elicited embarrassed laughs.

4. Simone de Beauvoir, *The Second Sex*, trans. H. M. Parshley (New York: Bantam Books, 1961); Anais Nin, *The Diary of Anais Nin*, ed. and trans. by Gunther Stuhlman (New York: Swallow Press, 1966).

5. Michelle Zimbalist Rosaldo and Louise Lamphere, eds., *Woman, Culture, and Society* (Stanford, Calif.: Stanford University Press, 1974).

6. Chandra left BU in the mid-1970s to take a position at the University of California, San Diego, where she still teaches. She has written three highly acclaimed books in the sociology of culture. Barbara moved to Seattle to take a research position at the Batelle Institute, where she has flourished.

7. Harry Braverman, *Labor and Monopoly Capital* (New York: Monthly Review Press, 1974).

8. Our first article, "Degraded and Deskilled," was published in *Social Problems* 15 (1977): 52–64. Arlene Kaplan Daniels's editorship of the journal undoubtedly had a great deal to do with its receptivity to our kind of research.

9. Sacks coined the term to refer to a type of leadership that involves building and maintaining connections necessary for organized resistance. See Karen Sacks, *Caring by the Hour* (Urbana: University of Illinois Press, 1988).

10. Carole Turbin, Chris Bose, Natalie Sokoloff, Myra Ferree, Carol Brown, Susan Lehrer, Roz Feldberg, and I have been with the group for the entire twelve years. Other past and present members include Fran Rothstein, Peggy Crull, Nadine Felton, Amy Srebnik, Amy Gilman, and Nancy Breen.

11. Christine Bose, Roslyn Feldberg, and Natalie Sokoloff, with the Women and Work Group, eds., *Hidden Aspects of Women's Work* (New York: Praeger, 1987). One unfor-

tunate aspect of my current residence in California is missing meetings of the group. Fortunately, Carole Turbin, who spent a year in California, and I have developed a close relationship intellectually and personally, and frequently discuss our work with each other.

12. I can be as dazzled and engaged by good work based on multiple regressions as by good work based on ethnography or historical research, but that doesn't mean I can do them equally well.

13. For example, the deanship of the College of Arts and Science was dubbed "the revolving deanship" by faculty critics because a series of incumbents resigned in frustration. Finally, an individual who many felt was unqualified for tenure was given tenure by Silber and installed as dean. In 1992 the attorney general of Massachusetts launched an investigation of Boston University management practices that forced the university to agree to make certain changes relating to the independence and oversight function of the trustees.

14. Many accounts of violation of academic freedom and normal academic practices have been published over the years in the *Boston Globe* in the period from the late 1970s until the present.

15. Examples include the elimination of sociology departments at Washington University, St. Louis, and the University of Rochester; unilateral downsizing at California State University at San Diego; and proposals for a severe cut at Yale.

16. The prospect of transcribing approximately 100 hours of taped interviews was daunting, but a good friend, Jean Twomey, became fascinated by the interviews and volunteered evenings to transcribing them. She transcribed one-third, I did another one-third, and I hired Japanese-speaking assistants to transcribe the remaining interviews. Jean and I spent many hours discussing the project. Her commitment and interest boosted me over what had been a formidable hurdle.

17. Evelyn Nakano Glenn, "Occupational Ghettoization: Japanese American Women and Domestic Service, 1905–1970," *Ethnicity* 8 (1981): 352–386; Evelyn Nakano Glenn, "The Dialectics of Wage Work: Japanese American Women and Domestic Service, 1905–1940," *Feminist Studies* 6 (fall 1980): 432–471.

18. Evelyn Nakano Glenn, *Issei, Nisei, Warbride: Three Generations of Japanese American Women in Domestic Service* (Philadelphia: Temple University Press, 1986).

19. My friend Liz Lyons, a lawyer, really bucked me up when I felt the most dispirited. Always a fighter and advocate, she was totally outraged by any violation of rights and by bureaucratic stupidity. She was completely partisan in my favor—an attitude I badly needed—and urged me to argue my grievance as aggressively as possible.

20. Ironically, Silber was impressed by the documents I wrote in support of my grievance and final appeal. He concluded his final letter of denial with the statement "You write very well" and said that I should therefore have no trouble finding another position! He apparently was unaware that his own provost stated in his letter of denial that my writing "verged on the ungrammatical."

21. Editors had not leaped at the chance to publish my manuscript, seeing the method as too hybrid or the topic as too narrow. I am therefore grateful to Mike Ames at Temple University Press for his early interest in and encouragement of my work-in-progress.

22. Evelyn Nakano Glenn, "Split Household, Small Producer, and Dual Wage-Earner," *Journal of Marriage and the Family* (February 1983): 35–46.

23. See Robert Blauner, *Racial Oppression in America* (New York: Harper and Row, 1972).

24. See, for example, Bonnie Thornton Dill, "Our Mother's Grief: Racial-Ethnic Women and the Maintenance of Families," *Journal of Family History* 13 (1988): 415–431; Evelyn Nakano Glenn, "Racial Ethnic Women's Work: The Intersection of Race, Class, and Gender Oppression, *Review of Radical Political Economy* 17 (fall 1985): 86–108.

25. For example, Patricia Hill Collins presented early chapters of *Black Feminist Thought* (Boston: Allen and Unwin, 1990), at one of the summer institutes in 1983. See also the collection of articles by scholars working with the Inter-University Group or the Memphis Center edited by Maxine Baca Zinn and Bonnie Thornton Dill, *Women of Color in U.S. Society* (Philadelphia: Temple University Press, 1994).

26. She currently teaches in history and African American studies at the University of Michigan.

27. One of the issues I have faced in doing this research is a hesitancy about speaking about African American and Mexican American women's experience. Women of color have been critical of white women interpreting our experience for us, and being Asian American does not automatically endow me with special understanding of other women of color.

*Barrie Thorne*

# Brandeis as a Generative Institution: Critical Perspectives, Marginality, and Feminism

*I*n the late 1960s and early 1970s, when second-wave feminist ideas began to take hold in U.S. sociology, the Brandeis graduate program was regarded as "good" but not at the top of the profession, with only one woman on the faculty. Yet out of that program came an unusually large proportion of the first generation of contemporary feminist sociologists.[1] Why? What was it about the Brandeis milieu that nurtured early connections between the women's liberation movement and sociology as an academic field? These autobiographical reflections start before but mostly dwell on that focal place and time; they have been enriched with a lot of help from my friends.

## From Mormonism to Social Science

Given the geographic, ethnic, and political distance, I am probably the only person from a Mormon background to have enrolled in the Brandeis graduate program in sociology. My family's history moves through nineteenth-century sagas of conversion to the Church of Jesus Christ of Latter-Day Saints (LDS); migration from England, Scandinavia, and small farms in the Northeast; arduous crossing of the Plains in wagons and on foot; and settlement in what are now the states of Utah, Idaho, and Arizona. When I was growing up in northern Utah in the 1940s and 1950s, we sometimes attended large family reunions where distant cousins were introduced as descended from the "first," "second," or "third" wife of a shared ancestral patriarch. If that great-(great, great) grandmother was known to have been the patriarch's "favored" wife, her descendants also seemed a little special.

Education became my family's route out of hardscrabble farming and into professional life. My maternal grandfather and my father each put themselves through Utah State Agricultural College and went on to get Ph.D.s (my grandfather, in economics; my father, in soil chemistry). My mother, Alison Comish Thorne, also earned a Ph.D., in consumer economics, from Iowa State, where she met my father at the L.D.S., or Mormon, Sunday School. They married in 1937, and my father, Wynne Thorne, took faculty positions first at Texas A&M and then at Utah State Agricultural College.

Mother used to say that she and Dad were a "pair-a-docs," but it was obvious that these docs had quite different opportunities. Dad rose through the faculty ranks and eventually became vice president for research at Utah State. Nepotism rules barred Mother from an academic career, although she occasionally taught at the university and in the 1970s, as a part-time lecturer, helped establish its women's studies program. She raised five children, wrote a column for *The Gifted Child Quarterly* (the label weighed as expectation), read philosophy and "great books" during the several hours each day that she tried to set aside from domestic routine, and actively worked for liberal causes in the conservative town of Logan. She became a mainstay of the local Democratic Party and League of Women Voters; led an unsuccessful 1950s campaign for fluoridation of the water supply; and in the 1960s helped organize a summer school for migrant farm children and federally funded antipoverty programs in northern Utah. She served on the Logan School Board for eleven years until, in 1971, after the U.S. invasion of Cambodia and the shootings at Kent State, she participated in the first antiwar demonstration in Logan's history. This led to rumors that "Alison Thorne is not patriotic" and her defeat in the next school board election.[2]

Our parents simply assumed that their five children—spaced in an older set of two, a gap of six years, and then three more—would do well in school. As the oldest, my brother and I got especially strong doses of the "n-ach" (need-for-achievement) that fuels cross-generational upward mobility. For me, good grades became both a ladder of opportunity and a self-inflicted whip. My "Book of Remembrance," a scrapbook designed for girls and filled with church-related categories, includes pages of neatly glued report cards from elementary school through junior high—a field of A's, qualified by a few minuses, and one seventh-grade C, the humiliation softened because it was in gym, a nonacademic subject. I used to take pride in the field of A's, but they now make me sigh over the years of obedience, self-suppression, and the obsessive wish to please.

The ladder of A's did help me climb out of "Happy Valley" (our sardonic teenage name for Cache Valley, where Logan is located) and into a scholarship at Stanford University. During the first semester, I felt like a scared hick, intimidated by students from prep schools and advanced place-ment classes, and I studied almost nonstop. I also fell in love with ideas. In an introductory philosophy course, Professor Mothershead persuasively ar-gued each position, and then after many of us had become believers, he unsparingly picked each one apart. It was like a roller-coaster ride, climb-ing up to belief in utilitarianism or logical positivism and then hurtling down the slope of disenchantment. However, one of the readings, David Hume's "On Miracles," had a lasting effect. I outlined the argument again and again and concluded that I could no longer believe in God or, there-fore, in the L.D.S. religion. This culminated a slow loss of faith that had begun with my parents' growing doubts and liberal attitudes and my expo-sure to varied beliefs at Stanford. Hume sealed it up, and in a series of small rebellions, I began to engage in forbidden practices, which I came to call my "sindrome"—drinking Coke, coffee, tea, and alcohol; smoking an occasional cigarette; and engaging in sex outside of marriage.[3]

Loss of religious faith coincided with my taking an introductory course in anthropology taught by George Spindler and Louise Spindler (she was one of only two women teachers in my undergraduate years; I had no women teachers as a graduate student). I loved the Spindlers' detached compari-sons, say, of the religious practices of the Menominee and the Navajo. That comparative approach, and the concept of "culture," gave me perspective on the totalizing world I had come from; I discovered, with fascination, that the Mormons were one of the "four cultures" that a team of anthro-pologists had studied in the Southwest. I decided to major in anthropol-ogy, with a minor in an honors program in social thought and institutions, organized by Charles Drekmeier, who had studied in the Social Relations Program at Harvard.

Over time, I became much more comfortable at Stanford. I especially loved the social thought seminar, cotaught by Charles and Margot Drekmeier and several faculty from other disciplines. Margot had a Ph.D. from Harvard and an inspiring relationship with ideas; however, she did not have an aca-demic appointment, and, as with my mother, I vaguely sensed the injustice of her institutional marginality. The seminar was held at the Drekmeiers' home in Palo Alto. I savored the framed picture of Sigmund Freud on their living room wall and the ritual glasses of sherry served as the evening's conversation began. Each year the seminar focused on a different theme—it was "freedom" during my junior year. We read Max Weber, Karl Mannheim, Freud, Herbert Marcuse, B. F. Skinner, and court cases on por-nography, and we threw around concepts like "repressive desublimation." My senior thesis, grandly titled "A Theory of Mind for the Sociology of

Knowledge," was a smorgasboard of ideas from Mannheim, Émile Durkheim, Max Scheler, George Herbert Mead, C. Wright Mills, Freud, and Norbert Weiner. I had discovered a taste for theory.

After graduation I followed the culture strand of my interests, and as the first woman from Stanford to win a Marshall Scholarship, I went to the London School of Economics to study social anthropology. My hopes were high, but the program, which mostly involved reading dull classics by Bronislaw Malinowski and E. E. Evans-Pritchard and memorizing kinship systems, was not what I had anticipated. I lived in a dreary undergraduate dorm purported to have central heating—even on the coldest days the radiators, at best, were lukewarm—and I felt lonely and uprooted. Instead of switching programs or simply deciding to quit, I became so depressed that I finally returned to the United States, where I stayed with my brother and his wife and worked as a secretary in the Princeton Physics Department. After the depression lifted, I reconsidered my future.

By sheer chance I ran into a friend from Stanford who had gone on to Brandeis to do graduate work in philosophy. She loaned me the catalog, and I discovered that the Brandeis sociology program focused on European social theory, my other intellectual passion (I felt burned by anthropology). I applied in early summer and went for an interview; Kurt Wolff and Robert Weiss nodded approvingly at the field of A's on my Stanford transcript and approved my late admission to the program. Weiss arranged for restoration of the Woodrow Wilson Fellowship that I had declined in order to go to England, and the pieces fell into place for a second chance at graduate school.

## Brandeis and Converging Marginalities

When I arrived at Brandeis in fall 1965, the sociology graduate program was only three years old; the university, founded in 1948 by an American Jewish group, was also relatively new. Although Brandeis was officially non-sectarian, the majority of faculty, students, and staff were Jewish, which created an ambience quite different from anything I'd previously experienced. The Mormon culture in which I had grown up, the WASP upper-middle-class ethos at Stanford, and my experiences in England had left me emotionally parched, and I drank thirstily from the affectivity and warmth I found at Brandeis. I loved emotional exuberance, as when Lewis Coser burst from his office and told me the results of my qualifying exams by calling out, "*Mazeltov!*" as he came to give me a hug. At first I was intimidated by loud and mutually interrupting patterns of argument, but I learned how to join in and found it energizing. I was moved by stories of the Holocaust, some told by survivors, and came to realize that words such as *angst* and *weltschmirz*, which I had encountered in my undergraduate reading, were part of a language of suffering that connected with human tragedy much more authentically than prepackaged and repressed Mormon styles of experiencing. The contrast felt like going from plywood to rich mahogany; from rigid and conformist dogma to depth, mystery, and risk.[4] I had never met people who talked so freely, and so often, about neuroses, and I started pondering my own. The Brandeis folks liked to hear Mormon stories, and they joked about my being the essence of goy.

In a time of lingering anti-Semitism at other universities, Brandeis welcomed Jews as both students and faculty. The department also welcomed women (including older and married women) as students, although not, as I will later discuss, as faculty. Between 1965 and 1971, about one-half of the sociology graduate students were women, and of those who completed Ph.D.s between 1966 and 1980, forty-six were women and forty-one were men.[5] In researching the history of women psychoanalysts, Nancy Chodorow uncovered a loose sociological principle that may help account for the much higher proportion of women students at Brandeis compared with other graduate programs in sociology. Asked why so many women entered the field of psychoanalysis in its early days, an elderly informant observed of the Austro-German culture from which she came that where they allowed Jews, they allowed women. When a range of groups are excluded from the top stratum, they may end up together in more marginal or lower-status places.[6] Of course, Jewish and female are overlapping social categories. Other racial ethnic groups were not well represented at Brandeis, although a few African Americans entered the sociology program over the years. There was also a steady stream of international students.

The Brandeis sociology faculty shared a sense of collective marginality. From the time of the school's founding, Brandeis welcomed refugees from Nazi Europe; Lewis Coser, Kurt Wolff, Paul Kecskemeti, Egon Bittner, and Herbert Marcuse (in the History of Ideas Program, but with close ties to sociology) were central to the intellectual life of the Sociology Department.[7] Everett C. Hughes came to Brandeis in 1961 to escape forced retirement from the University of Chicago. Maurice Stein, Philip Slater, Gordon Fellman, Jack Seeley, and Larry Rosenberg were self-proclaimed exiles from mainstream U.S. sociology (Larry told a story, which quickly became a legend, about having thrown his dissertation into Lake Michigan after becoming disillusioned with the highly quantitative training he'd received at the University of Chicago). The faculty often voiced C. Wright Mills's criticisms of the twin distortions—still prevalent in the 1960s—of grand theory, especially structural functionalism, and the abstracted empiricism perpetuated by large survey research empires at Columbia and Chicago.[8] The Brandeis faculty was determined to create a graduate program organized around a different kind of sociology.[9]

## Brandeis Sociology

The graduate curriculum required during my first year (1965–1966) laid out the core of that difference. Our methods requirements were minimal—a two-semester, hands-on course in field methods and a one-semester survey of research methods, skillfully taught by Robert Weiss. The other two required courses were in sociological theory. Lewis Coser taught the first semester, which included Durkheim, Georg Simmel, Marx, Weber, Robert Michels, Mannheim, and lesser-known theorists such as Scheler and Maurice Halbwachs. The second semester focused on contemporary theory and was taught by Maurice Stein, who assigned such authors as Mills, Marcuse, N. O. Brown, R. D. Laing, Frantz Fanon, and Marshall McLuhan. The other graduate courses focused on interesting and big ideas, whatever their disciplinary homes, rather than on a narrowly defined corpus of sociological literature. In addition to substantive seminars (e.g., sociology of family, taught by Slater; deviance and medical sociology, taught by Irving Zola; social institutions, taught by Hughes), there were many specialized offerings in social theory. I took a seminar in the sociology of knowledge from Kurt Wolff (who had been a student of Karl Mannheim), another on ideology and social movements from Paul Kecskemeti (Mannheim's brother-in-law), and an especially memorable seminar on the pretheoretical foundations of sociology, which Wolff organized around the philosophy of social science, phenomenology, and the writings of Alfred Schutz. The theory courses drew students from the History of Ideas Program, including Jeremy Shapiro and Shierry Weber, who became central to my Cambridge-based circle of friends. Jeremy and Shierry had studied with Theodor Adorno in Germany and Marcuse at Brandeis and were translating writings by Adorno, Marcuse, and Jürgen Habermas. Martin Nicolaus, an older and politically experienced member of our sociology graduate cohort, was working on the first English translation of Marx's *Gründrisse*. Wolff had published major English translations of Simmel's writing, and Coser had written about Simmel. Even Hughes, a quintessentially midwestern American, read German and had undertaken his own mimeographed translations of essays by Weber and by

Simmel. In short, graduate students at Brandeis felt directly and richly connected with European social thought.

This connection included a lively commitment to psychoanalysis as a social and cultural theory. Philip Slater and Gordon Fellman had come out of the Harvard Social Relations Department, which combined sociology, psychology, and anthropology and took psychoanalysis seriously. Psychoanalytically based social criticism was central to Stein's theory course, and many of us engaged passionately with efforts to combine Marx and Freud. Psychoanalysis wove in and out of daily conversations among graduate students. We even created a guessing game where one person would proclaim a behavior, such as "chewing your fingernails" or "reading on the toilet," and the others would offer psychoanalytic interpretations. We would then hunt up the behavior in Otto Fenichel's encyclopedic *A Psychoanalytic Theory of Neurosis* and the person who came closest to Fenichel's interpretation won that laugh-filled round.[10]

The Brandeis European theory tradition was unique among U.S. graduate programs in its emphasis not only on psychoanalysis but also on Simmel, the preeminent classical sociologist of everyday life, and on Schutz and Mannheim. We were trained to theorize everyday life, as well as larger structures, and to think of knowledge as perspectival. Our reading of Schutz led us to ponder such concepts as *Lebenswelt* (life world), multiple realities, phenomenological bracketing, and the situation of the ordinary knower. Phenomenology values everyday life, which, some of us later came to see, is often defined as women's realm. In concert with the sociology of knowledge, which also engaged us, phenomenology moves the knower from the Archimedean point of objective knowledge to a more situated understanding of the relation of knowledge, social location, and interests. Our graduate education exposed us to the roots of later feminist epistemological writings about gender and ways of knowing.[11]

As graduate students at Brandeis we pursued questions of daily life not only through courses on Simmel, Schutz, and psychoanalysis but also through intensive training in field methods. When the graduate program was founded in the early 1960s, the Brandeis faculty saw its mission as teaching "understanding," or *verstehen*, sociology, with an almost exclusive focus on qualitative methods. Many of the Brandeis faculty had used participant-observation and/or open-ended interviewing in their own research, and they had a strong and self-conscious connection to the old Chicago School of fieldwork (by the late 1960s Chicago had shifted to a quantitative mode). Hughes, who had taught a legendary graduate course in fieldwork at Chicago brought the course with him to Brandeis. It was taught collectively—when I took it, by Hughes, Slater, Zola, Fellman, and Sam Wallace—and was an intense and collective hands-on experience. The instructors sent us to Charlestown, a white working-class, mostly Irish Catholic community and gave us the initial charge of taking field notes on the sights and sounds of a census tract. We then worked in smaller groups, piecing together a community study. Learning to do fieldwork as a group was a great source of bonding; together we figured out how to take and analyze field notes and how to handle emotional, ethical, and political dilemmas. We shared adventures, anxieties, and laments. "How can I live for tomorrow when I'm taking yesterday's notes?" Marty Epstein whined one day in the graduate student room, and we burst into shared laughter.

Each of the instructors wrote very different comments on our field notes. Next to my shocked response at seeing two young men in a fistfight on the street, Slater wrote, "Are you taking an ingenue role?" (role or not, I was far from streetwise, and the sting of his comment carried multiple gender meanings). In the midst of my field notes describing Sunday services in a small Protestant congregation, I wrote that I liked the feel of singing hymns and sitting shoulder to shoulder in the pews because it reminded me of my Mormon childhood. The autobiographical aside whetted Hughes's interest, and he stopped me in the hall to ask about it, opening the first of many conversations and a lasting relationship of mentoring and friendship. As he did for so many other students, Hughes helped me use sociology to gain a more detached and appreciative understanding of a former identity that chased me around (one of his many imaginative conceptualizations).[12]

The practice of fieldwork concretely anchored our more theoretical readings in phenomenology, *verstehen,* and psychoanalytic sociology, juxtaposing philosophical depth and critical perspectives with the more pragmatic foundations of the original Chicago School of fieldwork.[13] The mix was exciting but also jarring; the European theory that Coser and Wolff taught veered toward the philosophical and abstract, while Hughes generated ideas through the concrete particulars of the social world. The contrast, which bears on different modes of theorizing, is vividly conveyed by a story Howard S. Becker tells about his own first year as a graduate student taking a course from Hughes at the University of Chicago. Becker came up after class and inquired, "Professor Hughes, what do you think of theory?" Hughes asked in return, "Theory of what?"[14]

In courses taught by Wolff, Coser, and Stein, we read and talked Theory, with a capital *T.* It was a mode I had come to love in the Stanford social thought seminar—engaging with the overarching frameworks of Marx or Freud, examining their assumptions, spinning out implications. Isaiah Berlin contrasts that systematizing mode, symbolized by the hedgehog, with the approach of the fox, who darts from insight to insight.[15] Hughes worked in the latter spirit. Rather than moving from a general framework, he used the process of analogy and juxtaposition to raise nuggets of insight, pointing, in the spirit of Simmel, to underlying social forms. Hughes taught with stories and Zenlike questions. For example, he opened the oral defense of a dissertation on rabbis who presided over marriages between Jews and gentiles by asking, "How are these rabbis like abortionists?" His answer: they do the marginal and devalued work of their profession.

Overall, the Brandeis intellectual milieu reinforced the value of connecting sociology with everyday life and experience and with critical consciousness. There was no sense in our training that objectivity meant erasing subjectivity or the personal interests of the researcher; indeed, the faculty openly discussed the passions that guided their own projects. Wolff was working on the sociology of evil; Slater, on issues of male narcissism in ancient Greek society, with a critical view of contemporary masculinity. Always a weathervane picking up the breeze of new ideas, Stein moved, over my years at Brandeis, from writing about McLuhan, to the counterculture, and finally to co-counseling. The faculty saw themselves not as advancing a science but as making sense of human experience and the problems of the time. They had no interest in policing disciplinary boundaries; instead, they taught ideas that engaged them, and they were openly critical, as Stein once phrased it, of "people who inhabit something called careers." In the Brandeis department there were no large, funded research empires, no steady demand for graduate student labor. The program was small, and students mostly subsisted on their own funding and individual fellowships, including, in the late 1960s, departmental NIMH training fellowships in field research methods.

The faculty encouraged us to pursue our own intellectual interests. Nothing was too grand or ambitious for study. For example, Nancy Jay developed a Durkheimian theory of sacrificial religions, Donna Huse wrote her dissertation on the theory and practice of dialectical rationality, and Jasminka Gojkovic wrote about ideology and politics in the sociology of art. Nor was anything too odd, offbeat, or seemingly trivial for serious sociological work. Hughes was working on a paper called "The Humble and the Proud" and often compared plumbers and physicians (both routinize other people's crises), saints and sinners (both go to extremes), and told us about former students who had studied taxi dance hall girls, furriers, cab drivers, and funeral directors.[16] He encouraged us to develop topics that engaged our own experiences, and in his wry and wondering approach to the human panorama, every experience counted. It was an easy step for Nancy Stoller to do fieldwork on the management of birthing in the Boston Lying-in Hospital, Lynda Holmstrom to interview dual-career couples, Barbara Carter to observe in a women's prison, and Natalie Allon to observe in a Weight Watchers' program. Because of this emphasis on daily life and the social contexts of knowing, we experienced less of the extreme "bifurcated consciousness" that Dorothy Smith has described as a woman studying sociological texts that erased many of her experiences.[17]

## The New Left and Women's Liberation

In 1967 I finished coursework, passed qualifying exams, and began to try on dissertation topics like a series of garments. The Vietnam War was heating up, and the threat of the draft was sending ripples of fear among students. In a tempestuous, all-university meeting, Brandeis faculty and students debated whether the university should release student grades to the Selective Service. Jack Seeley, then chair of sociology, passionately argued that the university should avoid complicity with the war in Vietnam. Meetings of that kind drew us into intense personal engagement with debates about the politics of intellectuals, universities, and the professions and the urgency of our own historical moment.

My friends and I began to participate in antiwar demonstrations, and I went through training to become a draft counselor with the Boston Draft Resistance Group. It occurred to me that I could combine the stances of activist and participant-observer by doing draft counseling and helping organize demonstrations while taking field notes on the side and eventually writing my dissertation on the dynamics of the movement. Although I pulled it off, this mix of purposes turned out to be less ingenious, and more fraught with risk, guilty feelings, and ethical dilemmas, than I had anticipated.[18] It inaugurated what has turned out to be a recurring personal tension between the social movement mode of passionate engagement—the collective stance of being "up against the system" with the goal of social change—and a detached and analytic mode that loosens the claim of singular beliefs and gives ballast against dogmatism and intolerance (and helped free me from Mormonism).

My first serious encounter with the idea of women's liberation took place at a national Resistance conference in Illinois in March 1969. A speaker from Chicago Voice of Women argued that the spirit of draft resistance, compressed in slogans like "Take control of your own life," could be extended to the oppressed condition of women. She invited the women to meet separately, and we talked, far into the night, about our secondary position in the movement and the ways in which our relations with one another were largely mediated through men.[19] After returning to the world of Boston-Cambridge, several of us decided to continue the discussion by forming a women's caucus within the New England Resistance. We invited others to join, and we met weekly in one another's apartments, improvising a form of consciousness-raising.[20] That fall we joined other women's collectives (as we called the groups of six to twelve that had sprouted in varied New Left spaces) and founded Bread and Roses, one of the first women's liberation groups on the East Coast.

The small-group structure of consciousness-raising created many nodes of intimacy and commitment in Bread and Roses. We also organized weekly mass meetings, occasional demonstrations (for example, on International Women's Day), and spontaneous and theatrical zap actions, as when a group of us protested the showing of pornographic movies at a trendy Cambridge movie theater. Various task forces focused on issues such as women and work, child care, and women's health (their efforts evolved into the widely read publication *Our Bodies, Ourselves*).[21]

By the early 1970s, women's liberation had become a vital presence in the student milieu in the Boston-Cambridge area, touching the lives and thinking of many, although certainly not all, of the women in the Brandeis graduate program. The self-conscious heightening of women's commitment to one another was a major emotional feat of the movement. Those of us who were heterosexual no longer waited around for men to phone for dates; we made, and kept, Saturday night commitments to be with other women. We developed a greater sense of conscious choice about our sexual and personal lives, our appearance (we threw out girdles and cosmetics and reclaimed our underarm and leg hair), and possibilities for education and employment.

A group of us from Brandeis who entered the field of sociology and the women's liberation movement more or less in tandem found that the worlds sometimes collided and at other times met with thrilling resonance. We became deeply bonded and together developed the chutzpah to start questioning the conventional categories of the field and the authority of our male teachers, while also getting their ultimate blessing, which was emotionally important to me, a connected daughter even as I rebelled.

Consciousness-raising and the early texts of the movement gave us insight into women's subordination and consolidated a series of pressing questions: Why were women so marginal as subjects and as practitioners in the field of sociology? Why did sociologists ignore women's lower wages, their channeling into devalued occupations, their exploitation in domestic labor, their sexual objectification? Members of our collective gave outreach talks on behalf of Bread and Roses in which we cited facts—for example, about employed women's lower wages and their disproportionate responsibility for housework—and criticized stereotypes of women as overly emotional and as male sexual objects. I helped give these raps, as we called them, to the women's auxiliary of a Jewish synagogue; the wives of Harvard Business School students; a group of junior college students; and, in an especially memorable encounter, a large undergraduate course on the sociology of the family at Harvard. The T.A. introduced us as representatives of "women's lib," unaware that two of the three speakers (Donna Huse and I) were also graduate students in sociology. The speaking of sociologically relevant insights from a committed and collective movement stance was a powerful experience. I liked the position of informed advocacy and the feel of working in concert together as we confronted audiences that were sometimes indifferent and even hostile.

During that same spring of 1970, some of us who bridged between Bread and Roses and Brandeis sociology decided to organize a departmental colloquium on women's liberation, in essence bringing our newfound insights and anger back to our home turf. Several years before, Nancy Stoller had recorded patterns of interruption in the graduate student room and found that men far outscored women. It was also obvious that the all-male faculty did most of the talking in colloquia, even when there was ample student attendance. We decided that when we opened the floor for discussion after our initial presentations on women's liberation, we would call only on women. The faculty quickly became impatient; Jerry Boime almost exploded from the pressure of not speaking. Finally, Slater managed to get the floor (I chaired the discussion and found myself calling him "Phil" for the first daring time). He said that he felt uncomfortable—like a little boy—and that the other men seemed to feel that way, too, perhaps because their only experience with women's voices being dominant was with their mothers. That was a stunning Oedipal moment, when one of our collective fathers said he felt like our son!

Although charged with tension, the colloquium also opened glimmers of recognition and support. The Brandeis faculty was eager to be up on political and cultural trends, and the women's movement raised fascinating intellectual questions. Some of the faculty had already warmed to the challenge of thinking about gender, especially Slater, whose book *The Glory of Hera* traced the origins of male narcissism to the anxiety of confined and subordinated mothers; long before others, he saw that the psychological emancipation of men ultimately depends on the liberation of women, and he understood the emotional threat of feminism to some men.[22] Boime was working on a theory of risk-taking as a basis of male bonding, as in revolutions and gangs, which he contrasted with the mode of civil society based on men and women joined in families. Hughes had long recognized patterns of discrimination; in his 1945 article "Dilemmas and Contradictions of Status," he unpacked notions such as "woman engineer" and "Negro doctor," observing that professions constrain the participation of entire groups in order to limit competition.[23] He was curious about this new wave of feminism and often observed that his mother-in-law had been a suffragist, as well as a judge, in Canada. Hughes often engaged in sociological reflections by typing notes on his manual machine; the pale and uneven letters bounced up and down instead of holding straight to the line. When I worked as his research assistant between 1969 and 1971 in a project on professional education, Hughes typed and gave me several notes that focused on gender. In one he mused about what each gender knows of the other's secrets, and in another he pondered the sociological significance of the fact that the biological dimensions of sex, unlike those of race, cannot be eliminated by group interbreeding.[24]

Intellectual engagement was one thing, the actual treatment of women another, and as feminist ideas spread, women graduate students became more and more angry at the absence of women on the Brandeis faculty. Helen MacGill Hughes and Rose Laub Coser, whom we initially got to know because they were married to our teachers, provided us with immediate examples of the barriers women sociologists faced as they sought steady employment and regular careers; nepotism rules and other patterns of sexism had continually blocked them from positions at Brandeis and at the other universities where their husbands had taught.[25] (By then I had had clearer insight into and anger about my mother's stalled academic career.)

In 1967 Rosabeth Kanter joined the Brandeis sociology faculty, which, except from 1958 to 1961 when Suzanne Keller was in the department, had been all male. Graduate students (women, as well as men) generally opposed the hiring of Kanter, as did some of the faculty. Later, as we developed feminist consciousness, some of us ruefully remembered the sexist comments that had been made at the time of Kanter's hiring and wondered if we, then in the position of daughters, could ever become sisters or full colleagues of the men who were our teachers.

Throughout the 1970s the hiring and retention of women faculty in the Brandeis department were shaky and uneven at best, a pattern that later cohorts of feminist graduate students loudly protested. In contrast, the senior faculty seemed to go out of their way to support several problematic junior male colleagues, showing a degree of tolerance and protection that would be hard to imagine in most other elite departments. Although unconventional in their masculinities, the Brandeis faculty were clearly a brotherhood, generous to women as students but uneasy about admitting women to equal positions of collegiality.[26]

## Learning from One Another

The intellectual milieu of Brandeis, which combined critical perspectives, theories of oppression, and an emphasis on personal experience and everyday life, was especially generative for feminist ideas. Our intellectual community remained distant and critical of the central theoretical fare of other U.S. sociology graduate programs—structural functionalism—which cast gender as role and stripped it of critical significance and systematic attention to inequality. Because we were trained in field research and not in survey methods, we were spared the snapping up of gender as a binary variable, another way in which feminist insights have been coopted in sociology.[27] The tools we acquired from Marxism, psychoanalysis, critical theory, the sociology of knowledge, and phenomenology turned out to be extraordinarily useful in theorizing women's oppression and the dynamics of gender. These were all, of course, "masters' tools" and thus, in Audre Lorde's compelling imagery, not fully suited for dismantling "the master's house" of androcentric knowledge.[28] But the theoretical perspectives we learned at Brandeis turned out to be well suited for feminist inquiry. The department had many women students, and the emergence of a feminist political milieu nurtured our personal, political, and intellectual bonds. Some of the faculty supported our engagement with issues of gender. Above all, the department's climate left us space to follow topics and interests of our own choosing.

My most vivid experience of this mix of support, useful tools, and, above all, learning from other women in a movement-inspired context began in fall 1971. In a reading course with Slater focused on the family, Marcia Millman, Nancy Chodorow, Nancy Jay, Janet Mendelsohn, and Ann Popkin discovered a notable gap in the literature. Much had been written about father-son, father-daughter, and, especially (Slater's focus), mother-son relationships, but there was almost nothing about mothers and daughters. The members of the reading group set out to explore that intriguing gap by forming a mother-daughter group of Brandeis women graduate students and other friends in Cambridge. The group met weekly or biweekly, with fluctuating membership, for the next three years. We used a mode of consciousness-raising, which we had learned through participation in the women's liberation movement, to talk about our experiences as daughters and also (a few) as mothers. The mother-daughter pairs were particularly welcome and on the spot; visiting mothers and sisters enriched our meetings and made us feel connected with one another's female family members.

The Mother-Daughter Group turned out to be a magical experience, linking the personal and the intellectual in an abundance of delicious moments. We talked, for example, about times when our mothers seemed to think they owned our (daughter) bodies, telling us how to wear our hair or going emotionally haywire over our acne or weight. Shifting outlooks, the mothers among us explored conflicted feelings about their own daughters' bodies. We discovered that the consciousness of the mother and of the daughter are totally separate, though intertwined, gestalts, even in the same woman, and that psychological boundaries between mothers and daughters are often problematic. We also talked about family secrets and why we kept them even after the death of everyone who might be shamed by the telling. In discussions that thundered with laughter and emotion, we shared our own family secrets and then explored the centrality of secret-keeping to family structure. We also discussed family alliances; dyads and triads; guilt, shame, and anger in mother-daughter relationships; and our fantasies of maternal caretaking when we had been sick or facing abortions. We discussed menstrual knowledge and its transmission, and we read and analyzed fairy tales. The Mother-Daughter Group, which drew upon consciousness-raising, psychodynamic understanding, and phenomenologial bracketing, inspired myriad creative efforts, including Nancy Chodorow's dissertation and my own interest in teaching and writing about families and later about the sociology of childhood. Harriet Rosenstein took off from our vivid discussions to write a short story about her family's secrets, which was published in *Ms. Magazine*, and Ann Popkin and Janet Mendelsohn created films about their grandmothers.

## From Then to Now

The Brandeis department became known as a place where students could pursue feminist interests, and during the 1970s a steady stream of women, some of them experienced political activists, went through the program and came to define themselves as feminist sociologists. I feel fortunate to have been at Brandeis when there was a catalyzing mix of structure (provided by the required courses in theory and fieldwork and by the presence of "straighter" faculty such as Hughes, Wolff, and Coser; Egon Bittner also gave this sort of stability to subsequent cohorts) and radical questioning of sociology and, indeed, of academics itself. In 1971 Slater, whose critique of mainstream U.S. culture, *Pursuit of Loneliness,* was reaching a wide audience, announced that he was going to drop out of academics and turn to doing therapy and writing of poetry and plays.[29] He was a major (transference) figure in the department, and his decision caused a real stir. Soon after, Larry Rosenberg also left the university to join a Buddhist community. Other faculty became immersed in antiwar politics, meditation, co-counseling, encounter groups, the Rajneesh community, and building of countercultural institutions. In 1969 Lewis Coser left for the State University of New York at Stony Brook, where Rose Coser also secured a tenured faculty position, and Everett Hughes took a second retirement and moved to Boston College in 1968, although he continued to teach part-time at Brandeis. Soon after, the department abolished required courses and preliminary exams, leaving graduate students, in effect, to put together their own versions of sociology. The department admitted many older students, some with advanced degrees in other fields and thus more able to make it through the loosely structured program. In a statement for the twenty-fifth reunion volume, Doug Harper (Ph.D., 1975) captured those odd, fragmented, and largely laissez-faire departmental times: "I recall delivering a seminar paper on the precapitalist forms of economic organization while in the next room the class was singing, 'We get by with a little help from our friends.'" By the early 1970s, the diverse quests of the Brandeis faculty had unraveled a sense of shared enterprise, and later cohorts of students complained about feeling anomic and being left too much on their own.

I feel lucky to have studied at Brandeis when the curriculum was more structured but critique was well under way; I came out attached to but also ambivalent about the discipline of sociology. The word *discipline* itself suggests the weighing down, the imposition of conventions, which can constrain creativity. In contrast, "Brandeis sociology" questioned mainstream conventions and valued interesting ideas, whatever their source; this freedom helped us raise and pursue feminist questions and catch the interdisciplinary winds of women's studies. But I have also come to value the coherence, continuity, and intellectual community that academic disciplines can provide.

Because I had come through a more structured program and had earlier training in the social sciences, I was better prepared than many Brandeis Ph.D.s to survive in mainstream contexts, a process that started in 1971 when I became an assistant professor in the Sociology Department at Michigan State University. My partner, Peter Lyman, is a political scientist. We searched for jobs together and felt fortunate to land in the same place. My marginality in the MSU department became clear soon after I arrived when a tenured colleague whom I'd barely met came into my office and announced, "It's all right for you to educate undergraduates, but you have no business training graduate students because you're not a scientist." I was speechless, and tears of hurt and anger sprang to my eyes. Later I wished I had told him, "Okay, you can have science; I approach sociology like an artist."

Gradually, like locating members of my ethnic group, I found a network of radical colleagues in and outside of the Sociology Department. Peter and I lived together for several years without marrying, which raised concern among some of our colleagues. Peter's longish hair was a focus of whispering in his department, my teaching in sandals led to comments in mine, and I relished the thought that in spite of my faculty status, I was still a bit of a rebel. I found other feminists around the campus, and together, with considerable opposition from an overseeing administrator, we began to develop an undergraduate concentration in women's studies.

During those early years, when I had to struggle for permission to create an undergraduate course in "sex roles," I turned to my Brandeis friends for support. Many of them were also in their first jobs and experiencing the "reality shock" (as Hughes called such gaps between schooling for work and the work itself) of the wider world of sociology. We packaged up syllabi and entire sets of lecture notes on the sociology of women, family, and feminist theory and shipped them across the country. These materials gave a sense of tangible reality to our critical perspectives; confronted with large lecture classes, we had materials to revise and draw from and to give us courage. Object relations theorists would say that we had the benign internal presence of the other at the lectern; we were not alone. I also discovered that building ties to other qualitative and feminist sociologists around the country gave me local leverage and lessened the risks of marginality.

Several men who were at Brandeis during the late 1960s and early 1970s have wistfully told me that after embracing critical approaches to sociology in graduate school, they ended up feeling isolated. There was nothing like the women's liberation movement to give them an ongoing sense of collectivity; there were no immediate political goals, such as challenging discrimination and articulating missing experiences, to propel them into academic careers.

The creation of feminist sociology propelled some of us much further into the discipline than we had ever anticipated. Working individually and collectively, we took up gender like a thick ball of yarn that unraveled into continuous insights and topics waiting to be knit. Over the years I moved from my dissertation interest in (as we would now phrase it) the gender dynamics of social movements, to research on women's and men's differing uses of language and speech, and then to more theoretical writing about feminism and families.[30] My interest in women, gender, and families and shifts in my own experiences as I became a mother eventually led me to ethnographic research with and conceptual rethinking of children and childhoods.[31] In addition to providing topics, the convergence of feminism and sociology gave me networks of collegiality and support and employment and career opportunities that my mother's generation had been denied.

Looking back over the three decades that have passed since I first entered the Brandeis graduate program, I am amazed at and grateful for the accomplishments of feminist sociologists. I also wonder if we have been coopted, if our efforts have mostly gone into constructing another segment of a discipline and careers we can congenially inhabit rather than transforming knowledge and making social change. The inner conversations continue between my activist self, who (in Hughes's memorable phrasing) testifies in and out of season, and the detached observer, who weighs in with ironic perspective.

## Notes

I wish to thank Nancy Chodorow, who began as coauthor but faded to supportive ghost-helper, for her substantial contributions to this essay. Alison Thorne, Avril Thorne, Judith Stacey, Marcia Millman, Kurt Wolff, Elizabeth Higginbotham, Shulamit Reinharz, Gaye Tuchman, Tony Bales, Marilyn Aronoff, Judith Adler, Doug Harper, and Nancy Stoller generously shared memories and insights. I have also drawn on statements by former students about "what the Brandeis experience meant to me" in the reunion volume "Brandeis University Sociology Department 25th Anniversary of the Graduate Program, April 11–12, 1987." This essay evolved from a talk I gave at that reunion.

1. This early, collective movement toward researching women's lives and experiences can be traced through Brandeis dissertations written between about 1969 and 1976 and then turned into books: Lynda Lytle Holmstrom, Ph.D., 1970, *The Two-Career Family* (Cambridge, Mass.: Schenckman, 1972); Nancy Stoller Shaw, Ph.D. 1972, *Forced Labor: Childbirth in America* (New York: Pergamon Press, 1974); Fatima Mernissi, Ph.D., 1974, *Beyond the Veil: Male and Female Dynamics in Modern Muslim Society* (Cambridge, Mass.: Schenckman, 1975); Nancy Chodorow, Ph.D., 1975, *The Reproduction of Mothering* (Berkeley and Los Angeles: University of California Press, 1978).

Chodorow's book won the American Sociological Association Jessie Bernard Award, as did three other books by Brandeis Ph.D.s: Judith Stacey, *Patriarchy and the Socialist Revolution in China* (Berkeley and Los Angeles: University of California Press, 1983); Judith Rollins, *Between Women: Domestics and Their Employers* (Philadelphia: Temple University Press, 1985); and Patricia Hill Collins, *Black Feminist Thought: Knowledge, Consciousness, and the Politics of Empowerment* (Boston: Unwin Hyman, 1989). Stacey received her Ph.D. in 1979, Rollins in 1983, and Hill Collins in 1984.

Marcia Millman, Ph.D., 1972, and Rosabeth Moss Kanter (who was hired in 1967 and was the sole woman faculty member in the Brandeis department until 1972) edited *Another Voice: Feminist Perspectives on Social Life and Social Science* (Garden City, N.Y.: Anchor Books, 1975), the first anthology focused on the exclusion and distortion of women's experiences in sociological knowledge. Sociologists who received Brandeis Ph.D.s between the late 1960s and the mid-1970s and who later published feminist books include Gaye Tuchman, Ph.D., 1969, *Edging Women out: Victorian Novelists, Publishers, and Social Change* (New Haven, Conn.: Yale University Press, 1989); Ruth Harriet Jacobs, Ph.D., 1969, *Life After Youth: Female, Forty, and What Next?* (Boston: Beacon Press, 1979); Barrie Thorne, Ph.D., 1971, *Gender Play: Girls and Boys in School* (New Brunswick, N.J.; Rutgers University Press, 1993); Marcia Millman, Ph.D., 1972, *Such a Pretty Face: Being Fat in America* (New York: Norton, 1980); Rachel Kahn-Hut, Ph.D., 1974, et al., eds., *Women and Work* (New York: Oxford University Press, 1982); Janet Mancini Billson, Ph.D., 1976, *Keepers of the Culture: The Power of Tradition in Women's Lives* (New York: Free Press, 1995); Kelly Weisberg, Ph.D., 1976, ed., *Women and the Law: The Social-historical Perspective* (Cambridge, Mass.: Schenckman, 1982); Mamie Garvin Fields, with (her granddaughter) Karen Fields, Ph.D., 1977, *Lemon Swamp and Other Places: A Carolina Memoir* (New York: Free Press, 1983); Shulamit Reinharz, Ph.D., 1977, *Feminist Methods in Social Research* (New York: Oxford University Press, 1992); Louise Levesque-Lopman, Ph.D., 1977, *Claiming Reality: Phenomenology and Women's Experience* (Totowa, N.J.; Rowman and Littlefield, 1988); Wini Breines, Ph.D., 1979, *Young, White, and Miserable: Growing up Female in the 1950s* (Boston: Beacon Press, 1992); Margery W. Davies, Ph.D., 1979, *Women's Place Is at the Typewriter* (Philadelphia: Temple University Press, 1982); Nancy Jay, Ph.D., 1981, *Throughout Your Generations Forever: Sacrifice, Religion, and Paternity* (Chicago: University of Chicago Press, 1992); and Lise Vogel, Ph.D., 1981, *Marxism and the Oppression of Women: Toward a Unitary Theory* (New Brunswick, N.J.; Rutgers University Press, 1983).

Sociologists trained at Brandeis have long been active in promoting feminist ideas within sociology. For example, Rachel Kahn-Hut and I have chaired the ASA Section on Sex and Gender, and Elizabeth Higginbotham, Ph.D., 1980, helped found the Memphis Center for Research on Women; in 1993 she and two colleagues (Bonnie Thornton Dill and Lynn Weber) won the Jessie Bernard Award for promoting work on race, social class, gender, and women in the South.

2. In the 1940s my mother began drafting a book manuscript on the importance of women sustaining their own values rather than conforming to expectations about neat housekeeping. Over the last decade she has rewritten the manuscript as a personal, family, and community memoir: Alison Comish Thorne, "Leave the Dishes in the Sink: Memoirs of a Liberal in Conservative Utah" (unpublished ms).

3. In 1980 the L.D.S. Church sought me out for excommunication. Since (along with my parents and siblings) I'd been a lapsed, or "jack," Mormon for many years, I was surprised at the heavy emotions that process unleashed: anger at the church elders and their nerve in actually holding an excommunication trial, which I refused to attend, and, after the anger settled, a feeling of soaring freedom. Increasingly annoyed by the church's shift to the fundamentalist right and especially by its subordinating treatment of women, my mothers and siblings formally revoked their memberships in 1993. My father, Wynne Thorne, died of cancer in 1979; he had long been estranged from the church.

4. In construction projects around the world, the L.D.S. "authorities," as the top (male) leaders are called, continue to use bland 1950s church architecture, a physical sign of the conformity and hierarchy basic to Mormon culture.

5. Information compiled from "Brandeis University Sociology Department 25th Anniversary of the Graduate Program." A loosely comparative set of statistics from the Department of Sociology at the University of California, Berkeley: from 1952 to 1972, one-third of the graduate students were women; of these, only one-quarter received doctorates, compared with one-third of the men. See Kathryn P. Meadow Orlans and Ruth A. Wallace, Introduction to Kathryn P. Meadow Orlans and Ruth A. Wallace, eds., *Gender and the Academic Experience: Berkeley Women Sociologists* (Lincoln: University of Nebraska Press, 1994), p. 2.

6. This observation and information come from personal conversations with Nancy Chodorow, who also supplied additional examples. When Margaret Lawrence, an early woman psychoanalyst and an African American, tried to get an internship in 1940, she ended up at Harlem Hospital, mostly with Jews, Italians, and a few other African Americans; all had been passed over by the more white, Protestant, mainstream New York hospitals. See Sara Lawrence Lightfoot, *Balm in Gilead: Journey of a Healer* (Reading, Mass.: Addison-Wesley, 1988). Another example, which suggests that exclusion by the top stratum may be a key dynamic, comes from Meyer Fortes, who observed, in a personal conversation with Nancy Chodorow, that in the late 1930s British anthropology attracted (and allowed in) Jews, women, and white people from the colonies; British gentlemen with anthropological interests went into the colonial service, which excluded people from these other backgrounds.

7. For the larger story, see Lewis A. Coser, *Refugee Scholars in America: Their Impact and Their Experiences* (New Haven, Conn.: Yale University Press, 1984).

Marcuse left Brandeis for the University of California, San Diego, just before I arrived at Brandeis, but his influence lingered. Kurt Wolff often invited graduate students to confer about their work at his home. After coffee and cake with his wife, Carla Wolff (also a German Jewish refugee and a great friend to many of us), Kurt would lead the way up the stairs to his book-lined study, where he invited the student to sit in an old and comfortable chair that, according to student rumors, once belonged to Marcuse. We students privately called it "the Marcuse chair," fancying that his vibrations infused the conversations that circled around it.

After reading a draft of this paper, Kurt Wolff wrote me that he has no recollection of such a chair. This points to the ambiguous and divergent nature of memories (it was Kurt's study, and I trust his, rather than my, memory of the lineage of its furnishings) and of gossip turned into shared mythology. Our belief that Marcuse had once owned the chair had real effects in the world.

8. C. Wright Mills, *The Sociological Imagination* (New York: Oxford University Press, 1959).

9. Shulamit Reinharz has traced the history of the Brandeis graduate program in "The Chicago School of Sociology and the Founding of the Graduate Program in Sociology at Brandeis University: A Case Study of Cultural Diffusion," in Gary Alan Fine, ed., *A Second Chicago School? The Development of Midcentury Sociology at the University of Chicago* (Chicago: University of Chicago Press, 1995), pp. 273–331. Three other feminist sociologists have written about their experiences in the Brandeis graduate program, in Ann Goetting and Sarah Fenstermaker, eds., *Individual Voices, Collective Visions: Fifty Years of Women in Sociology* (Philadelphia: Temple University Press, 1995): Lynda Lytle Holmstrom, "Working the Third Shift," pp. 251–270; Shulamit Reinharz, "Marginality, Motherhood, and Method: Paths to a Social Science Career and Community," pp. 285–302; and Gaye Tuchman, "Kaddish and Renewal," pp. 303–318.

10. Otto Fenichel, *The Psychoanalytic Theory of Neurosis* (New York: Norton, 1945).

11. Brandeis graduates, especially Nancy Chodorow (*The Reproduction of Mothering*), Patricia Hill Collins (*Black Feminist Thought*), and Shulamit Reinharz (*Feminist Methods in Social Research*), have made significant contributions to this branch of feminist theory.

12. Hughes referred to my struggles with Mormonism in "Teaching as Fieldwork" (1969): "One of my favorite graduate students is of Mormon family; she confesses to liking the collective warmth of sitting shoulder to shoulder in a great congregation of people all lifting up their voices in lusty song, as Mormons and Methodists do. She and I have this feeling in common, although neither of us subjects himself to the pressure for further participation that would come if we indulged the collective pleasure often. She has found other outlets for her love of collective activity and for the social idealism that is evidently part of her heritage. But hers is not the reaction of the alienated; it is emancipation without alienation. That is something teacher and students can share. It makes a base for mutual learning and teaching" Reprinted in Everett C. Hughes, *The Sociological Eye: Selected Papers* (New Brunswick, N.J.: Transaction Books, 1984), p. 573. Addendum from the student: I felt alienation, as well as emancipation.

13. In an interview quoted in Reinharz, "The Chicago School of Sociology," pp. 302–303, Paul Campanis, Ph.D., 1966, discusses the juxtaposition between the Chicago fieldwork tradition and European phenomenology and critical theories: "The Europeans in the department, especially Kurt Wolff and Lew Coser, grounded the philosophically shallow Chicago tradition in European philosophy. In particular, they sharpened its fuzzy pragmatism with more rigorous European phenomenology; on the other hand, the fieldworking Chicago tradition expanded the range of the armchair European phenomenologists to the actual perspectives of those of different social locations....The Chicago sociological tradition had always been more appreciative than critical, more wide-eyed with wonder that institutions could function at all than cynically squinting at what was wrong with their functioning."

14. From a personal conversation, May 1994.

15. Isaiah Berlin, *The Hedgehog and the Fox* (New York: Mentor Books, 1937). Lewis Coser also makes this point in his editor's introduction to *Everett C. Hughes on Work, Race, and the Sociological Imagination* (Chicago: University of Chicago Press, 1994), p. 14.

16. Everett C. Hughes, "The Humble and the Proud," in *The Sociological Eye*, pp. 417–430

17. Dorothy E. Smith, *The Everyday World as Problematic: A Feminist Sociology* (Boston: Northeastern University Press, 1987).

18. See Barrie Thorne, "Political Activist as Participant Observer: Conflicts of Commitment in the Draft Resistance Movement of the 1960's," *Symbolic Interaction* 2 (1979): 73–88.

19. I wrote a dissertation chapter on the contradictory experiences of women activists in the draft resistance movement as one source of the women's liberation movement as it emerged from the New Left. This became my first solo publication: Barrie Thorne, "Women in the Draft Resistance Movement: A Case Study of Sex Roles and Social Movements," *Sex Roles* 1 (1975): 179–195.

20. Priscilla Long, another member of that collective, has written an essay about those years: "Myself/Ourselves: Remembering the Women's Movement," to be published in an anthology of feminist memoirs edited by Ann Snitow and Rachel Blau dePlessis.

21. For a brief history of Bread and Roses, based on a 1978 Brandeis sociology Ph.D. dissertation, see Ann Popkin, "The Personal Is Political: The Women's Liberation Movement," in Dick Cluster, ed., *They Should Have Served That Cup of Coffee* (Boston: South End Press, 1979), pp. 181–222. The Boston Women's Health Book Collective, which continued this project after Bread and Roses dissolved, regularly updates *Our Bodies: Ourselves;* Simon and Schuster published the latest edition in 1996. For a discussion of *Our Bodies, Ourselves* as one of the "ten most influential books of the last 25 years," see Linda Gordon and Barrie Thorne, "Women's Bodies and Feminist Subversions," *Contemporary Sociology* 25 (1996): 322–325. Irving Zola, who was on the Brandeis faculty and a strong supporter of feminism for many years, came to be closely connected with the Health Book Collective and its work.

22. Philip Slater, *The Glory of Hera: Greek Mythology and the Greek Family* (Boston: Beacon Press, 1968).

23. Reprinted in Hughes, *The Sociological Eye*, pp. 141–150.

24. In June 1976 when I was living in Michigan, Everett wrote me from Cambridge: "Someone should study the attitudes of men to the women's movement. In the academic world, with things not looking very bright, there may be a half hidden anti-woman feeling....I predict also a campaign in favor of people whose publications are very technical and not related to any social cause. The more trivial the points made, the more scientific they will be classed. Some journal will be the prime scientific, least meaningful one; get into it to be promoted."

25. Helen Hughes and Rose Coser became active feminists and in 1973 jointly wrote the first American Sociological Association report on the status of women in sociology. Helen published two perceptive essays about her career: Helen MacGill Hughes, "Maid of All Work or Department Sister-in-law? The Faculty Wife Employed on Campus," *American Journal of Sociology* 78 (1973): 5–10; Helen MacGill Hughes, "WASP/Woman/Sociologist," *Society* 14 (1977): 69-80.

26. Kathleen Barry, who was on the Brandeis faculty in the 1980s, published a satire of her experiences, criticizing men sociologists who "prided themselves on having trained a generation of graduate students to be feminists" but who were "suspicious of anything calling itself feminist theory that is not marxist and/or freudian or critical or particularly socialist-feminist (feminist theory that does not come from the

feminism they reproduced)." See Kathleen L. Barry, "Tootsie Syndrome, or 'We Have Met the Enemy and They Are Us,'" *Women's Studies International Forum* 12 (1989) 387.

27. See Judith Stacey and Barrie Thorne, "The Missing Feminist Revolution in Sociology," *Social Problems* 32 (1985): 301–316; and R. W. Connell, *Gender and Power: Society, the Person, and Sexual Politics* (Stanford, Calif.: Stanford University Press, 1987).

28. Audre Lorde, "The Master's Tools Will Never Dismantle the Master's House," in *Sister Outsider* (New York: Crossing Press, 1984), pp. 110–113.

29. Philip Slater, *Pursuit of Loneliness* (Boston: Beacon Press, 1970).

30. Barrie Thorne and Nancy Henley, eds., *Language and Sex: Difference and Dominance* (Rowley, Mass.: Newbury House, 1975); Barrie Thorne, with Marilyn Yalom, eds., *Rethinking the Family: Some Feminist Questions* (New York: Longman, 1982).

31. Barrie Thorne, *Gender Play: Girls and Boys in School* (New Brunswick, N.J.: Rutgers University Press, 1993).

*Judith Stacey*

## Disloyal to the Disciplines:
## A Feminist Trajectory
## in the Borderlands

*I*t is more than a decade now since Barrie Thorne and I commenced a set of public discussions about the impact of feminism on sociology, which we summarized in an essay with the somewhat reproachful title "The Missing Feminist Revolution in Sociology."[1] The initial impetus for that project was my participation in a session at a National Women's Studies Association conference in 1982 that had the more politically specific, and, for its period, unremarkable title "Socialist-Feminist Perspectives on the Disciplines." Few feminist conferences or lecture series would be likely to adopt such a title today, nor would I be likely, if one did so, to be invited, or to agree, to assess sociology under such an aegis. I remain committed to the ideals of economic and gender justice and to those of political and cultural democracy that once undergirded my earlier socialist-feminist identity, but too much has happened in global geopolitics and in feminist theoretical developments to sustain my earlier comfort with the first political term or with the dual structure of such an identity.

Moreover, I can no longer imagine undertaking an essay that presumed that sociology, or any of the existing disciplines, was the appropriate terrain to excavate for a feminist revolution in knowledge. To anticipate discrete revolutions in discrete scholarly disciplines is to betray a decidedly unrevolutionary conception of the disciplinary constructions of knowledge. Had such a feminist "revolution" occurred in sociology, should it not have challenged the discipline's recognizable borders or "essence?"[2]

Shifts in feminist labeling fashions and in my own disciplinary self-conception index, I believe, a significant set of transformations within feminist political discourse, as well as in feminist relations to the disciplines. I discuss these transformations autobiographically by "reading" the trajec-

A version of this essay appeared in *Feminisms in the Academy,* ed. Domna C. Stanton and Abigail J. Stewart (Ann Arbor: University of Michigan Press, 1995). Reprinted by permission of the University of Michigan Press.

tory of my own work as a feminist sociologist as emblematic—perhaps some will think it symptomatic—of shifts that have taken place in theoretical and disciplinary fashions in women's studies and social theory more generally. To take this tack is to enact my current "disciplinary" location as an ambivalently postmodernist, reflexive ethnographer. Or, for those unsympathetic with what some have called "the postmodernist turn in anthropology,"[3] the fact that I take this tack may confirm the judgment of a hostile reviewer of my ethnography *Brave New Families,* who labeled its first-person narrative approach "self-indulgent."

Certainly my trajectory is unique, indeed in certain aspects, idiosyncratic, and I do not presume that the evolution of my own theoretical and substantive interests typifies that of feminist sociologists. The core of American sociology, if such a decentered discipline can be said to have a core, remains deeply positivist, while its diverse qualitative, interpretive, and theoretical schools have, in varying degrees, accommodated themselves to feminist inquiry without much evidence of conceptual turmoil. Thus, a great many, perhaps a statistical majority of feminist sociologists, continue to conduct valuable empirical research, often with significant policy implications, unaffected and unfazed by shifts in theoretical climates that I have found so compelling and unsettling.[4]

In fact, I believe that it is the idiosyncratic character of my feminist trajectory that might help to illuminate certain notable recent developments in feminist scholarship. My scholarship has always been centered not in sociology but on the disciplinary borderlands that have nurtured the intellectual audacity that feminists have needed to think our ways radically through the disciplines. But in this regard I have begun to find myself increasingly out of step. A great deal of feminist scholarship today seems more entrenched in and bound by academic disciplinary identities than it did when Barrie Thorne and I first recorded our reflections on feminist knowledge transformations.

The increased strength of disciplinarity observable in contemporary feminist scholarship can be read, of course, as a cheering index of our astonishing successes. In most humanities and social science disciplines today, feminist inquiry has achieved undisputable legitimacy—in some, a level of acceptability approaching normalcy—and the demographic trends seem irreversible. The Sex and Gender Section of the American Sociological Association, for example, has displaced the far-better-funded research subspecialty of Medical Sociology as the largest "subfield" represented in the organization. Sociology, like other social sciences and humanities disciplines, is a feminizing field.[5]

Yet I am worried, as well as cheered, by these achievements, for this success also breeds new intellectual and political dangers. Because so many feminists can now enjoy sympathetic collegiality and legitimacy within our disciplinary enclaves, there is less compelling impulse for extradisciplinary migrations. As it becomes increasingly possible for feminists to achieve (what was once unthinkable) a fully respectable and rewarded academic career within a conventional discipline, there is less incentive or demand for feminists to acquire counterdisciplinary language and research questions or to participate in the more transgressive forms of knowledge renovation that I still consider to be crucial. I worry that this may blunt the critical edge, as well as the public intelligibility, of our once-visionary project. Perhaps this anxiety signals my personal anomalous experience. For precisely during this period of feminization and of feminist incorporation in my official discipline, I have been experiencing my own work and identity as increasingly marginal to "actually existing sociology." Is it this traveler or her disciplinary itinerary that has provoked this anomaly?

Sketched schematically, my trajectory through my discipline travels from socialist-feminist historical sociology to feminist and "postsocialist" ethnographic sociology and interdisciplinary cultural studies. I have spent most of my research energies since my first year as a graduate sociology student at Brandeis University in 1973 studying family revolutions and always by transgressing disciplinary boundaries. The three books I have completed since then are preoccupied with a common set of substantive issues—gender, family, and rapid processes of broad-scale social change. They differ greatly, however, in their geopolitical settings, research methods, and textual products. The first, about peasant families and revolution in modern China, trafficked in historical sociology. The book that resulted was a theoretical analysis of secondary literature, organized chronologically and written in a conventional third-person narrative format.[6] My second book-length project focused on family change among white, working people living in postindustrial "Silicon Valley," California. After three years of commuter fieldwork, I wrote an ethnography in a first-person, reflexive mode that incorporated dialogic elements, organized the book somewhat novelistically, and dusted it with "post" words.[7] Unexpected political responses to that book induced me to write *In the Name of The Family: Rethinking Family Values in a Postmodern Age*,[8] which might be characterized as a contribution to political sociology, the sociology of knowledge, and cultural studies. Or it might better be described as my attempt to practice a form of "applied" feminist sociology by intervening more directly in the cultural wars being fought over "family values" in the United States. Indeed, I found the call to this form of intellectual activism so pressing that it led me to withdraw from a very different research project to which I had turned after completing *Brave New Families*—a collaborative study with feminist literary critic Judith Newton of male cultural critics.

As is evident, whatever coherence is discernible in my work lies in Left feminist political and theoretical domains rather than in specialized research topic, methodology, or epistemology. For better and worse, I work as a disciplinary dilettante. If the un-disciplined character of my academic affiliations is somewhat unusual, it has historic roots in the social movement that generated feminist scholarship. It seems crucial to note that when I entered the doctoral program in sociology at Brandeis University in 1973, I did so as a feminist who had already participated in establishing a women's studies program elsewhere.[9] Indeed, it was my "conversion" to feminism, my commitment to emergent women's studies, and my desire to study and build feminist theory that led me to abandon a doctoral degree in education that I had been pursuing and enter a social science discipline instead. Feminism was (and remains) my primary, and sociology a secondary, and, indeed, somewhat of an arbitrary, disciplinary affiliation. In fact, when in the early 1970s I looked for a disciplinary context in which to pursue my/our then-new interest in feminist theory, I applied for admission to doctoral programs in anthropology, as well as in sociology. As I look backward, it seems less surprising to me that I should have migrated from the historical to the anthropological borders of my nominal discipline than that it has taken me so long to do so.

My un-disciplined proclivities met few constraints in the Brandeis Sociology Department—a decidedly maverick program that foregrounded and enacted the decentered character of the discipline that was depicted in one of the first influential books I read about my new field—Alvin Gouldner's *The Coming Crisis in Western Sociology*.[10] Profoundly affected by the radical pedagogy and self-actualization ideals promoted by political and countercultural movements during the 1960s, the Brandeis faculty had eliminated a shared curriculum or set of degree requirements. Even more unusual for an American sociology department was its pervasive hostility to positivism. Interpretive sociology and theory were privileged at Brandeis, and the privileged body of theory for my cohort of New Left veterans was Marxism and its Frankfurt School elaborations. My sister graduate students and I quickly identified as socialist-feminists and steeped ourselves in the emergent Marxist-feminist "discourse," a term we had not yet heard.

We were trailblazing here. Although there were a couple of feminists on the Brandeis faculty, they were no more advanced in this then-nascent endeavor than we were. Consequently, my principal graduate school experience involved a form of collective self-education. With and without faculty participation, feminist graduate students formed study groups in which we made up a decidedly transdisciplinary approach to feminist sociology as we went along. I also benefited from an exhilarating extracurricular graduate education. By participating in one of the Northeast coast Marxist-feminist groups that emerged in the early 1970s, by teaching (while learning) "Marxism for Women" at a local grassroots women's school, and later, and most significantly, by serving for more than a decade on the editorial collective of the interdisciplinary journal *Feminist Studies,* I "interned" in feminist theory and developed my undisciplined approach to feminist sociology. The startling overrepresentation of Brandeis degree-holders among feminist sociologists who have published widely recognized work suggests the creative potential of a highly permissive approach to disciplinary training.[11]

This was the intellectual milieu that enabled the audacity of selecting for my dissertation topic a subject about which I had received no formal schooling—patriarchy and socialist revolution in China. Of course, the political milieu that fostered that decision was equally heady and is hard to recapture. Highly romanticized images of the Cultural Revolution in China and wildly inflated (or grossly understated) reports that "Women hold up half the sky" were being deposited on overly receptive shores of the anti–Vietnam War era by waves swelling in the wake of President Richard Nixon's historic thaw with China; these inspired enormous curiosity and enthusiasm among American socialist-feminists. Although twenty-five years had passed since the Chinese revolution, the Chinese Communists did not seem to have followed the disappointing precedent set by the Russian Bolsheviks in their earlier postrevolutionary backlash against family and gender policy in the Soviet Union.[12] I was eager to explore the sources and effects of the seemingly more resilient Maoist family revolution.

"Dual-systems" theory, the dominant socialist-feminist framework of the period, which presumed that gender and social class represent two distinct and interrelated systems of domination, influenced my original conceptualization of my study. Because dual-systems theory asserted the relative autonomy and equal significance of gender, it seemed then to be the most promising strategy for liberating feminism from the subordinate position in its "unhappy marriage" to Marxism.[13] Examining the history of the Chinese revolution through the lens of gender and family dynamics, my analysis pushed feminist claims for the fundamental significance and the relative autonomy of gender about as far as they could go. So far, in fact, that they upturned the dual-systems premise with which I had begun my research. The prerevolutionary agrarian crisis, I argued, was also inseparably a patriarchal peasant family crisis, and the resolution of that crisis through policies that built patriarchal socialism was a central vehicle for the victory of the Chinese Communists. Thus, I concluded, gender and class dynamics were inextricably intertwined in the Chinese revolution, and a fully feminist historical materialism, rather than a dual-systems model, was needed to comprehend this.

By the time I completed my study of the Chinese family revolution, I was dissatisfied not only with dual-systems theory but also with the abstract and secondary character of this research and book and their remoteness from the agency of women to which I was committed theoretically. This fed my determination that my next project would involve the sort of primary, "hands-on," qualitative research that I, like many feminists by the early 1980s, had come to presume was the privileged method for feminist research.[14] Coinciding with my newly expanded personal family commitments—the birth of my son in 1981—this conviction conspired to place geographic restrictions on my possible research fields. The demands and delights of delayed mothering, also characteristic of my generation of feminists, confined my field research options to locations accessible to my San Francisco Bay Area residence. In fact, it seems plausible to me that the emergence of what anthropologists George Marcus and Michael Fischer approvingly call "repatriated anthropology" in the United States may have been propelled by changes in the gender and demographic composition of their discipline as much as by a principled response to the politically troubled conditions of postcolonial ethnography.[15] The influx into anthropology of women whose family commitments were less portable or expendable than those typical of their male counterparts would in itself have fostered interest in formulating geographically accessible ethnographic questions.[16] Certainly, my own ethnographic impulses were about to be "disciplined" in this manner.

It was during this personal period of research transition that Barrie Thorne and I wrote "The Missing Feminist Revolution in Sociology," where, in a passing comment, we lamented the dearth of feminist sociologists who had chosen to work within the discipline's own rich, ethnographic tradition of community studies. This aside unwittingly foreshadowed the project I was soon to engage—my accidental ethnography of the families of white working people in California's Silicon Valley. Once again I began with a vintage socialist-feminist subject—working-class gender relationships under postindustrial conditions. Again, too, I began with a historical sociological orientation. In fact, in the project's initial stages I was collaborating with a historian. Our plan was to integrate a historical overview of occupational and demographic shifts in the region and the nation with my untrained conception of a conventional sociological qualitative research design involving numerous semistructured interviews. The political impetus for this research, however, contrasted sharply with the optimistic and innocent motivations for my China study. It was my mounting concern with the antifeminist "pro-family" backlash movement in the United States that had been credited by many for providing the grassroots kindling for the 1980s Reagan revolution.

Given my geographic constraints, it is fortuitous that I lived within commuter reach of an ideal research site for my project. Silicon Valley was not only a vanguard region of postindustrialization but also one where the demographic indices of family change were stark and where feminist ideology once had been articulate and politically consequential. Although I selected this research site for its vanguard features, I chose to study a population that I erroneously presumed to manifest the opposite tendencies. Like most white middle-class feminists, I regarded white and Latino working-class people as the most "traditional" in their family convictions and behaviors and thus the primary appreciative audience for the remarkably successful "pro-family" performance of the quite untraditional (and unsuccessful) Reagan family.

My formal research design, to interview a large sample of Anglo and Latino people working in and around the electronics industry, unraveled rapidly. As my book describes, two interviews that I conducted immediately after Reagan's landslide reelection in November 1984 profoundly challenged my own class and gender prejudices and provoked my surrender to the lures of an open-ended ethnographic quest. First, "Pam," a woman I had known for four months and thought to be a feminist, revealed to me her recent conversion to evangelical Christianity and her participation in Christian marriage counseling. One week later, "Dotty," a survivor of an often abusive, thirty-year-long marriage, surprised me with her feminist convictions. Abandoning my research plans, I spent the next three years conducting intermittent fieldwork among these women and their kin.

This accidental but, I later came to believe, overdetermined turn to ethnographic methods shifted my disciplinary cross-dressing impulses to anthropology (the discipline that Barrie Thorne and I had earlier rated comparatively high in our feminist transformation assessments), just when that discipline was turning reflexive about the power/knowledge nexus of field research and textuality.[17] This was also a period when postcolonial consciousness, in addition to demographic changes, had encouraged increasing numbers of anthropologists to cross-dress as sociologists studying "others" at home.[18] Here, however, I enjoyed an advantage as a sociologist. Most practitioners of "repatriated anthropology" in the United States were still struggling for full legitimacy in their discipline, in part, because foreign fieldwork has long been one of that discipline's best-equipped border guards patrolling the research terrain it shares with sociology.

Doing urban anthropology (or a postcommunity study) as a Jewish, secular feminist among born-again Christians and hard-living, crisis-riddled people more than sated my craving for engaged research. It also propelled me spontaneously to struggle with numerous ethical, political, and textual questions about representation and to engage with some postmodern feminist debates that, by the late 1980s, were beginning to migrate from literary criticism and the humanities into anthropology, and to a lesser extent into history, but not yet noticeably into sociology. I lost my feminist ethnographic innocence in the field, as I explain in an essay written in the midst of this upheaval, "Can There Be a Feminist Ethnography?"[19] Only a "partially" feminist one is possible, I concluded, intending both senses of the term and placing myself thereby in the camp of those who reject as utopian the claim that there is such a thing as a specifically feminist research methodology or even the view that any one method is specifically suitable for feminist research.

The partially feminist ethnography I wrote about Pam and Dotty (and me) bears the traces of these disciplinary and political transitions. I structured the book as two documentary novellas and wrote it, against resistance from my male editor, in a reflexive, first-person, and occasionally dialogic narrative style. The novellas, however, are sandwiched inside a more conventionally authoritative, third-person, interpretive sociological account of the history of family revolutions in the United States. Thus, in structure and style, this book enacts my ambivalent relationship to the postmodernist turn in feminist anthropology and exhibits an interdisciplinary feminist research and rhetorical stance.

The same tension besets the book's two central arguments. One is avowedly postmodernist, the other an empirically grounded revision of conventional sociological understandings of family and social transformations. I argued first that "the postmodern family" is a useful conceptual category for analyzing the transformation of gender and kinship that has accompanied and helped shape postindustrial society. Literary critics in a Humanities Institute seminar in which I participated while struggling for an interpretive vocabulary for my ethnography prodded me to develop a theoretical understanding of the elusive concept of "postmodern." Not surprisingly, therefore, I turned to humanists to explicate what I meant when I used the concept of "the postmodern family condition" to signal the collapse of a hegemonic family system. I found that I could readily apply art historian Clive Dilnot's answers to his own rhetorical question "What is the postmodern?" in an essay on postmodern culture to current family conditions in the United States. The postmodern, Dilnot maintains, "is first, an uncertainty, an insecurity, a doubt." Most of the "post-" words provoke uneasiness because they imply simultaneously "both the end, or at least the radical transformation of, a familiar pattern of activity or group of ideas" and the emergence of "new fields of cultural activity whose contours are still unclear and whose meanings and implications . . . cannot yet be fathomed."[20] The postmodern, moreover, is "characterized by the process of the linking up of areas and the crossing of the boundaries of what are conventionally considered to be disparate realms of practice."[21] Similarly, I argued that contemporary U.S. family arrangements are diverse, fluid, and unresolved and that *the* postmodern family is not a new model of family life equivalent to that of the modern family, not the next stage in an orderly progression of family history, but the stage in that history when the belief in a logical progression of stages breaks down. Donning unmistakable postmodernist drag, I even wrote: "Rupturing the teleology of modernization narratives that depict an evolutionary history of the family and incorporating both experimental and nostalgic elements, 'the' postmodern family lurches forward and backward into an uncertain future."[22]

The book's second major argument, however, remained a plainclothes historical-sociological one about family revolutions and vanguard classes. A major shift, I argued, has taken place in the class direction of U.S. family change. Most historians agree that the white middle classes were in the vanguard of the "modern" family revolution—that is, the transformation from a premodern, corporate, patriarchal family economy into a male breadwinner "companionate" family that transpired between the late eighteenth and the early twentieth centuries. Although the modern family pattern achieved cultural and statistical dominance, most working-class people attained the male family wage, their economic passport to that pattern, very late, if at all. I interpreted this to suggest that by the time, in the 1960s, that white working-class people got there, another family revolution was already well under way. Once again middle-class white families appeared to be in the vanguard; frustrated middle-class homemakers and their more militant daughters subjected modern domesticity to a sustained critique, at times with little sensitivity to the effects that our antimodern family ideology might have on women for whom full-time domesticity had rarely been feasible.

Thus, feminist family reform came to be regarded widely as a white middle-class agenda and white working-class families its most resistant adversaries. These, after all, had been the presumptions that led me to focus my study of postindustrial family change on white working-class people in the first place.

But this time appearances were deceptive. Field research convinced me that white middle-class families have been less the innovators than the propagandists and principal beneficiaries of contemporary family change. Instead, I argued that postindustrial conditions have reversed the trickle-down trajectory of family change once predicted by modernization theorists. By studying a family revolution ethnographically, I upturned many of my preconceptions about gender, class, and even born-again Christianity more profoundly than would have been possible using only the more distant research methods of historical sociology. I discovered on the ground, for example, that evangelical Christians are not monolithically antifeminist, nor are their family relationships uniformly "traditional" or patriarchal. And I observed firsthand some of the ways in which many evangelical women and even antifeminist women have been reinventing family forms as creatively as have many feminists. Feminists have received far too much credit and blame for instigating postmodern contests over the meaning of "the family," perhaps because we have done so much to challenge the "essentialist" connotations of the term.

Ethnographic research also brought "home" to me the grounds for pervasive ambivalence about postmodern family and social crises. Observing the everyday traumas and tragedies caused by the irrationality and injustice of contemporary occupational and social conditions reinforced my feminist and still democratic socialist beliefs that equitable, humane, and democratic gender and family policies could go a long way to alleviate the "surplus" family oppression that most women and many men suffer. But I no longer fantasize (as I did when I concluded my book on China with the claim that it had achieved a family revolution, but not a feminist family revolution) that even a feminist family revolution could put an end to family distress. There are human costs to the fruition of a fully voluntary sexual and kinship system that no social policy can fully eradicate. No nostalgic efforts to restore the "traditional" modern family system, however, can offer a more effective, let alone a democratic, resolution to family upheaval. For better and worse, the postmodern family revolution is here to stay.

The last chapter of *Brave New Families* ends on that note, indeed with that sentence. It acknowledges just cause for widespread ambivalence about postmodern family and social conditions but offers no parallel reflections on my own ambivalence about my current relationship to feminist sociology and postmodernist theories. The book itself does not end there, however. Displaying, perhaps allaying, some of my unresolved ethical-textual-political anxieties, I chose to end the book instead with an epilogue in which Pamela appears to have the provocative last word on my reading of her life: "You could never capture me." This somewhat disingenuous democratic gesture, which masks my asymmetrical control over the dialogic and textual conditions of its production, also signals the straddle position I came to occupy within and among contemporary debates about feminism and ethnography.

Even though my ethnographic rhetorical strategies in *Brave New Families* were somewhat reflexive, dialogic, and decentered, they produced a book that remained incurably humanist in the same sense that feminism and socialism have been humanist projects, committed to the emancipation of subjects who are comfortable naming themselves in gender and class terms. My humanist feminism sympathizes with the critique made by Francis Mascia-Lees, Colleen Cohen, and Patricia Sharpe of the premature forfeit of a female subject and of the frequent excesses of textual experimentation for its own sake sometimes found in "the postmodernist turn in anthropology."[23] Nonetheless, I am not willing to polarize feminism and postmodernism in this way, for I believe that feminism has been one of the enabling conditions for, as well as a generative force in, the development of theoretical developments often designated loosely as "postmodern." Gender crises embedded in the kinds of family revolutions I have studied through both historical sociology and ethnography have been among the important sources of the crisis of representation, the critiques of unified subjectivity, and the preoccupation with questions of difference, identity, culture, and authority that galvanize postmodern theories.

With this formulation of the relationship between feminism and postmodernist forms of knowledge in mind, I turned from the study of family revolutions to a project designed to explore the relationships between feminism and postmodernist cultural criticism by men. Migrating even further "afield" from most sociological projects, and adopting the surprising new feminist fashion here of studying men, I began collaborating with feminist literary critic Judith Newton on a project that combined ethnographic and literary critical approaches to contemporary fashions in cultural critique. Both my choice of collaborator and the linguistic shift evident in our defining this project as *cultural*, rather than *social*, criticism reflect and reinforce recent shifts in the primary locus of feminist and other radical theories. The historic collapse of "actually existing socialist societies" deepened a crisis in Marxist social thought. At the same time, and perhaps as a result, a right-wing intellectual backlash in the United States has directed much of its energies to an assault on feminist and multicultural challenges to the classic Western canon. Perhaps this explains why the gravitational center of critical theory seems to have swung from the social sciences to literary criticism and the humanities.[24] I worried about and wanted to understand this tendency even as I found myself participating in it. Thus, beginning with "the new historicism" in literary studies and with what some have termed "the new ethnography" in anthropology, Judith Newton and I began to study and rewrite the stories of the genesis of these discourses in ways that write feminisms into the narrative of these postmodern "turns," even if primarily as a displaced "other."[25]

As we navigated a route through the turbulent waters of postmodern feminist debates on men "in" or "and" feminism,[26] we pursued a middle course that we began charting while team-teaching a graduate seminar on feminist theory. With most of our students, we found many insights developed by feminist and other postmodern theorists persuasive and useful. Striving for ethnographic and textual reflexivity about the nexus of power and knowledge in cultural research and representation seemed crucial to us, as did efforts to historicize the conceptual vocabulary that feminists employ in our work. Feminists of color, along with other postcolonial, as well as postmodern, critics have taught us to mistrust dominant conceptual categories that falsely universalize the experiences and conditions of dominant subjects.[27] And like other feminists influenced by Michel Foucault, we had come to understand power to be productive, as well as repressive.

At the same time, however, we retained conceptions that some poststructuralist theorists eschew, still finding fruitful notions of agency, experience, resistance, and social referentiality, even if the social world that agents construct, experience, and resist has become one in which images dominate and, to a significant extent, constitute social reality. Thus, although I can no longer sustain the socialist-feminist confidence with which I once represented the narrative of family revolution in China, and I now find all metanarratives to be inevitably provisional, I nonetheless find them indispensable vehicles for representing relationships of power and injustice, such as those distributed along old-fashioned axes of gender, class, race, and sexuality. For this reason (and others), I am willing to employ, as Gayatri Spivak advocates, a "strategic" use of essentialism.[28] Indeed, I confess that, reminded during the Gulf War of the ubiquity of male associations with militarism and physical violence, I found myself entertaining more than strategic ideas about essentialism. I even dared publicly to interrogate mono-lithic refusals by most feminists, like myself, to consider the possibility that biology might provide more than a semiotic resource for the more lethal aspects of masculinity.[29]

As my trajectory was picking its undisciplined and anxious way through feminist and other bodies of postmodern social theory, my femi-nist colleagues in literary criticism began to report a mounting feminist back-lash in their discipline against the hegemony of poststructuralist theories, while some feminist critics of postmodern anthropology were beginning to move beyond critique to creative appropriations.[30] Meanwhile, ironically enough, my home discipline, sociology, began to exhibit early symptoms of postmodern courtship: sessions on postmodern selfhood and society began to infuse the annual meetings of the American Sociological Associa-tion; the November 1990 issue of *Social Problems*, the official journal of the Society for the Study of Social Problems, an organization and publication heretofore more noted for its liberal and Marxist sensibilities, featured "Three Papers on Postmodernity and Panic" (one by the 1991–1992 president of the organization), followed by "Two Papers on Feminism, Language, and Postmodernism"; and the theme of the 1992 meetings of the SSSP was ex-plicitly "Postmodernity as a Social Problem: Race, Class, Gender, and the *New World Order*."

Interestingly, perhaps perversely, just as the postmodern theory in-dustry seemed to be outsourcing some of its knowledge production sites from a humanities "core" and an anthropological "semiperiphery" to here-tofore peripheral sociology, "cultural studies" was migrating from Birming-ham, England, to displace postmodern theory, as well as feminist theory, as the favored sign and institutional site for left-wing inter-, trans-, and counterdisciplinary intellectual work in the United States. The rise of cul-tural studies over the past few years has been meteoric, with new centers, institutes, conferences, journals, graduate programs, and even undergraduate majors proliferating, despite the severe, often devastating, impact of the economic crisis on higher education.

From a sociological standpoint, it is interesting to note that the stan-dard, and generally male-authored, genealogies of cultural studies locate its roots in the 1970s Birmingham Centre for Cultural Studies, an interdis-ciplinary project in which sociology, particularly of a critical Marxist cast, played an integral part. However, sociology failed to survive the late 1980s transatlantic crossing of this intellectual vessel, which disembarked prima-rily in humanities settlements. Perhaps this is partly because many of the indigenous roots of cultural studies in the United States can be found in feminism, ethnic studies, and American Studies, projects in which litera-ture and humanities scholars increasingly dominate. From this perspec-tive, I found it oddly comforting to observe anthropologists at their 1992 meetings organizing plenary sessions to express, and to analyze the sources of, their own widespread feelings of marginalization from the vortex of multicultural and cultural studies discourses, intellectual territory in which many anthropologists presumed proprietary disciplinary interests.[31]

This displacement of postmodern theory by cultural studies seems to be coinciding with a notable transfer of intellectual energies from gender and class—the foundational cross-bars of socialist feminism—to race and sexuality as the privileged sites of radical theorizing. What is more, this shift from gender and class to race and sexuality is evident not only in the United States version of cultural studies, broadly defined, but even within women's studies and feminist theory. So fully has feminist attention to dif-ferences among women and to conceptions of multiple subjectivities dis-placed unitary formulations of gender differences between women and men that it has become challenging to decide whether one still can identify an intellectual terrain that remains a specifically *feminist* project. By 1994 I found myself naming the graduate seminar in contemporary feminist theory that I teach "Different Differences and Significant Others: The Decentering of Gender in Feminist Theory."

In fact, what many feminists of color came to label "white feminist theory" has been so successfully mainstreamed into most of the humanities and a few of the social sciences that queer theory and multiculturalism are displacing feminism as the primary targets of conservative backlash. Former New Leftist turned neoconservative intellectual entrepreneur David Horowitz made the vanguard role of queer theory explicit in "Queer Revolution: The Last Stage of Radicalism," a rather loathsome diatribe he presented at a self-consciously backlash session of the 1992 meetings of the American Stud-ies Association. Parodying the *Communist Manifesto*, Horowitz began: "A specter is haunting the American academy, the last refuge of the political left. It is the specter of queer theory."[32] He proceeded to portray queer theory as the final assault by radical theories of social construction on nature, nor-malcy, and civilization, thereby transferring to queer revolution the privi-leged status of pariah once "enjoyed" by feminism. Similarly, the widespread political backlash against affirmative action, both on and off U.S. campuses, seems to be directed more vocally against compensatory remedies for racial than for gender imbalances.

The rhetoric and outcomes of recent and current electoral campaigns in the United States reflect these shifts, as homophobia and racism are proving to be far more potent resources than sexism for galvanizing back-lash voters. Tangible feminist gains in the 1992 "Year of the Woman" coin-cided with anti–gay rights victories in Colorado and in Tampa, Florida, and a frighteningly close call for a draconian antigay proposition in Oregon whose language about perversity and abnormality is echoed in the David Horowitz pamphlet. Likewise, Year of the Woman hoopla helped to mask the Democratic Party's active suppression of its traditional racial equality and antipoverty discourses in favor of universalist appeals to a "forgotten" middle class, not so subtly coded as white. As I compose these thoughts in the midst of the 1996 electoral season, the Democratic Party has dropped the mask. Party strategists openly count upon sustaining the gender gap advantage Democrats enjoy among women and pro-choice voters as a cru-cial component of a reelection constituency. At the same time, however, President Bill Clinton has signed two pieces of historic, and in my view heinous, backlash legislation that directly pander to popular prejudice against gays and lesbians and the disproportionately nonwhite poor—the Defense of Marriage Act, which defines marriage as an exclusively hetero-sexual right, and the repeal of our already paltry system of federal welfare entitlements for the poor.

I have indulged these meditations on recent shifts in politics and theory trends at some length because they have impinged on my own recent work as well. The multifaceted national cultural wars have pulled my work in unanticipated directions. In fact, ironically enough, ever since December 1992 when one of these discourses "hailed" me, as an Althusserian might say, by name from the op-ed pages of the *New York Times,*[33] I have found myself drawn irresistibly back to "the family." A surprising new campaign for family values, spearheaded by social scientists, subjected *Brave New Fami-lies,* my feminist ethnography about postmodern family life, to hostile at-tention, inadvertently drawing me away from my ethnographic project on cultural studies and into the fray of public intellectual combat over family research and politics.[34] Having been cast by the campaign in the role of a dissident respondent, I began to map its institutional, rhetorical, and po-litical frameworks. What began as a cartographical project, a reflexive soci-ology of knowledge treatment of political and intellectual developments inside and outside the academy that drive and configure the neo-family values campaign gradually generated an unanticipated book. I self-consciously undertook to write *In the Name of The Family* to intervene in contemporary representational struggles over family politics that now op-erate at the boundaries of social science, the media, and political discourse. At the same time, and to the same ends, I began working with an interdisciplinary group of family scholars and clinicians, many of whom evince little interest in, or patience with, the favored rhetoric and theories of cultural studies, to form a Council on Contemporary Families. The council plans to serve as a research and education clearinghouse that will work to challenge misleading social scientific claims made "in the name of the family" that have been used to justify reactionary political initiatives.

My recent engagement with a decentered genre of feminist cultural studies in the academy helped alert me to the social significance of the cultural campaign for family values and furnished me with analytical resources for examining its mastery of the politics of representation. For example, where once I might have read Dan Quayle's assault on Murphy Brown in straightforward terms of gender, now I could readily perceive that she functions as a multilayered cultural code signifying racial, sexual, and social class meanings at least as potently. However, to directly challenge these meanings, to engage, that is, in a kind of applied cultural studies in the public arena, I have had to bracket my academic investments in cultural studies. After all, it is my disciplinary status as a credentialed, and decidedly modernist, sociologist that legitimates my scholarly authority to engage in the cultural politics of *the family*.

These disciplinary and political disjunctures provide "disloyal" feminists like myself paradoxical new constraints against and opportunities for interdisciplinary work. The increased disciplinarity, specialization, and sheer magnitude of feminist scholarship makes cross-disciplinary feminist discourse ever more difficult. At the same time, however, feminism has become a significant presence in cultural studies, a key site of interdisciplinary theory and politics, but one in which sociology is even more marginal than anthropology. Meanwhile, backlash movements against the liberatory politics of gender, race, class, and sexuality have achieved so much success in the public arena that they now threaten to render the flourishing academic project of feminist cultural studies, as well as all forms of critical inquiry, either an irrelevant or endangered activity.

I conclude these reflections on my travels in feminist disciplinary borderlands with thoughts provoked by Avery Gordon, a decidedly postmodernist, "disloyal" feminist sociologist and cultural studies scholar, in her discussion of disciplinary impediments to writing ethnography and literary fictions as sociology: "Perhaps the key methodological question is not: what method have you adopted for this research? but what paths have been disavowed, left behind, covered over and remain unseen. In what fields does field work occur?"[35]

Looking back over my travels to, from, and within the study of family revolutions, I have no desire to disavow my undisciplined migrant labors in cross-fertilized feminist fields, least of all those that challenge arbitrary and increasingly atavistic disciplinary divisions of knowledge. Indeed, I worry rather less about the consequences of my personal disloyalty to the disciplines than about the costs to feminism of what strike me as increasingly conducive conditions for disciplinary loyalty now evident in the social sciences and humanities. Yet I find comfort, as well as concern, in my conviction that these will provide a fertile "field day" for an emerging generation of feminist cultural studies theorists who must confront the challenge of keeping success from spoiling academic feminism.

## Afterword

Not long after I had written an earlier version of the preceding essay for a multidisciplinary women's studies lecture series and volume on the impact of feminism on the disciplines, I received the invitation from Barbara Laslett and Barrie Thorne to contribute to the conference that yielded this volume an autobiographical essay that applies "a life history methodology" to "the recent history of feminist thought within sociology."[36] Although my response claimed that I had recently completed such a piece—an earlier version of the preceding essay—for a different venue, rereading that essay, I discovered how few of the "life history" dimensions, that is to say, of the intimate motivational dimensions of my trajectory, I had chosen to reveal. Regard this Afterword, therefore, as a kind of thin overlay relief map to the essay it follows. Adding a layer of personal texture and tone to the essay's more composed reflections on my theoretical and political autobiography, it hints at some of the extratextual desires, vulnerabilities, anxieties, obsessions, and happenstances that inevitably undergird, but are repressed by, more conventionally processed representations of intellectual biography.

Once pressed by Barbara and Barrie to think more confessionally about my research, I allowed the subtitle of *Brave New Families*, at the time my most recently published book, to bring an instant blush to my face. For I immediately recognized the private double entendre of the "stories of domestic upheaval in late twentieth century America" that I had simultaneously signaled and masked therein. My own family history is marked by upheavals that intersect with, at times in boldface, at others less overtly, many of those I tell in the ethnographic portions of that book, as with the broader social trends the book interprets. Indeed, I could readily produce a reductionist, but not false, narrative about how my more than two-decades-long intellectual preoccupation with family revolutions, as well as the best-honed undergraduate course I teach on the making and unmaking of the modern family, were propelled by the painful discrepancy between the sentimentalized 1950s family ideology that was culturally dominant during my teen years and the grittier texture of life in my troubled natal family.

I lived my childhood and adolescence in New Jersey during the 1940s and 1950s, suffering the underside of Ozzie and Harriet Land in an "intact" lower-middle-class modern family. Until both children had begun their own first marriages, my mother, a frustrated, socially ambitious, intermittently full-time homemaker, sustained an overtly hostile, incompatible marriage to my father, a distant, depressed, working-class breadwinner, for fear of the serious social stigma and economic risks of divorce. My quotidian, experiential curriculum documented the hollowness of the modern family ideal, but, like most children, I fancied my own family's pain no critique of the institution, but an anomalous, and disgraceful, instance of its failure. In consequence, it was a family pattern I felt compelled to replicate until liberated by the "domestic upheavals" of the 1960s.

A true product of 1950s gender culture, I possessed no educational or career goals of my own but devoted my undergraduate years in the early 1960s to seeking a husband. In June 1964, immediately after graduating from the University of Michigan, I married a medical student and moved with him to Chicago, where I spent the next three years teaching social studies in secondary schools, earning what we young working wives of student doctors in that period called our Ph.T. degrees (putting hubby through). The synergistic effects of *Sputnik,* Vietnam, civil rights, marijuana, and, later, feminism gradually rescued me from this ill-suited, feminine life course.

*Sputnik* inspired the National Defense Education Act, which, among other things, funded summer enrichment programs for public school teachers. Because I was beginning to be drawn into the mounting cultural and political maelstroms of the mid-1960s—the antiwar, civil rights, cultural revolution—I enrolled in an intensive summer institute at the Chicago campus of the University of Illinois to study what was then called Negro history. There an inspirational, attentive professor helped awaken and fuse my too-long-suppressed intellectual, political, and erotic passions. During politically volatile 1968, I completed a master's degree program in U.S. history at that same university, writing an M.A. thesis, "The Martyrdom of Malcolm X." I also divorced my first husband, joined the Gene McCarthy for President campaign, and enrolled in a doctoral program in history teacher education at the University of Chicago.

Thus, I had already divorced, as had my parents by then, and had begun to develop a left-wing political consciousness when feminism en tered and redirected my life in 1970. "Feminism provided an analysis and rhetoric for their discontent, and it helped each woman develop the self-esteem she needed to exit or reform her unhappy modern marriage" and to pursue educational and occupational interests of her own, I would write twenty years later about Pam and Dotty, the central subjects of my ethnography, neglecting to indicate the autobiographical roots of this insight.[37] So profoundly did feminism alter my own consciousness and commitments that it has been my vocation ever since.

As I construct this more psychological reckoning of my interest in family change, the decade of work I committed to studying China reads almost as a displacement in which a remote geographical and abstract analytical plane allowed me unthreatening means with which to contend with unresolved, no doubt irresoluble, personal preoccupations with questions of familial repression and with the possibilities and limits of liberation. In such a reading, *Brave New Families* represents the nearest facsimile of an intimate "life history methodology" as this family sociologist is willing to record in print. That project was precipitated, as I hint in its pages, by the collapse in 1984 of my feminist-inspired joint household in Berkeley, California—a household that had survived longer than my, or many other, first marriage(s). Its failure catapulted me uneasily into the first nuclear family household of my adult years.

As I read backward, additional displacements become visible. For example, I first drafted this autobiographical Afterword in December 1992, one week after viewing Spike Lee's film about Malcolm X. I could not help but notice that Lee's masculinist, idealized treatment of the slain black nationalist hero bore an uncomfortable resemblance to the one I had produced in the M.A. thesis written during my prefeminist black history period. The naive, well-intentioned, white female college student whom Malcolm, in his separatist phase, rebuffs in the Spike Lee film reminded me that the interpersonal effects of black nationalism facilitated my long retreat from a central focus on racial politics and scholarship, as well as my turn to what I later learned to regard as white feminism.

Intriguingly, two decades later I once again chose to study men. And although this time I did so through feminist lenses, the project on male cultural critics revived my long-standing, but for too long subordinated, interest in race. I suspect that the coincidence of my then eleven-year-old son's budding adolescence with my own approach to the midlife "change" that Germaine Greer was more willing than I to celebrate seeded some of the furrows I began raking over in those newer fields.

From this perspective, however, my collaborative project on men could also be read as an abortive attempt to escape *the family*. I'm reminded of another of my published titles, which evokes another blush. "Are Feminists Afraid to Leave Home?" I queried rhetorically in 1986 in a review essay of works by Betty Friedan, Jean Bethke Elshtain, and Greer herself, which I termed "conservative, profamily feminism."[38] Retrospectively I see that I, too, only managed to escape the lure of "the family" for a few years before I found myself irresistibly called back to work that truly does feel like home. My current research, writing, public speaking, and organizing on the politics of family values seem to draw on and satisfy a remarkably extensive range of my intellectual, emotional, and political identities.

Intellectually, this project requires the sort of disciplinary disloyalty, or dilettantism, I have honed over decades. For example, the sources I drew on to write the last chapter of *In the Name of The Family*—"Gay and Lesbian Families Are Here; All Our Families Are Queer; Let's Get Used to It!"—which was solicited for inclusion in a family policy collection, ranged from literature in child development, demography, critical legal theory, the daily print media, and feminist theory, to online postings from political action groups and episodes from TV sitcoms such as *Roseanne* and *Friends*. Moreover, this project attends equally to those "tc" (theoretically correct) Four Horsemen of feminist cultural studies—gender, race, class, and sexuality. Even more compelling, I suspect, are some of the emotional and political functions this project serves. It enables me to fuse scholarship with political activism on issues of profound personal salience. I confess to taking a portion of perverse pleasure from engaging in intellectual-political combat against the family values brigades while occupying the "subject position" of a married, heterosexual, working mother. No doubt, this derives from my 1960s era investments in a countercultural identity, as well as that era's idealistic injunction to "keep the faith."

Nor would I deny that on a more personal level, this project provides me continual opportunities to reflect on and reconsider my own kinship history and strategies. Apropos, I am concluding this Afterword exactly one week after giving the word to old and new colleagues that I have decided to accept a new academic position at USC . My son will be entering his junior year of high school when I assume this position, and my own, perhaps overly child-centered, family values prevent me from uprooting him from the community and school that he does not wish to leave. In consequence, I will soon join the ranks of long-distance, commuter marriages as we negotiate a dual-household family strategy. Despite the misgivings and anxiety with which I anticipate this challenge, I also look forward with some pleasure to the opportunity it will give me to "divide the k'ang," as the joint

Chinese families I once studied described the process of household division. After more than a quarter century of domesticity, I am ready to savor some of the privileges of inhabiting a part-time "home of my own." This stage of my personal and professional life history will have to take clearer shape, however, before I would disclose in a scholarly venue any more than this about its meanings.

## Notes

My thanks to Sarah Fenstermaker, Judith Newton, Domna Stanton, Abby Stewart, Barrie Thorne, and Susan Gerard for helpful responses to an earlier draft.

1. Judith Stacey and Barrie Thorne, "The Missing Feminist Revolution in Sociology," *Social Problems* 32 (April 1985): 301–316.
2. Barrie and I discuss this issue at greater length in a postmortem commentary on our earlier essay: Judith Stacey and Barrie Thorne, "Is Sociology Still Missing Its Feminist Revolution?" *ASA Theory Section Newsletter* 18 (summer 1996): 1–3.
3. Frances E. Mascia-Lees, Patricia Sharpe, and Colleen Ballerino Cohen, "The Postmodernist Turn in Anthropology: Cautions from a Feminist Perspective," *Signs* 15 (Autumn 1989): 7–33.
4. Even the most cursory, arbitrary list suggests the continued vitality and value of contributions by feminist sociologists whose work thus far displays little interest in postmodern theory disputes—for example, Barbara Katz Rothman, Lenore Weitzman, Carole Joffe, Ruth Milkman, Arlene Kaplan Daniels, Maxine Baca Zinn, Arlie Hochschild, Kristin Luker, Evelyn Nakano Glenn, Judith Rollins, Lillian Rubin, Diana Russell, Candace West, Barbara Reskin, Rosanna Hertz, and Marcia Millman. The *American Sociological Review,* the major, and primarily positivist, journal published by the American Sociological Association routinely publishes feminist articles on such issues as female employment, fertility, family behaviors, status attainment, political behaviors, deviance, and gender attitudes. Feminist work permeates *Social Problems,* the more qualitative and critical journal published by the less mainstream Society for the Study of Socialist Problems, and Sociologists for Women in Society publishes its own journal of feminist sociology, *Gender and Society.*
5. In 1994 the Sex and Gender Section had 1,271 members, which was 200 members more than the Section on Medical Sociology, which is currently the second largest specialty section of the ASA (data provided by American Sociological Association). The proportion of sociology Ph.D. degrees awarded to females increased from 33 percent in 1977 to 51 percent in 1989 (National Science Foundation [NSF], "Science and Engineering Degrees, 1966–1989: A Source Book" NSF 91-314 [Washington, D.C.: 1991], NSF, Table 54). Compare this 50 percent increase and achievement of female numerical dominance with the 20 percent increase of Ph.D. degrees awarded to females in all fields: In 1980, 30 percent of all Ph.D. degrees in the United States were awarded to females, and in 1990 the proportion had risen to

36 percent (National Research Council, "Summary Report 1990: Doctorate Recipients from United States Universities" [Washington, D.C.: National Academy Press, 1991].) These figures for completed doctoral degrees likely understate the feminization trends evident among currently enrolled graduate students in sociology and other fields.

6. Judith Stacey, *Patriarchy and Socialist Revolution in China* (Berkeley and Los Angeles: University of California Press, 1983).

7. Judith Stacey, *Brave New Families: Stories of Domestic Upheaval in Late Twentieth Century America* (New York: Basic Books, 1990).

8. Judith Stacey, *In the Name of The Family: Rethinking Family Values in a Postmodern Age* (Boston: Beacon Press, 1996).

9. In 1971 I joined women faculty and students at what was then called Richmond College of the City University of New York in implementing a women's studies program. As I was an instructor in education, I developed a course, "Women in Education," that inspired my first feminist publication, Judith Stacey, Susan Bereaud, and Joan Daniels, eds., *And Jill Came Tumbling After: Sexism in American Education* (New York: Dell, 1974).

10. Alvin Gouldner, *The Coming Crisis in Western Sociology* (New York: Basic Books, 1970).

11. To name just an arbitrary sample of feminists who have received degrees from the Brandeis sociology department: Nancy Chodorow, Barrie Thorne, Marcia Millman, Lise Vogel, Gaye Tuchman, Judith Rollins, Elizabeth Higginbotham, Patricia Hill Collins, Nancy Shaw, Wini Breines, Marjorie Davies, Shulamit Reinharz, Fatima Mernissi, Lynda Holmstrom, Natalie Allon, and Elizabeth Long. Barrie Thorne provides a longer list and an insightful analysis of the conditions at Brandeis that fostered this feminist renaissance in "Feminist Sociology: The Brandeis Connection," a presentation she gave at a symposium in April 1984 honoring the twenty-fifth anniversary of the department's graduate program, and in her essay in this volume.

12. Because early Bolshevik efforts to undermine patriarchal sexual and family practices were rescinded after the Soviet regime consolidated its power, most social scientists theorized that revolutionary gender policies were strictly instrumental and short-lived. Reactionary gender and family policies would inevitably follow the consolidation of state power by a formerly revolutionary regime. See, for example, Rose L. Coser and Lewis A. Coser, "The Principles of Legitimacy and Its Patterned Infringement in Social Revolutions," in Marvin B. Sussman and Betty E. Cogswell, eds., *Cross-national Family Research* (Leiden: Brill, 1972).

13. Heidi A. Hartmann wrote the essay that galvanized attention to theoretical relations between feminism and Marxism: "The Unhappy Marriage of Marxism and Feminism: Towards a More Progressive Union," in Lydia Sargent, ed., *Women and Revolution.* (Boston: South End Press, 1981). An important early anthology of dual-systems theory was Zillah Eisenstein, ed., *Capitalist Patriarchy and the Case for Socialist-feminism* (New York: Monthly Review Press, 1979).

14. I discuss some of the feminist literature extolling the virtues of interactive field research in "Can There Be a Feminist Ethnography?" *Women's Studies International Quarterly* 11 (1988): 21–27.

15. George E. Marcus and Michael M.J. Fischer, *Anthropology as Cultural Critique* (Chicago: University of Chicago Press, 1986).

16. I am grateful to Abby Stewart for initiating a provocative dialogue on this issue with me and others.

17. The collection that canonized the reflexive, experimental turn in anthropology was James Clifford and George Marcus, eds., *Writing Culture: The Poetics and Politics of Ethnography* (Berkeley and Los Angeles: University of California Press, 1986). It was foreshadowed, however, by numerous earlier essays and ethnographies, most of which are surveyed in Marcus and Fischer, *Anthropology as Cultural Critique*. Of course, as Barrie Thorne has properly reminded me, my turn to ethnography in itself need not have propelled me outside sociology, where there is also a rich, honorable tradition of ethnographic work starting with the early twentieth century urban studies of the Chicago School and continuing in the community studies tradition to which our earlier essay pointed. Once again the primacy of my feminist, antidisciplinary grounding proved decisive.

18. In addition to the works discussed by Marcus and Fischer, see Michael Moffatt, *Coming of Age in New Jersey: College and American Culture* (New Brunswick. N.J.: Rutgers University Press 1989); Faye Ginsburg, *Contested Lives: The Abortion Debate in an American Community* (Berkeley and Los Angeles: University of California Press, 1989); and Patricia Zavella, *Women's Work* and *Chicano Families* (Ithaca, N.Y.: Cornell University Press, 1987). A vanguard instance is one of my favorite ethnographies: Barbara Myerhoff, *Number Our Days* (New York: Dutton, 1978). For a fine collection of feminist anthropological studies of the United States, see Faye Ginsburg and Anna Tsing, eds., *Uncertain Terms: Negotiating Gender in American Culture* (Boston: Beacon Press, 1990).

19. For other analyses of the quest for a feminist research methodology, see Gloria Bowles and Renate Duelli-Klein, *Theories of Women's Studies* (London: Routledge and Kegan Paul, 1980); Sandra Harding, ed. *Feminism and Methodology* (Bloomington: Indiana University Press, 1987); Elizabeth Gross, "Conclusion: What Is Feminist Theory?" in Carole Pateman and Elizabeth Gross, eds., *Feminist Challenges: Social and Political Theory* (Boston: Northeastern University Press, 1987), pp. 190–304; and Liz Stanley and Sue Wise, *Breaking out: Feminist Consciousness and Feminist Research* (London: Routledge and Kegan Paul, 1983).

20. Clive Dilnot, "What Is the Post-modern?" *Art History* 9 (June 1986): 245.

21. Ibid, p. 249.

22. Stacey, *Brave New Families*, p. 18.

23. Mascia Lees et al., "The Postmodernist Turn."

24. Thus, humanists, rather than social scientists, took much of the initiative in organizing Teachers for a Democratic *Culture* (TDC, my emphasis), mobilized to defend multicultural and feminist curricular reforms against the anti–political correctness campaign of the National Association of Scholars and other reactionary groups. The organizational meeting of TDC was held at the December 1991 meetings of the Modern Language Association.

25. Judith Newton and Judith Stacey, "Learning Not to Curse, or Feminist Predicaments in Cultural Criticism by Men: Our Movie Date with James Clifford and Stephen Greenblatt," *Cultural Critique* 23 (winter 1992–1993): 51–82. I find it gratifying that other feminists have challenged genealogies of postmodernist theory and cultural studies that marginalize feminist contributions. See, for example, Meaghan Morris, *The Pirate's Fiance: Feminism, Reading, Postmodernism* ( London: Verso, 1988);

Susan Bordo, "Feminism, Postmodernism, and Gender Skepticism," in Linda J. Nicholson, ed., *Feminism/Postmodernism* (New York: Routledge, 1990); Elizabeth Long, "Feminism and Cultural Studies," *Critical Studies in Mass Communications* 6 (1989): 427–435; and Cathy Schwichtenberg "Feminist Cultural Studies," *Critical Studies in Mass Communication* 6 (1989): 202–209.

26. Much of the academic debate about the proper preposition, conjunction, and character of the two terms was initiated by Alice Jardine and Paul Smith, eds., *Men in Feminism* (New York: Methuen, 1987). See also Joseph A. Boone and Michael Cadden, eds., *Engendering Men: The Question of Male Feminist Criticism* (New York: Routledge, 1990).

27. The critical literature on this theme is vast. See, for example, Maxine Baca Zinn, Lynn Weber Cannon, Elizabeth Higginbotham, and Bonnie Thornton Dill, "The Costs of Exclusionary Practices in Women's Studies," *Signs* 11 (1986): 290–303; Chandra Mohanty, Ann Russo, and Lourdes Torres, eds., *Third World Women and the Politics of Feminism* (Bloomington: Indiana University Press 1991); Gloria Anzaldúa, ed., *Making Face, Making Soul: Haciendo Caras* (San Francisco: Aunt Lute Foundation, 1990); and bell hooks, *Feminist Theory: From Margin to Center* (Boston: South End Press, 1984).

28. Gayatri Spivak, *The Postcolonial Critic: Interviews, Strategies, Dialogue* (New York: Routledge, 1990), p. 10.

29. I first raised this issue while serving as a commentator at the "Unraveling Masculinities" conference at the University of California, Davis, in February 1991. A revised version of the commentary was published as "Toward Kinder, Gentler Uses for Testosterone," *Theory and Society* 22 (1993): 711–721.

30. Four particularly influential critiques of the critical excesses of the antiessentialist "club" are Barbara Christian, "The Race for Theory," *Cultural Critique* 6: 51–63; Bordo, "Feminism, Postmodernism, and Gender Skepticism"; Diane Fuss, *Essentially Speaking: Feminism, Nature, Difference* (New York: Routledge, 1989); and Tania Modleski, *Feminism Without Women: Culture and Criticism in a "Postfeminist" Age* (New York: Routledge, 1991). At the November 1990 meetings of the American Anthropological Association, Francis Mascia-Lees, Patricia Sharpe, and Colleen Cohen, the authors of the widely discussed feminist critique of postmodern anthropology, gave, or rather performed, a paper that was decidedly reflexive about its textual, as well as political, dimensions. They did so, moreover, at a session on feminism and postmodernism organized by Mascia-Lees.

31. This was the basic premise of the entire panel "Multiculturalism and the Concept of Culture" and other panels. See, for example, Sherry Ortner, "Anthropology's War of Position" (Paper presented at American Anthropological Association meeting, San Francisco, California, December 1992).

32. David Horowitz, "Queer Revolution: The Last Stage of Radicalism" (Studio City, Calif.: Center for the Study of Popular Culture, 1992), pamphlet.

33. A widely circulated op-ed by David Popenoe, "The Controversial Truth: The Two-parent Family Is Better," *New York Times*, December 26, 1992, p. A13, identified me as an ideological exception to an emergent consensus among social scientists that two-parent families are superior.

34. I had been collaborating with Judith Newton in a study of male cultural critics when the op-ed just mentioned appeared, followed quickly by other articles by

family values advocates that identified *Brave New Families* as an example of mis-guided feminism and liberalism. I discuss the orchestrated character, as well as the substance of this campaign, at length in *In the Name of The Family*.

35. Avery Gordon, "Feminism, Writing, and Ghosts," *Social Problems* 37 (November 1990): 499.

36. The lecture series was sponsored by the Women's Studies Program of the University of Michigan in Ann Arbor. It resulted in publication of Domna Stanton and Abigail Stewart, eds., *Feminisms in the Academy* (Ann Arbor: University of Michigan Press, 1995). I am quoting language in the invitation to participate in the conference "The Missing Feminist Revolution in Sociology Reconsidered," convened by Barbara Laslett and Barrie Thorne at UC Berkeley, February 1992.

37. Judith Stacey, "Backward to the Postmodern Family: Reflections on Gender, Kinship, and Class in the Silicon Valley," in Alan Wolfe, ed., *America at Century's End* (Berkeley and Los Angeles: University of California Press, 1991), p 23.

38. Judith Stacey, "Are Feminists Afraid to Leave Home?: The Challenge of Conservative Profamily Feminism," in Juliet Mitchell and Ann Oakley, eds., *What Is Feminism?* (London: Basil Blackwell, 1986): pp. 219–248. This was an expanded version of "The New Conservative Feminism," *Feminist Studies* 9 (fall 1983): 559–583.

*R. W. Connell*

# Long and Winding Road

$\mathcal{S}$ocial theory grows out of the material detail of life as much as it comes from the abstracted conversation of theory-makers. And theory must, in the end, return to everyday practice. The project here is to explore the territory from starting points in personal experience.

Being a foreigner and a man, I do not have the experiences that most of the other authors in this book discuss. I do have a relationship with their story: American feminism has been important to me and to people with whom I have worked. The narrative frame in which participants retell their struggle is not available to someone who was not even in the country for most of it. My story is necessarily about intersections, not continuities. Making a virtue of necessity, I have borrowed from Australian author Frank Moorhouse the idea of "discontinuous narrative" and from British authors Carolyn Kay Steedman and David Jackson the idea of an autobiographical documentation of gender that repeatedly opens out a narrative for theoretical inspection.[1]

An outsider nonnarrative is likely to highlight issues different from those of an insider narrative. Two are, for me, unavoidable: the significance of American corporate wealth and cultural power and the personal and public response to feminism by men. Neither is simple; I hope to document some of their crosscurrents.

These issues involve strong emotions, among them humiliation and resentment, fear and admiration, pleasure and solidarity. Barbara Laslett argues convincingly for giving full weight to emotions. But how? The conventions of academic prose are designed to exclude emotions, not convey them. I have therefore drawn freely on other genres and techniques of writing.[2]

The story starts with my first encounter with North American sociology about twenty-five years ago; goes on to Australian universities, the growth of feminism there, and my adventures in a new sociology department; moves to Europe and the international publishing business; and returns to the North American academic world in recent years.

## The Patriarch in the Woodwork

*The scene is set at the end of the 1960s, at a Famous American University, in the office of a Very Famous Scholar. Enter a young man, just married, just off the plane from a distant country, just done with a Ph.D. thesis. He is about to join the department as an unpaid temporary postdoctoral fellow and find out what sociology is like in one of its world centers. A legacy from a great-aunt has funded an expedition by the couple to this side of the world. The young woman will, as it turns out, keep the ship afloat for a year doing clerical work at a consulate.*

*The Very Famous Scholar looks up from his correspondence, turns from his desk, smiles, and reaches out his hand. The young man is thrilled to shake it. The wood paneling, the leaded windows, the ghosts of sociologists past, frame the moment. The Very Famous Scholar kindly asks about intentions. The young man launches into hopes and plans for the year. About three minutes into the recitation, the Very Famous Scholar reaches a decision, swivels back to his desk, and continues signing his correspondence.*

## Conferenceville

*By Greyhound across the continent, to the annual meetings of two associations.[3] In 1970 only working-class people and students travel by bus. The dirt and indifference of Greyhound terminals are memorable. So is the dawn sunlight blazing on the mountains behind Salt Lake City.*

*Friends among the graduate students have arranged a bed in the city where the ASA conference is being held. So I know one or two people there; and I have an Australian friend to meet who knows his way around the radical student network. But the mass and anonymity of the conference are overpowering. The entire membership of the Sociological Association at home would fit into one of this conference's parallel sessions. The corridors are turbulent, full of business, none of which is my business.*

*I have bought a spiral-bound notebook and start filling it with field notes. There are so many sociologists that they have to be accommodated like a tourist invasion. So instead of the seedy functionality of university classrooms where Australian conferences are held, this one rejoices in the commercial splendor of a giant hotel.*

*The busiest place in the conference is an enormous book bazaar. Neatly dressed publishers' representatives stand around in little booths trying to get their texts adopted in the sociologists' courses, while the sociologists try to get the publishers interested in their proposals for books. I get my first picture of the scale of*

*American publishing and the economic stakes in higher education here. Some of the texts are familiar; the publishers also market them at home.*

*I also get a glimpse of employment practices. In another large room is the meat market. Hundreds of people are undergoing public humiliation, advertising their need for a job, putting their life courses on show in loose-leaf books for anyone to see.*

*The conference sessions themselves are a continuous display of professional power and status. An interesting paper on a topic close to my Ph.D. is delivered by a woman of about my age to an audience of about seven. A panel including a masculine Name I had heard even in Australia has a larger attendance, though I don't know exactly how big—I can't get in the room; several hundred people at least are there before me.*

## Commentary

The Very Famous Scholar, I thought at first, had simply decided I was not going to be part of his clientele. I was neither his student nor a resource for his research program. The insult was certainly a display of academic power.

There was more, of course, not least the hegemony of the United States. The term "hegemony" derives from the classical Greek term for the leading state in a military coalition. At this time, the United States was leading an alliance in Vietnam in which my country was a minor participant, a fact of which the Very Famous Scholar was certainly aware. This hegemony extended deep into academic life. Indeed, that is why I was there and not sitting on a rock in the Blue Mountains evolving an Australian sociology from my own inner consciousness. The Very Famous Scholar was, as Louis Althusser had put it not long before, merely the bearer of a structure.

More exactly, structures—though this took me longer to see. The scene would not have played the same way if the Very Famous Scholar had been a woman. Or, probably, if I had been. The authority on display amid the polished wood, and the way it was exerted, had a lot to do with gender.

So did the collective processes of the annual meeting. The Names competing for prestige were masculine. The profoundly alienated, market structure of the conference as an institution—notionally an occasion for the *sharing* of scientific knowledge—reflected a public world predicated on the gender division of labor, and massively dominated by men. I know now that a feminist movement was developing in the ASA, but I did not know it then. The first meeting of Sydney Women's Liberation had been called just before we left on the flight to the United States.

But there was something more, which took even longer to see. If the Very Famous Scholar was bearing a structure that day, so was I. The nervous young man was also a competitor in the struggle for gendered authority, and the Very Famous Scholar was doubtless bright enough to see that and a whole lot more experienced at its moves.

If I was one of seven at my comrade's paper, I was also one of hundreds turning up to hear the Name. Reeling around the carpeted corridors of the Sociology Hilton, I, too, was a beneficiary of the gender order that underpinned its glittering horror. My wife was working for me to be there.

There is truth in Dorothy Smith's account of the academic world as a sector of a patriarchal power structure producing abstracted knowledge through texts that substitute for concrete knowledge.[4] Yet her imagery is all too mild to capture the lunatic divisiveness of that world and the tangled dynamics producing academic masculinities as ways of surviving and operating in it.

My path into academic jobs involved learning certain gendered practices (such as ferocious concentration on writing tasks at the expense of human relationships) and rejecting others (including such conventional masculine items as enthusiasm for sport and sexual aggressiveness). In the context of a higher education boom, I was rapidly appointed to senior positions. The trip to the United States and some publications in American journals were no small part of my qualifications.

Senior appointments gave access to some resources needed by a movement to democratize higher education. We thought of it at the time as creating liberated zones in universities. I was, I think, the first New Left professor (i.e., head of department) in Australia, acutely conscious of being on the establishment's ground and wary of cooptation. Both my access and my resistance were gendered.[5] I was fighting against hegemonic masculinity at the same time as I deployed its techniques. I think this gained me a reputation for eccentricity, if not psychopathology: oddly dressed, long in the hair, humorless, by turns quiet and abrasive. In the mid-1970s this trajectory was complicated, but also clarified, by the growth of Australian feminism.

## Learning

*It is 1974, at the conference of another venerable institution run by men, the Australian and New Zealand Association for the Advancement of Science (ANZAAS). Feminism is gaining footholds in the academic world, and here is one. A program of sessions on "the Australian family" has been organized by Madge Dawson. The topic sounds traditional; the content is not. It includes countercultural, gay, and feminist critiques of the family.*

*The lineup of speakers is diverse. I am one, equipped with a not-very-diverse paper, a quantitative report on sex differences in adolescence wittily called "You Can't Tell Them Apart Nowadays, Can You?" My statistics echo back off the walls of the University of New South Wales, formerly University of Technology, with architecture to match.*

*There is no flood of requests for copies. Nevertheless, the paper becomes part of Madge's second coup: a special issue of the ANZAAS journal* Search, *usually packed with geomorphology and rabbit virology. Not only does the symposium turn into a special issue, but also the special issue turns into a book. Interest in gender questions is building.*

*Madge is one of a group of women, older than the Women's Liberation activists, who have been very important in getting feminist concerns onto academic agendas. Madge published the first study of the position of women vis-à-vis Australian higher education,* Graduate and Married. *This book was the product of collaborative work by a group of women in Madge's adult education class, a precursor of many later discussions of feminist research methods.[6] I met her through the peace movement and the Labor Party. I learned from her some important lessons about how tolerance and tough-mindedness, good humor and militancy, might be combined.*

*By the early 1980s, feminism was the leading intellectual force in Australian sociology—ignored by some established men, resisted by others, yet plainly the liveliest area of research, publication, and student interest, and finding support from women and men in almost every sociology department. The person who probably did most to make this possible was someone not conspicuously a feminist, Jean Martin. She was the best sociologist in the country in the decades when Australian academic sociology was being established, and she set up the largest department. Although her writing was mainly about community and migration, a thread of argument about family relationships and women's influence ran through it from the 1950s onward.[7] Toward the end of her life, she was explicitly researching the social position of women, and she inspired a great deal of research by other women.*

*I met her only a few times. The earliest was when I was an undergraduate history student. Jean Martin was the first live sociologist I had seen, and I asked her for a list of books to read. I thought that, unlike the history I was learning, sociology might say something of relevance. I don't have her list any more, but I remember that it emphasized field research and was mostly American.*

## The Patriarch in the Abattoir

*With the new chair, which I took up in 1976, some resources could be expected from the university's normal staffing processes. Several feminist courses had recently started in other departments on campus, mostly operating on a shoestring budget. Resources for feminist teaching and research would leap if we directed some of sociology's expected growth into the area of sexual politics. The question was how best to do it.*

*So perhaps twenty-five people sat around the walls of an upstairs meeting room in the Behavioural Sciences building, newest of the concrete bunkers from which Australian higher education defied the world. From one window we could see the Harbour Bridge across seven miles and a thousand gum trees; from another we could see a big wattle tree that exploded each year in golden flower. Amid this patriotic riot we—mostly women, both students and academic staff from half a dozen departments—debated with a good deal of vigor and humor the options of a broader interdisciplinary program or a narrower but deeper concentration within the sociology discipline. We eventually decided to put our new resources into the latter. A decisive argument came from women in other departments who did not want the men in their areas, beginning to feel pressure to include material about women in their "mainstream" courses, to be let off the hook.*

*So gender and sexuality were defined as one of the core areas for the new sociology program, and I drafted up course proposals and staffing requests. Which in good academic time were approved. Within a few years a group of academics concerned with gender and sexuality had formed. There were a research program, a group of graduate students, and a flow of publications.*

*The irony of a male head of department pursuing a feminist agenda was not lost on my fellow patriarchs in the professoriate, or on my colleagues in the department, or on the students. For the most part, the situation was a source of energy; I felt supported, and I was able to support. But there were built-in tensions. It was not a happy coincidence that I was assigned by the departmental meeting to teach the course that centered on feminist theories of patriarchy (its usual convenor being on leave) at the time a separatist current was strengthening in Australian feminism.*

*I tried to run the course as a lectureless, self-managed forum where ideas could be pooled, joint research and reading planned, and conceptions of patriarchy debated, without an agenda predefined by me. The department at that time made regular staff-student reviews of each course after it had run. We sat in a dark downstairs room, and for the two meetings and several hours we spent reviewing my course, the place felt like an abattoir.*

*Some (at least) of the students said that they had been let down by the course. Some said its structurelessness involved an abuse of power. It is generally difficult for students to criticize the professor; and when I argued against the criticisms, it seemed like further abuse. I don't pretend to give an impartial account of this; the memory is very painful. Perhaps the most interesting criticism was that by not giving a course of lectures, I had withheld knowledge and thus preserved patriarchal power. For my part, I felt that certain things being said were false, others distorted. I felt for the first time under factional attack, and it seemed as if in the final analysis I was being carved up for being the wrong gender. The other academic members of the department were divided by conflicting commitments and loyalties. Some put a lot of energy and kindness into trying to mend the situation. The aftertaste was still bitter for me. An agreement was reached, then not fully observed. In following years the department made sure I was not called on to chair that course again. And I don't think I have ever taken such risks again in teaching.*

*Some of my students in another course about this time decided that for their collective research project they would interview men in their lives and around campus. It was the first research project on masculinity I had anything to do with, maybe the first in the country. All members of the group were women.*

## Commentary

Other essays in this volume have spoken of pioneers and mentors. Older women serve as models and mentors not only for younger women. In a paper about young men involved in Green politics who were trying to reform masculinity, I remarked that most of them had formative encounters with women's strength,[8] and I guess I was unconsciously referring to myself as well.

The point may apply more broadly. The current strength of feminism in Australian sociology is partly an outcome of the alliances women have been able to make. These historically were partly determined by the influence *on men* of women such as Jean Martin, Madge Dawson, and Jean Blackburn. (Jean Blackburn, an architect of Australian educational reform, among other things, coauthored a 1963 study, *Australian Wives Today*, and the very influential 1975 national report *Girls, School, and Society*.)[9]

Such alliances may not be comfortable for either side. Being a male friend of feminism (in Australia, unlike the United States, one does not speak of men as feminists) is a contradictory situation; tension can be expected. As a minor example, a man in this situation gets to hear many expressions of casual, and sometimes not so casual, hostility toward men in general, including the penis jokes mentioned by Gary Dowsett.[10] The clash that developed around my teaching was not exceptional, though, of course, it had its specific local causes. Difficulties of that kind, with a fair chance of emotional injury, can be expected whenever there is sustained involvement of men with feminist projects.

Nor is there a simple way around or through these contradictions—except giving up the attempt to make an alliance work. The pleasures of separatism for men have now been discovered by the followers of Robert Bly, the author of *Iron John,* and other leaders of the masculinity cults that developed in the 1980s out of men's consciousness-raising groups, New Age culture, and Jungian therapy. All-male gatherings, "warrior weekends," and reconstituted initiation rituals among men are central to their search for the "deep masculine"—an entity that, however powerful and shaggy, seems too shy to emerge in the presence of women.[11]

Engagement is much more demanding, but it is possible. Alliances can be sustained, despite the inevitable tensions and injuries, wherever there are shared commitments. Such commitments most commonly rest on principles with a certain universality—the cause of humanity, the principle of justice, the goal of equality.

Ironically, radical theory over the last thirty years has put a lot of energy into dismantling principles of this kind: from the Althusserian denunciation of humanism, to the postmodern scorn for grand narratives and the poststructuralist valorization of difference. Radical identity politics hopes to overcome division by generating coalitions, and rainbow coalitions have certainly been formed. But what will hold people in those coalitions when they meet rocks in the road? We will need unconditional commitments. We will need theorizing that moves across boundaries and between standpoints and even finds, like Pauline Johnson's *Feminism as Radical Humanism,* unexpected common ground.[12]

## The Materiality of Theory

*I am sitting in a small room at the back of a brick house in south London, looking at a row of brick houses across a row of backyards, some with dogs that do not observe curfew. We are living with a close friend who has been fighting for women's interests in British trade unions, a long and grinding struggle. For globe-trotting intellectuals, London is the place to be in 1984: a woman prime minister is in power; the miners are on strike. It is the year of George Orwell, the year our daughter is born, the year of writing* Gender and Power.[13]

*Literally writing, with a pen. I have a sensuous relationship with the text flowing slowly onto the page, not just a cerebral one; a relationship compounded of body, clothes, chair, ink, paper spread on the table, stillness of the room, light falling from the window, scurries in the backyards. These physical matters seem to be part of the way ideas solidify and sharpen, the way prose gets shaped.*

*The baby is involved with this text-making, sharing a lot of it asleep in a carry cot on the floor behind me. She gradually swims up to the top end and gets stuck with her head in a corner, at which point her grunts and gurgles change tone, I get up and lift her back to the bottom, and she starts the journey again. Sometimes the grunts turn to grousing, a familiar aroma steals across the room, and it is time for a paragraph break.*

*I mostly do the midnight feed, which gives Pam the chance of a solid sleep and me an excuse to be up late. I like writing at midnight. With the house still, and no lights on but the desk lamp (bad for the eyes!), I seem to be in the middle of a vast, dark space stretching out in all directions to the stars and nebulae. The only things sounding in it are the words I write and the grunted comments of the next generation.*

## Men's Studies

*The world turns;* Gender and Power *is published; other comments appear. There are twenty-seven reviews that I know of, from New Zealand to Finland. What is most striking is the difficulty many journals and reviewers have in categorizing the book. Can't be social theory because it's not about Marx and Weber. Can't be women's studies because it's written by a man. Must be jelly 'cause jam don't shake like that.*

*Seven journals work out a solution that completely throws me when I see the first reviews. Because it's about gender, and because it's by a man, it must be men's studies. (True, it does contain three pages setting out a condensed model of masculinity.) So* Gender and Power *is rolled into review essays covering a bunch of Books About Men, or samples of The New Men's Studies, as a sardonic feminist reviewer puts it.[14] I have not felt so firmly positioned since the days when reviewers decided that because I wrote about class, I must be a Marxist.*

*Feminist teachers prove to be more interested than feminist editors. The book comes to be used as a text in a number of courses, and the publishers have recently shown me the list to help me in thinking about a second edition. Most are in women's studies programs.*

## Commentary

Although men come to support feminism for a great variety of reasons, in most cases of which I know, personal relationships with women have been important. Few men, gay or straight, have no close ties to women. Often men have dense networks of ties to mothers, daughters, wives, lovers, sisters, grandmothers, nieces, coworkers, neighbors, and friends. There are interests and motives in abundance here. For instance, I have a fairly close relationship with our daughter, and however well or badly I manage it, this relationship defines a political interest. I want a world that will give her the respect and resources it will give the sons of our friends living across the road. To produce that world means supporting feminism. The arithmetic is not very difficult.

As with a good many other Australian intellectuals, my earliest political commitment was to the labor movement and socialism. The kind of socialism I learned from my mother and father, from Labor Party members such as Madge Dawson, and from reading (George Orwell's *Homage to Catalonia* especially) was about equality, courtesy, respect, and human solidarity rather than about modes of production and commentaries on *Capital*. It still seems to me that a commitment to equality is the litmus test in politics. Given this beginning, it is not hard to see the next step when the facts of gender inequality and the abuse of women are, to use a title of Orwell's, "In Front of Your Nose."[15] They were in front of my nose because I loved, lived with, and worked with feminist women. I have done my best to put the same facts in front of a lot of other men's noses.

The proboscis theory of men's support for feminism has one great flaw: it presupposes that they are willing to read. Orwell's point was precisely that people often are not. Hegemonic masculinity and patriarchal ideology provide a whole repertoire of routines for evading the obvious in gender relations. Here are a few: declaring gender inequality a fact of nature (helped on by sociobiologists); exaggerating the gains made by women (helped on by "PC" backlash campaigns); exaggerating the woes of men (helped on by Bly); mobilizing homophobia (on the principle that any man who sympathizes with women must be a fag—note how the Religious Right, in retreat on abortion, is targeting gays with new vigor); projecting onto minorities (helped on by racists—the current demonizing of immigrants and "violent criminals" in the United States is striking).

In this field of ideological struggle, there is plenty of work for men as well as for women. No applicant will be turned away.

The success of patriarchal ideology depends not only on how vigorously it is contested in public, but also on how receptive or resistant people are in their personal lives. I doubt we will ever see capitalist patriarchy overthrown by revolutionary masses led by drag queens in quite the way projected by Italian gay theorist Mario Mieli.[16] But we do need to look closely at the fissures, tensions, and contradictions in gender, and at the occasions and potentials they offer for political action.

So far as concerns men, this is now happening in the research on masculinity that has multiplied, and strikingly improved in quality, in the last few years. I have put energy into this work, and have done my best to help other men, and women, engaged in it. This research has begun to feed into practice, for instance, in work against rape and domestic violence, in education, and in relation to AIDS. The applications are still on a small scale, but the demand for ideas is certainly there, and I think this activity will grow. The need is so clear that I have grown a little more sympathetic to the idea of "men's studies"—which at first appalled me and still worries me—to the extent that it provides a venue for this kind of strategic research.

## Back in the ASA

*Another tourist palace, glittering even harder as we approach the end of Reagan's administration. This time I am present by official invitation, to take part in a thematic session about gender in American sociology. I am not exactly a Name, but at least an Object of Interest, possessor of a strange accent and exotic foot- notes, as well as being a man doing gender. I feel like an ambassador from Mars. This is silly. A number of people here are familiar with my work, and that is why I have been invited.*

*The room where the panel is to speak seems dark (all my memories of ASA annual meetings seem to involve dark interior spaces; Erik Erikson would love them). It is full to overflowing; I hear that sex and gender is the most buoyant area of the ASA's membership, and this certainly looks like it. About nine-tenths of those in the room are women.*

*The presentations are followed closely by the audience. I do my bit about American sociology and my bit for Australian sociology, passing out reading lists of Australian work in the area and inviting people to get in touch to be networked. The session ends, the people swirl out into the corridor, and this time I am full of business.*

*Later in the conference, as a thematic session presenter and foreign guest, I am invited to a presidential reception in a hospitality suite of the hotel. I sit on the bed in my room on the fourteenth-floor-that-is-really-the-thirteenth, looking out over the urban core of Atlanta (a cluster of high-rise banks and hotels oddly re- sembling a fleet of spaceships), and have a crisis of my New Left conscience. Should I go? Do I join the Names and finally abandon the People? Is this my final sell- out—not even for thirty pieces of silver, just eighteen pages in the presidential*

Book of the Conference? Well after the time for the reception to start, I convince myself I ought to go, if only to be Ambassador from Mars. So I set off, dressed as little like a banker as possible.

The reception is in another dark place. The room seems to shimmer with a gray mist. Through it I can make out Names in silvery suits, scores of them, and they are the same Names as twenty years ago, but somehow changed, paler and more lined. They all seem to know each other and are talking quietly but deter- minedly. Most of the women present are wearing another kind of costume, move deftly through the mist, and offer drugs to all who come. I am courteously intro- duced to the association's senior officers, inquire about its finances, am waltzed into a technical discussion of conference fund-raising behind the cheese plate. The mist thickens, the voices rise. My panic threshold is reached and I shake hands and run for it.

## Boardrooms

The paper did appear in the Book of the Conference.[17] I admired the president then, and admire him still. Not all of the people at the reception were Names; not all of them were men. Most of the academic women did, however, wear suits, in semiotic opposition to the maids.

Months after that reception, I sat in an elegant room in another American city at a lunchtime feminist seminar where a considerable weight of jewelry was present. Its main element was gold.

## Commentary

American sociology has declined in size, and perhaps in influence, since the 1970s;[18] but it remains the most wealthy and powerful body of soci- ologists in the world. My second conference experience was as clear on that point as the first. Sociology is better entrenched institutionally in the United States than in countries like Australia. And it is far more settled in its ways, fully equipped with origin myths, heroes, sacred sites, canonical texts, and ritual disputes. Feminist revolutionaries face a tougher proposi- tion here than in many other places.

The feminist presence at this annual meeting, then, registers a con- siderable success. Women are much more visible in the organization, every major publisher's booth has its women's studies list, and the conference agenda gives ample space to gender and sexual politics. Sociology here and now is a venue for women's experiences, for truths about sexuality and inequality, in a way it certainly was not a generation ago. Moreover, the success of American academic feminism becomes a resource in other countries. The cultural and economic power of the United States helps legitimate feminist work there; American feminism means literature, models, and sometimes direct personal support for feminism in other parts of the world.

Intellectual influence on the men in the metropole, however, is more elusive. In this respect the revolution is still missing. Most men attending the annual meeting do not come to the sessions on gender. Most theory sessions trundle down the old tracks. American sociology long ago found it could deflect critique by defining each criticism as a new specialty. This mechanism is clearly operating to contain feminism.

Perhaps, too, the seductions of power operate more intensely here in the imperial center than in a small university system in the colonies. As American feminism has won battles, accumulated resources, and pressed on into the academic establishment, it has begun to take on more of the coloration of the American ruling class. Beyond radical and liberal and socialist and cultural feminisms, we seem to be getting corporate feminism.

Listening to the gold jewelry, I realized I was now sitting square in the middle of the privilege that the labor movement had been formed to fight against. Twenty years ago I was demonstrating in the streets against this. Other people in that room had done the same. I do wonder about the meaning of the current turn of theory away from material inequalities and toward complexities of language, relativist epistemologies, and issues of identity, as the movement enters the house of power.

## Notes

1. Frank Moorhouse, *The Americans, Baby: A Discontinuous Narrative of Stories and Fragments* (Sydney: Angus and Robertson, 1972); Carolyn Kay Steedman, *Landscape for a Good Woman: A Story of Two Lives* (London: Virago, 1986); David Jackson, *Unmasking Masculinity: A Critical Autobiography* (London: Unwin Hyman, 1990).

2. Among my sources are "memory work," in June Crawford, Susan Kippax, Jenny Onyx, Una Gault, and Pam Benton, *Emotion and Gender: Constructing Meaning from Memory* (London: Sage, 1992); and prose techniques borrowed (with trepidation) from James Joyce and Patrick White.

3. The title of this section is, with a tip of the Akubra hat to Frank Moorhouse, *Conference-Ville* (Sydney: Angus & Robertson, 1976).

4. Dorothy E. Smith, *The Conceptual Practices of Power: A Feminist Sociology of Knowledge* (Boston: Northeastern University Press, 1990).

5. My access also involved class and ethnic privilege; I came from the Australian-born Anglophone professional bourgeoisie, had an elite education, and had enough money to launch the trip to the United States.

6. Madge Dawson, *Graduate and Married* (Sydney: Department of Adult Education, University of Sydney, 1965); Madge Dawson, ed., *Australian Families* (Australian and New Zealand Association for the Advancement of Science, 1975).

7. Perhaps her finest work was Jean I. Martin, *Refugee Settlers* (Canberra: Australian National University Press, 1965).

8. Robert W. Connell, "A Whole New World: Remaking Masculinity in the Context of the Environmental Movement," *Gender and Society* 4 (1990): 461.

9. Australian Schools Commission, *Girls, School, and Society* (Canberra: Schools Commission, 1975).

10. Gary Dowsett, "I'll Show You Mine, if You'll Show Me Yours: Gay Men, Masculinity Research, Men's Studies, and Sex," *Theory and Society* 22 (1993): 70.

11. For fuller discussion of this movement and its context in masculinity politics, see R. W. Connell, *Masculinities* (Berkeley and Los Angeles: University of California Press, 1995).

12. Pauline Johnson, *Feminism as Radical Humanism* (Sydney: Allen and Unwin, 1994).

13. R. W. Connell, *Gender and Power: Society, the Person, and Sexual Politics* (Stanford, Calif.: Stanford University Press, 1987).

14. Christine Griffen, review of *The Making of Masculinities, Changing Men,* and *Gender and Power, Feminist Review* 33 (1989): 103–105.

15. George Orwell, "In Front of Your Nose," in *Collected Essays: Journalism and Letters,* vol. 4 (Harmondsworth: Penguin, 1970), pp. 150–154. I am not implying that Orwell was any supporter of feminism! Quite the reverse was true.

16. Mario Mieli, *Homosexuality and Liberation: Elements of a Gay Critique* (London: Gay Men's Press, 1980).

17. R. W. Connell, "The Wrong Stuff: Reflections on the Place of Gender in American Sociology," and "Notes on American Sociology and American Power," in Herbert J. Gans, ed., *Sociology in America* (Newbury Park, Calif.: Sage, 1990), pp. 155–166, 265–271.

18. Enrollment statistics for undergraduate majors and Ph.D.s were compiled by the national office of the ASA.

*Desley Deacon*

# Brave New Sociology?
# Elsie Clews Parsons and Me

$\mathcal{D}$iana Trilling, in an extraordinary passage in her recent autobiography, writes of her childhood in New York in the early part of this century that "fear is the emotion I remember best." "I grew up in a fear culture," she goes on.

> Here are some of the things of which I and the grown-ups around me were afraid: lightning, thunder, wind, heavy snow, driving cars, driving in cars, horses, snakes, worms, germs, poisonous plants and berries, electrical appliances, gas and gas fixtures, fire, cows, bulls, all boats including rowboats, swamps, quicksand, flies, mosquitos, bees, Greek ice cream parlors, bats, mold, rust, gangrene, spiders, caterpillars, strange cats and dogs, mice, rats of course, canned goods, bad fish, damp, drafts, whooping cough, blood poisoning, influenza, infantile paralysis, ruptured appendices, syphilis, other people's towels or tubs or toilet seats (much the same as syphilis), subways, bananas, tomatoes, oranges, oysters, fruit pits, and medicine taken even once in excess of a prescription, any two medicines taken in conjunction, foods in unusual combination with other foods, deep water, undertow, waves, leeches, toads, eels, dyes, hospitals, insanity, imbecility, brain fever, pinkeye, ghosts and ghost stories, cemeteries, Saint Vitus' dance, the poorhouse, lockjaw, rabies, heredity, sunstroke, trains, gypsies, beggars, intermarriage, leprosy, lice, nits, pimples (related to syphilis), anything swallowed without sufficient chewing, ice water, the dark, burglars. I put last what was the most embracing of my fears: burglars. Burglars were anything that menaced me in the dark or when I was alone.

"Fear is at present out of fashion," Trilling goes on to observe; "it has been largely replaced by anxiety. I am constantly surprised by the fearlessness of people today, especially young women; they move about as if the world held no terrors for them." For Trilling, fear had a certitude about it: fear is "something specific which proposes, if not always reliably, the existence of a cure." But anxiety is "more diffuse and seldom offers a cure or escape." Anxiety is something to be managed, lived with, while fear leads only to negative action that keeps people in their place: "If I am afraid of deep water, I can stay on shore; if I am afraid of snakes, I can avoid the places where they are known to congregate."[1]

Alongside her bundle of fears, Trilling also felt an intense longing "for someone or something which could not be named, a transcendence, I suppose, of my capacity and experience."[2] Tragically, the tension between this longing to move beyond her circumscribed experience and her fear of the forbidden and dangerous led to the paralysis of agoraphobia for much of her young married life.

Trilling's list would not look very different from the things I was supposed to be frightened of as a child growing up in Australia in the 1950s. I would add some sexual fears: of washing my hair while menstruating, of not being popular with boys, of becoming pregnant out of wedlock, of being too thin (yes!), of being too clever; but Trilling's text suggests that these could well have been added to her list. I would also add some political ones: communism and Asia, with its falling dominoes. These barely hovered on the periphery of my secure childhood, but they manifested themselves in the adult community around me in a suspicion of anyone foreign, particularly the "Balts" (an all-encompassing term for the refugees from Eastern Europe who had to earn their right to live in the land of the free with two years' labor on the roads), the "Dagos" (the Italian immigrants we allowed the privilege of working in our new manufacturing industries), and even the "Poms" (British immigrants, who unfortunately had a propensity to "whinge" and want to return home).[3]

What the United States in 1910 and Australia in 1950 had in common was that they were self-satisfied, rule-bound societies, confident that they had found the key to prosperity and progress. The message they tried to pass on to the next generation was that you were safe as long as you stayed within the boundaries they set; but if you ventured into the deep water, into the places where the snakes congregated, or into the dark, or if you ventured out alone, you were in dangerous territory. At the same time, the United States of the 1910s and Australia of the 1950s were societies in the process of swift and dramatic social change, as evidenced by the presence of the Balts, Dagos, and Poms in my Australian childhood. In the United States, Trilling could sense the possibilities for new experience and new rules that these changes brought with them; but her childhood experiences and the new certainties of 1930s prevented her from exploring them. My own childhood in rural Australia gave me a sturdier sense of efficacy and a greater disdain for certainties that experience showed me were false. When snakes were swiftly dispatched by my mother and darkness and unlocked doors were my only experience of night and strangers, I could readily be skeptical of the other fears as well. I was also luckier than Trilling in my times. As a "clever" girl with only a minimal desire to conform to the old rules, I found the doors of newly expanded universities opening in front of me and employers newly anxious for educated workers competing for their first female employees. With little effort on my part, I became a pioneer— the first woman employed in my particular government agency, the first to be groomed for high-level policy work, the first to be married, the first to be nine months pregnant at the office, the first working mother.

Yet I found myself completely unprepared for the opportunities that opened up to me; and that world was completely unprepared for me. I was surrounded by competent women as a child and was by far the most able student at my small rural school. But there were invisible rules about how that competence could be applied that made no sense to me. These rules lay very lightly on me as a child. After all, in a school of seventy pupils it is hard to put two cricket teams together if you exclude the girls. When I first encountered the rules in their explicit, organized form at boarding school at the age of fourteen, I was incredulous; and I am still bitter at the totally inappropriate ideological training that school provided. Only my own sense that my "brains" gave me alternatives pushed me on to university, while all my friends got married or started to save for trips overseas, the Australian girl's standard prelude to "settling down."

I had no idea what to do with my university education. Books had been the only key to interpreting the social rules I found so curious, so I decided to study English; and a counselor suggested I do honors, an elite stream that involved a fourth year and a thesis. I did not know at that time that this was the all-important gateway to graduate work. I found English totally foolish. Its formalistic approach and its emphasis on disembodied creativity in no way satisfied my desire to understand social life, and it was not until I discovered sociology a decade later that I recognized what I had been looking for in those four sterile years. But I did well, even in politics, where my complete ignorance was rewarded with an *A*, while my politically active male friends gained *C*'s. (This made no difference for the men. One of these is now minister for education in the state government, and the other is a millionaire corporate lawyer.)

When I graduated, I was sought after by a number of prospective employers and chose to join a new training program for top-flight policy work in the federal civil service. Again, I had no idea of how to make use of this opportunity. Nor did the well-intentioned men who hired and were supposed to be training me. We all carried the baggage of stereotypes about what women should and should not do. This was accentuated by the absurd situation we were in institutionally. Under the laws that governed the civil service, married women could not be employed, and women who married had to resign. Like every woman of the mid-1960s, I was determined to get married. When I did marry a year after I was recruited, I continued as a "temporary" until I went overseas with my diplomat husband. The law changed while I was abroad, and my male colleagues, unfailingly affectionate and accommodating, always had a job ready for me when we returned from overseas postings; and they could not have been more supportive after my first son was born. But my "brilliant career" was never anything but a job, and I was never anything but a well-treated "pet." (Rosabeth Moss Kanter's *Men and Women of the Corporation* captures my experience brilliantly and is still one of my favorite pieces of feminist sociology.)[4]

I did not have a word for what I was in the 1960s. I thought of myself as unusual, deviant in some sort of commendable but uncomfortable way; my father thought me misguided; my husband's colleagues, in what must be one of the most intractable institutions of all—the diplomatic service— thought me uncooperative. We were abroad for much of the late 1960s and early 1970s, and I missed the formative bonding experiences of my generation: the movement opposing the Vietnam War and the enthusiasm for a New Left emancipatory Marxism/socialism that often went with it. I read Germaine Greer's *The Female Eunuch* in medieval Malta in 1971 with a shock of recognition; but I was totally unprepared for the change that had taken place in Australian society when I returned in 1973. It was as if the whole world had been taken over by people just like me. I was soon absorbed into the feminist movement and for the first time began to find a language to speak about my own experience. The pleasurable feeling of having comrades-in-arms was an important part of the exhilaration of that period. But feminism to me was always a movement to allow women to be different in whatever way they wanted to be, to jettison the old rules, and to rid ourselves and others of the old fears and stereotypes.[5]

It was during this exhilarating and unsettling period that I was introduced to sociology. We had returned from a short and very unhappy posting in Saigon, from which my two small sons and I were evacuated in April

1975 by air force *Hercules* aircraft. I was in despair about my life as a diplomatic wife, and my civil service "career" had finally fizzled out. I was hired for my knowledge of the local political-bureaucratic scene by an American sociologist at the Research School of Social Sciences at the Australian National University who was carrying out a major study of Australian elites. I loved sociology from the start. It dealt with the questions I had been asking all my life, and like feminism, it gave me a vocabulary that helped make sense of my experience. I rapidly absorbed the new feminist sociology, anthropology, and history.[6]

By the time *Elites in Australia* was finished, I had decided to go on to graduate school. In the Australian system, graduate students are expected to come adequately prepared by a first-class honor's degree to plunge straight into their dissertations. There are no graduate courses, and the candidate spends three years writing what is expected to be a major piece of work under the supervision of only one member of faculty. My coauthorship of *Elites in Australia* and two undergraduate classes in sociology were considered adequate preparation for this rite of passage. Luckily, I was appointed as tutor in the department at the same time, and I was able to complete my education in sociology on the job.[7]

This unconventional path to sociology meant that I was totally unsocialized into what was in Australia a new and very inchoate discipline divided between an abstracted empiricism imported from the United States and an indigenous New Left/feminist wing of whom Bob Connell was the undisputed leader. My dissertation was supervised by a male colleague and friend (there were no women in the department), who brought his considerable critical acumen to the task but knew nothing at all about my topic. My most important audience was my peers. Apart from my fellow (male) tutors, who were sympathetic and generally involved in New Left projects, this was an interdisciplinary network of young and enthusiastic feminist scholars on my own campus and around the country who rapidly came to know one another.[8]

I have always been grateful for the creative marginality this situation gave me. It allowed me to become a historian, as well as a sociologist, and to find a methodology and theoretical position that emerged from my own experience of the data. Two moments stand out from the learning process that was my dissertation. The first happened very early on and was decisive in determining the direction of my work. I was putting together some basic background material for what was to be a study of contemporary women in managerial work inspired by Rosabeth Kanter. Looking up the late-nineteenth-century occupational censuses to get a timeline, I began to notice anomalies. I read the footnotes to the tables and then the explanatory text. What I discovered was that New South Wales government statistician Timothy Coghlan had radically changed the definition of women's work in 1891 and revised the figures from previous censuses to match. Then a young "water walker"—to use Kanter's delightful phrase—Coghlan had gone on to write the standard economic history of the period, and his figures and his vision of women's place had become the received wisdom about women "never working" that had hovered over my early life and career. Curiously, this discovery led me back to that bizarre "marriage bar" that had blighted my early career, for Coghlan turned out to be the architect of that policy, which one of his cohort of Young Turks then brought into the federal civil service. These series of revelations about an innovating intellectual and his cohort crystallized my interest in the social construction of knowledge about gender and the role of state institutions in disseminating these ideologies. Above all, however, the story of Coghlan and his cohort focused my attention on the human agency, ambitions, and desires that constructed what were then usually referred to in monolithic terms as "the state" and "the new middle class."[9]

The second moment occurred much later in the project. I had already labeled Coghlan definitively as the sociological version of a male chauvinist pig when I came across a warmly worded letter from the leading feminist of the period thanking him for all the work he had done for women. When I got over my shock, I returned to the data and found a much more complex picture of his motivations and the gender order of the period than I had previously seen. This jolt to my own assumptions led me to the more nuanced and historically specific view of masculinity that the dissertation finally conveyed.[10]

I concluded this study of the gender order, the state, and the new middle class with a profound sense of the precariousness of the social order, its constant construction and reconstruction through the wills and desires of its members, its discontinuities, and its variability. In other words, I had found none of the predictability and certainty that my 1950s upbringing had tried to convince me of. I also came away with a fascination with biography, the life history of exemplary figures, such as Coghlan, who seem to embody the experiences and choices of a generation and in the process manage to invent the future.

*M*y dissertation was immediately accepted for publication when I finished it in 1986, and it was published in 1989 as *Managing Gender: The State, the New Middle Class, and Women Workers, 1830–1930*.

By this time, however, I had moved to the United States to marry the senior sociologist I had worked with in Australia, and I had discovered the limits of marginality. As an Australian teaching in an American studies program and a sociologist working among colleagues trained in the humanities, a foreign scholar finding her way in a new invisible college, and a mother, daughter, sister, and friend living an ocean away from family and longtime companions, I found myself longing for the first time for certainty and stability and anguishing over the discontinuities and disloyalties of my life. My "traitorous location" suddenly and unexpectedly became a burden to me that I have often wished desperately to rid myself of.[11]

My companion through these travails has been Elsie Clews Parsons. I first met Parsons on the cover of Rosalind Rosenberg's *Beyond Separate Spheres* in 1982. I was drawn to her image like iron filings to a magnet before I knew anything more about her. Her cool, level gaze; her exquisite dress, which I now know probably came from Worth; and—more than anything—the baby on her lap spoke to me across the gap of eighty years and many more geographical miles. I could see immediately that she was a pioneer of new gender arrangements because professional women at the turn of the century did not usually marry and have children. When I read Rosenberg's chapter on Parsons, I was pleased to find that she had been a sociologist, one of the first to get a Ph.D., from Columbia University in 1899; that she had taught at Columbia through two pregnancies; that she had been the mother of four children; and that she had become a very successful anthropologist and the first female president of the American Anthropological Association. At a time when I was launching myself as a sociologist, and was myself the mother of two young boys, I felt as if I had gained a new colleague. When my new trajectory took me to an American studies department in the United States as a feminist historical sociologist of knowledge, it was almost inevitable that I should write about her. Ever since I had discovered the pivotal role of Timothy Coghlan in my book on gender and the state, I had been interested in using biography to explore the exceptional person who is, as we so inadequately put it, "before his or her time." "No one is ahead of his time," Parsons's contemporary Gertrude Stein pointed out, "it is only that the particular variety of creating his time is the one that his contemporaries who also are creating their own time refuse to accept. . . . That is the reason why the creator of the new composition . . . is an outlaw until he is a classic." Biography allows the sociologist to see the outlaw in relation to her times; and I badly wanted to understand how an outlaw manages to persist in creating in the face of her contemporaries' refusals.[12]

As I became more involved in Parsons's life, I became aware of the emotional struggles that lay behind her successful career. As a sociologist of knowledge, I was particularly interested in the way those struggles forced her to think through and articulate the theoretical positions that under-pinned her intellectual and personal life. What interested me was how Parsons dealt with being a woman living in the shadow of the certainties—and fears—of the late nineteenth century. Eerily, her battles seemed to echo my own belated reckoning with my legacy of the 1950s. And what heartened me was the serenity with which she persisted, once she had worked through her anguish, in a life deliberately based on uncertainty. In a period of intense personal and professional soul-searching, she became my companion and guide.

*E*lsie Clews Parsons was born into a wealthy New York family in 1874, the same year as Gertrude Stein, whose life history paralleled Parsons's in important ways. Her generation were the first modern Americans, irrevocably cut off from the past by the trauma of the Civil War, by the massive transformation of the nation through the processes of industrialization, urbanization, and immigration, and by the Darwinian intellectual revolution. Her family shared the self-satisfactions and fears of the late-nineteenth-century bourgeoisie, but the family's roots in tradition were shallow, and Parsons escaped a thorough socialization into their culture. The radically modified women's college in the form of Barnard College, with its close association with Columbia University, and the professionalizing cultures of the research university and the settlement house provided alternative models for Parsons, which she eagerly took up. Although she faced resistance from her family and her future husband, her early career from B.A. to M.A. to Ph.D. in the new disciplines of sociology and education and her activities in the settlement house movement were the confident moves of a young modern little troubled by the past. Even when she married in 1900, after much hesitation, and continued her teaching career at Barnard and Columbia and her settlement work through two pregnancies, she saw herself as an inventor of the future, consciously demonstrating what a modern marriage could be. The confident photograph that had drawn me to her initially was taken during this period.[13]

Parsons began to feel the social weight of the past seriously for the first time in 1906. Her husband, Herbert, had been elected to Congress at the end of 1904, and Elsie had used their move to Washington to break her ties with the closely linked worlds of university-based sociology and the settlement house. She now envisaged a much more outspoken role for herself, where she would use journals of social comment and the conversation of Washington society as forums for the propagation of new ideas. In particular, she wanted to talk about sex.

Parsons's observations of tenement house life, her students' sociological fieldwork, and the hostility she and other working mothers encountered had convinced her that sexual mores were more resistant to innovation than any other area of social life. A series of tragic personal events during 1906 convinced her of the urgent need to find a new approach to sexuality. In April 1906 her third child died two weeks after birth. Six weeks later she was again pregnant, and, troubled and unwell, she struggled through a pregnancy that ended in the loss of a second baby in February 1907. Early in 1906, as she was recovering from the death of her baby, her beloved friend Stanford White was shot dead by the husband of a former lover, and ugly stories of his extramarital sexual activities were revealed to a salacious public. Then as the year unfolded, the marriage of her friend Katharine Dexter McCormick was revealed as a sexual tragedy of major proportions, which illustrated starkly the consequences of sexual repression and reticence.[14]

Parsons had immersed herself in the burgeoning comparative literature on the family and sexuality while teaching a course on the family from 1902 to 1904, and she was eager to apply the literature's new message of cultural relativity to problems of contemporary sexual life. In a series of articles during 1905 and 1906, Parsons argued for frank discussion and acceptance of the moral and physical aspects of sex relations, including pregnancy, divorce, prostitution, and birth control. She quite deliberately linked the issue of women's emancipation with the cause of free speech. "In primitive communities taboo is a far-reaching and most effectual instrument and preservative of group tradition," she pointed out. "In modern civilization there are not a few survivals of taboo in out of the way mental corners, but the taboo of direct reference is perhaps the sturdiest." "In no other class of subjects . . . is taboo on clear thinking so onerous . . . and failure to 'think thru' so practically disastrous, as in our sex morality," she argued. "There is an ethical, as well as intellectual, obligation in seeing things as they were and are before concluding what they ought to be." Defending herself against the accusation that no "decent" woman would publicly discuss such subjects, she argued that no one else could carry out the task of improving attitudes toward sexuality. "Men merely because they are men, live or are reputed to live too firmly encased in glass houses to lead in the stone-throwing." The unmarried, the divorced, the unhappily married, and the childless woman are also handicapped in such a discussion. As a privileged woman who was happily married with children, she had a duty, she pointed out in a dictum she followed throughout her life, to speak out and act in situations where other women would be more severely sanctioned, especially if, she added, they were familiar with the morals of other peoples or had directly observed different economic or cultural classes in their own society.[15]

Speaking out on sexuality and defending free speech were the province of anarchists and freethinkers, not of wives of congressmen. It is not surprising, therefore, that her book *The Family* (1906), which ended with a plea for trial marriage, regulation of births, and economic independence for women, all—I might add—in the cause of preserving monogamous marriage, was greeted in many quarters with horror. On the day of its publication, a leading newspaper declared that "no more radical declaration from the pen of an author relating to matrimony has been published." Over the next few weeks, Parsons's ethics were reviled in newspaper after newspaper as "the morality of the barnyard," "absurd," "pretentious," and "diabolical," and the book was condemned from New York pulpits during Thanksgiving Day services.[16]

*P*arsons was devastated by the tirade her book unleashed. For the first time she had come face to face with the fears and certainties that Trilling found so omnipresent in her childhood during this period, and she had discovered the limits of acceptable behavior. Worried by the possible effect of this publicity on Herbert's career, and weakened physically and mentally by the loss of the second baby in February 1907 and the termination of another pregnancy soon after, Parsons was effectively silenced. Over the next few years she struggled with the shadow of fear that hung over her life. This struggle against the safety of the conventional life manifested itself most forcefully and distressingly in her obsessive jealousy over Herbert's friendship with Lucy Wilson, the conventionally feminine wife of a Washington colleague, which began in 1909 as Elsie anxiously awaited the outcome of another pregnancy. One of the tenets of the "experimental" marriage she had embarked on with such misgivings was that she and Herbert should remain individuals, each with her or his own lives, interests, and friends. But she found that in practice she was unable to be detached about Herbert's admiration of another woman, especially when she realized that his admiration was based on that woman's eagerness to lose her own personality in his. "All her little conjugal ways pleased him," she wrote in a fictionalized account in 1913. "So did her conventionalities with him." What was more galling, perhaps, was her realization that Herbert merely tolerated, rather than approved and supported, those activities in which she most directly expressed her individuality. "Do you realize that apart from the family and the routine of life all my energy and a very large part of my interest have gone into writing which you have never shown the slightest interest in?" she wrote him in 1912. "That my first book you didn't read, my second, published anonymously (you being still in public office when it went to print) you didn't even know about and the one I am writing now and talking to every one but you about (for, as it is popular, I get help from all sides) you also ignore? Your indifference or even antagonism once certainly hurt my vanity, but now I have no vanity about writing. But now as always to have you absolutely out of so large a part of my life is cutting." "I suppose cowardice is my reason," Herbert replied, acknowledging the truth of her accusation. "I feared that there would be so many points on which we would not agree that life would run more smoothly if I did not cross them. I have tried to be tolerant in other ways & thought I had been, though I could not always smile at it."[17]

Parsons strenuously resisted the decline in physical, mental, and moral strength that threatened her during these six years of anguish. In 1907, wrestling with terrible "fear-thoughts" in the wake of her double defeat as a radical intellectual and a mother, she found particularly helpful William James's 1906 presidential address to the American Philosophical Association, "The Energies of Man." Drawing on the doctrine of action formulated by the young Italian pragmatist Giovanni Papini, James examined the problem of habit-neurosis that inhibited the full development of mental and physical resources. "The human individual lives usually far within his limits; he possesses powers of various sorts which he habitually fails to use. He energizes below his maximum, and he behaves below his optimum," James pointed out. "In elementary faculty, in coordination, in power of inhibition and control, in every conceivable way, his life is contracted like the field of vision of an hysteric subject—but with less excuse, for the poor hysteric is diseased, while in the rest of us it is only an inveterate *habit*— the habit of inferiority to our full self—that is bad." But the vicious cycle of "psychasthenia" can be broken, he argued, by means of excitements, ideas, and efforts, which can be used to break down "the barriers which life's routine [has] concreted round the deeper strata of the will," "gradually bringing its unused energies into action."[18]

Parsons read James's address soon after the death of her baby. During this stressful period, she took his advice to heart and made every effort to use her rage and despair as a stimulus to action. She had always found physical outdoor activity liberating mentally and socially. Over the next few years she increasingly turned to strenuous trips as a means of shaking off her depression. At first she tried to interest Herbert in the sort of travel she craved, but he had little inclination for such jaunts, and the few they took together were not successful. In 1910, after a year in which Herbert's friendship with Lucy Wilson had strengthened and Herbert Jr., her third living child, was born, Parsons found the perfect companion in George Young, a secretary at the British Embassy in Washington. An authority on Turkish law who had traveled by horseback all over the Middle East, George Young came from an aristocratic family who shared a "brilliant contrariety" and a love of physical adventure. Young taught Parsons the delights of pushing herself to the limit, canoeing and walking in wild unknown country.[19]

With renewed faith in her own mental and physical strength, Parsons made a trip to the American Southwest that was to be a turning point in her life. With a new sense of purpose, she began to prepare herself for a career in anthropology. In a notebook labeled "American Ethnology SW," the page marked "Plans" included a list of things she had to learn. Along with Spanish, cooking (which she tried but never managed), cross-saddle riding, and masonry, she noted, "Practice with pistol, with compass." Throughout the following year she read voraciously about the Southwest, established contact with the anthropological museums in Washington and New York, rode, canoed, and camped with Young, despite the pregnancy that ended with the birth of her youngest son in September 1911.[20]

Parsons's sense of purpose and efficacy was strengthened by the new movement among women that was beginning to be called "feminism." This movement distinguished itself from the nineteenth-century "woman movement" by its emphasis on individual self-development and action; its focus on psychology and sexuality; its outspoken, "unladylike" stance; and its determination to make allies of sympathetic men. Parsons and her friends Katharine Dexter McCormick and Alice Duer Miller immediately recognized themselves as "feminists." By the time she returned to New York at the end of 1911, after Herbert had lost his congressional seat, Parsons found she had a readymade network of "restless" women like herself and an enthusiastic audience—both men and women—for her views. In the feminist group Heterodoxy, she and Alice Duer Miller joined a group of unorthodox women whose friendships survived until their deaths. And in Greenwich Village and in the numerous discussion groups and little magazines that sprang up eagerly to debate the new sexuality, the new family, and the new ethics, her terse, witty iconoclasm was quickly in demand. The confidence she gained from this sense of support helped Parsons to bring her simmering jealousy of Lucy Wilson out into the open and precipitate a crisis in her relationship with Herbert. In a long and frank discussion during the 1912 summer, Herbert confessed that her "new ways" puzzled him and that he had begun to realize that "travel, things new & unconventional are necessary for your enjoyment." For her part, Parsons admitted that he was unable to share her "new experiences, my new ideas, and feelings, my fresh impressions of persons and places." "My trips and my occasional flirtations . . . keep me from making uninstitutional demands on you which you wont or cant meet," she wrote him depairingly. In a fictionalized account, Parsons spoke of this period as marking the end of her love for Herbert. She continued to suffer jealousy until Lucy faded from the picture sometime in 1916 (interestingly enough, after Lucy divorced her husband) and always retained a strong affection for Herbert; but over the next few years she deliberately diffused her emotional life among her work, her children, and her friends, some of whom became lovers. Her fieldwork became particularly important to this process of emotional diffusion. It is significant, I think, that she finally found "her" place for intensive ethnographic work at Zuni, New Mexico, during the period when Herbert was in Reno with Lucy Wilson in his capacity as her divorce lawyer.[21]

*P*arsons's re-creation of herself as an anthropological fieldworker was not just a retreat from painful personal problems. Anthropology gave her the ideological and structural reinforcement she needed to successfully challenge orthodoxy and habit. Her foray into fieldwork in the Southwest brought her into contact with a group of young anthropologists based in the American Museum of Natural History and Columbia University. Over the next few years these young men, Robert Lowie, Alexander Goldenweiser, and Pliny Goddard, became her close friends and colleagues, welcoming her as a kindred spirit into the discipline they were reconstructing.[22]

The weapon that Parsons's new friends and colleagues used in their critical project was positivism—not the system-building positivism of Auguste Comte or Herbert Spencer, but what Robert Lowie called the "chaste" positivism of Ernst Mach. Mach was an Austrian physicist and historian of science, born in 1838, whose work had an enormous impact on turn-of-the-century scientific and artistic practice. "Physics is not a church," Mach argued; and he insisted that even the most useful theoretical system, such as Newtonian mechanics, must be continually challenged and historicized. Mach used historical inquiries and studies of perception to question the bases of knowledge claims and to critique accepted scientific concepts. He rejected metaphysical speculation and theorizing—

demonstrating what postmodernists call an "incredulity toward metanarratives"—and reminded scientists that all knowledge was based on experience. For Mach, knowledge was a provisional processing of experience for the purposes of survival. All we can know is given through our sensations, he argued. All our ideas—including those of space, time, body, and ego— are personal cuts into the chaos of sensations according to current need, to be discarded in the face of new experiences and new needs. For Mach, theories are "like withered leaves, which drop off after having enabled the organism of science to breathe for a time." The metanarratives implicit in words, concepts, classifications, and theories are therefore temporarily useful fictions that must be discarded before they became impediments to adaptation to new conditions.[23]

Mach's insistence on tearing down current systems was highly attractive to the modernist avant-garde, to revolutionary political groups, to innovative intellectuals, and to the women and men who were beginning to call themselves "feminists." In emphasizing experience as the only legitimate source of knowledge, Mach's critical positivism eliminated the weight of history and validated the idea of starting over—the idea of the "new" that was the basis of modernism. It also validated the search for experience itself, as a way of seeking a wider basis for formulating useful knowledge, thereby underpinning the restlessness and continuing search for the new that characterized the modern. The emphasis in Mach's positivism on the provisional character of all knowledge initiated a wholesale critique of language and conceptual, classificatory, and theoretical systems. It brought the body back in as an important factor in the constitution of knowledge: if all we can know comes through the sensations, the body obviously cannot be ignored. And it treated the ego as but one among many useful fictions subject to reconceptualization. "The Ego cannot be saved," Mach wrote in 1886.[24]

Mach's lucid and engaging work electrified the generation that came to adulthood at the turn of the twentieth century. Albert Einstein acknowledged the profound influence of Mach's critique of Newtonian concepts on the development of his Special Theory of Relativity in 1905. The young Polish scholar Branislaw Malinowski and the promising Austrian novelist Robert Musil both wrote their doctoral dissertations on Mach. And in Russia, Machism was such a serious rival to Marxism that Lenin was impelled to devote his *Materialism and Empirio-Criticism* to challenging it in 1909.[25]

*M*ach's impact was particularly strong in the United States, where he saw William James's pragmatism as "the coming frontier" of a critical positivism that would "wash metaphysics out of philosophy." One of Elsie Clews Parsons's new friends, Alexander Goldenweiser, had discovered Mach's work as a student of James's at Harvard in 1902. When Goldenweiser joined the graduate program in anthropology at Columbia, he and fellow students Robert Lowie, Paul Radin, and Morris Cohen formed a reading group in which they read the leading new positivists, Karl Pearson, Ernst Mach, Henri Poincare, and Wilhelm Ostwald—seeking, like others of their generation, for a new worldview better suited to their rapidly changing circumstances.[26]

As Jewish immigrants with backgrounds in the European intelligentsia, Goldenweiser, Lowie, Cohen, and Radin could be characterized as secure outsiders, a status that allowed them to be critical of established intellectual thought and able to tolerate the uncertainties implicit in Mach's approach to knowledge. When Parsons met Lowie and Goldenweiser in 1910, they were embarked, under Mach's inspiration, on a wholesale critique of the central concepts and theoretical systems of nineteenth-century ethnology. As Lowie put it in a call to arms in 1914:

> Like the generation of thinkers that preceded ours, we are living in an age of revolt, but the object of our revolt is different from theirs. Our predecessors fought tradition as arrayed against reason. We have the task of exorcising the ghosts of tradition raised in the name of reason herself. There is not only a folklore of popular belief, but also a folklore of philosophical and scientific system-mongers. Our present duty is to separate scientific fact from its envelope of scientific folklore.[27]

Parsons had much in common with these young Jewish intellectuals. An outsider by virtue of her gender and radicalism, and secure by virtue of her wealth and social position, she found their deconstructive project highly sympathetic. Through them she found a supportive group of colleagues and friends, who later included Franz Boas and the three women she helped move from their secretarial positions in Boas's office into fieldwork and professional anthropology, Gladys Reichard, Ruth Bunzel, and Esther Goldfrank.[28]

Through Lowie and Goldenweiser, Parsons also found in Mach's ideas a crystallization of her own attempts to overcome fear and to fashion a more complex and flexible approach to life and work. Over the next few years she used Mach's ideas as the basis of her critique of the situation of women and as the charter for the new way of life she created for herself. Between 1912 and 1917, at the same time as she established herself as an anthropologist, Parsons set out her critique in a series of popular books, articles, and unpublished manuscripts that could be considered as manifestos for the new feminism. Drawing on a variety of ethnographic material, assembled with a cool irony, she mocked the past, celebrated the speed of change, and looked forward to what she called "An Unconventional Society"—a future society that science would help bring about by undermining the influence of "the Elders." Along with Gertrude Stein, who was experimenting with an entirely new use of language, Parsons set out to "kill what was not dead, the nineteenth century which was so sure of evolution and prayers, and esperanto and their ideas."[29]

Although her focus is always on women, or rather on the relationships between women and men, Parsons's critique is embedded in a general conception of social freedom in which people are no longer swallowed up by safe identities defined by age, sex, class, married status, or nationality. Just as Mach had freed modern physics from outmoded and unnecessary concepts and categories, Parsons's project was no less than to free people from the imprisonment of social categories. Human beings have a passion for classification, she argued in *Social Freedom* in 1915, and a fear of anomalies—in other words, a fear of those people who are unclassified or unclassifiable. The social categories are obsessive and imperial, she wrote, spreading over the irrelevant. "The modern Chinaman, however feminist he may be, cannot avoid referring to darkness or cold or the evil side of the world by the same word he uses for woman. Nor can he write the ideograph for wrangling or intrigue without using the character for woman." Not only are the classifications imperial; they also arrest innovative thought. "The classification once made is still binding," she pointed out, "more binding than the bandages [the feminist Chinaman] is now removing from the feet of his daughters."[30]

The urge to classify, the fear of social change, and social control are closely interrelated, Parsons argued in *Social Rule* in 1916. "The social categories are an unparalleled means of gratifying the will to power. . . . The classified individual may be held in subjection in ways the unclassified escapes." In particular, classification by sex maintains the segregation of the sexes, preventing women from encroaching on men's territory. With the ironic use of ethnographic materials typical of her style, Parsons pointed out that "in certain New Guinea tribes during times of religious excitement the village is deserted by the women; they have to take to the woods. With us it is the woods, sometimes men say, which are no place for women." "The streets of Seoul were once taboo to women by day," she observed drily; "there are streets of New York once taboo to them at night."[31]

Given the power of classification, Parsons argued, feminism's main objective is "the declassification of women as women, the recognition of women as human beings or personalities." "The more thoroughly a woman is classified the more easily is she controlled," she pointed out. "The *new woman*" therefore "means the woman not yet classified, perhaps not classifiable." This unclassified, unclassifiable woman is new not only to men but also to herself. For women were, from Parsons's observations of her own social milieu, more conventional than men. Parsons had a deadly eye for the conventionalities of daily life that women maintained to uphold the distinctions between the sexes, and she delighted in turning Lucien Lévy-Bruhl's concept of "primitive thinking" on its head by demonstrating the "magical" and "sentimental" basis of the thinking of society women. She was especially scornful of what she called the "antifeminist suffragist." Drawing on her own acquaintances who were strenuously involved in the campaign for the vote in New York State, she defined the antifeminist suffragist as "she—or he—who sees in enfranchisement an expression for sex, not an expression for personality." "Is not every attitude of the anti-suffragist taken in the assumption that politics is a function of sex, a kind of secondary sex function?" she asks. The suffragist who argues for the vote on the basis of the difference women would make as women is no different from the antisuffragist. What is more, suffragists who do not rebel against the conventionalities of daily life undermine whatever political gains they may make. "Anxious beyond measure for the vote," she wrote, "such a woman remains wholly unperturbed by the constraints of her daily life." "Is not chaperonage a more important question for women than suffrage?" she asked.[32]

       *B*asic to Parsons's feminism was the notion of experience as the source of knowledge, adaptability, and power. The female traveler and the female stranger epitomize for Parsons the modern, independent woman. As Parsons pointed out in 1914, in terms reminiscent of Trilling's "burglars": "In no culture have women shown desire to do anything which requires running the risks of being alone. Women hermits are extremely scarce, there are few women explorers, there are no women vagabonds. . . . Rarely indeed do women go off by themselves—into the corner of a ballroom, into the wilderness, to the play, to the sacred high places of the earth, or to the Islands of the Blessed. Penelope stays at home."[33]

Feminism, for Parsons, is therefore an "adventure" involving the crossing of boundaries and the challenging of classifications. In the ideal "Unconventional Society" that she set up at the end of *Fear and Conventionality* (1914), Parsons placed the principle of fearless and unrestricted travel at the center of her vision. "The viability of the world will be taken advantage of," she predicted. "The habit of living in lairs will die out and . . . we shall live at large, going where it is best for us to be, unperturbed by novel experience and not safeguarded against it."[34]

For Parsons, one of the most important outcomes of the lifting of the social categories was the possibility of substituting "personality" for a more rigidly defined "ego." "The ego must be given up," Mach had argued. The ego should be a makeshift, designed for provisional orientation and for definite practical ends; but it more often took on a fixed quality that was "insufficient, obstructive, and untenable." Mach's view of the ego as a theoretical construction, like the category "woman," opened the way for Parsons's view of the "personality." A personality did not have any preconceived characteristics or consistency. Instead, it was a heterogeneous bundle formed by the spontaneous reaction of its various facets to their environment. In conditions of social freedom, men and women would have a wider scope in their expressions of self, and these different expressions would be more frankly expressed in their relationships. "The day will come," Parsons wrote in her unpublished "Journal of a Feminist, 1913–1914,"

> when the individual . . . [will not] have to pretend to be possessed of a given quota of femaleness or maleness. . . . This morning perhaps I feel like a male; let me act like one. This afternoon I may feel like a female; let me act like one. At midday or at midnight I may feel sexless; let me therefore act sexlessly. . . . It is such a confounded bore to have to act one part endlessly. Men do not resent being treated always as men because, in the first place, of the prestige of being a man and because, in the second place, they are not treated always as men. And yet men too may rebel some time against the attribute of maleness. . . . The taboo on a man acting like a woman has ever been stronger than the taboo on a woman acting like a man. Men who question it are ridiculed as effeminate or damned as perverts. But I know men who are neither "effeminate" nor perverts who feel the woman nature in them and are more or less tried by having to suppress it. [Some day, she concluded,] there may be a "masculinism" movement to allow men to act "like women."[35]

Parsons saw sexual relationships as particularly bound by conventions, and she looked forward to greater frankness, sincerity, and privacy between the sexes under conditions of social freedom. "Between a relationship all sex as in the ante-feminist past and the entirely sexless relationship of the Professional Feminist . . . I don't see much to choose from," she wrote in "Privacy in Love Affairs" in 1915. "Why keep sex so tagged and dock-eted? So shunted off from human relations? Sex is a part of every personal-ity, and into any personal relations between a man and a woman it naturally enters—more or less. Whether more or less is to be decided for itself in each case, otherwise a relationship is not private at all, it's impersonal, a status relationship, a relationship of the old order."[36]

The greatest opportunity for the expression of personality, according to Parsons, was between friends because friendship is "so regardless of con-ventions, so heedless of status." Friendship cuts through social barriers and insists on a highly personal interaction, it is nourished by difference, and it does not expect unbroken companionship. Because of all this, friendship is more imaginative, alert, spontaneous, and joyful than other relationships. Marriage, in contrast, tends to obliterate all expression of personality. In a chapter of *The Old-Fashioned Woman* (1913) mordantly titled "One," Par-sons documented ideas of conjugal identity across cultures. And in an ar-ticle in the *New Republic* in 1916, she asked the question "Must We Have Her?" arguing that "a husband or a wife is a personal taste" that should not be forced on others. She made a plea, therefore, for separate invitations as part of "a new, less institutional, more personal form of intercourse." "The separate invitation," she argued, "would contribute . . . somewhat like the separate dressing room or the separate bank account, to the establishment of personal decency and dignity."[37]

$f$or Parsons, then, the most important role for sci-ence in bringing about an "Unconventional Society" is by clarifying con-cepts and questioning classifications. In this new society, "differences in others will no longer be recognized as troublesome. . . . Nor will presump-tions of superiority or inferiority attach to differences *per se*. Exclusiveness will cease to be a source of prestige. Blind efforts to produce types . . . will be condemned. Intolerance will be a crime. . . . Variation will be wel-come. . . . Complete freedom of personal contacts will be sought. [And] the play of personality upon personality will become the recognized *raison d'etre* of society instead of the greatest of its apprehensions."[38]

Parsons's feminist project in her writing from 1912 to 1917 was to free the concept of the self from the prison of categorization. Judith Ryan has demonstrated in *The Vanishing Subject* that the fragmentation of the self was a major preoccupation of modernist writers under the influence of Mach and William James. Interestingly, it is the women Ryan discusses—Gertrude Stein and Virginia Woolf—who were the most accepting of "the world without a self." For Woolf, release from the "damned egotistical self" is a liberation that allows the development of a fluid subjectivity that is better able to challenge patriarchy.[39]

Parsons's life was, from 1910, a deliberate attempt to create a life without a self, to reconstruct her own life as a new woman who was unclassified and unclassifiable. She deliberately cultivated an adventurous life physically, intellectually, and emotionally; a wide range of experience; and a variety of unfamiliar situations that forced her to interact in spontaneous, rather than conventional, ways. Anthropological fieldwork provided her with the ideal vehicle for the sort of multifaceted self she wanted to create. After 1911, when her sixth and last child was born, she spent at least part of each year in the field, beginning with work in the American Southwest that culminated in the monumental *Pueblo Indian Religion* (1939); moving on to Mexico in the 1930s (*Mitla*, 1936); and reaching, just before her death in 1941, to Ecuador (*Peguche*, 1945).[40] Interspersed with these field trips were folklore-collecting expeditions close to home along the Atlantic coast while her children were young and later sweeping through the West Indies, Egypt and the Sudan, and Spain and Majorca. These trips were deliberately both physically and mentally challenging. And they always combined work and play. Her fieldwork and her wealth allowed Parsons to divide her life among several homes—winter in New York; summer in Newport, Lenox, or Maine or somewhere in the field. And she cultivated a wide variety of relationships—as wife, mother, lover, colleague, stranger, and friend—allowing none of them to dominate or interfere with the other.[41]

Parsons's practical experiment in destroying the concept of "woman," and with it the idea of the unified self, was a difficult one that met with considerable opposition, first of all from her husband, and later from her lover Robert Herrick, who analyzed their relationship negatively in his 1932 novel *The End of Desire*. However, she found an understanding and supportive group for her project among her anthropological colleagues. Although they teased her about her "dual nature," pursuing social "propaganda" in the winter and anthropological research in the summer, they found in her "propaganda" an expression of their own vision—a vision that had to be excluded from the dry factual reportage of their "scientific" work. Franz Boas acknowledged the similarities of their projects when he inscribed his photograph to her in 1936: "To Elsie Clews Parsons, fellow in the struggle for freedom from prejudice."[42]

Perry Anderson has suggested that modernism flowered in the space between the still usable classical past, a still indeterminate technical present, and a still unpredictable future. Mach's critical positivism captured exactly the uncertainties and possibilities of this space; and it is here that Parsons's pragmatic feminism emerged, grasping the fragility and indeterminacy of the self and turning this into a source of emancipation. For Parsons, Mach's dissolving self was an important resource through which she could reconstruct her life as a form of permanent revolution, forever escaping definition and imprisonment by the expectations of others. And the members of her anthropological reference group, who understood and shared her project, provided the supportive environment that helped her sustain it.[43]

*I*n her presidential address to the American Anthropological Association in December 1941, which, tragically, was read by her friend Gladys Reichard after her sudden death two weeks before, Parsons characteristically made an excursion into the "borderland" between anthropology and social philosophy. In her usual challenging manner, she tackled the question of current demands on social scientists for prediction by pointing out its basis in fear of uncertainty. "Delphic or Inca oracles, geomancy, astrology, scapulamancy, throwing seeds, bones, shells, cards, or apple peels, palmistry, more politely called chiromancy, games of chance played to a system, dream lore, weather signs, omens and auguries of an infinite variety, pyramidology, Bible prophecy, *all* ideologies and practices concerned with life after death—the urge to know what is going to happen penetrates and colors culture deeply and variously," she points out. "Uncertainty is painful, the hardest of all things to bear, a panic breeder, which may be why concepts of faith and preordainment develop, why both science and divine revelation are popular, and why statesmen, particularly in wartime, give so many assurances of what is, or is not, going to happen next year or a thousand years hence." Refusing to submit to panic, Parsons had devoted herself to what could be called a sociology of uncertainty: what she herself, in her presidential address to the American Folklore Society in 1919, called "The Study of Variants." Too much social science expressed, in her opinion, "group will-to-power, the desire to have people like yourself or to have them amenable to immediate group ends." If we want cultural inventiveness and experiment, tolerance for group differences, and appreciation of their value, she pointed out, we have to understand why certain cultural variations or inventions "take" and others do not; and to do this we have to pay as much attention to differentiation as to similarities.[44]

In her lifelong study of cultural variants, Parsons relied heavily on folklore and ceremonial as windows into what she called "the mental processes in the culture." But she turned increasingly to biography as a means of seeing a culture from the inside and understanding its variability. In "The Imaginary Mistress," written in 1913 during her period of personal anguish, she turned her ethnographic gaze inward onto her own obsessions and fears. In her anthropological work she continually experimented with ways of incorporating accounts of the lived experience of the people she was interacting with into her more "objective" descriptions of ceremonial. From the beginning she conveyed a sense of the contested nature of the "reality" she was reporting through footnotes detailing the different points of view of her various informants. By 1920 she was incorporating a section on "Town Gossip" in her Pueblo studies; in it she drew sharply observed portraits of community members in the process of constructing and reconstructing that "reality." In *Peguche,* the study of an Ecuadoran Indian town she was engaged on at her death, Parsons vividly portrayed the changing culture of the town through the eyes of Rosita Lema, the young woman who was "the most enterprising person in all Peguche." Fittingly, Rosita's story was left unresolved at Parsons's death. Parsons was able to analyze the factors that helped Rosita to change, adapt to, and capitalize on new circumstances and those that kept her chained to old ways; but Parsons was not able to predict whether the outcome was going to be a triumph or a tragedy.[45]

Throughout her life Parsons wanted passionately to be "a carrier of culture, not its freight." With William James, she felt that the only certainty was that "man *engenders* truths" on a "malleable" world "waiting to receive its final touches at our hands." Convinced that "in our cognitive as well as in our active life we are creative," her sociology of uncertainty used biography to explore the processes of invention and innovation; and she saw biographies as human documents that allow us to extend our experience beyond the safe and the familiar. By forcing us out of the mold of our preconceptions, and opening us to new possibilities, biographies were, to her, one important means of inventing ourselves and creating the future.[46]

It was the willful sense of an invented self that attracted me to Parsons when I saw her photograph on the cover of Rosenberg's book fifteen years ago. That still resonates to me now. But what I have learned to appreciate through a close study of her life and work is the social responsibility of her constructive and fearless approach to the fragmented, discontinuous, and rapidly changing nature of modern life. As James pointed out, the pragmatic way adds "both to our dignity and our responsibility as thinkers" (and, Parsons would add, as livers of lives). Unlike the young Diana Trilling, whose life had grown, to borrow William James's words, "into one tissue of impossibilities," Parsons's anger and despair carried her "over the dam" of conscience and convention, allowing her to seek creative solutions to contemporary problems with an experimenting intelligence. Coolly and deliberately, but with a deep underlying passion, she used her life and work to engender on the world the truths she thought important. Parsons is obviously not me; nor am I a new version of the young Trilling. But Parsons has helped me over the dam by introducing me to a more self-consciously pragmatic approach to life and scholarly work that seems to suit my life-long role as stranger and exile. If novelist Michael Ondaatje is right that we live in an age of migrants, in which most of us are in a place we did not come from, Parsons has reminded me forcefully of the possibilities—and responsibilities—inherent in that role. Perhaps, with her help, I can help create "the new composition."[47]

## Notes

1. Diana Trilling, *The Beginning of the Journey: The Marriage of Diana and Lionel Trilling* (New York: Harcourt Brace, 1993), pp. 3–4.
2. Ibid., p. 4.
3. For the 1950s model of emphasized femininity, see Ann Game and Rosemary Pringle, "The Making of the Australian Family," *Intervention* 12 (1979): 63–83; Ann Game and Rosemary Pringle, "Sexuality and the Suburban Dream," *Australian and New Zealand Journal of Sociology* 15 (1979): 4–15; and R. W. Connell, *Gender and Power: Society, the Person, and Sexual Politics* (Stanford, Calif.: Stanford University Press, 1987), pp. 226–228
4. Rosabeth Moss Kanter, *Men and Women of the Corporation* (New York: Basic Books, 1977). Miles Franklin's *My Brilliant Career* (Sydney: Angus and Robertson, 1901), which Gillian Armstrong made into a well-known movie, is a classic account of a similar failed attempt at a career in turn-of-the-century Australia
5. Germaine Greer, *The Female Eunuch* (New York: McGraw-Hill, 1971).
6. Michelle Zimbalist Rosaldo and Louise Lamphere, eds., *Woman, Culture, and Society* (Stanford, Calif.: Stanford University Press, 1974), was the most important book in my induction into social science. I seriously considered going into anthropology, but my apprenticeship in sociology made it easier to continue in graduate work in that field.
7. John Higley, Desley Deacon, and Don Smart, *Elites in Australia* (London: Routledge and Kegan Paul, 1979).
8. These women continue to be an important part of my international "invisible college." R. W. Connell, *Ruling Class, Ruling Culture: Studies in Conflict, Power, and Hegemony in Australian Life* (Melbourne: Cambridge University Press, 1977), was the bible of the New Left intellectuals when I first began reading sociology. His extremely influential reinterpretation of Australian history, written with Terry Irving, *Class Structure in Australian History: Documents, Narrative, and Argument* (Melbourne: Longman Cheshire, 1980), and his *Which Way Is up? Essays on Sex, Class, and Culture* (Sydney: George Allen and Unwin, 1983), provided me with both a model and a target in my graduate work. An Australian dissertation is examined by three outside examiners who have had nothing to do with its preparation. Bob Connell was the chair and only sociologist on my examining committee. The other members were feminist social historian Marian Aveling (Quartly) and civil service historian Brian Dickey.

9. See Desley Deacon, "Political Arithmetic: The Nineteenth-century Australian Census and the Construction of the Dependent Woman," in Barbara Laslett, Sally Gregory Kohlstedt, Helen Longino, and Evelynn Hammonds, eds., *Gender and Scientific Authority* (Chicago: University of Chicago Press, 1996), pp. 103–123; and Desley Deacon, "State Formation, the New Middle Class, and the Dual Labor Market," in Gwen Moore and Glenna Spitze, eds., *Women and Politics: Activism, Attitudes, and Office-holding* (Greenwich, Conn.: JAI Press, 1985), pp. 247–266. These two articles won the Australasian Women and Politics Prize in 1983 and 1984.

10. However, Bob Connell was, justifiably, still not satisfied with my treatment of masculinity.

11. Desley Deacon, *Managing Gender: The State, the New Middle Class, and Women Workers, 1830–1930* (Melbourne: Oxford University Press, 1989).

12. See Desley Deacon, *Elsie Clews Parsons: Inventing Modern Life* (Chicago: University of Chicago Press, 1997); Rosalind Rosenberg, *Beyond Separate Spheres: Intellectual Roots of Modern Feminism* (New Haven, Conn.: Yale University Press, 1982); Gertrude Stein, *What Are Masterpieces* (Conference Press, 1940), p. 27, quoted in Bruce Kellner, Introduction to Bruce Kellner, ed., *A Gertrude Stein Companion: Content with the Example* (Westport, Conn.: Greenwood Press, 1988), p. 4. My other important companions have been the community of feminist scholars, who have read my work (even when it was about Australia), helped me get travel money and fellowships, asked me to write papers, and generally welcomed me and my biography.

When I began work on Parsons, her grand-nephew Peter H. Hare had recently published *A Woman's Quest for Science: Portrait of Anthropologist Elsie Clews Parsons* (Buffalo, N.Y.: Prometheus Books, 1985), based on Parsons's private papers, which he had deposited in the American Philosophical Society Library. For Parsons's life and work, see Barbara A. Babcock and Nancy J. Parezo, eds., *Daughters of the Desert: Women Anthropologists and the Native American Southwest, 1880–1980: An Illustrated Catalogue* (Albuquerque: University of New Mexico Press, 1988), pp. 14–19; Barbara A. Babcock, Introduction to Barbara A. Babcock, ed., *Pueblo Mothers and Children: Essays by Elsie Clews Parsons, 1915–1924* (Santa Fe: Ancient City Press, 1991), pp. 1–27; Barbara A. Babcock, Foreword to Elsie Clews Parsons, *Tewa Tales,* ed. Barbara A. Babcock (1926; Tucson: University of Arizona Press, 1994), pp. v–xix; Paul Boyer, "Elsie Clews Parsons," in Edward T. James, Janet Wilson James, and Paul S. Boyer, eds., *Notable American Women* (Cambridge, Mass.: Harvard University Press, 1971), pp. 20–23; Desley Deacon, "The Republic of the Spirit: Field Work in Elsie Clews Parsons's Turn to Anthropology," *Frontiers* 12 (1992): 13–38; Mary Jo Deegan, "Elsie Clews Parsons," in Mary Jo Deegan, ed., *Women in Sociology: A Bio-bibliographical Sourcebook* (New York: Greenwood Press, 1991), pp. 320–326; Judith Friedlander, "Elsie Clews Parsons," in Ute Gacs, Jerrie McIntyre, and Ruth Weinberg, eds., *Women Anthropologists: Selected Biographies* (Urbana: University of Illinois Press, 1989), pp. 282–290; Ramón Gutiérrez, Introduction to Elsie Clews Parsons, *Pueblo Indian Religion,* vol. 2 (1939; Lincoln: University of Nebraska Press, 1996), pp. v–xix; Louis A. Hieb, "Elsie Clews Parsons in the Southwest," in Nancy J. Parezo, ed., *Hidden Scholars: Women Anthropologists and the Native American Southwest* (Albuquerque: University of New Mexico Press, 1993), pp. 63–75; Barbara Keating, "Elsie Clews Parsons: Her Work and Influence in Sociology," *Journal of the History of Sociology* 1 (fall 1978): 1–10; Alfred L. Kroeber, "Elsie Clews Parsons,"

*American Anthropologist* 45 (1943): 252–255; Louise Lamphere, "Feminist Anthropology: The Legacy of Elsie Clews Parsons," *American Ethnologist* 16 (1989): 518–533; Nancy Oestreich Lurie, "Elsie Clews Parsons," in *International Encyclopedia of the Social Sciences,* ed. David L. Sills (New York: Macmillan, 1968); Morris Opler, "Elsie (Worthington) Clews Parsons," *New Encyclopaedia Britannica* (Chicago: University of Chicago Press, 1943–1973); Gladys Reichard, "Elsie Clews Parsons," *Journal of American Folklore* 56 (1943): 45–56; Leslie Spier, "Elsie Clews Parsons," *American Anthropologist* (AA) 45 (1943): 244–251; Pauline Turner Strong, Introduction to Elsie Clews Parsons, *Pueblo Indian Religion,* vol. 1 (1939; Lincoln: University of Nebraska Press, 1996), pp. v–xxvii; Leslie A. White, "Elsie Worthington Clews Parsons," *Dictionary of American Biography* (New York: Scribner, 1932–1964), pp. 581–582; Rosemary Levy Zumwalt, *Wealth and Rebellion: Elsie Clews Parsons, Anthropologist and Folklorist* (Urbana: University of Illinois Press, 1992).

The American Philosophical Society (APS), Philadelphia, Pennsylvania, holds two Parsons collections: (1) Ms. Coll. #29 contains the bulk of her personal correspondence, some professional correspondence, manuscripts, financial papers, and photographs; (2) 572/P25 contains professional correspondence, notebooks, and manuscripts. A third collection of personal and professional papers is held in the Parsons Family Papers at the Rye Historical Society, Rye, New York.

13. Elsie Worthington Clews, "On Certain Phases of Poor-relief in the City of New York" (A.M. thesis, Columbia University, 1897); Elsie Worthington Clews, *Educational Legislation and Administration of the Colonial Governments* (reprint, New York: Arno Press, 1971). For her students' fieldwork, see Elsie Worthington Clews, "Field Work in Teaching Sociology," *Educational Review* (September 1900). Elsie Clews married Herbert Parsons on September 1, 1900. Her daughter Lissa was born August 1901 and her son John, August 1903. For the Columbia milieu, see Robert W. Wallace, "The Institutionalization of a New Discipline: The Case of Sociology at Columbia University, 1891–1931" (Ph.D. diss., Columbia University, 1989). For women's colleges, see Helen Lefkowitz Horowitz, *Alma Mater: Design and Experience in the Women's Colleges from Their Nineteenth-century Beginnings to the 1930s* (New York: Knopf, 1984). For settlements, see Allen F. Davis, *Spearheads for Reform: The Social Settlements and the Progressive Movement, 1890–1914* (New Brunswick, N.J.: Rutgers University Press, 1984). For settlements and social science, see Mary Jo Deegan, *Jane Addams and the Men of the Chicago School, 1892–1918* (New Brunswick, N.J.: Transaction Books, 1988).

14. Katharine married Stanley McCormick, the youngest of the brothers who controlled the International Harvester Corporation in 1904. When Katharine was preparing to enter graduate school in 1906, Stanley began to display acute signs of mental instability. He was hospitalized and remained in confinement until his death in 1947. A sensitive man brought up by his puritanical mother never to touch his body, he was so troubled by masturbation that he had rigged up a harness to prevent his hands from touching his genitals while sleeping; and he had apparently been unable to consummate his marriage with Katharine. Katharine's direction and funding of scientific work in an attempt to find a cure for Stanley led to the development of the contraceptive pill sixty years later. See James Reed, "Katharine Dexter McCormick," in Barbara Sicherman et al., eds., *Notable American Women: The Modern Period* (Cambridge, Mass.: Harvard University Press, 1980), pp. 440–442; and Ellen Chesler,

*Woman of Valor: Margaret Sanger and the Birth Control Movement in America* (New York: Simon and Schuster, 1992), pp. 429–452.

15. Elsie Clews Parsons (ECP), "A Plan for Girls with Nothing to Do," *Charities* 13 (March 4, 1905): 545–549; "Girls with Nothing to Do: A Rejoinder from Mrs. Parsons," Letter to Editor, *Charities* 15 (October 28, 1906): 124–125; "Penalizing Marriage and Child-bearing," *Independent* 60 (January 18, 1906): 146–147; "Sex Morality and the Taboo of Direct Reference," *Independent* 61 (August 16, 1906): 391–392; "Little Essays in Lifting Taboo," unpublished manuscript, pp. 1–4, APS. In 1900 sex reformer Ida Craddock had committed suicide rather than face another prison sentence for the publication of her pamphlet "Wedding Night," and Moses Harman, editor of the anarchist *Lucifer, the Light-Bearer,* had been jailed in 1905 for his pamphlet "The Right to Be Born Well." For repression of discussion about sex, see Heywood Campbell Broun and Margaret Leech, *Anthony Comstock: Roundsman of the Lord* (London: Wishart , 1928).

16. ECP, *The Family: An Ethnographical and Historical Outline with Descriptive Notes, Planned as a Text-book for the Use of College Lecturers and of Directors of Home-reading Clubs* (New York: Putnam's Sons, 1906). See *New York Herald,* November 17, 18, 19, 1906; *Evening Sun,* November 17, 1906; *Sun,* November 18, 1906; *New York Daily Tribune,* November 18, 1906; and *World,* November 19, 1906.

17. ECP, "The Imaginary Mistress" (1913), unpublished manuscript; ECP to Herbert Parsons (HP), August 6, 1912; HP to ECP, August 7, 1912, APS.

18. William James, "The Energies of Man," *Philosophical Review* 16 (January 1907): 1–20, esp. 13, 17–19; ECP to HP, March 19, 1907, APS. For "fear-thoughts," see ECP to HP, June 25, 1907, APS.

19. See Deacon, "The Republic of the Spirit."

20. Notebook, "American Ethnology SW," APS.

21. ECP-HP corres., April 3–August 26, 1912, APS; ECP, "The Imaginary Mistress"; Deacon, "The Republic of the Spirit." See Judith Schwarz, *Radical Feminists of Heterodoxy: Greenwich Village, 1912–1940,* rev. ed. (Norwich, Vt.: New Victoria, 1986).

22. Paul Radin, "Robert H. Lowie. 1883–1957," *AA,* 60 (1958): 358–375; Robert H. Lowie, "Reflections on Goldenweiser's 'Recent Trends in American Anthropology,'" *AA* 43 (1941): 151–163; Alfred L. Kroeber, "Pliny Earle Goddard," *AA* 31 (1929): 1–8; William N. Fenton, "Sapir as Museologist," in William Cowan, Michael K. Foster, and Konrad Koerner, eds., *New Perspectives in Language, Culture, and Personality* (Philadelphia: Benjamins, 1986), pp. 215–240 (for Goldenweiser).

23. Ernst Mach, *The Science of Mechanics: A Critical and Historical Exposition of Its Principles* (1883; Chicago: Open Court, 1893); Robert H. Lowie, "Ernst Mach," *New Republic,* April 9, 1916, pp. 335–337; Jean-Francois Lyotard, *The Postmodern Condition: A Report on Knowledge* (Minneapolis: University of Minnesota Press, 1984), p. xxiv; Mach, quoted in Philipp Frank, "The Importance of Ernst Mach's Philosophy of Science for Our Times," in Robert S. Cohen and Raymond J. Seeger, eds., *Ernst Mach: Physicist and Philosopher* (Dordecht: Reidel, 1970), pp. 219–234; Robert S. Cohen, "Ernst Mach: Physics, Perception, and the Philosophy of Science," in Cohen and Seeger, eds., *Ernst Mach,* pp. 126–164, esp. pp. 128–129.

24. Ernst Mach, *Contributions to the Analysis of Sensations,* quoted in R. von Mises, "Ernst Mach and the Empiricist Conception of Science," in Cohen and Seeger, eds., *Ernst*

*Mach*, pp. 245–270, esp. p. 263. For feminism, see Nancy F. Cott, *The Grounding of Modern Feminism* (New Haven, Conn.: Yale University Press, 1987).

25. Ronald W. Clark, *Einstein: The Life and Times* (New York: World, 1971), pp. 37–39; Robert J. Thornton, "'Imagine Yourself Set Down. . . .': Mach, Frazer, Conrad, Malinowski, and the Role of Imagination in Ethnography," *Anthropology Today* 1 (October 1985): 7–14; Cohen, "Ernst Mach," esp. pp. 156–160. For a comparison of Mach, *The Science of Mechanics* and Mach, *Contributions to the Analysis of Sensations* with Friedrich Nietzsche, *The Will to Power* (London: Foulis, 1909), nos. 252, 289, 287, 291, see Frank, "The Importance of Ernst Mach," 232–233. For Mach's influence on literature, see Malcom Bradbury and James McFarlane, eds., *Modernism: A Guide to European Literature, 1890–1930* (New York: Penguin, 1991).

26. James gained an impression of "pure intellectual genius" when he had four hours of "unforgettable conversation" with Mach in 1882. Mach dedicated *Popular-wissenschaftliche Vorlesungen* (Popular scientific lectures), 4th ed. (1910) to James. See Erwin N. Hiebert, Introduction to Ernst Mach, *Knowledge and Error: Sketches on the Psychology of Enquiry* (Boston: Reidel, 1976), pp. xiii, xxvi, xxviii, xxix. For reading group, see "Letters from Ernst Mach to Robert H. Lowie," *Isis* 37 (1947): 65–68; Cora Du Bois, ed., *Lowie's Selected Papers in Anthropology* (Berkeley and Los Angeles: University of California Press, 1960); Robert H. Lowie, "Relations with Boas," Robert H. Lowie papers, Department of Anthropology, University of California at Berkeley; Robert H. Lowie, "An Ethnologist's Memories," *Freeman* 1, 2 (August 11, October 6, 1920): 517–518, 85–86; Robert H. Lowie, "Reminiscences of Anthropological Currents in America Half a Century Ago," *AA* 58 (1956): 955–1016; Robert H. Lowie, *Robert H. Lowie, Ethnologist: A Personal Record* (Berkeley and Los Angeles: University of California Press, 1959); Harry Hoijer, "Paul Radin, 1883–1959," *AA* 61 (1959): 839–843; and Morris Raphael Cohen, *A Dreamer's Journey: The Autobiography of Morris Raphael Cohen* (Boston: Beacon Press, 1949).

27. Robert H. Lowie, "Social Organization," *American Journal of Sociology* (AJS) 20 (July 1914): 68–97.

28. See Melville J. Herskovits, *Franz Boas: The Science of Man in the Making* (New York: Scribner's, 1953); and Theodora Kroeber, *Alfred Kroeber: A Personal Configuration* (Berkeley and Los Angeles: University of California Press, 1970). For Bunzel, Goldfrank, and Reichard, see Babcock and Parezo, *Daughters of the Desert*.

29. Gertrude Stein, *Wars I Have Seen* (New York: Random House, 1943), 21, quoted in John Malcolm Brinnin, *The Third Rose: Gertrude Stein and Her World* (New York: Addison-Wesley, 1987), p. 16; Lisa Ruddick, *Reading Gertrude Stein: Body, Text, Gnosis* (Ithaca, N.Y.: Cornell University Press, 1990). For ECP on the "Elders," see "Sex and the Elders," "A Warning to the Middle Aged," and "War and the Elders," *New Review* 3 (1915): 8–10, 62–63, and 191–192.

30. ECP, *Social Freedom: A Study of the Conflicts Between Social Classifications and Personality* (New York: Putnam's, 1915), p. 1.

31. ECP, *Social Rule: A Study of the Will to Power* (New York: Putnam's, 1916), p. 2; ECP, *Social Freedom*, p. 25.

32. ECP, *Social Rule*, pp. 54–55; ECP, "Feminism and Conventionality," *Annals of the American Academy of Political and Social Science* 56 (November 1914): 47–53, esp. 47–48; L. Lévy-Bruhl, *Les Fonctions mentales dans les sociétés inférieures* (How na-

tives think) (Paris: Félix Alcan, 1910). Herbert Parsons was a leader of the male supporters of female suffrage.

33. ECP, "Feminism and Conventionality," pp. 48–49. See also ECP, "The Supernatural Policing of Women," *Independent* 72 (February 8, 1912), pp. 307–310. For Mach's observation that physics was only experience arranged in economical order, see Raymond J. Seeger, "On Mach's Curiosity About Shockwaves," in Cohen and Seeger, eds., *Ernst Mach*, pp. 60–61.

34. ECP, *Fear and Conventionality* (1914; reprint, Chicago: University of Chicago Press, 1997), pp. 205–218, esp. p. 210. For fear of strangers as a contemporary psychosis, see ECP, "Avoidance," and "Teknonymy," *AJS* 19 (1914): 480–484, 649–650.

35. ECP, "Journal of a Feminist, 1913–1914," unpublished manuscript, p. 115, APS.

36. ECP, "Privacy in Love Affairs," *Masses* 6 (July 1915): 12. See also ECP, "Sincerity in Love Affairs," unpublished manuscript, [July 1915], APS.

37. ECP, "Friendship, a Social Category," *AJS* 21 (1915): 230–233; ECP, *The Old-fashioned Woman: Primitive Fancies About the Sex* (New York: Putnam, 1913); ECP, "Must We Have Her?" *New Republic* 7 (June 10, 1916): 145–146.

38. FCP, *Fear and Conventionality*, pp. 209–210.

39. Judith Ryan, *The Vanishing Subject: Early Psychology and Literary Modernism* (Chicago: University of Chicago Press, 1991), p. 226. Woolf attributed this "damned egotistical self" to James Joyce.

40. ECP, *Pueblo Indian Religion*; ECP, *Mitla, Town of Souls and Other Zapoteco-Speaking Pueblos of Oaxaca, Mexico* (Chicago: University of Chicago Press, 1936); ECP, *Peguche, Canton of Otavalo, Privince of Imbabura, Ecuador: A Study of Andean Indians* (Chicago: University of Chicago Press, 1945).

41. See Deacon, "The Republic of the Spirit."

42. Robert Herrick, *The End of Desire* (New York: Farrar and Rinehart, 1932). For Boas, see Zumwalt, *Wealth and Rebellion,* p. 122.

43. Perry Anderson, "Modernity and Revolution," in Lawrence Grossberg and Cary Nelson, eds., *Marxism and the Interpretation of Culture* (Urbana: University of Illinois Press, 1988), pp. 317–333, esp. p. 326.

44. ECP, "Anthropology and Prediction," *AA* 44 (July–September 1942): 337–344; ECP, "The Study of Variants," *Journal of American Folklore* 33 (April–June 1920): 87–90. ECP died unexpectedly on December 19, 1941, following a routine appendectomy. She had just returned from a field trip to Ecuador in apparent good health.

45. ECP, "The Study of Variants," p. 89; ECP, *Peguche,* p. 13.

46. ECP, "A Pacifist Patriot," review of *Untimely Papers,* by Randolph Bourne, *Dial* 68 (January–June 1920): 367–370, esp. 370; William James, "Pragmatism and Humanism," in *Pragmatism: A New Name for Some Old Ways of Thinking* (New York: Longmans, Green, 1907), reprinted in *William James: Writings, 1902–1910* (New York: Library of America, 1987), pp. 591–605, esp. p. 599.

47. James, "Pragmatism and Humanism," p. 599; James, "The Energies of Man," pp. 3–5; Michael Ondaatje, *The English Patient: A Novel* (New York: Knopf, 1992); Gertrude Stein, in Kellner, ed., *A Gertrude Stein Companion,* p. 4. For notions of stranger, outsider within, traitorous identity, fractured identity, and exile, see Patricia Hill Collins, *Black Feminist Thought: Knowledge, Consciousness, and the Politics of Empowerment* (New York: HarperCollins, 1991); Sandra Harding, *The Science Question in Feminism* (Ithaca, N.Y.: Cornell University Press, 1986); Sandra Harding, *Whose Sci-*

*ence? Whose Knowledge? Thinking from Women's Lives* (Ithaca, N.Y.: Cornell University Press, 1991); and Mary Lynn Broe and Angela Ingram, eds., *Women's Writing in Exile* (Chapel Hill: University of North Carolina Press, 1989). For the alternative notion of interpreter, see Zygmunt Bauman, *Legislators and Interpreters: On Modernity, Post-modernity, and Intellectuals* (Ithaca, N.Y.: Cornell University Press, 1987).

*Susan Krieger*

# Lesbian in Academe

*N*ot long ago, a graduate student called to interview me for a master's thesis on experiences of lesbian and gay sociologists. She was interested in the effects of being gay on their academic lives. Was prejudice an issue? What happened in their universities and over the course of a career? I agreed to do the interview, but I told no one about it, for I felt I ought not to speak with her. Although I do have relevant experiences as a lesbian, I have always felt these experiences are not supposed to matter. Being a lesbian is, internally, a source of strength to me, but I feel it is a private choice I have made with full knowledge that this choice must often be hidden. Although I know discrimination exists in academic settings, and that I have experienced it, it feels to me as if it violates a code to turn around and point this out. It violates the code of accepting the conditions of my chosen status, and I fear something awful will happen to me as a result—the homophobia, or discrimination, that affects me will get worse.

Such a fear of making things worse by calling attention to them probably accompanies any stigmatized minority status or sense of personal vulnerability. With homosexuality and, in particular, lesbianism, the secrecy aspect of the status stands out more than in some other cases, for it is assumed that homosexuality can be hidden, that an individual can pass (as straight), and often should, thus disappearing as gay. One consequence of passing is that in becoming invisible to the outside world, one often becomes invisible to oneself. Lesbianism adds to the invisibility, since lesbians are women, and women and their choices are often viewed as unimportant and so they are not seen. When I seek to identify experiences I have had as a lesbian that have affected my academic career, I often feel I am pointing to something not there, or to a factor that does not matter much, or that should not be pointed to anyway because it is too private.

Initially, when I thought about speaking with the interviewer, I was apprehensive because of the nature of the subject, although I was interested to speak about it. We scheduled a time to conduct the interview on the phone long-distance. When the interviewer called and our discussion began, I immediately became afraid, much as people I have interviewed have become afraid. I feared what would happen to me as a result of this research. Specifically, I feared having it known in the outside world that I was a lesbian, odd as that my sound, and worse, having it known that I had recently acted like one.

My fear was particularly acute at that moment because of an incident that had occurred the spring before when I had denied permission to a hostile male graduate student to take one of my courses. The class was a feminist research seminar. He was opposed to studying women. He felt wronged by me and took his case to university administrators and to the campus newspapers, which published stories sympathetic to him. Several months later, articles drawing from the story that appeared in the campus right-wing newspaper were published in a national newsmagazine and in a local city paper, disparaging me for denying permission to the male student.

At the time of the incident, several feminist faculty members had publicly criticized what I had done. The class to which I had denied the male student access suffered internally—many of the students were scared, and the process of learning was disrupted. Although I had thought the controversy would be over when the course ended, the next fall the campus ombudsperson called me into her office because two women graduate students who had been in my course—one of whom, I suspected, was a closet lesbian—needed to pursue the matter. They had spoken with the ombudsperson, not mentioning the incident of the male graduate student, saying only that they wished to complain about my approach to teaching. That winter, ten months after I had denied permission to that one man, my teaching contract was not renewed for an upcoming three-year term. The next spring, both of the courses I was teaching were affected when the students in them were unusually homophobic in their responses to me. Hard to prove as related to any of this, but disturbingly coincidental, just when the male student's story hit the campus papers, both my car and my lover's car began to be repeatedly stolen and vandalized in front of our house. "Anyone hate you?" asked the police officer who came out to investigate. "Give any student an 'F' recently?"

When I spoke with the interviewer on the phone, all these events were on my mind. Thus, I was afraid perhaps far more than the situation of a master's thesis warranted. I was sure that people would know it was me in the thesis the interviewer would write, or in an article based on it, or they would hear about me through researchers' gossip networks. They would know I had said no to a man, and they would expect the same, or worse, from me. I would be seen as a person who is unsafe to hire, as a betrayer of the trust that holds up the system. No one in the whole country, I felt, would ever hire me again if they knew.

I may have had an exaggerated expectation of adverse consequences from a master's thesis, but I did not, I think, have an exaggerated fear. There are consequences of saying no to men. The instance of my saying no to the male student had already unleashed a set of them for me. This incident became controversial, in large part, I felt, because it raised the specter of my being a lesbian—a separatist, a man-hater, not a male-aligned woman, a woman who risks being denied male privileges and who is, therefore, vulnerable. Even though I felt my lesbianism had affected what happened to me, it was difficult for me at the time of the controversy, and even after, to identify the consequences I experienced as related specifically to my being a lesbian. For example, during the more recent spring term, when I saw students in one of my classes avoid looking directly at me at times when I expected they would, or when they had trouble talking about the content of *The Mirror Dance,* my book on lesbians, I thought I was probably a bad teacher, or that I was feeling distant from the students, or maybe the students were right that there was not much provocative in my book to discuss. I did not think the students were afraid of me because I was a lesbian, or that this fear was related to the controversy of the year before when I had said no to the male graduate student.

The previous year, after I denied the male student permission, I had felt the silences that set in during class discussions, the fragmentation of morale, and the various oppositions to me, and I had thought, similarly, that I was not doing well as a teacher, or as a person, that the students had really different values than mine, or that they simply did not like me. I did not think, "I am a lesbian. I have said no to a man publicly. They are scared of me, of being like me, and of losing the support of men." When I heard the conservative women faculty members at the meeting in which my case was discussed asking, "What do you mean by woman-centered?" and "Why didn't you take care of this man?" I felt hurt, and I was not sure why they were picking on me. I knew I was a lesbian and they were straight, and that this made a difference, but exactly what difference was hard to determine when the challenges were so indirect.

Now I told the interviewer about my fears concerning this still troublesome incident and what might yet happen to me, and she agreed to substitute another example when she wrote her thesis and article, rather than saying what I had actually done. I felt cowardly requesting her to hide my situation, and I hoped such a change would not harm the truth. We next discussed the many more usual circumstances when it is not clear to me whether my being a lesbian is affecting responses I receive. When I see women secretaries and administrative staff in university offices looking at me, for instance, I always wonder, Am I attractive to them, or frightening? Do they see me as a woman, or a lesbian—a mannish woman? What difference is it to them? What about the male administrators who pass judgment on my hirings and interview me, do they see a woman who is a lesbian and, therefore, threatening to them? Do they assume that because I am a lesbian, I will not do their bidding, and, therefore, who needs me? What about male students—is it only a facade when they defer to me, or seem to like me? Do they fear that because I am a lesbian, I will not like them? What about other women faculty, whether friendly on the surface, or formal and distant—does my lesbianism scare them? No one speaks of these things. The women students, who am I to them? "Are you afraid of me because I am a lesbian?" I asked one woman student who kept challenging me in class this past spring. "No," she swore up and down, she was not. Some of her best friends were lesbians. That just could not be.

When I did not get my teaching contract renewed, the obvious reason was that the university was having a budget crisis and lecturers were easy to eliminate. It seemed to have nothing to do with my being a lesbian, maybe it had something to do with my being a woman, certainly nothing to do with my having said no to the male student the year before. Usually when my contracts are not renewed, they say it is because of the nontraditional nature of my work. When I am not hired, that is also the reason given. I have found it is very hard to put a finger on anything important that has ever been denied me as a sociologist and say, "This is because I am a lesbian." There always seem to be other, better reasons. The lesbian part of the picture always disappears, as it does, for instance, when gay people say, "We are just like you. We have families. We raise children. We want to be loved." Yet we are different, or else why the consequences? Why the choice to be a lesbian in the first place?

When our cars were repeatedly stolen and vandalized, the police finally decided it might be a hate crime, but the hate crime squad never came out to get the facts. The threat hung there, unsolved. This type of crime, we were told, was usually impossible to pin down. If my hostile male graduate student had any link to our cars being attacked, I concluded, I was not going to find out. I was not of the mind to send the cops after him. Why stir up the antagonism? The police, were they to question him, would probably find nothing to link this shy, ivory-tower, third-year graduate student to car thieves.

So I said to the woman interviewer, feeling very tense just then about my prospects for another job, thinking about the cars, and wondering about the ways I sometimes think people look at me in hallways, "I might as well walk around in black leather and chains. I might as well rub it in. Maybe that would be better than being nice about it." She laughed. We both laughed. It was the highest, most intimate moment of the interview. I felt the interviewer, too, had had this thought. She was also a lesbian, as well as a good interviewer. It was a funny image—the two of us who had never met, talking on the phone, each imagining the other in black leather and chains walking around her relevant university wearing a sign saying, "lesbian (hates men, rejects being feminine, seeks to seduce other women)," or with a star symbol conveying the same meaning emblazoned on her forehead. We discussed how we each tried to hide it, but we always felt other people knew.

During the interview, I wished not to remember facts of my past. The interviewer tried repeatedly to get me to go back through the experiences of my career in a chronological way, beginning with graduate school, to trace the effects of lesbianism or discriminatory treatment related to it. I was reluctant to trace myself in that way. Instead, I felt mostly the jeopardy of my present. We did, however, identify some events of the past. There again, it felt to me like secrets I was not supposed to tell, for fear others would think I was betraying the system or acting improperly by speaking. My secrets, however, are probably not uncommon. On my first job, for example, as a visiting assistant professor, a senior male faculty member wrote me a note after my interview. It was on a pretty little card with a pressed, dried flower included in it. I figured he had some sort of fantasy, and that it was harmless. When I arrived to take the job at the start of the fall term, he picked me up at the airport and drove me around to look at houses. The damage was soon done. The first night, when he offered, I refused to stay with him at his house. Two days later, when I took an apartment that he drove me to see, I again refused his offer to spend the night with him, explaining that I was a lesbian. He quickly disappeared. Later in the semester at a faculty and graduate student party, I remember the rose-colored sweater I was wearing and how he kept looking at my breasts. Not long after that, the faculty of my department considered the continuation of my appointment. He strongly opposed it and his senior position helped to put an end to me at that university. Of course, other reasons were given—the nature of my work, for instance.

I am not saying that sleeping with male faculty members is a way to get ahead. I am saying I think it might have helped had I been wearing black leather and chains. At least, the betrayal element would then be missing. This man would have known who I was from the start. But then, again, men do not always accept what they see.

From that first job, I moved to a position at another university, again as a visiting assistant professor. I remember I did not attend a faculty party at the start of the year. The night of the party, I wondered whether I should have gone. Generally, I did not socialize with the members of my department in a way that suggested it mattered to me, and at that university such socializing might have mattered, since the faculty were unusually young; they were all my age or younger. But I was a lesbian. Moving to a new town, I had sought out other lesbians for my social life. When I finally went to a faculty party late in the fall, I came and left quickly. I still remember the dark interior of the male faculty member's house where the party was held. The living room was crowded and I was not interested in meeting people's wives. I had another party to go to that night, at a gay woman's house, and I had a lesbian lover who was waiting to go there with me. I walked through the straight faculty party quickly and did not engage anyone in conversation of more than a few syllables. I was glad not to have to take all that very seriously.

At that second university, there was, again, a senior male faculty member, although he was younger than the senior male at the first school. He came over to my house one night after a preliminary show of interest. I knew why he was coming and I planned to tell him I was a lesbian. I hoped we might be friends. That was my first experience with a man who takes it as a challenge when told that a woman is a lesbian. After I informed him, there was some wrestling on a bed that served as a couch in the living room, and finally he gave up.

Three of us had been hired that year as visiting assistant professors. One of us would be kept on. It was not me, and it was not the nicer of the two men. It was a man who had a dark brown beard, and who, when he got dressed up, wore a white linen suit, and whose wife had recently left him. There was nothing particularly wrong with him. He was more like the man who had come over to my house than like anyone else on the faculty.

The man who came over that night was one of the three male faculty members who formed the committee that decided on who to hire permanently for the organizational position. They made their decision before Christmas, although the appointment would not start until the next academic year. For some reason, they wished to make a decision quickly. I remember walking to my car one day not long after I was told that I would not be hired, thinking that if it took a dress to get a job, I would wear one to my next interview. I would ask people I knew if a dress would make a difference, and if so, I would do what I had not been willing to do before and get one. As it turned out, I did not wear a dress to either of the job interviews I went to that year, and I did not get either job. I never took seriously wearing a white linen suit like the bearded man who got the job in my department, but a vision of myself in a white suit, looking just like him, often occurred to me.

At one point, I visited each of the three men who formed the committee that made the hiring decision, and asked them why I did not get the job. I was told that the bearded man was more conventional. He was more the straight-line organizational type and could bring members of the nonuniversity community into the department's organizational program. I had brought nonuniversity people into my courses as guests, and I felt hurt that what they were saying was not true of me. I had probably already brought in more nonuniversity people than he had, but that was not the point.

These are blatant examples, two cases where a man I rejected sexually later rejected me in an institutional sense. Most cases are less clear. The clear ones, it seems to me, are less hurtful. At least they are less hurtful emotionally at the moment of their occurrence. In the long run, however, any rejection, or loss of a job, has consequences. In the second university, the job I did not get was one I very much wanted. I had developed attachments to people there and to that part of the country. I still think about how my life might have been different had I been able to stay. By this second time, too, I was beginning to feel that I should expect rejection when people got to know me, as they do when one is a visitor rather than a set of credentials on a curriculum vitae. Whether or not I was rejected because I was a lesbian, I felt I had been rejected because I was myself.

There are other less clear examples of experiences in which my being a lesbian has been tied to rejection, or to my being held at a distance by others. I have taught temporarily at a variety of universities, for instance, and I have noticed that my social circles are not those of the heterosexual women around me. They have husbands and I do not, and this often seems to be the problem. I sometimes feel hurt because the lesbian/straight divide limits the friends I can have at any place. The effect is not necessarily institutional disadvantage, since women do not have great advantages in universities. Mostly, I feel a loss. I notice the lesbian/straight divide and I never like it. It is another invisible presence, something supposedly not a matter of gay and straight, but of personal choice, and assumed not to be of much importance. Yet it is important to me, for I lose relationships with other women.

Another kind of example concerns my research, since I have done work on the subject of lesbians in *The Mirror Dance* and in articles about lesbian identity and about researching lesbians.[1] When I think about my work, I usually do not think it is marked by the fact that I have studied lesbians. However, it must be and, of course, this must make a difference. What if I had studied something else? Banks, for instance, or government, or men and women in high-technology industries? When I first did the research for *The Mirror Dance,* I felt I had a great advantage: here was a fascinating community of lesbians, and as a member of it, I had access as an insider. I did not think that a study of lesbians, because it is about a "marginal" group of women, would have marginalizing consequences for me within sociology. Yet even in feminist and women's studies, I would find the study of lesbians would set me apart, carrying with it the same discomforts that lesbianism does: a discomfort with sex between women, a fear of being called man hating, and a fear of losing ties with men and of losing privileges from men.

I would discover that there is a deep-seated fear, which can lead to hostility, both in women's studies circles and elsewhere, as if lesbians would take over the institution if granted more than minimal courses to teach and minimal faculty positions. When known to be an academic couple, lesbians are often closely scrutinized, more so than heterosexual couples in the same university. I have found such scrutiny to be intimidating, especially when used as a device of institutional control. It has seemed to me a shocking invasion of privacy. But then the boundaries of women, whether as individuals or as a couple, are often not respected. Unfortunately, I think, it still pays to be invisible, whether for financial reasons or to defend against the hostility and homophobia of others entering into one's private life. Self-protectively, I have tried to be quiet and to keep to myself in the institutions where I have worked, but I have not been able to be invisible.

If studying lesbians, and studying them as I do—visibly, like a woman, speaking in the colloquial, dealing with the personal—has disadvantaged me, however, I have tended to overlook that disadvantage. What I study, and how I study it, has seemed to me so much my choice, and my virtue, that I have a blind spot when it comes to thinking that others might devalue my work because of its subject, or because of my own life. But they do. After one hiring meeting, in particular, which occurred a few years after *The Mirror Dance* came out, I was told that the faculty, all men but one, did not find my work interesting or exciting. No wonder, I thought.

If I have been marginalized—disregarded, devalued, pushed aside—because I have studied lesbians, I have never felt I could do much about it, which may be one reason I have ignored it. I have also felt that judgments about my work that reflect a bias against lesbians are not judgments about me—that they do not really affect me personally, or cause me to think less well of myself. However, that is probably not true.

Responses to my work are responses to its style and content—and to me—which sometimes confuses me, and often obscures the lesbian issue for me. Yet I do think that my experimenting with narrative form is related to my perspective as a lesbian. *The Mirror Dance,* written in an unusual multiple-person stream of consciousness style—from the points of view of the seventy-eight women I interviewed—reads like gossip, like overhearing women in a small town talking about themselves and each other: "There was a lot of gossip, said Emily. It was not ill intentioned. It was Hollywood-type gossip, infatuation—'Last night she was seen with her.' She make hopeless attempts to control it sometimes."[2] There is a lesbian feel to this gossip, joined with a sense that *The Mirror Dance* breaks barriers of convention by inventing its own style of expression, as do many lesbians, and as I did in attempting faithfully to depict this lesbian community.

My subsequent study, *Social Science and the Self,* which argued that the social scientific observer should be acknowledged more fully in our studies, dealt, too, with lesbianism, but in a more indirect way. In large parts of *Social Science and the Self,* to illustrate my thesis, I spoke about my personal experiences related to my work, and I spoke about being a lesbian. This study was unusual in that it combined my self-reflections with discussions of self and knowledge by women artists—Georgia O'Keeffe and Pueblo Indian potters. The book concluded with discussions by eight feminist scholars whom I interviewed about self-expression in their work. Four of these eight scholars were lesbians. Except for one, however, I did not identify them as lesbian in the book, in part because they did not mention it when I interviewed them, and in part because I thought identifying them would cause readers to discount what they said. I feared readers might view their comments as the peculiar views of lesbians, rather than as more broadly relevant. I do not know if I would closet my choice of subjects again, but that I did so bears noting because it illustrates how easily lesbianism becomes invisible. It seems not to matter, or it seems to be something that should not be singled out for fear of adverse consequences.

The issue of closeting lesbianism aside, *Social Science and the Self* raised questions about narrative form: how is this study to be categorized? How does valuing self-expression and originality change a sociological work? How does speaking from a woman's view change social science? Although I did not explicitly discuss the issue of a lesbian approach to knowledge in *Social Science and the Self,* I think that being a lesbian and seeking women's perspectives—especially nonconforming ones—go together for me. To a significant extent, both *The Mirror Dance* and *Social Science and the Self* are lesbian expressions. They break away from male academic forms and seek to use an inner female voice in ways that challenge conventional expectations. *The Mirror Dance* presented a collective lesbian voice. In *Social Science and the Self,* I articulated my own individual voice more, and I sought out individual statements from others. In both studies, I was concerned with the difficulties of women's efforts to create their own forms of expression.[3]

Recently, I have been asked by people who know my work and its concern with lesbianism, "Given the current rage for lesbian and gay studies, why don't you have a regular job by now?" I was startled, at first, to be asked this question. It caused me to think about why I have not been swept up in this wave of popularity. Although I am a lesbian, I am not a particularly trendy or entrepreneurial one. I think that the current vogue for gayness in academia, including the interest in "queer theory," will further other women who play the male academic game far more so than I do, and those who already have security, or a high status, at a university. It is deceptive, I think, to see those few token lesbians who are rewarded for studying lesbians, and then to assume that everyone will be rewarded, or that I will be.

As a writer and scholar, I am marked by who I am. Although I wish it were otherwise, I may never become a conventional success in terms of salary, position, and popularity. In part, this is because, for me, being a lesbian is part of a desire not to fit a mold. My lesbianism, which is central to my work in general, has different value premises than those aimed at proving I can do as others do. Queer theory, like much that becomes popular in academic circles, is male theory, which may account for its appeal.[4] I wish to express a female sensibility. Further, it seems to me that any trend in scholarship, whether female or male, brings with it its own kind of standardization. I may always be slightly too different from what is standard to be fully embraced in the academic world, even as a representative of a minority. My lesbianism, in some way, stands for my difference. I do not mean by this to understate the costs to me of that difference. I have sought to follow my own values in my work, but I have never wanted to be penalized for doing so.

Finally, I wish to speak of homophobia. It runs through all my experiences like an invisible thread. It seems not to determine something major, like whether or not I receive a job, but rather to consist of small slights toward which I try to turn the other cheek. Yet the small slights have a way of building. Last spring, for instance, I heard, by word of mouth, a piece of anonymous gossip about a woman graduate student I knew and liked. It was introduced to me as something too horrible for the student herself to speak of. The item was this: a senior male faculty member on the dissertation committee of the woman student—who may, or may not, have been a lesbian—had suggested that the student seek my advice for some part of her study because it was about lesbians, and I was a lesbian. The awful part, according to the gossip, was the way the faculty member referred to me when he made his suggestion. He spoke with his hand held up to his face, looking off to the side, as if he were speaking of something dirty, and in a snide tone. "You know," he said of me, "she's an out lesbian," with the emphasis on "out." When I heard this story, I was not horrified but, rather, I felt let down. So what? I wondered. What is wrong with being known as a lesbian? The student, however, was so hurt and frightened by the remark that she never came to ask me for advice.

I usually think it is not the gestures like this man's, in which the scorn is on the surface, but those in which the scorn is covered up that are more serious in their consequence. The covered-up affronts are more difficult to identify and thus to deal with. I tend to think I am more hurt by the student in a classroom who sits across from me in silent distrust because she wishes not to be homophobic, but still is, than I am by the man in the background who disdainfully tells a graduate student to look me up, and also, I suspect, votes negatively on my hiring. However, the two are related. The student keeps her distance because the man is there. The man speaks his mind because no one stops him. I may not be hurt when told of the man's scorn, but I am hurt by the graduate student when, in not seeking my advice, she seems not to value me. Homophobia has a hidden nature because it is a fear. Acts that stimulate that fear are interrelated. They are also, I think, disabling. I have found the repeated job rejections I have experienced to be disabling, not only externally, but internally, in terms of my self-confidence and ability to do my work. However, I know that those who attempt to conform, to be invisible, also are disabled by not being able to be themselves in their work.

When I think about hurts of the academic system, I do not usually think I have been hurt because I am a lesbian. I think of things I can see more easily, and of explanations that have nothing to do with my choosing women. My main hurt in academia is lack of a regular job—a full-time, full-status position. I also think I have been hurt because of the ways people have spoken to me over the years about my not having such a job. They make comments such as: "I wish I could have all that time off." "If you just were willing to move." "You are happier this way." "You would not be so productive if you were full-time employed." "You don't do mainstream work, what do you expect?" meaning, of course, "you deserve what you get." I feel hurt by these words, to the point of tears, every time I hear them. Over time, however, I have learned to speak back to the words and eventually to focus on the insensitivity of the speaker: "This person does not realize, she does not know. I do deserve. I would be more productive. I am not happier. I have reasons for not moving, and for not taking just any job." Yet the hurt continues.

I have learned to think of my hurt in the academic world as very much related to the nature of my work—to my unconventional choices about what my work is, and where I do it. I have also learned to see this hurt as related to a larger economic circumstance that has existed since the time I completed my degree. I did my graduate work at a time of plenty. The academic world subsequently became more constricted, and it came to have less room for people like me. Such an economic explanation seems, at times, very clear to me. I see it with pain, but I see it.

What I almost never see is that my choice to be a lesbian is significant in all this. I can see that being a lesbian is an element in the whole bundle that is me, but it is hard for me to feel that this lesbian element is more important, say, than my refusal to keep moving for a job, or my penchant for doing things my own way. However, I now think I must take into account how I felt in the interview with the master's student, how great my fear was, how strong my denial, how shocked even I was by my own constant dismissal of the facts of my past and present. By the end of the interview, I was sweaty and tired and I wanted to stop early. "These are things I do not like to think about," I kept telling the interviewer. "These are things I do not want to know," and yet I know them.

In the past, I have viewed parts of my lesbian experience as incidents not to be spoken of in the same breath as I speak of my academic career.[5] I have feared I would be making the situation worse for myself by speaking of events that are too petty or too private. I feared that just as I dismiss the importance of these events, others would too. Yet my being a lesbian is not a private, or separate, part of my life. It is not separate for me, nor for those who respond to me. It is not unimportant for any of us. As a lesbian, I choose women over men, I align myself with women, and I often deny men access to me. To the extent that I do so, I am alternately vulnerable, threatening, and disposable in a system where male-based choices and alliances are the important ones. My experience is not that of every lesbian, but there may be elements of it that others may share, such as the sense of having a stigma that is accepted, and a pain that is not felt, or of having a wish that black leather would solve the problem, or simply wishing that the system had other rules.

## Notes

A version of this essay also appears in Susan Krieger, *The Family Silver: Essays on Relationships among Women* (Berkeley and Los Angeles: University of California Press, 1996), pp. 155–68. *The Family Silver* includes essays on feminist teaching, lesbian experiences in work and family settings, and the sociology of gender. For conducting the interview described in "Lesbian in Academe," I want to thank Nicole C. Raeburn; for editorial help, I thank Estelle Freedman.

1. In addition to *The Mirror Dance: Identity in a Women's Community* (Philadelphia: Temple University Press, 1983) and *Social Science and Self: Personal Essays on an Art Form* (New Brunswick, N.J.: Rutgers University Press, 1991), my other previous works dealing with lesbianism are "Lesbian Identity and Community: Recent Social Science Literature," *Signs* 8:1 (1982): 91–108; and "Beyond 'Subjectivity': The Use of the Self in Social Science," *Qualitative Sociology* 8:4 (1985): 309–24, reprinted in *Social Science and the Self*, pp. 165–83. Lesbian community responses to *The Mirror Dance* are discussed in "Snapshots of Research," in *Social Science and the Self*, pp. 150–64.

2. Krieger, *The Mirror Dance*, p. 25.

3. Lesbian bases for theories of knowledge are discussed in Sandra Harding, "Thinking from the Perspective of Lesbian Lives," *Whose Science? Whose Knowledge? Thinking from Women's Lives* (Ithaca, N.Y.: Cornell University Press, 1991), pp. 249–67; Diana Fuss, "Lesbian and Gay Theory: The Question of Identity Politics," in *Essentially Speaking: Feminism, Nature, and Difference* (New York: Routledge, 1989), pp. 97–112; and Teresa de Lauretis, *The Practice of Love: Lesbian Sexuality and Perverse Desire* (Bloomington: Indiana University Press, 1994), which offers a theory of lesbian subjectivity as part of an exploration of the inner psychic roots of lesbian desire and sexuality. In my view, all works that seek to identify ways that lesbian existence, subjectivity, or social life are unique point to bases for lesbian theories of knowledge. For a review of other lesbian scholarly literature, see the notes to *The Family Silver*.

4. A discussion of "queer theory as male theory" can be found in Terry Castle, "A Polemical Introduction; or, The Ghost of Greta Garbo," in *The Apparitional Lesbian: Female Homosexuality and Modern Culture* (New York: Columbia University Press, 1993), pp. 12–15; says Castle, "When it comes to lesbians, many people have trouble seeing what's in front of them" (p. 2). Teresa de Lauretis, similarly, notes "a failure of

representation, an enduring silence on the specificity of lesbianism in the contemporary 'gay and lesbian' discourse," *Differences* 3:2 (1991): vii. Donna Penn speaks of a queer "erasure" of lesbian experiences in "Queer: Theorizing Politics and History," *Radical History Review* 62 (1995): 24–42. Jacquelyn N. Zita discusses potential dangers for women in "the attempt to create an interdisciplinary area of queer studies," including the silencing of women's views and the "camping up of gender and the gutting out of feminism" (p. 262). She suggests that perhaps "a new rebellion of bride resisters is in order" (p. 271), in "Gay and Lesbian Studies: Yet Another Unhappy Marriage," in Linda Garber, ed., *Tilting the Tower: Lesbians, Teaching, Queer Subjects* (New York: Routledge, 1994), pp. 258–76.

A similar concern with the invisibility of women appears in Marilyn Frye, "Lesbian Feminism and the Gay Rights Movement: Another View of Male Supremacy, Another Separatism," in *The Politics of Reality: Essays in Feminist Theory* (Freedom, Calif.: The Crossing Press, 1983), pp. 128–51. Frye says of lesbians and gay men, "we deviate from very different norms" (p. 130) and points out that gay male effeminacy, and the male impersonation of women, displays no love of women, but rather is a "casual and cynical mockery of women." For women, "femininity is the trapping of oppression," while for men, it is more often "a naughtiness indulged in…by those who believe in their immunity to contamination" (p. 137).

5. For discussions of experiences of other lesbian faculty, some of them similar to my own, three recent important collections are Toni A. H. McNaron, *Poisoned Ivy: Lesbian and Gay Academics Confronting Homosexuality* (Philadelphia: Temple University Press, 1996); Beth Mintz and Esther D. Rothblum, eds., *Lesbians in Academia: Degrees of Freedom* (New York: Routledge, 1997); and Linda Garber, ed., *Tilting the Tower: Lesbians, Teaching, Queer Subjects* (New York: Routledge, 1994); see especially Mary Klages, "The Ins and Outs of a Lesbian Academic," pp. 235–42, for a discussion of job interview experiences. An important earlier collection is Margaret Cruikshank, ed., *Lesbian Studies: Present and Future* (Old Westbury, N.Y.: The Feminist Press, 1982); see especially Jane Gurko, "Sexual Energy in the Classroom," pp. 25–31, for a discussion of "particular sexual dynamics set off by a lesbian teacher" and of a pattern of unusually high student expectations that a lesbian teacher will be an especially good mother, often followed by a letdown (pp. 29–30). An important overview based on a recent study of sociologists is Verta Taylor and Nicole C. Raeburn, "Identity Politics as High-Risk Activism: Career Consequences for Lesbian, Gay, and Bisexual Sociologists," *Social Problems* 42:2 (1995): 252–73, including a discussion of how engaging in lesbian and gay scholarship has affected individual careers.

Additional personal accounts by lesbians include: Elenie Opffer, "Coming Out to Students: Notes from the College Classroom," in R. Jeffrey Ringer, *Queer Words, Queer Images: Communication and the Construction of Homosexuality* (New York: New York University Press, 1994), pp. 296–321; Judith McDaniel, "Is There Room for Me in the Closet? Or, My Life as the Only Lesbian Professor," in Margo Culley and Catherine Portuges, eds., *Gendered Subjects: The Dynamics of Feminist Teaching* (Boston: Routledge, 1985), pp. 130–35; Rebecca Mark, "Teaching from the Open Closet," in Elaine Hedges and Shelley Fisher Fishkin, eds., *Listening to Silences: New Essays in Feminist Criticism* (New York: Oxford University Press, 1995), pp. 245–59; Jacqueline Taylor, "Performing the (Lesbian) Self: Teacher as Text," in Ringer, *Queer*

*Words,* pp. 289–95; and Ruthann Robson, "Pedagogy, Jurisprudence, and Finger-Fucking: Lesbian Sex in a Law School Classroom," in Karla Jay, ed., *Lesbian Erotics* (New York: New York University Press, 1995), pp. 28–39.

Henry Abelove discusses dilemmas posed by postmodernism for the teaching of lesbian and gay subjects, in "The Queering of Lesbian/Gay History," *Radical History Review* 62 (1995): 44–57; the idea of queering is also explored in Julia Wallace, "Queer-ing Sociology in the Classroom," *Critical Sociology* 20:3 (1994): 176–92. For accounts of teaching at many levels, see Kevin Jennings, ed., *One Teacher in Ten: Gay and Lesbian Educators Tell Their Stories* (Boston: Alyson, 1994). For experiences of students as well as of a lesbian teacher, see Harriet Malinowitz, *Textual Orientations: Lesbian and Gay Students and the Making of Discourse Communities* (Portsmouth, N.H.: Boynton/Cook Publishers, 1995).

*Sarah Fenstermaker*

# Telling Tales out of School: Three Short Stories of a Feminist Sociologist

*I*t has always troubled me that in most sociological analysis, once a story is told, there appear to be no lapses, few apparent contradictions, and no loose ends. Such is the nature of all stories, I suppose, but it has always seemed to me that sociological storytelling should reflect a bit more of the complication, confusion, and misfirings that are so characteristic of human affairs. Social life *is* complicated, after all, in its endless collision of structure and accident. And yet as I am called on to account for my own life, I find two very different but nonetheless equally tempting approaches to take. The first packages the life neatly, where both event and motive are explained, employing some tidy framework—be it psychological, historical, developmental, or what have you. My traditional sociological training makes me easy with this one. The other approach is to resist such neatness and to tell a life as largely orchestrated by circumstance and opportunity and informed only a bit by contemplation and self-reflection. But at once the scholar resists: "Don't bring me field notes, I hear myself (and the ghosts I carry with me) saying. "Tell what's *really* going on. Tell a *story*."

The tension between the two approaches of course recapitulates the quandary for all sociological analysis—the value of life history—and poses one compelling question for this volume: what is the relation between individual biography and history, the connection between individual agency and social structure? Philip Abrams suggests that the quandary is not solved until what he calls a "sociology of process" supplants our old dualities of action and system. He writes, "Society must be understood as a process constructed historically by individuals who are constructed historically by society."[1] Individuals, the history that makes them, and the history they make are unique not because they emerge at particular moments, or because they are crafted in specific fashion, but because they are the outcome of a unique process, itself a product of individual action and social structure. I will offer up three stories of a single life—three strands—that simultaneously and reciprocally construct the unfolding of a historically situated set of individual experiences. Each strand highlights one autobiographical theme—the emotional, the political, or the intellectual. Each serves as context for the next and moves the whole forward. Within each operates the institutional backdrop for the individual experience told, as well as the telling itself. Together they will form the next story—told another time— an as-yet-unrealized unfolding.

## An Emotional Story

As I begin this story, I am struck by the fact that the person about whom I write feels no longer to be "me." She is the one who did most of the achieving to make my story solicited, and she is the one on whom this strand must center. But I think of her now as an earlier self—present, sometimes even palpably, but no longer visible, and no longer in control. But I remember her very well. Up until a decade ago, virtually all my life choices were fundamentally influenced by a crippling fear of being discovered, found out, called to account—and abandoned. Today the symptoms might be labeled agoraphobia. Then the fear took whatever courage I could muster to mask and control it. It shaped my occupational and marital choices, my political identities, and also all the qualities I value in myself that now remain as its legacy.

A boy from an upper-middle-class Indianapolis family, my father studied engineering at Purdue and later studied law for a time. Eventually, the Depression and the wishes of a domineering father compelled him to join the family firm, which sold concrete-reinforcing steel. He remained there and in his seventies retired as CEO. My mother, the product of a Norwegian immigrant who was (I am told) an exceptionally charming vaudevillian/inventor/drinker and a working-class girl from Long Beach was raised in Depression Manhattan by her mother and a widow friend. My grandmother, having separated from her "good-for-nothing" actor husband worked as New York City telephone operator (by night), while "Aunt" Alva worked as a New York public school teacher (by day). Together they made a family. My mother spent her childhood days at the movies or in the New York Public Library, with the goal, simply, to read all its books. And perhaps she was dreaming of the secure life she was to win when, in college in the Midwest, she met and married my very "steady" father. An unhappy

housewife, mother, and (always) transplanted New Yorker, my mother began writing when I was in elementary school. (She remembered with great
fondness when I returned from school one day and informed her that I had
on some form designated her occupation as "writer.") She published a number of short stories, one novel, and two volumes of poetry. She died recently, at seventy-five, still active as a short fiction critic and poet.

I always wanted to be a doctor—a *real* doctor. When I was growing
up in the 1950s, most people didn't query white upper-middle-class girls
about their aspirations beyond wife and motherhood. But I remember that
beginning about the age of three I told anyone who asked, "Pediatrician."
All things medical fascinated me. My own pediatrician was a rather
forbidding-looking woman—with the most gentle touch imaginable—and
looked every inch the pioneer she needed to be when, newly minted from
Cornell Medical School she opened her pediatric practice in 1927. By the
time she treated me, she had a vastly successful but not particularly lucra-
tive practice in the sleepy, provincial Indianapolis of my childhood.

I was often ill as a child, plagued by asthma, allergies, and uncon-
trolled eczema. I spent enough extra time at Dr. Souter's office to decide
that doctoring kids like me was the most exalted of adult activities. I am
sure now that this aspiration was in large measure my seeking out the most
powerful adult position possible—the beginning of a much longer search
for buffers to the vulnerabilities I believed life imposed.[2] (I also wanted to
be a boy, no doubt for the same reason.)

My illness, and the stultifying life package my mother confronted day
to day, made her communicate extraordinary ambivalence, guilt, and excessive indulgence to me, her last and most troubled child. An insidious
emotional dance resulted: as I demanded more of my mother's time, she
deeply begrudged more time in the process. With that came her guilt, and
indulgence of me, and so it went. I read this bundle of always unspoken
but powerful multiple realities, but their constant denial made the emotional ground very unsteady. I reacted with debilitating anger, depression,
and crippling dependence. By the age of seven, I was the officially designated "difficult" child, acting out every emotion apparently forbidden to
my parents and my older brother and sister.

My siblings' emotional inheritances are different, and both carry scars
from our brand of family dysfunction. For me, this early drama carried
with it a certifiable case of schoolphobia, complete with a private tutor and
no clear sense of what was bothering me or when it would stop. It was
around then that I realized that no adult would save me. I was either going
to kill myself or hide the fear and reenter the world. For twenty years

thereafter, I carried the secret fear that someone would find out I wasn't entitled to that decision to be in the world. It was at that time that my parents recall that I just—thankfully—"improved."[3]

Since things were invariably what they seemed and *not* what they seemed, I was bequeathed a fascination with and some talent for discerning the "hidden" realities, the variety of "real" truths, and the ambiguous message. This fascination has fueled my interests in sociology and specifically the powerful sociological vantage of social construction, the nature of stigma, and the backstage qualities of anything—especially work organizations. In all of that, it is always the *process* of it that is so compelling to me. The outcomes are visible, but the hidden realities lie elsewhere. Or so it appeared. I also came away with a good comic sense, and the ability to make people laugh—both to control and to deflect attention from what I feared they would see: the awful reality I always imagined was obvious without such distractions.

## A Political Story

My discovery of inequality and my sense of myself as a political person illustrate the complicated dovetailing of institutional structure, historical period, and individual personality. Race inequality—a reality hidden with the help of white denial—compelled my interest in a very personal way in high school. My father, a Republican moderate, and my mother, a liberal Democrat, sent my older brother and sister, as well as me (in the mid-1960s), to the oldest (and most venerated) public high school in town. My father himself had attended that school, and since its founding as "Indianapolis High School" just after the Civil War, Shortridge High School boasted of its students' achievements: many National Merit scholars, one of only a handful of student-run daily newspapers, a world-class choral music program, a state championship basketball team, and many distinguished alumni. During the 1950s and 1960s, it was also situated in the middle of the black community and was pointed to with pride as a successful "experiment" in racial integration. But it was an embattled time for the school, with its African-American population increasing and many parents taking their children elsewhere, to "safer," whiter high schools. Its practical and indelible contribution to my political socialization came in its defensive packaging of school pride with an unlikely analysis of the need for racial equality, equal rights, and the possibility of social change, made with others.

Since that time I have met no one else who experienced such notions reinforced during their high school pep rallies or any who were called on to defend her or his school against racist attacks. But for me and my class-mates, it was certainly a moment of political imprinting that in one way or another affected each one of us. Thereafter, nearly every other Left political idea that came my way—from the now tame notion of interracial dating, to Malcolm X (before the movie), to antiwar protests, to the Black Panther Party, to the Women's Liberation Movement and guerrilla theater—all seemed in some way to be a simple extension of those early messages about racial justice.

Much prodded by a radical high school history teacher who thought her alma mater perfect for me, I mustered what little taste for adventure I had to go away to school—Goucher College for Women, just outside Balti-more. My most vivid memories of it are not of the classroom but of dormi-tory rooms full of women analyzing, planning, arguing endlessly about the Vietnam War. And the soundtrack was rock and roll.

After a brief developmental stop at Gene McCarthy's "Children's Cru-sade," ending the Vietnam War consumed most of our energies.[4] And with it came the wonderful first Marxist notions about class, its connection to race inequality, colonialism, and American imperialism. (No women, no thought given to gender equity. Only invisibility.)[5] During my sophomore and junior years at Goucher, I attended meetings of the New University Conference (NUC), a national organization for academics mobilized around antiwar/anti-imperialism activities. Since Goucher had no graduate students, undergraduates were invited to participate. This allowed me the chance to watch (most of us undergrads were too intimidated to speak) faculty from Goucher and Johns Hopkins plan, argue, and build coalitions with other Baltimore groups around antiwar politics. Baltimore was close enough to Washington to allow us to be part of all the Student Mobilization demon-strations in 1968 and 1969, and from those we came away with not only an exaggerated sense of our own political agency, but also a clear feeling that our individual actions were indeed related to historical (and historic) events. In no other political activity or political time since have I felt that so strongly.

Some exposure to feminism and women's liberation also came during the end of my three years in Baltimore. Through NUC, I had got to know Florence Howe, my academic adviser, and it was she who first introduced me to the notion of gender inequality.[6] Interestingly, the news of women's liberation had simply not got out to my sociology classes—although it some-times creeped into Alice Rossi's family seminars. When I began to really listen to Florence, I responded immediately to the intellectual argument. After all, I must have always known about power differentials; it was no accident that I had wanted to be a boy so long ago. I had also been a good athlete in school and remembered my resentful confusion over the state of affairs where once a girl reached high school, there were simply no team sports available. But it was not until the next year that the arguments for women's liberation would begin to take on real meaning.

That same year, I met Richard Berk—also through NUC—when he was then a graduate student at Johns Hopkins studying with Peter Rossi. A very short courtship (much of it during political meetings or in the pizza parlors afterward) resulted in marriage that same year. I followed Dick to Northwestern, where he took a job as assistant professor in sociology and where I was to finish my last year as an undergraduate. I always wince a little when I think of 1970: at age twenty finding a feminism that would direct me for the rest of my life *and* marrying because I believed I was unable to live on my own. I needed a champion, and Richard Berk was simply the most powerful person I could imagine. Luckily, he thought so, too. I also changed my name. It took all of a week to regret that decision and seventeen years before I changed it back.

If my memories of Baltimore revolve around antiwar activity, my memories of Evanston (and Chicago) revolve around the heady days of "early" feminism. From the moment we arrived, I was gratefully swept up into the activities of the new Evanston chapter of the Chicago Women's Liberation Union (CWLU, then two years old). The CWLU was an extraordinarily successful model for feminist organizing. Each of eight to ten chapters in Chicago met weekly and determined its own agenda via the (then-new) consciousness-raising, or "speaking bitterness" format. My memories of this time, and via this method, are of developing an ethical/political framework for living as a feminist. Twenty-five years later, that framework remains fundamentally unchanged. Coupled with the consciousness-raising work, however, was the expectation of the union that local chapters would engage in ("direct") political action. Located in Evanston, and drawing largely from white undergraduate and graduate populations at Northwestern, our chapter was by far the least diverse with respect to class, age, and race. Other chapters had members with very different sorts of experiences. Our membership in the union kept us in touch and at least exposed, if not accountable to, a certain kind of class- and race-conscious feminist-socialist politics that we would not have explored on our own.[7] Second-wave feminism and I were far too young to appreciate what the CWLU was accomplishing, but now, years later, it remains for me the best example of what feminist organizing and coalition building can achieve. I will be forever grateful to every woman in that group for what I learned from them and for giving me a safe and stimulating place to first explore feminist thought.

This early period in the CWLU's history was fraught with tension surrounding the feminist "abandonment" of the antiwar movement and the women who stayed behind to work in it. And even those of us who continued to participate in antiwar work but who would no longer commit to a "male-identified" movement were very ambivalent. The end of the war resolved a great many of these doubts, as my political identity as a feminist activist and my intellectual identity as a sociologist developed simultaneously and felt, for the time being, compatible.

## An Intellectual Story

After I had completed my final undergraduate year as a "special student" at Northwestern, my decision to enter graduate school was surely based on the same "safety-first" principle I had employed since I was three: namely, the greatest measure of security against the possibility that my entitlement to take up space would be questioned. I had already achieved some sense of security in marriage, and this career choice seemed right. I did seem to be able to fool my instructors very well. And sociology's puzzles were compelling. As an undergraduate, I chose sociology because I was at home with its focus on inequality. It was only later I understood that my fascination with it came from the sense it gives of revealing the secrets of social interaction—another sort of power I so desperately lacked as a child.

Early 1970s Northwestern was just right for me. The faculty welcomed me with open arms and set about determined to treat me as a student and not a wifely appendage. I am grateful to that collection of (mostly) unreconstructed men for what I now know is quite a difficult undertaking, primarily since it must be done day to day and by each individual. At twenty-two, I was far too young and terrified to give the faculty much guidance myself. Throughout my graduate career they did their best to make me feel that I was being judged independently of Dick. As a result, I developed a glimmer that not *everything* I achieved was a fluke or someone else's misunderstanding of my true abilities.

This was likewise true of the graduate cohorts with whom I spent time. Even though it was clear that my marriage to Dick meant that I might have capitalized on a kind of privileged familiarity with faculty that they did not share, I never got a sense of unease or resentment about my position. And there were reasons for that. We were all young and still very much in the 1960s mode of a studied resistance to authority. Equally important, the last gasps of the War on Poverty provided enough money to support fully almost all graduate students, and this kept the relations among us relatively noncompetitive. Finally, *my* friends were our friends, and our friends were primarily graduate students. Dick was not a particularly social person, and I was still intimidated by most faculty. Anita and Barry, Ellen and Jack, Mike and Pam, Kate and Bruce, and Bill and Barb were all graduate student couples or graduate students and their partners. All this served to mute, and even mask, for all of us what privileges I actually benefited from.

In the early 1970s, the Northwestern sociology faculty was congenial, clever, quick, on the rise, and devoted to graduate training. The faculty fancied themselves more creative than their colleagues at Chicago and far more eclectic than the "factory" in Madison. With the exception of my last years, when Arlene Kaplan Daniels and Janet Lever were hired, the department employed only one woman, Janet Abu-Lughod, a fine scholar, but one with whom I had little contact. So I was left with a group of men who gave a sort of training that was (unbeknown to me at the time) characteristically "Northwestern" in character. For me, the intellectual atmosphere was determined by my associations with John Kitsuse, Howard Becker, Allan Schnaiberg, and Arnold Feldman. John taught me how to think as a sociologist, Howie taught me how to do sociology, Allan instructed me in method and meaning, and Ackie schooled me in Karl Marx. Each had an intellectual and personal history that placed him *in* the club, but not quite *of* it. That alone made them fascinating teachers.

I worked with and for John Kitsuse for two years, completing my master's thesis with him before he moved to UC Santa Cruz. There was probably no other person who affected my early scholarship more. From him I came to know what sociology's distinctive gifts were and that sociology and sociologists do best when they limit their vantage to the study of social life as a social process subject to change, situated interpretation, and relations of power. In short, John Kitsuse taught me the wonders of taking the "natural" unfolding of social organization as the sociological problematic. It was only a matter of finding the right tools for the problem.

At that time, the graduate program was marked by the legacies of the older midwestern, pragmatic approach to sociological training. The department required one quarter of qualitative methods in the fall of a student's first year, taught by Howard Becker, intellectual heir to Everett Hughes, to be followed by a two-quarter statistics series, taught by Allan Schnaiberg, who had been a student of Dudley Duncan at Michigan. Since ours was a theory-light program, we were required only to take one quarter of classical theory with Arnold Feldman. Thereafter, students were strongly discouraged from submitting secondary data analysis for a thesis or doctorate. We had to get our hands dirty.

The presence of Howard Becker at Northwestern granted a central role to qualitative methods both among the faculty and within the graduate curriculum. This curriculum communicated to us that qualitative methods had not only a legitimate but also an *equal* standing in the profession. At Northwestern we came to believe that methods should be driven by sociological problems and not the other way round. Graduate students were admonished if it appeared that they treated methodological techniques as tricks, toys, or political statements. In fact, we were taught to look with disdain at all researchers who "unzipped" their tools before the problem was found. Moreover, for many students there was an expectation that our research would employ a variety of methods. This early exposure to the issues surrounding problem and method—cart and horse—has made a fundamental difference in my reaction to the development of the discipline and to the work that I would craft as feminist sociology.

Methodological tools and approaches change so rapidly, and, when applied sensitively, are so subject to the exigencies of the problem that the notion that one learns how to "do" qualitative or "do" quantitative is just one more delusional notion from conventional sociological practice. Our training was certainly traditional in many respects, but it was cast as a social, shifting matter always subject to dialogue and change. With so much organized doubt and equivocation, I believe we came away with a productively unconventional epistemological stance. Howard Becker and Allan Schnaiberg taught not only a collection of techniques but also a way of thinking about problems and a way of looking at social life. Allan, who for his outlook we affectionately dubbed "Eeyore," saw all methodological decisions situated with others, each with a downside, each a product of compromise. There was no right solution, only the one that seemed to solve the very worst problems at the moment. From Howie we learned that nothing is as it seems and that sociological meaning lies in the workings of the social group; it is seldom derived theoretically.

This early exposure to ethnography, the privileging of experience, and profound skepticism about social research I now believe introduced us very early to how James Clifford described ethnography: the "discipline's impossible attempt to fuse objective and subjective practices."[8] Yet Howie Becker in particular conveyed the thrill at the "discovery" or "unearthing" of an unrevealed story—hidden in among the characters who inhabited one's field site. After nearly twenty years of feminist exploration of the relation between subject and researcher, and the constructed nature of their collaborations, whether I am using logit regression or an interview, I have not fully shaken that feeling that I can discover a preexisting social reality once hidden to everyone else. Since then, and in my own teaching, I have elaborated on and greatly complicated those early lessons, but they remain nonetheless a foundation for my feminist scholarship in sociology, as well as a rationale for their own critique.[9]

As I reflect on this period, I am not sure how I managed to deny all the inconsistencies that must have been so obvious in my life: I was attending at least two meetings a week that involved women's liberation—either consciousness-raising or some sort of political action; soaking up the discipline of middle-class white men; finding some way to accommodate to the idea (and practice) of marriage; and meeting every two weeks with a number of graduate women in sociology (among them Kate Berheide, Demie Kurz, Eleanor Lyon, Pamela Richards, and Judy Wittner) to pose the question, What *would* a sociology look like if women's experience were really present in it?

At that time, any implications for my own life were lost on me: my general acquiescence to the sociology I was being taught, my heterosexual/marital privilege as I moved effortlessly through a department where my husband held power over all my friends, and my newfound feminist consciousness, which I fancied was free from political or personal contradiction. The *intellectual* was political, but there, in suburban Evanston, as I pulled age, race, class, and heterosexual privilege around me like a blanket, the personal was political only for other women. This was hardly a time when I *could* confront such contradictions. I was functioning in the world. I was fooling everyone—still my most difficult and absorbing accomplishment.

Individual struggles aside, I believe there is a cohort of white, baby-boom academics like myself who, being younger in the early 1970s, were swept into feminist scholarship without the wisdom that came from the day-to-day adversities experienced by older women. Perhaps for us, feminism and the decision to be feminist scholars came *first* and were based largely on intellectual excitement and an aversion to inequality, felt deeply, but *theoretically.* When adversity came later, it was then experienced *in the context* of a feminist analysis of where it came from and why. In short, it was as if the "problem with no name" was named *first* and the problem came later.

My study of household labor was begun in graduate school. Richard Berk, Catherine Berheide, and myself received funding from NIMH's Center for the Study of Metropolitan Problems, administered by the late Elliot Liebow. It was Elliot who took a chance on granting major funding to our national survey of four hundred women and their husbands on the content, allocation, and affect surrounding household labor. In retrospect, I cannot imagine how Elliot marshaled the arguments to defend the funding of that study. In those days the topic was not only treated as unfit subject matter for the sociology of work but was also very often greeted by male sociologists with a level of resentment and anger that simply could not be fathomed by taking the subject matter at face value. When looked at as work, household labor and its division were sociologically illegitimate and downright unspeakable.[10]

At that time, the sociological study of household work was only mentioned with any frequency in the old family studies of "power" and marriage. Who does what in the household was conceptualized as one more set of indicators of power. It was always assumed that if one did housework and child care, one had less power than if one didn't, presumably because no one with any power would ever do any.[11] Among feminists, only Mirra Komarovsky's, Helena Znaniecka Lopata's, and (in a new vein) Ann Oakley's research had treated the subject in any but the most condescending way.[12]

The Cornell school of "old" home economics, led by Kathryn Walker, has a distinguished history of studying the "nuts and bolts" of housework. It is unique for the way in which it takes the work of women on its own terms, and it is to that work that we initially turned for guidance.[13] At this time, too, the "wages for housework" flurry in Great Britain was picking up steam, only to have its moment a few years later on U.S. daytime talk shows. Its academic counterpart was developing a fascinating debate within the Marxist community about the status of household work under capital. We did not become aware of this literature until we were well into our study, and mainstream sociology barely gave it a passing nod. Ann Oakley's work and our project had much in common, despite their differences in scope, methodology, and locale. In both projects, housework was *work* and thus subject to a sociological analysis informed by the experiences of other work and workers. This was hugely important from a theoretical point of view, for this made it possible for household work to be viewed as something that is not derivative of or inseparable from the family. With this shift, household work could be studied within the family as a *particular work context*. And following that, once the work was made visible as *work*, the women who do such work were made visible as *workers*. That they were also wives and mothers could then became the theoretical context in which the experience of those *workers* could be analyzed. There were many such insights that emerged from our project begun in Evanston. But it was Ann Oakley who first distinguished between (husbands') "help" and (wives') "responsibility" as the way in which men and women view their household labors.[14] It is a seemingly simple distinction but ultimately proved to be an analytically powerful entry into women's actual experience of their work lives.

If my sociological training at Northwestern left me fascinated with the organization of work and the power relations implied in it, if it encouraged looking backstage, if it gave me a variety of tools to study work experience and a healthy skepticism about data, then the study of household labor was certainly what I was prepared for. And what I have found over the last twenty years is that it was the invisibility, illegitimacy, and isolating qualities of household work itself that drew me to both the scholarship and the feminism I developed around it.

It was no accident that Kate Berheide and I would begin a study of household work with an ethnography. We were doing what we had been taught, both by Northwestern-style sociology and by Chicago-style feminism. We reasoned that since we knew so little about what the work was, who did it, or how people felt about it, we would observe and interview household workers. We talked to women, and we watched them work.[15] I had yet to understand that from a professional point of view I was far from the mainstream because for me sociology was about method, rigor, and creativity. From that early fieldwork, and the intensity with which the women spoke to us, however, I understood that I was revealing a hidden reality— one that existed side by side with the ones that were so obvious. At the age of twenty-four, and for the first time, I was discovering the culture of adult women. And it felt as if we were writing some of that culture out of its invisibility.

I was also forced to look behind my own carefully crafted privilege: at women like my mother and their frequent bouts of despair, at poor women who faced agonizing choices each day but who could never reveal their struggle, and at the women of color who cleaned one house by day and another by night. From this early work we developed an elaborate survey instrument and two diary instruments for the national study, but for me that beginning "in the field" helped keep all the other methods accountable to women's experiences.

I will not recount the substance of that research for this essay or the way in which Richard Berk and I worked to make a productive collaboration to write about household labor. I will end this story by describing a crisis in my attempt to complete the major product of the work begun in 1974. I believe the struggle I went through marked the beginning of my independence as a feminist scholar and firmly connected me to the feminist project thereafter.

When Dick Berk and I arrived at UC Santa Barbara in 1976, I intended to plunge into the business of getting tenure. Instead, I had to win back the job I had been promised initially. The year before, Dick and I had both interviewed for the available jobs at UC Santa Barbara, at full professor and assistant professor, respectively. Things went well, and we returned to Evanston believing that the department was very enthusiastic about our appointments and that we would be given job offers. Unlike other places we had considered, the faculty at UC Santa Barbara seemed able to discern my talents as distinct from Dick's and appeared to be enthusiastic about what I would bring to the department. That same week Dick Flacks called with verbal offers. Three weeks after that he called again. This time it was to convince me that for the sake of "expediency" I should sign a one-year contract for an appointment to lecturer. He explained that the extra departmental reviewers had expressed misgivings about granting a full professorship to someone as young as Dick, and because I was his wife, my appointment to assistant professor would further complicate matters. Flacks assured me that it would be "no problem" to change my status to assistant professor, even before the end of that first quarter. Knowing nothing about UC or the yawning chasm between ladder and temporary appointments, I trusted the process, and with the Oath of Allegiance to California, I also signed a contract to be a lecturer.

What followed was a year reaping the consequences for what I had done. In response to campus review agents' "concerns," my work was subjected to another complete review, and senior members of my department would grill me (sometimes at odd hours and places) to establish exactly how much of my own dissertation I had written. In addition, my dissertation committee was called on individually to testify in writing that I had actually done my own work. A full year later I was appointed to the job for which I had interviewed. Moral: real institutional mistreatment at the hands of bullies teaches lifelong lessons—if one survives.

During the next few years, Dorothy Smith often made wintertime visits to UCSB Sociology to consult with our two resident ethnomethodologists, Don Zimmerman and Thomas Wilson. She would talk about her own work in progress with whomever seemed interested. My breathless reaction to her work and my fervent wish for Dorothy's good opinion made me return to an earlier incarnation as a shy and quite inarticulate graduate student.

But after those visits, her ideas stayed with me as I struggled to speak more bravely through my own work.[16] At that time I read "A Sociology for Women" and, later, "On Sociological Description" as one lost returns home.[17] There the real problematics of feminist research are addressed directly: it was the first thing I had read that actually articulated how a feminist might work as a researcher; it voiced the discomfort we feel when—in the name of sociology—we so distort the experiences of women that they are later unrecognizable, even to us; and not since I had first read Marx had I had such a strong feeling of truth *revealed* and my thinking forever altered. This might have been a tremendously liberating intellectual moment, but to return to an earlier story, my own reticence as a scholar overwhelmed the guidance Smith's work offered to me. So I resisted its effect on me, even as I began to rethink my own way of working.

In the early 1980s (just after I was awarded tenure), I was anxiously trying to complete the analysis of "who does what"—the allocation of household labor and employment time.[18] The statistical analysis was finished, complete with an elaborate set of footnotes wherein I worked through all my methodological ambivalences and doubts. And I was satisfied with it. The theoretical chapter, which had taken me months to write, was exhaustive and critical, if a bit tentative. What was not written was the punchline. Howie had always asked us, "What is this story *about?*" I had dutifully revealed the dimensions of what I called a "gendered" allocation system. I had used some novel methods and relatively sophisticated quantitative techniques and had come up with original findings. I had employed a microeconomic model of the household and in critique of it had painted an empirical picture of gender inequality that at least one feminist reviewer would later criticize as "too gloomy." I had said that there is *less* to

> the division of labor than the system that we may fancy it to be: one marked primarily by rational specialization, substitution, and cooperation. . . . Men and women may share a work environment but do not share much of its work; they may share a living space, but the maintenance of that space affects primarily wives. Thus, [there is] an intimate relation between work and gender that is revealed through the division of household and market labors.[19]

But however arduous and complicated the trip had been, I was simply not convinced it had been necessary. I could not fathom why, regardless of every biographic characteristic I could tease out of the data, wives did so damn much work and by their own report thought it was *fair.* I was stuck. I had run out of answers since the only answer offered by my own discipline was "norms." I thought it was at least faintly ridiculous to go to all the trouble I had to analyze the dynamics of the allocation of household labor and end the story with the explanation that "norms made them do it." There are certainly worse shaggy dog stories in sociology, but I didn't want the shame of adding another. Moreover, I knew that one couldn't explain a variable with a constant. But to have answers of my own was far too threatening, for they required a self that was simply not equal to the task. I lost a year: writing and rewriting, waiting and waiting.

My revelation did not come in a blinding light, but it came nonetheless. I had been talking about and teaching Dorothy Smith's ideas, particularly about the research process—repeating questions in however many ways I could imagine to whomever would talk to me about them: How does one, as feminist and scholar, place oneself in the process and keep allegiance to those with whom one constructs and reconstructs their lives? What does the researcher actually *do* in a sociology for women? What does "beginning from the standpoint of women" really *mean* for the practicalities of research? I had slowly come to feel, if not articulate, that my own private notions about the practice of feminism as a way of living held clues to how scholarship might be done in its goal to begin from the standpoint of women. There, one's vantage begins from a new center—women's experiences—and returns ultimately to that center.

What this meant for me in the darker moments with my own research is that I had lost the point where I had begun so long ago—watching women straighten their living rooms, boil hotdogs for the kids, and fold the laundry. It felt like a "lost" reality, but in fact I had given it away through the process of analysis and in my need to avoid the costs of speaking in my own voice. And I was paying the price, for now I had no satisfactory reference point with which to return to the questions on which my work turned. As a feminist, I knew only that I could not conclude that my respondents had been "falsely conscious" or simply irrational.

I resolved to suspend my own (and everyone else's) sociological judgment and assume that if women had told me that the division of household labor was "fair," I must assume that it *was* fair. My question then had to be, What reality determined that to be a rational response? The question put this way provided the shift in vision I had been seeking, and it was compelling enough intellectually to counter my reticence. The result was the application of some powerful theoretical notions (at that point, in 1983–1984, unpublished) from Candace West and Don Zimmerman that we, and especially Candace and I, have been engaged with ever since.[20] I was able to conclude that because gender relations—the doing of dominance and submission—are an everyday proposition, then gender may serve as a warrant for household members' claiming particular relationships to, or stances toward, household labor. When the time comes to allocate household members' labor, there are available a host of "good reasons" that husbands, *regardless* of other considerations, should be market specialists, and wives either household specialists or modern-day generalists, devoting time to both work sites. Ultimately then, and from day to day, work and gender combine, and the division of household labor becomes the activity around which each can determine and capacitate each other. It is within these two interwoven structures that household members make their choices and get the business of living done.[21]

This was really the scholarly beginning where I first risked a voice. What I was saying seemed to affirm, rather than violate, the truths of the hidden realities I had become so adept at perceiving, whatever the reaction from others or the consequences of voicing them. It was an intellectual stance that was not motivated by the familiar fears. Risking this sort of vulnerability was very new, but it was liberating and loaded with possibility. The emotional, the political, and the intellectual were for a moment, in some sort of balance, a single story.

## Afterward/Afterword

It is now more than a decade since that liberating lesson about feminism, method, and voice. A child, a divorce, the experience of mothering, the worst isolation I have known, the company of women from many disciplines, and a progressive working of fear to a closing have all followed. With that sort of rebuilding and struggle has also come a new sense of the possibilities when the emotional, the political, and the intellectual are in greater harmony. By way of conclusion, the example of my efforts in my campus Women's Studies Program should illustrate.

As I became a more senior feminist in my own department and on my own campus, I began to be called on to work in more interesting ways for women. Over time this generated a partial shift in my own activism away from the community outside the university and toward the one within it.[22] I learned not only that I had some facility for administration, but also that those predilections were very much connected to my old sociological fascinations: for backstages, work and organizations, and collective action.

This refocusing of my energies enhanced the other greatly preoccupying work that my feminist colleagues and I began in 1986: the establishment of a multidisciplinary undergraduate program and major in women's studies. About fifteen to twenty primarily senior women faculty and staff from a variety of humanities, science, and social science departments began to meet regularly to discuss the prospect of such a program. Over the prior decade, we had all received requests from students to establish a major, and every once in a while we would come together to review the notion and reject it. Because of UC Santa Barbara's unique development from a conservative postwar teacher's college, the campus was very slow to appoint women on the ladder faculty and even slower to promote them. We token appointments, working away in our own departments and disciplines to establish feminist footholds, never felt we could mount the sort of program that would offer *us* anything but the guarantee of overwork, burnout, and further isolation. This situation meant, however, that once we *did* believe there was a critical mass of faculty to staff a cross-disciplinary program, there were feminist curricula in many departments on which the program could be founded, and the faculty who would propose and run such a program were senior, influential, and networked. Such a delay worked to great advantage.[23]

The abiding lesson from this "Judy come lately" development is that in large measure we established this program for ourselves as feminist scholars. We reasoned that, after all, we had full-time jobs and we were already overworked, so anything like a new program that would partly divert us from the struggles in our mainstream departments would have to be unique to the campus and uniquely satisfying to us. It is this that informed the goals of the program: to bring feminists across the disciplines into a scholarly dialogue that was relatively unfettered by the male-defined departmental cultures we had suffered under; to allow for the development of a multi- (even inter) disciplinary and cross-cultural curriculum that excited us as teachers; to provide a rigorous, affirming intellectual experience for women's studies majors; and, finally, to develop a program supported well enough by the campus community to make us want to lend our energies to it.

In the year prior to the approval of the program, I emerged as the likely candidate for chair, and so I spent a great deal of time shepherding the proposal through the necessary gatekeepers and securing money and permanent positions to get us up and running. Thereafter, I served as chair of the Women's Studies Program for three years, later as associate dean of the Graduate Division, and I am now serving as vice chair of our Academic Senate.

Each success, small and large, and each moment of productive collaboration, whether with college secretaries, vice chancellors, or chairs of other departments, confirmed a growing sense of my own agency, my ability to communicate vision, and the compelling intellectual rationale for cross-disciplinary feminist scholarship. Most important, however, such experiences have left me with a belief in possibilities that I only pretended as a younger person—a belief in things yet imagined in myself and in the future of feminist scholarship.

## Notes

Thanks to Howard Becker, Evelyn Nakano Glenn, Ann Goetting, Valerie Jenness, Ursula Mahlendorf, Robyn Posin, and Candace West for their valuable suggestions. Thanks also to Patty Forgie, Ellen Lopez-Gomez, and Holly Unruh for clerical assistance.

1. Philip Abrams, *Historical Sociology* (Ithaca, N.Y.: Cornell University Press, 1972), p. 227.
2. I abandoned the aspiration to be a doctor one day in high school. I remember I discovered that a great deal of math was required in medical school, as well as something called organic chemistry. I was convinced I couldn't manage the math. With barely a ripple, and with no one noticing—let alone refuting—my conclusion, I let go of any notions of a medical career. I have never had another career aspiration quite like that one; all subsequent ones were bound to the limitations imposed by my fears or subject to the complicated maze of opportunity, accident, and logistics.
3. In retrospect, and with the help of a more removed analysis of the situation, I see that it is likely that my response to the perils of the outside world were manifested fears projected by my mother. Here, birth order, the sensitivities of a precocious youngest child, the politically predatory 1950s, and my mother's own fears of the world fundamentally fixed my first set of disabilities and compensations.
4. In 1968 when Eugene McCarthy, Democratic senator from Wisconsin, entered the Democratic presidential primary race, he ran as the most progressive candidate and enlisted a large corps of young people to stump for his antiwar candidacy. Dubbed the "Children's Crusade" by the press, we proved to be quite a fickle group. Very late in the primary game, Robert Kennedy entered the race and readily wooed and won the support of most young McCarthy supporters. But it was Gene McCarthy who took the initial risk and framed the issues.
5. I should qualify this point by saying that the experience of a woman's school was among the most significant to my development as a feminist. The environment at Goucher, where women's intellectual growth was the business of the institution, allowed us to feel entitled to our own education, very often for the first time. I knew countless women who came to that college with virtually no sense of their own intellectual worth and left forever changed.
6. The summer before I left Baltimore, Florence hired me to begin the work that was to became the Feminist Press.

7. I do recall, however, that the Evanston chapter had a certain sort of "radical" reputation for taking a tough stand on the membership of Marxist-Leninist women and for urging the CWLU to confront the issue of "sexuality" (i.e., lesbianism).

8. James Clifford, *Writing Culture: The Poetics and Politics of Ethnography* (Berkeley and Los Angeles: University of California Press, 1986) p. 109.

9. The anxiety surrounding Howard Becker's methods class has bound Northwestern graduates to each other like no other experience. Twice a week the incoming cohort sat in a circle with Howie where we discussed our field projects, about which most of us were terrified. We were expected to have our first set of field notes at the *second* week's class meeting and every week thereafter until the final project was due ten weeks later. And, to my students' horror today, he did not allow us the use of tape recorders for interviews. I still marvel at our being able to establish a project, spend most of our waking hours working on it, and turn in a substantive analysis at the end of ten weeks. How did he get us to do all that? Many master's theses were born this way, mine among them, and not a few dissertations. Class time was spent discussing particular ethnographic issues that we were facing at that moment in the field. Each problem would bring some sort of parable from Howie to illustrate whatever lesson he wanted us to learn. These were typically based on his own ethnographic work—usually either Howard S. Becker, *Boys in White: Student Culture in Medical School* (Chicago: University of Chicago Press, 1961); or Howard S. Becker, *Outsiders: Studies in the Sociology of Deviance* (New York: Free Press, 1967)—but sometimes on any of the Chicago crowd who worked with Everett Hughes. I loved these stories and the romantic connections they made from me to the discipline. After all, I reasoned, this bridge to the Chicago School very quickly got me from Becker to Hughes or from Becker to Blumer to Mead!

10. I am still searching through my office to find a copy of our first ASR review. Berk, Berheide, and myself had submitted our first piece on who did what in the household. It was rejected outright. See Catherine White Berheide, Sarah Fenstermaker Berk, and Richard A. Berk, "HouseholdWork in the Suburbs: The Job and Its Participants," *Pacific Sociological Review*, 19 (fall 1976): 491–518. I do remember that one of the reviewers sounded furious as he explained all the things *he* did around the house. Later, of course, household work came of age and mainstream sociology repackaged it as "hot." For examples, see Melvin Kohn and Carmi Schooler, *Work and Personality: An Inquiry into the Impact of Social Stratification* (Norwood, N.J.: Ablex, 1983); and Denise D. Bielby and William T. Bielby, "She Works Hard for the Money: Household Responsibility and the Allocation of Work Effort," *American Journal of Sociology* 93 (fall 1988): 1031–1059.

11. Robert O. Blood Jr. and Donald M. Wolfe, *Husbands and Wives: The Dynamics of Married Living* (Glencoe, Ill.: Free Press, 1960).

12. Mirra Komarovsky, *Blue Collar Marriage* (New York: Random House, 1962); Helena Lopata, *Occupation: Housewife* (London: Oxford University Press, 1971); Ann Oakley, *The Sociology of Housework* (New York: Pantheon Books, 1974).

13. See, for example, Kathryn E. Walker and Margaret E. Woods, *Time Use: A Measure of Household Production of Family Goods and Services* (Washington, D.C.: Center for the Family of the American Home Economics Association, 1971).

14. Oakley, *The Sociology of Housework.*

15. For discussion, see Sarah Fenstermaker Berk and Catherine White Berheide, "Going

Backstage: Gaining Access to Observe Household Work," *Sociology of Work and Occupations* 4 (winter 1977): 27–48.

16. I will never forget one moment in the hallway outside Don Zimmerman's office, I believe in 1979. There I was uncharacteristically revealing my fears to Dorothy and Don about an invitation I had received to present a paper on household labor to a very small group of eminent sociologists in Washington, D.C. (see Sarah Fenstermaker Berk, "Some Behavioral Consequences of Women's Labor: A Nonrecursive Model," in Ida H. Simpson and Richard Simpson, eds., *Research in the Sociology of Work*, vol. 2 [Greenwich, Conn.: JAI Press, 1983], pp. 33–67. I got very useful words of wisdom from each of them. Don said, "Just do what you do." Dorothy said, "Just remember they're all baboons." I did and they were.

17. Dorothy Smith, "A Sociology for Women," in Julia A. Sherman and Evelyn T. Beck, eds., *The Prism of Sex*, (Madison: University of Wisconsin Press, 1983); and Dorothy Smith, "On Sociological Description: A Method from Marx," *Human Studies* 4 (Winter 1981): 313–337.

18. Sarah Fenstermaker Berk, *The Gender Factory: The Allocation of Work in American Households* (New York: Plenum, 1985).

19. Ibid., p. 165.

20. Candace West and Don Zimmerman, "Doing Gender," *Gender and Society* 1 (Winter 1987): 25–151. For examples of later work, see Sarah Fenstermaker, Candace West, and Don Zimmerman, "Gender Inequalities: New Conceptual Terrain," in Rae L. Blumberg, ed., *Gender, Family, and Economy: The Triple Overlap* (Beverly Hills, Calif.: Sage, 1991), pp. 289–307; Candace West and Sarah Fenstermaker, "Power, Inequality, and the Accomplishment of Gender: An Ethnomethodological View," in Paula England, ed., *Theory on Gender/ Feminism on Theory* (Chicago: Aldine, 1993), pp. 261–279; and Candace West and Sarah Fenstermaker, "Doing Difference," *Gender and Society* 9 (winter 1995): 516–523.

21. Fenstermaker Berk, *The Gender Factory*, pp. 205–206.

22. This may be a pattern, particularly for white academic feminists, where as one gets more senior and influential, one's political work is focused more narrowly on the academic community. We do, after all, wish to work where we believe we can make the most difference. There are stultifying downsides to such choices, of course, but they can sometimes effectively blend one's intellectual and political struggles.

23. Sometimes the compulsive good citizenship that women academics are known for can pay off. In the decade before, many of us had accumulated both significant goodwill and political capital (from across the campus and its mix of political persuasions), which we could now cash in on behalf of the program. Just as our intellectual talents varied, so, too, did our spheres of influence: whereas some had friends in administration, others had influence in the Academic Senate, and so on. As a result, the entire campus community publicly supported the program's establishment.

*Lynn Weber, Elizabeth Higginbotham, and Bonnie Thornton Dill*

# Sisterhood as Collaboration: Building the Center for Research on Women at the University of Memphis

This essay explores the connections between the development of the University of Memphis Center for Research on Women and the personal biographies of its three founders: Bonnie Thornton Dill, Elizabeth Higginbotham, and Lynn Weber.[1] From its inception in 1982, the center was distinctive among women's research centers. Two of its founders were African-American women and one was a white southern woman. It was the first center funded by the Ford Foundation at a regional comprehensive state university rather than at an established research university. Its central mission—to examine the intersections of race, class, and gender—was a direct outgrowth of our scholarly pursuits, as well as of our biographies. All of us are sociologists and have realized the vision for the center through collaborating on both sociological research and teaching that are centered in an agenda for social change.

We begin this essay with a discussion of several themes that characterize our common scholarly visions, action strategies, and personal histories. This presentation is followed by biographical vignettes and substantive discussions of our scholarly works and our activism through the Center for Research on Women.

## Themes in Our Biographies, Theory, and Practice

Several themes characterize the collective vision of race, class, and gender that we developed and nurtured in conjunction with many other teacher/scholar/activists around the nation. These themes so powerfully contributed to each of our biographies that when the Ford Foundation gave us the opportunity to propose a women's research center in 1982, we had no problem articulating our broad mission and goals.

First, we each knew at a deep personal level that race, class, and gender are *power relations* of dominance and subordination that are socially constructed and historically specific and that are *primary* forms of social organization. We knew this because these truths were central to our lived experiences of multiple dimensions of oppression as African-American and working-class women and to the social histories of the post–World War II period, when we came of age as sociologists. We each, in fact, pursued sociology to understand and to change the injustices we abhorred. The fact that by 1982 no existing women's research center or research tradition had yet articulated such a stance meant only that we had a greater challenge. We never doubted the correctness of this basic belief.

Second, we knew our mission would be to validate and promote the views of women of color, working-class women, and other groups that experienced oppression along multiple dimensions. To understand the nature of race, class, and gender, we needed to encourage and promote scholarship about oppression by many individuals and groups that had faced oppression and been silenced in dominant culture scholarly traditions, as well as in the newly emerging scholarship on women.

To us, gender had always been significant within the context of race and class: it was never salient in isolation from race or class as a source of our own sense of what structures our worlds, limits our options, or provides opportunities. The opportunity to establish our center provides a case in point. In 1981, the Ford Foundation extended an invitation to Bonnie to develop a proposal for a center for research on women at the University of Memphis. It seemed apparent to us that a combination of factors, including Bonnie's scholarly work, her race, her gender, and her location at a *southern* university at a particular historical moment, rather than any single factor, influenced this invitation. Notwithstanding the significance, perhaps primacy, of race and class in our worldviews, our scholarly production and activism have most forcefully affected and found acceptance among the now very large community of feminist sociologists and women's studies scholars.

Although our articulation of race and class occurred within this gendered context, white middle-class women's experiences and the scholarly positions articulated from their standpoints rarely resonated with our own. When we found them useful, it was most often as a counterpoint that clarified our own places by demonstrating differences in perspective produced by race and class privilege among women. The preoccupation among many white feminists with finding "common ground" or a set of "universal" women's experiences to "bind us together as women" was never, and is not now, an exercise we deemed worthwhile.[2]

We never doubted, however, the necessity and value of working together with many diverse groups to gain scholarly insight and to promote social change. We shared a desire to learn from groups different from our own. A basic mistrust of a power structure whose portrayals of our groups rarely conformed to our experiences led us to question dominant culture images of other subordinate groups.

We are aware of the power of individualism, status rankings, and competition in shaping the worldviews, career paths, and personal goals of the U.S. middle class.[3] By the time all three of us met, we had already successfully survived college and graduate school, had attained faculty status, and had thus been exposed to the reward system in academia that paralleled that of other middle-class occupations. However, our working-class, African-American, and female socialization had taught us to value collaboration, collective action, and social justice, values that find few legitimized outlets in academia.

Although as director Bonnie was the most visible representative of the center to foundation officers and university administrators, as a mother of a two-year-old son and newborn twin girls she knew that she could not and did not want to envision and create a unique research center single-handedly. Instead of acting alone, she collaborated with Elizabeth and Lynn, and they consulted other women-of-color scholars and collectively created the vision for the center. Even after the proposal was developed and the center was well established on the basis of a strong alliance and shared roles and responsibilities, it took a number of years for people to see that the center was always the product of a collective effort of the three of us, our staff, and our national network.

All three of us had fairly extensive experience in crossing social barriers, building coalitions, and standing up for principles we believed in—as presidents of our high school classes and student bodies and as leaders in many organizations and arenas from civil rights to sports. We had learned to accept and appreciate difference; to use our marginality, "outsider-within" statuses, and multiple memberships to bridge social divides; and to be especially critical of stances that emanated from privileged standpoints or stances that each of us might take that emanated from our own privilege.

Finally, even though we each experienced painful restrictions on our lives based on race, class, and gender, we also experienced uncommon levels of direct involvement with white middle-class and elite worlds. We not only crossed the race, class, and gender social boundaries that most of our young cohorts did not, we also learned to function well in those places where we stood out as different because of our race, class, and/or gender.

In the discussion that follows, we hope to illustrate some of the ways that these themes emerged through our lives and shaped both our scholarship and the character of the Center for Research on Women.

## Historical Context for Development of the Center

In 1982 when the center was established, there were approximately twenty-five other women's research centers nationwide. Most had been started with Ford Foundation funding as early as 1972. By the early 1980s, the field of women's studies had made important inroads into the academy, but its impact had been most visibly and forcefully felt in the humanities, particularly in English through the Modern Language Association. Women of color offered sophisticated critiques of the white middle-class male biases in all fields, including sociology, but sociological scholarship on race relations, social class, and gender continued to develop in almost complete isolation from each other. Race relations scholarship explored race from the perspectives of men, gender scholarship explored gender from the perspectives of white women, and social class scholarship explored class from the perspectives of white middle-class men. All obscured the perspectives of workers and of people of color.[4] The irony of ignoring groups whose experiences typically reflected the confluence of all three major dimensions of inequality was captured in the oft-cited title of one of the first anthologies about black women's studies: *All the Women Are White, All the Blacks Are Men, but Some of Us Are Brave: Black Women's Studies.*[5]

In the early 1980s, black women were beginning to make their voices heard in discussions of women's lives.[6] Bonnie Dill was among the first black women scholars whose critical perspective on race and gender was published in a major feminist journal.[7] Her presentation at the Seventh Scholar and the Feminist Conference at the Barnard College Women's Center in 1980 gained the attention of the Ford Foundation program officer for women's studies, Mariam Chamberlain. A version of Dill's keynote address later appeared in *Feminist Studies.*[8]

Chamberlain and Dill began discussions about establishing a research center at the University of Memphis as part of the foundation's dual interest in developing centers in southern universities that addressed race and gender. Bonnie initially received a small grant to support the work of the Inter-University Research Group Exploring the Intersection of Race and

Gender.[9] This group laid much of the groundwork for the center. Later Bonnie and Lynn, in collaboration with Elizabeth, applied for and received an initial three-year grant from the Ford Foundation for core support for the Center for Research on Women at the University of Memphis. At the same time, a center at Duke University and the University of North Carolina, Chapel Hill, and one at the University of Washington were established with Ford Foundation funding. The Women's Research and Resource Center at Spelman College was established around the same time through a grant from the Mott Foundation. Each of these centers identified race and gender as central components in their missions, but each center developed a distinct, yet complementary approach.[10]

## Biographical Statements: Growing Up

By the time we met one another, we had each become highly skilled at negotiating the boundaries of race and class. Our biographies are replete with experiences in which we were outsiders, an "other," different from the majority of people in the particular settings of school, work, or sports. Through these experiences, we became adept at crossing class and racial borders and at communicating with diverse groups of people, including white middle-class men and women. We were each acutely aware of the pain and isolation that accompany being seen as outsiders, but we also knew the basic human desire for connection and belonging.

When we first sat down to think about this article with one another, we discussed our lives or, more accurately, reminded each other of life stories we had shared over many years of friendship. We did make one rather funny new discovery about ourselves: Bonnie had been the president of her high school senior class, and Elizabeth and Lynn had been the presidents of their all-girls high school student bodies. Furthermore, we each attributed those elections at the time, as well as many other leadership roles we played later in our lives, to our marginality and to the border-crossing skills we had developed to survive on the margins.

### Elizabeth Higginbotham
*I grew up black and working class in New York City. I was the second of five children and the oldest daughter. My father was a bartender at a jazz club in the Village and later a waiter in hotels, where he served at various functions, such as weddings, lunches, breakfasts, and dinners. In his younger years, he had been a Pullman porter, riding back and forth across the country.[11] My mother entered paid employment after I entered junior high. She had a retail sales job at a*

department store and later was a secretary with the New York public school system.

My father often talked about his work, his working buddies, and the class relationships of the job. When I was in the second and third grades, I vividly remember my father's friend Larry coming by the apartment every day to travel with my father to work. It seemed so nice that I have since always felt that work should be shared with your friends—an aspect of working-class life that I wanted in my middle-class position. In fact, I was shocked by the isolated nature of academic life when I began my first full-time faculty position at the University of Pittsburgh. I made the decision to move to Memphis so that working with my friends Lynn and Bonnie would become a reality in my professional life. Lynn shared this distinctly working-class view of work with me, and we often fondly referred to taking our lunch pails to work in the center's "factory" together.

My family moved from Harlem to lower Manhattan when I was five. Childhood summers were spent in Pittsburgh with my grandparents and extended family, and later moves (family and individual) took me to other neighborhoods and regions. These moves were important in my life since they meant entering different settings where I had to learn what was expected of me and to exhibit appropriate behaviors.

My formal education began in a public elementary school on the East Side of Manhattan in 1953. This neighborhood, now the East Village, was overwhelmingly working class but ethnically and racially mixed. Even though I grew up outside the black communities of New York, I was very aware of race since I was often the only black student in my classes. This early experience also exposed me to other people of color (Puerto Ricans and Asian Americans) and a host of first- and second-generation white ethnic students.

After Thanksgiving in 1960, my family moved to the Upper West Side of Manhattan, where my world grew to include middle-class young people. This neighborhood had a mixture of racial and social class tensions and intimacies. I transferred to Joan of Arc Junior High School and spent the remainder of the seventh grade in a diverse classroom. There were middle-class and working-class students, as well as students from a range of racial and ethnic and cultural backgrounds. I enjoyed this class, where my propensity to challenge myself by reading the longest book, memorizing the longest poems, and tackling major projects was appreciated by all, even those students who selected an e. e. cummings poem, "The Fog," over Robert Frost's "The Wall." Our English/social studies and homeroom teacher, Mrs. Witte, made us all feel appreciated and welcomed.

It was in that junior high school that I was "selected" by teachers and administrators for mobility. In eighth grade, another black classmate, William, and

I were taken out of our diverse class and moved to a predominantly white class. For the eighth and ninth grades, William, Evelyn, and I were the three black students in an "enrichment track" class. This meant crossing many borders, but I enjoyed the educational challenges, as well as learning about the lives and families of other students. The classroom was a cooperative setting where we worked together on course projects, committees, and field trips. Even though I was always conscious of representing the race in this very small fishbowl, I appreciated the community of teachers and administrators who exposed us to classical music, museums, plays, and musicals and encouraged us to see the city as a resource for us all.

I decided to attend the district all-girls high school, Julia Richman High School, because it was reputed to have a very solid college preparatory program. Over my three years in high school, I watched the high ability academic courses become more white and middle class, as even I drifted into the regular academic program in my senior year. As a senior, I took advanced placement history and fought to gain access to college preparatory English. In retrospect, I can see that I was disengaged from many courses because of the way they were taught, and I therefore put my attention elsewhere. I became involved with New York High School Friends of SNCC (Student Nonviolent Coordinating Committee), and that made the high school years tolerable and provided me with an important way to connect to race issues. I also developed my leadership skills in this arena. In my high school, I was active in the Human Relations Club and very visible as a political person. As a senior, I was elected president of the student government organization.[12]

With a mixed high school record and a consistent ability to botch standardized tests, I started college at the Borough of Manhattan Community College in 1966. This was an exciting year since I was able to connect with students from around the city who, like me, were smart but alienated by the routines and memorization of high school. I had wonderful teachers, and often my classmates and I took discussions out of the classroom to the coffee shop, located on the ground floor of the office building that was then our campus.

After one year, I transferred to City College of New York. Open enrollment did not come to the City University until 1971, so during my three plus years on campus, I was one of a few students of color. Again, I felt highly visible, but in retrospect I can see that my New York public education and years of working gave me a broad experience. I moved into and out of working- and middle-class settings and across racial and ethnic lines. Although this experience generated many questions about social systems, it also fostered a comfort with being different and an ability to build coalitions and communities in different settings.

*Bonnie Thornton Dill*

*Growing up on the South Side of Chicago in the 1950s taught me a lot about race and class. Both of my parents were professionals who had grown up in Chicago; like many of their contemporaries, they were the first in their families to have the opportunity to complete college and a professional education. My father was a pharmacist who owned his own business; my mother, a schoolteacher, later owned and operated an independent nursery school. Although both my parents were products of the Chicago public schools, my mother's experiences as a teacher there convinced her that she wanted a different kind of education for me. So beginning in nursery school and continuing through twelfth grade, I attended the University of Chicago Laboratory School.*

*Although my classmates were overwhelmingly white, my neighborhood community, church, and social life were unmistakably rooted in African-American culture until high school. Through these sources I learned black history, culture, and social life. At the dinner table and at social gatherings, I heard discussions about improving conditions for "the race." The names of notable African Americans, such as Ida B. Wells, Percy Julian, Benjamin Mays, Paul Robeson, and Mary McLeod Bethune, became familiar to me at an early age. There was no questioning that education was the key to achievement, that contributing to the improvement of the race was expected, and that I had a rich legacy to inspire and sustain me.*

*The nurturance and pride with which I learned about race in my family and immediate community contrasted sharply with the ways I learned about race from living in Chicago. Chicago in the 1950s was a racially divided city. My parents purchased a home in a section called Englewood in 1944. They were among the first African-American families on the block. Within a few years all the white people had moved out. This was a typical pattern in the so-called integration of Chicago: block busting, distinct racial and ethnic neighborhoods, and white flight. In fact, the block just north of us was divided in the middle by elevated railroad tracks. Only white people lived on the other side of the tracks. Interestingly, my mother told me of a conversation she had with a white woman who resided in that area and boasted that the Catholic parish had bought up vacant homes in that neighborhood in order to ensure that no black people moved in. Even if apocryphal, this story conveys the racial divisiveness that characterized the city. I never rode through that neighborhood without feeling apprehension and a sense of threat. As children out at play, we never ventured over there.*

*Another incident that is my earliest personal remembrance of racism occurred at the neighborhood swimming pool. I was perhaps six or seven at the time, and one hot summer afternoon my mother took me to the local public pool to swim. I joyfully jumped into the water, and soon there was a group of white teens yelling at my mother to get me out of the pool before they threw me out. My mother looked at me and told me not to move. So I didn't move, but I must admit that at that moment I would have preferred to be any place else but there. Eventually we left, but that night my mother wrote letters and made phone calls to the mayor and numerous other local public officials. By the following summer, the pool was integrated Chicago style: black folks swam there, and white folks left.*

*There were many aspects of my early life that made me keenly aware of class differences in the African-American community. My extended family consisted of mostly working-class and a few middle-class individuals. Those differences were the source of conflict and jealousy within the family at the same time that they were a source of pride and defined patterns of family support and assistance. Our neighborhood, too, although consisting of mostly stable working-class and middle-class African-American homeowners, was not without tension. The oldest girl from one of the least stable families on the block teased and taunted me about attending a private school. I now recognize this as class anger and resentment, but it sometimes made neighborhood play unpleasant. On a broader scale, many of the problems of joblessness and low income that my parents and their friends discussed and sought to address were problems resulting from both racial discrimination and lack of economic resources. My parents believed strongly in cooperative economics and had been founders of a consumer cooperative that ran a grocery store and a savings and loan association and now operates a senior citizen housing complex.*

*Being one of a few African-American students in a predominantly white private school was not as alienating as it might be today, partly because I had such a strong and rich family, community, and social life—particularly during elementary school. In high school, however, I became acutely aware of the two separate and conflicting worlds in which I lived and the challenges of trying to maintain both of them. My conflict became palpable, as most high school conflicts do, around the lunch table. I had many different friends in high school and ate lunch with different people—sometimes with my African-American friends and sometimes with my white friends. One day, however, my black friends informed me that they were having a private club meeting and that I couldn't join them. After that happened repeatedly, I began to eat lunch regularly with my white friends. Although I remained friendly with the African-American girls and continued to be involved with them socially outside of school, I was not in their inner circle, nor were they in mine.*

*My access to and engagement with white friends at school exposed me to a variety of life experiences. My best friend's family was Jewish and had escaped from Poland through France during World War II. Another friend's father was a rabbi. Several other friends had parents who were faculty members at the*

University of Chicago. My connections with groups of both African-American and white students was an important factor in my being elected senior class president.

## Lynn Weber

Early in life I developed a strong image of life as the interplay of insiders and outsiders: as an Irish Catholic raised in predominantly Protestant Nashville, Tennessee; as a student in an extremely rigid mission elementary school; as a working-class state champion tennis player in the middle-class world of tennis; and as a straight A student and leader in my all-girls working-class high school. Adult experiences in college and in my career as a sociologist remade my worldview in some ways, but notions of power and privilege, exclusion and oppression were already there to be named and refined, but not to be denied or doubted

My daddy was a steamfitter and my mom a secretary at the Internal Revenue Service. Although he was never active in union politics, my father was a union member, a fairly uncommon experience in the working-class South. Both my parents worked very hard to provide an opportunity for me and my younger brother and sister to "get ahead," and college attendance was the route they encouraged.

Catholics in Nashville were very aware of our outsider status. I grew up knowing that "we" (my family and others) were in hostile territory surrounded by Protestants (they were generically all alike to me) and a mysterious organization called the KKK that put us in the same despised category as "colored people" (with whom I had some experience) and Jews (with whom I had absolutely no experience).

My schoolmates were all white, though ethnically quite diverse, and so were my best friends: Lucia was Irish, Debbie was Lebanese, and Cheryl was Italian. But our greater reality was the common thread of our differentness from the larger community. Because we went to school on different buses (from public school children) and wore uniforms, we were easily spotted as outsiders in our neighborhood. But the outsider pain of exclusion and derision by the dominant culture was coupled with a strong insider sense of community belonging and moral rightness.

At my elementary school, a mission school taught by French Canadian nuns whose only other mission school was in Africa, we observed a strict code of silence. Except when we were outside at recess, we never spoke unless called on by a teacher, and then we were required to stand whenever we spoke. Whenever an adult entered our classroom, the entire class stood and remained standing until given permission to sit. Our conduct was constantly monitored by teachers or by designated students when teachers were not present. We were punished for ever speaking: on the bus, in the bathroom, in the cafeteria, in the hallways, in the church, and, of course, in the classroom. Our parents reinforced the rigid authoritarianism of the schools. Misbehavior at school also brought punishment at home.

During elementary school, I wanted desperately to be good, to avoid breaking the rules, and to avoid punishment. At the same time, the system fostered in me an "us" (students) versus "them" (adults) mentality. I walked a fine line between these worlds: to conform and thus to please teachers and when that conformity brought the desired and dreaded designation as monitor, not to rat on my classmates. To become a turncoat who betrayed other students was both a reward for good behavior and a threat to solidarity and friendships. In contrast, my brother rebelled and faced daily punishment. Thus, very early in life I began to see that things simply weren't always fair and that young people could do very little about it. At the same time, the Catholic emphasis on racial and economic justice heavily influenced my worldview. My decision to attend college seemed, in fact, somewhat like a copout, the Peace Corps or direct social service being the more worthy routes (short of entering a convent).

Sports was, for me, a source of great enjoyment and accomplishment and was ultimately a ticket to visit the middle class. I began my interest in sports as the only girl in my neighborhood play group of six. We played all the major sports in season: football, basketball, and baseball. As I got older, even though my father was a coach, I was excluded from Little League Baseball because I was a girl, despite several coaches' pleas to the national association to let me in. My family's response was to enroll me in free tennis (a sport for girls) clinics in the public parks. I was good at tennis, too. From the age of twelve, competitions pulled me into a world of rich, white, country-club people all over the South. I experienced this world in a very different way than my middle-class contemporaries did. My tennis friends and competitors never came to my side of town to practice. Instead, along with black women domestics, I often rode the bus an hour across town. As city and state champion for several years, I traveled and stayed with wealthy people all over the region who housed tournament participants for free. During those years from twelve to twenty-three, I constantly crossed the boundary from working-class home to middle-class school and to middle-class country club almost daily. No middle-class friend or competitor ever crossed my way.

## Biographical Statements: Entering Sociology

We each entered graduate school in sociology in the 1970s to pursue our dual commitments to promoting social justice and to securing decent middle-class employment. We knew, however, from our personal experiences and from the social movements of the times that the formal educational system could not be counted on to embrace our perspectives and meet our needs. We would have to make these things happen on our own. We each entered our programs with primary interests in race and class. As we pursued our degrees, courses in gender were only beginning to be offered on the graduate level. Bonnie and Elizabeth each took a graduate seminar focused on gender issues. Bonnie read early feminist literature in her course and realized that it did not speak to women's realities as she knew them. For Elizabeth, a few of her sociological seminars included feminist social science works. She also participated in a research seminar on gender where other participants studied the lives of white middle-class women, while the two women of color focused on the lives of women of color.

Our graduate schools provided us with skills and credentials, but these were not settings where we flourished. Gender and race barriers were firmly entrenched in our graduate departments, which had lifted barriers of admission but did not embrace the perspectives that women, working-class people, and people of color used to understand social life.

### Elizabeth Higginbotham

*I squeezed my undergraduate degree at City College in between the various part-time jobs necessary for my survival. Therefore, graduate school was a unique opportunity for me to finally have the time for the reflection and interaction with other students that my peers in graduate school had had in their college years. Bringing skills and interests from my political work in SNCC in 1971, I organized a racially integrated women's consciousness-raising group. Later I pulled together a support group of women-of-color graduate students in the Boston/Cambridge area. In addition to helping each other survive and write dissertations in overwhelmingly white graduate departments, we openly discussed our families, schooling experiences, upward social class mobility, and relationships across gender, race, and class. In these peer networks I learned far more about issues that were important to me and critical to my survival than I learned from graduate faculty at Brandeis.*

*Although many of the white graduate students at Brandeis did not attend regional and/or national professional meetings until they were looking for jobs, I was encouraged by an undergraduate professor to begin attending these meetings early in my graduate career. In this way I followed developments in the study of U.S. race relations, content that was missing in the graduate curriculum at Brandeis. I also established a network of relationships with graduate students of color at other institutions and received encouragement and support from senior black colleagues in the discipline. Their support and encouragement were critical to my survival as a graduate student.*

*My part-time teaching experiences and interaction with students and fac-*

ulty at the University of Massachusetts at Boston motivated me to complete a doctorate. But it was my interactions with other people of color that actually gave me the social, emotional, and intellectual resources to secure that goal. While building and operating within a network of graduate students of color, I met Bonnie Thornton Dill, a graduate student in New York who was also working on black women. Initially, Cheryl Townsend Gilkes, then a graduate student at Northeastern University and now associate professor at Colby College, heard Bonnie Dill deliver a paper at the 1975 annual meetings of the American Sociological Association in San Francisco (that year my meager earnings did not permit me to travel to the annual meetings). Cheryl, excited by the work of this sister graduate student, made copies of Bonnie's paper for members in our Boston group. I contacted Bonnie, and we met at the 1976 ASA meeting in New York City. Our budding group of black women sociologists nurtured and guided each other's work in the absence of senior mentors in our institutions knowledgeable about gender and race. We organized panels at regional and national meetings to present our work and expand our network. In 1979 we took pride as four in our group completed dissertations.[13] We continued to support each other as we launched our careers.

## Bonnie Thornton Dill

I entered graduate school in sociology at New York University in 1972 after working for seven years in New York City. My first job after college was with the federal Office of Economic Opportunity. I continued to work in the War on Poverty at both the federal and local levels for several years. After earning a master's degree in human relations, I became a counselor in the SEEK Program (the special admissions program for African-American and Latino students of the City University of New York) at Bernard M. Baruch College. My work in organizing community corporations, setting up family planning programs, and counseling students of color had given me hands-on experience with the problems that sociological theories purport to address. I came to graduate school looking for theories that would help me understand and make sense of what I had learned about racism and poverty. I also came to sociology because I knew I had a different story to tell about African-American families than the one that was sweeping the country at the time under the title of the "Moynihan Report."

I began my work in sociology as a part-time student, convinced that if I did not like it and if it did not provide me with a way to address the issues I was concerned about, I would not continue. I had been an English major in undergraduate school and was unfamiliar with the discipline of sociology. Once I read C. Wright Mills, however, I was hooked: hooked on the idea that biography and history were keys to understanding people in society. I entered the field when conflict theory was displacing functionalism, and that shift explained a lot of the world as I came to know it. It also fit with my desire to use sociological theory as a tool for social improvement and social change.

I entered graduate school determined to study African-American families, but I did not expect to find much expertise about them within the institution. I knew from the outset that I would have to build my own support networks. As I became more engaged in the field, I sought other graduate students who shared my interests. Several of my efforts to exchange work and get feedback were unsuccessful, but once I met Elizabeth Higginbotham and Cheryl Townsend Gilkes, I found myself among a group of developing young scholars who became career-long allies, colleagues, and friends.

Through graduate school, I learned to be part of a long-distance network and to use the annual sociology meetings as a point of connection. When I moved from New York to Memphis, I took my network and networking ideas with me. From the start, Lynn Weber and I got along. Like me, she had gone to graduate school with interests that could not be fully accommodated there, and she had created her own concentration in race. Her scholarly and personal interest in race was our first point of connection, and over the years we discovered many others. It was inevitable, then, that when Elizabeth came to Memphis in 1979 to visit, she, Lynn, and I would begin to work together.

## Lynn Weber

I changed majors eight times in my four years of undergraduate work at Memphis State, trying biology, math, social work, and psychology before settling in on sociology the semester before I graduated in 1971. I pursued sociology to understand some of the tremendous social issues of the time: racism, war, and poverty. During work on my master's at Memphis State and my doctorate at the University of Illinois, Champaign-Urbana, my attitude toward graduate school was that it was a necessary evil en route to a secure job and decent pay in a field I liked. I looked on it as an evil because I was acutely aware of the political nature of the process and the way it influenced every aspect of graduate education from entry to exit.

Early in my M.A. program, for example, the new chair of the department of sociology actively campaigned to deny tenure to a faculty member. Although I was unaware of these men's struggles, I was the only student called by both sides to testify in an appeals committee hearing. I saw the whole sordid affair as an exploitation of relatively powerless students in the petty, foolish, and unnecessary power games that faculty play. I still feel the same way about most university politics today.

My class, region, and gender were each explicitly presented as barriers to *my continuing down one path or another throughout my education. For example, my undergraduate professors told me that because an undergraduate degree from Memphis State was a liability, only after completing a master's would I be able to compete with undergraduates from top universities to get into a "good" doctoral program.*

*When I did enter the University of Illinois, my advisory committee in the second semester indicated that I would need to take more coursework than other graduate students because my undergraduate institution was southern and its faculty was "unknown." My faculty advisory committee made this decision after I had completed my first semester with four A's, no incompletes, a fellowship, and a part-time job. At the time, I had already begun to systematically study inequities of power within the classroom. As a participant-observer and unbeknown to the faculty, I conducted a power analysis of a team-taught theory seminar. The results clearly showed the ways that the frequency and content of communications varied with the status of the speaker.*

*Despite my being a straight-A student in graduate school, I never wanted to revel in or repeat my educational experiences, so I set my mind to getting out as fast as I could. Even though I had studied race and worked on a study of social class identification, it was not until I met Elizabeth and Bonnie that I first began to see clearly the connections between my work and my self.*

*I will never forget my deep-seated feeling of liberation as I came to know Bonnie Dill after she joined the Memphis State faculty in 1978, two years after I had. I came to feel what I had never imagined possible before: that there could be a sociology/professional colleague who frequently shared my views and interests. More important, when we did not agree, I learned from her different perspective. She was the first colleague I had ever had who related to me as an equal with respect. The relationship meant so much to me that I grew in leaps and bounds in self-confidence, in intellectual creativity and risk-taking, and in productivity.*

*The relationship affected me in ways that I did not comprehend. When Bonnie was absent for a semester after the birth of her twin girls in 1980, for example, I carried on my daily work much as I had before she came. I had no soulmate at the office, but I frequently visited her and the children at her home and helped with regular outings. The first week after her return, we entered the sociology building after having lunch. An African-American woman on the house-keeping staff proclaimed down the entry hall for all to hear: "It sure is good you [Bonnie] got back. She was so sad while you were gone! She's smiling again." I had no idea that my feelings were so different and visible. I had discussed them with no one. Of course, it was not my faculty colleagues but a member of the housekeeping staff who saw the change in me and reflected it back.*

## Points of Connection/Building the Center/Intellectual Vision

As we came to know each other across our diverse backgrounds, our intellectual interests in social inequality, our critical perspectives on power structures, our desire to be scholar activists, and our multiple experiences of oppression all became central points of connection among the three of us. The people we were and the instincts we followed led us to trust one another in our critical stances toward the mainstream of sociology as a discipline and of the academic institutions where we worked.

The Department of Sociology at the University of Memphis, where Lynn began her career in 1976 and which Bonnie joined in 1978, was overwhelmingly white and male. And virtually all of the men had wives who bore primary responsibility for home and family lives. During her first few weeks on campus, Bonnie was invited to lunch by three of her male colleagues. When they arrived at the cafeteria, all three of them pulled out lunch bags with sandwiches their wives had prepared. Bonnie recalled: "I was astounded to think this was supposed to be my professional reference group. Every morning before I went to work, I was getting food and formula together for my five-month-old son, and my husband was busy going to work himself. There was no one to make lunch for either of us."

Bonnie and Lynn supported each other's efforts to manage the demands of family while maintaining scholarly productivity and quality teaching. Many early meetings to plan the center's work were conducted at Bonnie's house while feeding and caring for babies. When Elizabeth moved to Memphis in 1983 and joined the center she had helped to frame, she needed support as a single woman to keep endless work demands from consuming her entire life. Our everyday lives in the department mirrored our places in the discipline, and the encouragement we gave each other to value our personal lives while pursuing our careers was so important to our survival that we knew it would be key to the survival of other women. We had already become good friends before we initiated the center, but as we shared our work and lives over time, we became sisters.

Our center's collective vision was developed through interactions among ourselves and other members of our intellectual and activist communities at the University of Memphis, in the city of Memphis, and across the nation. By sharing our individual wishes, assessing our strengths, and identifying our communities' needs, we set out to nurture a national and local community of scholar-activists working for social change for women of color and working-class southern women. Because we are sociologists, our center was then, and remains, grounded in a sociological perspective.

The process through which we came to an understanding of our common vision for the center and for our individual roles within it was much more chaotic and ambiguous. Because we were clearly creating a new kind of institution in a unique location, we found no models that guided us very far toward our goals. When Elizabeth and Lynn, for example, wrote a proposal to the National Institute of Mental Health (NIMH) for research on upward mobility among black and white women, no one at the University of Memphis State had ever before submitted a successful research proposal to NIMH. The Office of Sponsored Programs gave us the closest examples they had on file: two National Institutes of Health grant proposals, one on hearing aids and a second on blood hemoglobin.

At that time, much of what we attempted, either in our scholarship or in other projects, felt like walking into a void. Who knows how you'll get through it or where you'll be when you do? Many of the things we did as a nationally focused, externally funded program had never been done before at the University of Memphis. Often new rules and procedures were developed as a result of our actions.

During the first five years of the center's operation (1982–1987), for example, the university had no written procedures or standard practices for such common grant issues as allocation of indirect costs, faculty buyouts, obtaining of space, and renovation of space. Each grantee negotiated in private with several levels of higher administration (chair, dean, vice president for sponsored programs, vice president for academic affairs), and it was never clear exactly with whom we should negotiate. Frequently, we would reach an agreement with the dean of arts and sciences only to learn a few months later that the vice president for sponsored programs would not carry through on some aspect that involved (or came to involve) his office. Because administrators rarely agreed to put anything in writing, we constantly faced crises as issues we thought were settled arose when someone's paycheck was not cut or travel not approved. And even though administrators appreciated the money and the visibility of the grants that we brought to the university, they did not believe that our center, or women's studies as a whole, would survive for five years. So they were never willing to invest in our operation the way that they did in other centers on campus, such as the Center for Earthquake Research and Information (CERI) or the Manpower Research Center. As we sought to figure out how to negotiate the system, the director of CERI was, in fact, quite helpful and was also very frustrated with the uncertainties in the system.

Given this high degree of uncertainty, the processes we developed reflected the creative tension of oppression and activism as we experienced it in individual and collective ways. In a system that had historically devalued our people and our work, we acted because our individual and collective survival depended on it. Regularly sharing our personal experiences and studying the histories of oppressed groups were means through which we found in an uncertain world one certainty: the necessity and value of the struggle for justice.

Because of the limited resources available to us at the University of Memphis, we decided that our mission had to be narrowly focused and clearly defined. We knew that we and others sharing our vision needed a place that would give priority to a social structural study of race, class, and gender. We sought to legitimate the academic and activist pursuits that we and many others had engaged in for so many years.

In 1982, with Bonnie Dill as director and Lynn Weber as associate director, we formally announced our mission in our first newsletter: "This Center's first commitment is to advance, promote, and conduct research on working-class women in the South and women of color in the nation." We further stated that our enterprise would be defined through our actions. "Our activities of our first eleven months reflect the ways in which we see ourselves vis a vis the community of researchers, writers, and teachers who make up our target population, the University community in which we hope to become an increasingly important unit, and the Memphis community in which we live and work.[14]

During those first eleven months, we hosted a one-day workshop on women and work in the South; established a national advisory board; initiated a clearinghouse of scholars conducting research on women of color and on southern women; with local community activists, cosponsored a women and religion conference; produced a newsletter and a national and local mailing list; sponsored meetings of the Inter-University Research Group Exploring the Intersection of Race and Gender; planned our first summer institute, hosted our first visiting scholar, Elizabeth Higginbotham; started a series of working papers; established ties with many groups across the country; and began to develop research grant applications. We also provided a minority voice in the development of the National Council for Research on Women, a new coalition of twenty-eight centers for research on women.

On the home front, we also dealt with the institutional bureaucratic and political demands of hiring staff, identifying and renovating space, and establishing ourselves as a new unit on our campus. We also maintained

our involvement in campus committees and programs (e.g., women's studies and black studies) and taught two courses a semester.

Through the challenges of our first years, our intellectual vision became ever more focused and clear. We maintained our commitment to studying social structural systems of inequality embedded in race, class, and
gender relations and their ramifications for social life. Examining the diversity of social experiences across systems of oppression was a natural outgrowth of this focus. Through this process we demonstrated the importance
of multiple perspectives representing the views/insights/voices of those in
different relations of power for a more complete and accurate understanding of social reality. The basic truth of this principle was reinforced in our
everyday lives as we struggled together to develop our careers and build
the Center at the University of Memphis.

*Scholarship*

Because we wanted our scholarship to reflect the complexities of the social
world as we experienced and observed it, we sought to find new ways to
develop insights, design and conduct research, and write within a perspective integrating race, class, and gender. Thinking and writing together were
two of the ways we gained clarity. And we did this in an academic environment that favored individual achievement over collaborative efforts.

The Inter-University Group Exploring the Intersection of Gender and
Race opened the dialogue about gender and race. Within this group—Bonnie
and Elizabeth, along with Cheryl Townsend Gilkes, Evelyn Nakano Glenn,
and Ruth Zambrana—we rethought the influence of racial oppression on
women's lives by examining various groups of women in different
racial-ethnic communities. Lynn was often an informal participant in this
group and played a critical role on the faculty of the center's first summer
institute on women of color in 1983. That summer institute brought together graduate students and faculty, most of whom felt isolated in their
respective institutions because they lacked colleagues with whom to share
their work on women of color.[15]

We agreed that in feminist circles we often found ourselves surrounded
by middle-class white women who were unwilling to confront the racist
assumptions of women's studies. Even though we had each learned a lot
through placing women in the center of scholarly analysis, we were dissatisfied with the position of women of color and working-class women, who
were still on the margins. Along with Maxine Baca Zinn, a visiting scholar
at the center during summer 1984, we wrote a critique of exclusionary
practices in women's studies that was published in *Signs*.[16] We hoped that

making white feminists aware of their biases would prompt them to take issues of race and class more seriously.[17]

Extending the critique of white middle-class biases in women's studies was just one step on our scholarly journey. We also found ourselves critiquing work within several other subfields of scholarship. Although we found useful insights in historical and contemporary work in ethnic studies, male biases pervaded these fields. And even though scholarship on working-class women was growing, it was mostly historical and focused more on the employment and social lives of white women. Through careful analysis, critique, and selection, however, we used each of these scholarly traditions in our work.

We integrated our focus on race, class, and gender into this scholarship. We did not agree with the critique of the family as completely as many women's studies scholars did at the time, for example, because this paradigm ignored important aspects of family life for people of color. In some respects our families did constrain women, but we often felt more constrained by patriarchy in the public sector. Additionally, our families had often been sources of strength and refuge in a hostile society. Because racism and discrimination often pushed women of color out of the household and into the marketplace, we became particularly interested in employment, especially in the segmented labor systems in which women of color were found. Bonnie's research on black women domestics explored the working conditions, as well as the economic survival strategies, of these women.[18] Elizabeth and Evelyn Nakano Glenn looked at patterns whereby women of color performed reproductive work inside and outside of individual homes, often enabling middle- and upper-class white women to avoid this work.[19]

We were also interested in the ways in which state supports and private-sector benefits extended to families varied by race and class. Racial oppression made the history of motherhood for women of color decidedly different from that of white middle-class women.[20] This thinking provided the intellectual framework for Bonnie's exploration of female-headed families in mid-South rural counties. Bonnie, along with Michael Timberlake and Bruce Williams, secured funding from the Aspen Institute to examine the relationship among family structure, state supports, and community resources in the coping and survival strategies of low-income single mothers.[21]

Both Elizabeth and Lynn began to look to sociology to help them understand the upward class mobility struggles that they and other colleagues shared. In dissertation research, Elizabeth had been one of the first people to study social class differences among educated black women. Lynn was just completing a major project on American perceptions of class.[22] Both of those projects, in combination with life experiences, left them with many questions about the ways that race and gender shape the mobility process.

At the time, little was known about the social mobility process for white women and even less for black women and other women of color. They were typically either excluded from the research, or race and class were confounded in the same study; most often studies of minorities were on poor and/or working-class populations, and studies of white people were on middle-class populations. So Elizabeth and Lynn designed a joint research project to explore variations in the process of educational and occupational mobility in a wide range of areas, including the current work, family life, and health of black and white women professionals, managers, and administrators.[23]

They organized a team of graduate assistants and conducted focused life history interviews with two hundred black and white women of the baby-boom cohort (ages twenty-five to forty) who were employed full-time as professionals, managers, or administrators in the Memphis metropolitan area from 1985 to 1987.[24] Successful completion of this project was possible, in part, because the center had developed such strong ties to our local community, especially among black women. As we recruited participants, we called on women contacts and friends across the city to assist us in providing the contacts and assurances that black women were much more likely to need to feel comfortable in participating. Our study of the differences in methods required to recruit subjects is reported in a *Gender & Society* article that has been widely reprinted.[25]

The experiences of these black and white professional and managerial women have certainly painted a different picture from the dominant culture image of the mobility process based on research on white males. First and foremost, these women are not detached, isolated, or driven solely by career goals. Relationships with family of origin, partners, children, friends, and the wider racial community significantly shape the ways they envision and accomplish mobility and the ways they sustain themselves as professional and managerial women. For these women, for example, social mobility involved not only competition but also cooperation, community support, and personal obligations.[26]

*Teaching*

In addition to our scholarship, our commitment to creating space for multiple perspectives extended to our teaching and our relationships with students. We each desire to change education, making it more relevant to people like ourselves. With funding from the Ford Foundation, the Fund for the Improvement of Post Secondary Education, and the University of Memphis, we sponsored nine national workshops and/or summer institutes that highlighted the new scholarship on race, class, and gender. Most participants have been social science, history, and humanities educators, scholars, and graduate students.

We established an online database of bibliographic citations to social science research on women of color and southern women and continue to make this information available in printed bibliographies. We also maintain resources for curriculum change, publish working papers on curriculum issues, and biannually publish a newsletter that seeks to teach people about new scholarship. Center professional staff, primarily Lynn and Elizabeth, consult with other universities, colleges, and community colleges to aid in faculty development.

Through this combination of action/experience and research, we seek to "transform the curriculum," to develop a more inclusive curriculum by expanding the guiding vision, disciplinary knowledge base, and pedagogical strategies. In our work with faculty, we provide access to new race, class, and gender information that is relevant to their work; a broad vision of what an ideal, inclusive curriculum might contain; and pedagogical strategies to develop classroom climates that are open and positive for the diverse students in them.

We recognized the need for strong links among peers, and Elizabeth designed a model for our summer institutes and workshops whereby participants share their research and teaching issues in small groups, as well as in larger forums. Because we knew that people supporting each other as they develop research and teaching agendas was important, we facilitated exchanges across race, class, and gender among faculty so that faculty could do the same for their students. In this work, we have been trial-and-error learners, grateful for concrete feedback from workshop faculty and participants.

Lynn used her long-standing interest in classrooms and power to develop methods of promoting positive race, class, and gender dynamics in the classroom. She began work in this area in graduate school and extended it early in her teaching career to examine relationships between white faculty and black students. Building on experience and scholarship on race relations and small groups, she developed a variety of strategies for promoting positive race, class, and gender dynamics in the classroom.[27] They include ground rules for classroom discussion that acknowledge the presence of hierarchies in the classroom and ask students to show respect for one another in their communication. This work has helped many faculty around the nation understand how they can use their power in the classroom to establish the type of climate that would support learning across diversity.

### Building an Institution: Collaborative Work and Rewards

Because we were committed to work that incorporated the multiple perspectives of those in different power relations along race, class, and gender systems, we employed a collaborative model for our practice, as well as for our scholarship. And because collaborative work is often devalued in academia, where the ideal scholar is an isolated man working alone to write some great work or make some discovery, our collaborative practice is often deeply problematic within university hierarchies where issues of professional recognition and reward are concerned.

In developing the center, we were committed to sharing power and responsibility, yet little about the institution allowed for this model of functioning and organization. The lack of fit between our vision and the institution's structure proved to be a constant source of strain and tension. So it was critical for us to clarify and resolve issues among ourselves in order to present a united front to administrators and colleagues in the Department of Sociology and Social Work. Our resolve was based on our shared vision of goals for the center, our individual and collaborative research, and our commitment to our personal growth. Often achieving unity among ourselves meant challenging each other to be the best that we could be. Submitting grant proposals and being evaluated, for example, were never pleasant for anyone, particularly for Lynn, whose sense of fatalism made it difficult for her to believe that major granting agencies would fund us rookies. Yet Elizabeth realized that part of preparing a grant proposal was providing the emotional support to collaborators so that they could do their best writing: "I often had to find optimism I did not know I had." Together we pushed one another to do our best work, and as rookies we took reviewers' comments seriously and prepared a proposal that was initially funded for two years. After we completed data collection, we applied and secured an additional two years of funding. This commitment to one another, to getting through difficulties by resolving issues among ourselves, was central to our ability to build the center within the university.

As we worked together, we watched and learned as each of us faced different treatment from University of Memphis faculty, administrators, and students. Daily we went out from the safe space we created for ourselves in the center and later reported to each other the reactions we received from all quarters. We analyzed these encounters for their race, class, gender, and regional content and planned our next actions accordingly. This process was informal but systematic and necessary to our survival in a system that we often experienced as hostile and obstructionist. The process also solidified our friendships and commitment to one another and our goals.

The tension between our vision for the center and the structure of the institution played itself out in many ways throughout the years. Our institutional location and reporting structure, for example, changed four times in ten years. The University of Memphis administrators' ongoing ambivalence about where our unit should be located was reflected in the initial decision to establish the center as an independent unit reporting directly to the dean of arts and sciences and equivalent to departments and yet to exclude us from meetings of heads of departmental units and from routine administrative communications on the grounds that since we were not a teaching unit, much of the discussion at the meetings would not be relevant to us. It was not until 1987, our fifth year, that we received any base budget support from the institution.

From the beginning, Bonnie, the founding director, and Lynn, the associate director, attended all meetings with university administrators together to represent the center, the only unit in the institution to do so. As soon as we received a nominal base budget from the university, however, the center was moved into the Sociology Department, and we were told that only one person could now report to the dean. We were not invited to meetings with arts and sciences chairs and directors. We were sometimes dealt with directly, sometimes through the sociology chair, and sometimes not at all. As a result, we became much more vulnerable to an increasingly hostile Department of Sociology.[28] We continued to request and receive meetings with the dean but were not fully informed of all administrative issues and processes. It took critical changes in higher administration for our status on the campus to improve.

In 1991, when V. Lane Rawlins became president of the University of Memphis, he recognized the importance of women's studies as an interdisciplinary field—and as a labor economist, he acknowledged the realities of race and gender discrimination. Because he wants the university to serve the greater metropolitan area, including a central city that is 50 percent African American, the new administration is more appreciative of our programming, curriculum work, university service, and research publications focused on race, class, and gender than were past administrations. As the climate shifts, we become more involved on the campus in efforts to recruit and retain women faculty and faculty of color. We have also clarified our administrative location and routinized lines of reporting.

Over the years our personal and professional issues frequently clashed with the way things were done at the university. What made a difference for us in confronting these obstacles was that because we supported one another, these struggles were not as isolating and devastating as they could have been and typically are for faculty who lack colleagues to communicate with about their problems and who have a structural analysis from which to critique their situations.

In 1993 we received two major awards from the American Sociological Association: the Jessie Bernard Award, in recognition of how our collective work had enlarged the horizons of sociology to fully encompass the role of women in society, and the Distinguished Contributions to Teaching Award. We were nominated by our colleagues, people who had worked with us and/or attended our institutes and workshops. These awards acknowledged the impact of our work and research on the teaching of groups that are traditionally devalued and marginalized. And they recognized the legitimacy of the collaborative model we had worked so hard to develop and maintain. We appreciated this acknowledgment that we had successfully achieved one of our major goals: to create a place where work on race, class, and gender was unquestionably viewed as not just legitimate but also as crucial to the development of social theory. Unlike our experience as isolated graduate students, we are now secure in a large network of scholars who actively support one another in their work.

Finding a true voice to represent a self-defined standpoint is critical to the survival of oppressed groups. Finding this true voice is equally important for the survival of individual members of those groups. Our own experience of oppression and the skills we developed over our lifetimes guided us in our quest to find our own standpoints. We worked together to create a community centered in Memphis. We listened to and worked to help one another find our own unique lenses for viewing the world. We know all scholars, regardless of race, gender, and social class, need communities where they are insiders, where they are cherished for who they are and how they see the world, and where they are encouraged to share that vision and perspective with colleagues, students, and other communities.

## Notes

We wish to thank Jean Bohner, Arlene Kaplan Daniels, Barbara Laslett, Barrie Thorne, and Lynet Uttal for their comments on an early draft of this essay. We also appreciate the efforts of Melissa Fry in preparing the final copy for publication.

1. The University of Memphis was named Memphis State University until July 1994. In the text of this essay, we refer to the new name of the institution, but to be historically specific and retain the flow of the biographical narratives, we use the old name in these statements.
2. Ironically, it is that very search for a "common agenda as women" that leads many white middle-class women to continue to see the inclusion of oppressed groups as necessary at the same time that they cannot fully incorporate those groups. The very basis for the inclusion is the search for a way to ignore the race and class realities of the lives of women of color and working-class women. These efforts often lead to mistrust and ill will, certainly not to a common agenda.
3. Reeve Vanneman and Lynn Weber Cannon, *The American Perception of Class* (Philadelphia: Temple University Press, 1987).
4. Ibid.; Rick Fantasia, *Cultures of Solidarity* (Berkeley and Los Angeles: University of California Press, 1987); Betsy Lucal, "Class Stratification in Introductory Textbooks: Relational or Distributional Models?" *Teaching Sociology* 22 (1994): 139–150.
5. Gloria Hull, Patricia Bell Scott, and Barbara Smith, eds., *All the Women Are White, All the Blacks Are Men, but Some of Us Are Brave: Black Women's Studies* (Old Westbury, N.Y.: Feminist Press, 1982).
6. Toni Cade, *The Black Woman* (New York: Signet, 1970); bell hooks, *Ain't I a Woman* (Boston: South End Press, 1981); LaFrances Rodgers-Rose, ed., *The Black Woman* (Beverly Hills, Calif.: Sage, 1980).
7. Bonnie Thornton Dill, "The Dialectics of Black Womanhood," *Signs* 4 (1979): 543–555.
8. Bonnie Thornton Dill, "Race, Class, and Gender: Prospects for an All-inclusive Sisterhood," *Feminist Studies* 9 (spring 1983): 131–150.
9. This initial research group was composed of Dill, Higginbotham, Cheryl Townsend Gilkes, Evelyn Nakano Glenn, and Ruth Zambrana. The grant from the Ford Foundation provided them with funding for books, summer stipends, and travel for three group meetings held between 1981 and 1983. Afterward, in 1984, the group had a Problems of the Discipline Grant from the American Sociological Association.
10. For a discussion of the Spelman Center, see Beverly Guy-Sheftal, "A Black Feminist Perspective on Transforming the Academy," in Stanlie M. James and Abena P.A. Busia, eds., *Theorizing Black Feminisms: The Visionary Pragmatism of Black Women* (New York: Routledge, 1993), pp. 77–89.
11. By World War I, Pullman employed approximately twelve thousand black people, making it the largest single employer of black workers in the country, according to William Harris, *Keeping the Faith: A. Philip Randolph, Milton P. Webster, and the Brotherhood of Sleeping Car Porters, 1925–1937* (Urbana: University of Illinois Press, 1991). These men were employed as sleeping car porters. Led by A. Philip Randolph, the Brotherhood of Sleeping Car Porters struggled for better working conditions. Many

of these men and their wives, often working in Ladies Auxiliaries, became key leaders in their communities and many worked in the early civil rights movement in the North and South. For additional reading on the topic, see Jack Santino, *Miles of Smiles, Years of Struggle: Stories of Black Pullman Porters* (Urbana: University of Illinois Press, 1989).

12. Deborah Gray White succeeded me in that position. She is currently a professor of history at Rutgers, State University of New Jersey, and author of *Ar'n't I a Woman: Female Slaves in the Plantation South* (New York: Norton, 1985).

13. In addition to Higginbotham, Gilkes, and Dill completing dissertations in 1979, Regina Arnold, now associate professor at Sarah Lawrence College, also finished her doctorate from Bryn Mawr.

14. Bonnie Thornton Dill, "Director's Comments," *Newsletter Center for Research on Women, Memphis State University* 1 (December 1982): 1.

15. In addition to the members of the original research group and Lynn Weber, the faculty for the first summer institute on women of color were Esther Chow, professor of sociology, American University; Leith Mullings, professor of anthropology, Graduate Center for the City University of New York; Maxine Baca Zinn, professor of sociology, Michigan State University; and Lea Ybarra, professor of sociology and an administrator at California State University, Fresno.

16. Maxine Baca Zinn, Lynn Weber Cannon, Elizabeth Higginbotham, and Bonnie Thornton Dill, "The Costs of Exclusionary Practices in Women's Studies," *Signs* 11 (winter 1986): 290–303.

17. This article, which was designed to speak directly to white feminists, was encouraged by Barbara Gelpi, then the editor of *Signs*.

18. Bonnie Thornton Dill, "The Means to Put My Children Through: Child-rearing Goals and Strategies Among Black Female Domestic Servants," in Rodgers-Rose, ed., *The Black Woman*, pp. 107–123; Bonnie Thornton Dill, *Across the Boundaries of Race and Class: An Exploration of Work and Family Among Black Female Domestic Servants* (New York: Garland, 1994).

19. Elizabeth Higginbotham, "Laid Bare by the System: Work and Survival for Black and Hispanic Women," in Amy Swerdlow and Hanna Lessinger, eds., *Class, Race, and Sex: The Dynamics of Control* (Boston: Hall, 1983), pp. 200–215; Evelyn Nakano Glenn, "From Servitude to Service: Historical Continuities in the Racial Division of Paid Reproductive Labor," *Signs* 18 (1992): 1–43.

20. Bonnie Thornton Dill, "Our Mothers' Grief: Racial-Ethnic Women and the Maintenance of Families," *Journal of Family History* 13 (1988): 415–431.

21. Bonnie Thornton Dill and Bruce Williams, "Race, Gender, and Poverty in the Rural South: African American Single Mothers," in Cynthia M. Duncan, ed., *Rural Poverty in America* (New York: Auburn House, 1992), pp. 97–109; Michael Timberlake was a professor of sociology at the University of Memphis until 1991; he is now professor and chair of the Department of Sociology, Anthropology, and Social Work at Kansas State University. Bruce Williams is an associate professor of sociology at the University of Mississippi.

22. Vanneman and Cannon, *The American Perception of Class*. This earlier work was important in clarifying our vision of social class as a complex economic, power-based relationship with key structural and psychological consequences.

23. This research was supported by National Institute of Mental Health Grant MH38769.

24. This research experience was key for graduate assistants on the project. Our institution offers only a master's in sociology and other social sciences. Thus, this study was a unique opportunity for students to actually participate in a major research project. They were trained in interviewing and issues of confidentiality of human subjects. Then they participated in design, testing, recruiting, collecting data, and cleaning the data for analysis. Their insights were helpful in coding data for quantitative and qualitative analysis. Furthermore, the actual interviews with middle-class black and white women in the city provided students with insights into what was behind the success of individuals who could be role models. Several graduate assistants from the project continued their education beyond the master's.

25. Lynn Weber Cannon, Elizabeth Higginbotham, and Marianne Leung, "Race and Class Bias in Qualitative Research on Women," *Gender and Society* 2 (December 1990): 449–462. This article describes a methodology that is a model for conducting research that does not confound race and social class. The article has been reprinted in two anthologies and is widely cited by people interested in multiracial research.

26. For a longer discussion of the race, gender, and traditional mobility research, see Elizabeth Higginbotham and Lynn Weber Cannon, "Rethinking Mobility: Towards a Race and Gender Inclusive Theory," Research Paper 8 (Memphis, Tenn.: Center for Research on Women, Memphis State University, July 1988).

27. Lynn Weber Cannon, "Ground Rules for Classroom Discussion," *Women's Studies Quarterly* 14 (spring–summer 1990): 126–134.

28. Several members of the department became hostile to many new developments in sociology, including the emphasis on improved undergraduate teaching and progressive scholarship in areas such as world systems and stratification, as well as in race, class, and gender.

*Marjorie L. DeVault*

# A Second-Generation Story

*I* am not a feminist pioneer. My intention in begin-
ning this way is not to indulge in self-deprecatory apology but to provide a
statement of historical context. As an early "daughter" of second-wave feminist scholars, my work and career have developed within a fragile, uneven,
but steadily strengthening feminist community in the academy. In many
ways, I have worked with a kind of comfort that I recognize as part of the
privilege of coming later: I have been helped by feminist scholars before
me, socialized into the profession by powerful mentors who are also feminists, and supported (for the most part) in my attempts to resist disciplinary tyranny. I have also learned to accommodate to the demands of the
profession, and my adjustments to an academic career often sit uneasily
beside my feminism. The community that supports my work often seems
dangerously fragile. Finding a place in the discipline felt like a risky bet
until quite recently; the fact that I have entered the field successfully is a
source of pride and also cause for reflection on why I have been sorted in
rather than out. I try to tell a story here that examines my historically situated self and that displays some of the conditions of my entry into both
feminism and sociology.

## Growing up: Cultural Contradictions

I was born in 1950 to white middle-class parents who had constructed a
traditional family of the era.[1] My parents, raised in mostly rural midwestern
environments, valued education. My father, who went to college to become
a music teacher, was encouraged to continue with graduate work and soon
became a college teacher specializing in mathematics education. My mother,
whose college work in art had been interrupted by their marriage, took up
the work of a faculty wife (enthusiastically at first, I think, and then with
increasing ambivalence). I was their first child, obedient, smart, and shy. I
was much loved and, for better and worse, shaped by the values of the

prevailing culture of my era and class. A kindergarten evaluation (preserved in my mother's lovingly detailed record of my development) encapsulates the contradictions of middle-class girlhood in that time: "Marjorie is extremely well-adjusted. I have never seen her cry or get upset, though she sometimes sucks on her skirt."

I was encouraged to apply myself academically, to think of myself as "special," and to make my own decisions. But it was never very clear where that decision-making might lead. For a while (during the Kennedy era), I remember that I aspired to what seemed a very influential post: politician's wife. I was a responsible, intelligent, and conscientious student, drifting toward a promising, if hazy, future. Gender patterns in this sort of middle-class family were just beginning to fracture: I remember, in my early teens, overhearing adult voices in heated discussion of *The Feminine Mystique*. Soon, a wave of painful divorces would begin in such families.

Politically, I grew up alongside the 1960s, just a bit too young (and too timid) to participate fully in the movements of the time. Off to college in 1968, I watched the activism of the period mostly from the sidelines, drawn away from classes and out to the streets only at moments of crisis—spring 1970, for instance, when U.S. troops invaded yet another Southeast Asian country and students like me were killed by soldiers on their campus.

I remember—just barely—that during those years "women's liberation" came to our campus one day: a group of slightly older activists from somewhere in the East, traveling through the country with a workshop for women. I remember, dimly, that I attended, with my roommates, that we sat on the floor and talked. And I remember that the discussion continued back in the dorm well into the night.[2] This early appearance of feminism was anomalous in my life, however. I was about to slide into marriage to my high school sweetheart, too early and far too blithely. It didn't take long to discover that this marriage would not work. I struggled with various accommodations: I became domestic, tried to suppress my ambition. And I wish I could say that I rebelled and left, but in fact it was his unhappiness that finally moved me along. I hadn't yet learned to be angry in any effective way.

## Discoveries

In my first year of college—1968—I discovered social science in an introductory psychology course taught by a very young woman faculty member. (I remember this young woman very vividly and sympathetically: in the image I retain, she sometimes trembled while lecturing. She was one of the four faculty women who taught me in that college, each of whom I can visualize now in precise detail. Significantly, I remember in this vivid way hardly any of the faculty who were men.) We were to write term papers, and after choosing the topic "subliminal perception," I went to look for the material referenced in our textbook, articles in a journal so esoteric sounding that I was sure the school library wouldn't have it: the *Journal of Abnormal and Social Psychology*. Of course, I found it, on the fourth floor, in a little garret at the top of what seemed a very musty branch of the old library.

My discovery in that garret was what captured me for social science and, eventually, sociology. I discovered that scholars argued back and forth about topics such as subliminal perception and that psychologists engaged in the most interesting exercise: they designed experiments to convince each other of their views. I spent many hours working on my paper, poring over dirty old journals, tracing debates back and forth. It was a time of private, intense emotion, an awakening to the excitement and creativity of scholarly work. I sensed then that scholarship could be a kind of conversation, and I wanted to be part of it. The tone of slightly illicit pleasure in this account captures the edge of ambivalence I felt in this discovery. I was still caught in the dilemmas of my socialization, unwilling to fully acknowledge my ambitions but equally unwilling to put them aside.

A few years later, around the time I was divorced, I discovered feminism. I did not join a consciousness-raising group or engage in political action. Instead, I encountered the women's movement in its academic context. I was then pursuing a master's degree in curriculum and instruction, with the idea of becoming an elementary school teacher (one of the failed strategies for accommodation to my marriage), and faculty members at my institution, the University of Wisconsin at Madison, were just beginning to bring feminist content to the teacher training program. I read about gender stereotyping in children's readers, began to think about my own life, and experienced that profound feminist "click" of awakened consciousness. I began to get angry, and—more important—I had a theory to explain why. I learned, for example, that women were socialized into a double bind: that being a "normal woman" was incompatible with being a "normal adult." And that men expected—and would demand—that women serve as audience for men's actions rather than becoming actors themselves. I remember long, solitary walks during that time, when I tasted these new insights and emotions and considered what they meant. And I remember discovering feminist writings that spoke directly to these feelings: Judy Chicago, Doris Lessing, Marge Piercy, the alternative journal *Country Women,* and others. I began to work on becoming a conscious, independent woman, and I found this project tremendously energizing.

With other women in the Department of Curriculum and Instruction, I began to explore what feminist scholarship might be. In the early 1970s, I was a member of that department's first graduate course in women's studies, "Issues in Sex-related Differences in Curriculum and Instruction," a seminar offered by Elizabeth Fennema, who had already begun to challenge the prevailing wisdom about girls' mathematics performance.[3] We had a wonderful time, but there were lurking anxieties; it seemed odd and a bit risky, then, to give serious attention to women and girls. Several times, I heard Liz, in the course of telling about the seminar, offer a laughing apology. "Well," she would say, "these students have to take the blame for all this." Smiling, we would correct her: credit, not blame! But I was struck by the sense of vulnerability that produced this kind of nervous joke.

Abandoning my plans for elementary teaching, I wrote a master's thesis that analyzed students' experiences in the university's two-year-old introductory women's studies course.[4] And then I left school, uncertain what would come next. By that time—the late 1970s—feminism had touched everyone in my family of origin. My parents were divorced, and my mother was establishing herself as a painter. She and I were especially close during this time; we encountered feminism together and shared books, friends, and ideas about our work and our fledgling careers. My sister Ileen was also becoming a feminist scholar: she was one of the first women's studies majors at the University of California, Berkeley (Judith Stacey, whose essay appears elsewhere in this volume, was one of her first women's studies teachers), and she is now a feminist labor historian.[5] We developed these common interests in different ways and times: she was radical while I was married, then moved toward labor studies when I was discovering feminism. But we finished our graduate work at nearly the same moment, found jobs at roughly the same time, and published books in successive years. Now we live in the same region and share professional networks, as well as the puzzles and frustrations of writing, teaching, and institutional politics. I suspect that my siblings and I were all looking for some integration of the implicit gender split we observed in the family: while Ileen and I followed our father into academic work, our brother became a musician and is active in the feminist men's movement.

## Learning a Discipline (and Resisting It)

My feminism, then, was in place before I became a sociologist. In fact, I chose sociology rather casually—it was one among several possible fields—and in 1978, with little knowledge of what it would mean, I entered the

Ph.D. program at Northwestern University. I knew only that I would do feminist scholarship, that the "sociological imagination" seemed relevant (I'd read C. Wright Mills), and that the department seemed hospitable.[6] I met briefly with Arlene Kaplan Daniels, who would later become my thesis adviser, and she extended an enthusiastic invitation. We talked about her research on women as volunteer workers and an ongoing study of returning women students. "I'm just having a great time," I remember her saying, "and you're welcome to run alongside and join the fun!"

This sense of joining a collective project captures my experience of feminism in sociology during those years. Some might assume that, coming in a second generation, I had "training" to be a feminist sociologist, but it didn't feel that way. When I think of my development as a feminist scholar, I do not think primarily of coursework and mentoring relationships (these seem much more crucial for my development as a sociologist). Instead, the story I construct from those years is one of lessons learned from the "hidden curriculum" of my graduate program and of a collective intellectual project of resistance to the discipline in its traditional construction. This project was supported by an emerging feminist community, but it often felt like a private struggle.

In many ways, Northwestern provided a most congenial environment. I remember, with gratitude, that faculty gave us lots of freedom, took student work seriously, and insisted that we take it seriously, too. I saw the faculty as engaged and productive scholars who paid attention to each other's work. There were classroom experiences that are still vivid for me, as well as the extended student discussions over coffee that are so central to most graduate study. It was a program that left room for challenge to the disciplinary canon, and I found among the faculty and my graduate student colleagues a willingness to listen sympathetically to my questions about how women might be made more visible in sociological work.

I can also easily recall becoming aware of a pervasive and frightening atmosphere of sexism. I watched as two outstanding junior faculty women, Janet Lever and Naomi Aronson, were denied tenure, and I noticed that the two senior women were curiously distant from the centers of the graduate curriculum and departmental decision-making. Slowly, I began to see the institutional pressures that excluded women and the questions I wanted to ask. I was cheered and inspired by the presence of women faculty: I watched Arlene at work and learned from her example, and I was moved by Janet Abu-Lughod's elegant and forceful address to the Northwestern faculty, "Engendering Knowledge: Women and the University."[7] But as I came to know women faculty, I shared not only ideas but also their experiences of discomfort and marginalization as sociologists. The lives of junior faculty women were especially frightening; I wondered, often, if I could survive in the profession and if survival would be worth the pain that seemed inevitable.

During my time at Northwestern, the formative collective experiences for graduate students were Arnold (Ackie) Feldman's classical theory course and Howard Becker's fieldwork seminar. In the theory course we read Karl Marx, Max Weber, and Antonio Gramsci. I entered the program with virtually no sociology and began to read the first volume of *Capital*. I remember the sense of wonder that Ackie's close readings of this text could produce and my pleasure in discovering that sociology could dissect inequality with such precision. In the fieldwork seminar, we simply began to work. "Go out there and start writing field notes," Howie told us. "Just write down everything you see." So we went out, wrote voluminous notes, and then came back to class to work on making sense of them.

These were very different classroom experiences. I remember Feldman pacing in front of the class, delivering extremely dense lectures that we tried to transcribe as completely as possible. It was difficult for most of us to formulate questions; usually one or two students (often Marxists from other countries) were prepared to grasp the point quickly enough to discuss it, and the rest of us struggled just to keep up. We were taught to read Marx and Weber as complementary, completing each other's analyses so as to encompass both class and status inequalities. We did not hear much about gender (though we could ask or write about it, and some of us did). And theory appeared to be men's territory. It was almost always men who participated in the extra reading groups and who went on to work with Feldman. Nevertheless, the two courses I took with him were important for me. I was challenged to produce a rigorous kind of analysis that really explained something, showing how it happened. And I was given a set of theoretical tools. For several years I started every project with a ritual re-reading of the several hundred pages of notes I had produced in these classes.

Becker's fieldwork seminar met in a special classroom furnished with dilapidated easy chairs. He began each class as if he had no plan at all: "So what's been happening?" he might ask. And from whatever we had to say, he would make a lesson in fieldwork. Some people were frustrated by this style of pedagogy, feeling that nothing much was happening, but I found these sessions utterly enchanting. As the weeks went by, we could see projects developing, analyses arising from our confusions in the field. Howie pushed us; there were simply no excuses for not getting started. He conveyed a tremendous respect for the work we were doing, finding the seeds of significance in our beginners' attempts at observation. He insisted that it was all very simple: we could just figure it out and write it down. And he pointed out that no project was really complete until it had been written up for publication. Here, too, gender did not appear unless we asked. Howie was impatient with the idea that one might come to a project with a feminist agenda; he didn't believe in agendas and didn't want to talk about them.

Some students veered toward one or the other of these approaches; many of us yearned to "have it all." Given this foundation (and this desire), I was more than ready for Dorothy Smith's visit to Northwestern in winter 1983 as guest lecturer for a quarter. Several of us had been reading her work with great interest, and women faculty in the department had arranged a visiting lectureship. We organized a seminar and Dorothy taught her own work, week by week, laying out for us the development of her thought about sociology, its problems, and the promise for women of a revised and stronger form of sociological analysis. With several friends, I studied this material in a nearly fanatical way. We met early to prepare for each class and again later to discuss what had happened in each session. Laboring over Dorothy's dense prose, I copied long excerpts into my notebook and composed lists of questions to ask in class. Whenever Dorothy spoke, I was there.

During Smith's visit, I began to envision a sociology that was more satisfying than any I'd known: it would build on materialist principles, retain a commitment to the world as people lived it, and insist that women's varied situations be kept in view. Dorothy's approach, more than any other, seemed to offer possibilities for moving beyond feminist critiques of established sociology and beginning to build something new. There were lessons in the hidden curriculum as well. For example, one of the startling revelations of the seminar lay in discovering its meaning for Dorothy: that this was her first opportunity to present her work so thoroughly as a unified body of thought and that she needed our response as much as we wanted to hear her words. The experience also supported my sense of feminist scholarship as collective project. One day in class, when I'd asked another earnest and anxious question about how to do this kind of sociology, Dorothy just smiled for a moment. "Well, Marj," she finally said, "I don't have all the answers. You'll have to figure some of this out for yourself."

My research topic, the invisible work of "feeding a family," arose from the feminist theoretical agenda I'd brought with me to sociology, as well as from questions about my own gendered experience. I'd been fascinated by the feminist idea that women's absence from most scholarly writing had shaped the assumptions and concepts of every discipline. I wanted to study aspects of life that "belonged" to women and to consider what it would mean to take those activities and concerns as seriously as we take the perspectives that arise from men's experiences; for this reason, I began to think about housework. There were, at that time, several sociological studies that took housework seriously, applying the perspectives that sociologists of work applied to paid jobs.[8] I was enormously grateful for these early studies, but I also tested them against my own experience—a fundamental feminist move—and felt that something was missing.

I was living at that time in a stormy, exciting, and ultimately disastrous relationship with a man who had become quite incapacitated by chronic depression. During the years we spent together, he became increasingly helpless; I was terribly ambivalent about the partnership but strongly committed to caring for this person I had loved so intensely. Life felt very difficult during those years; I brooded a lot about how to respond to his troubles, and I remember in one moment of reflection thinking that the womanly experience I wanted to capture in my work was this incredibly delicate craft of caring for others.

I did not go directly to my typewriter. Instead, I muddled along wondering if I would ever develop an acceptable thesis topic, experiencing a prolonged period of depression myself, and slowly beginning to write about women and food. I couldn't say what I was up to: I wrote about supermarkets, the health food movement, dietitians, food stamps, and food journalists. And I kept coming back to the household work of providing food. Stubbornly, I held onto my own experience and my intuitive sense of topic, which didn't seem to fit with the topics available in the discipline. My first clear statement of my topic came from my reading outside sociology, when I was able to point to Virginia Woolf's novel *To the Lighthouse* and say: "It's what Mrs. Ramsay does at her dinner party! Of course there isn't a name for it—that's the whole point." I wrote an essay about Mrs. Ramsay, and finally I was able to begin an ethnography of the unpaid work of "feeding a family" with some confidence that I might capture what made it so compelling for women.[9]

I wanted a feminist as my thesis adviser, and I chose to work with Arlene Kaplan Daniels. We shared a central concern for excavating those womanly activities rendered invisible or trivialized by social theory derived from the concerns of privileged men. Arlene's own work at that time was concerned with the "invisible careers" of women volunteers who became civic leaders.[10] This study was leading her toward a more general analysis of varieties of "invisible work," which she presented as her presidential address to the Society for the Study of Social Problems in 1987.[11] In that piece, she synthesized writings by feminists (and others) about a wide range of nonmarket activities, arguing for an expansion of the concept of work as a crucial step in the project of including women's contributions more fully in sociological analyses of work and the social order.

Arlene's writing on invisible work displays the kind of strategically doubled vision that I absorbed from working with her and that I now see as crucial to my development. As a feminist, Arlene saw the promise of rethinking the grounding concepts of the discipline; as a sociologist, she conceptualized the innovative work that feminists were developing in terms that located it in relation to core questions of the discipline. Perhaps because she had long been a student of the professions, Arlene insisted on the importance of placing oneself firmly and clearly inside the discipline; she insisted that I write a dissertation that was not only innovative but also acceptable in the terms of the discipline.[12] These lessons were sometimes uncomfortable: I confess that I was often impatient when she counseled me cheerfully to become an "occupations and professions man"; I understood, but could not quite accept, the conditions that produced this advice (see her account elsewhere).[13] But I do believe that to steer the tricky course between innovation and acceptance is the most essential task for a feminist scholar: even though our aims may be transformative, innovative writing is recognized and appreciated only if it can be located successfully, somewhere, in relation to existing work.

My account of Arlene's mentorship would not be complete without some mention of the personal texture of our relationship—the complex and lively breadth of our interaction. One of my vivid memories: each time I put a chapter in Arlene's mailbox, I would soon afterward hear her extravagant voice booming down the hall as she skipped toward my office. "Marj, my dear Marj!" she would shout. "You finished another chapter! You deserve a reward; what would you like? A box of chocolates? Or shall I take you for sushi lunch tomorrow?" Sushi lunch was my favorite, so we would stroll down the street together, and I would have my reward. It felt wonderful. To emphasize this kind of help is not to trivialize Arlene's intellectual contribution to my work; rather, I mean to emphasize her recognition that intellectual work is best sustained through attention to emotional, as well as intellectual, needs. While I was her student, I ate and shopped with Arlene, as well as joining her at feminist lectures and meetings. She introduced me to her colleagues and "talked up" my work. I watched and learned as she helped to build a feminist world within the discipline and pulled me into that world.

## Collective Work

My scholarship has always depended on the support of women colleagues
and could not have developed as it has, I believe, without my relationships
with other women. Twice, I've enjoyed long periods of intensive "partnered"
reading and thinking. In graduate school, I worked with Sandra Schroeder
and for several years after graduation with the late Marianne (Tracy) Paget.
In neither case did we work collaboratively on joint projects or even on the
same topics. But in both cases we shared feminist commitments, interests
in experimentation and resistance, and some affinity in our styles of thought.
In both cases, we paid loving attention to each other's work, read and talked
about everything we wrote, and tried to hear and coax out for each other
what we meant to do in our work.

Sandy and I scheduled weekly meetings throughout our dissertation
work (a practice that amused us since we were housemates most of that
time and shared an office as well); we considered each other essential, though
unofficial, members of our dissertation committees. Tracy and I began our
work together by reading all the work of Dorothy Smith that we could find,
and we agreed that it made a difference to study her writing as a coherent,
extended body of thought (the way students are routinely taught to understand canonical male theorists). We talked about reading other women sociologists in this way (inspired in part by the work that Shulamit Reinharz
was doing to reclaim women sociologists of the past), but that project was
precluded by Tracy's untimely death in 1989.[14]

These intense working relationships seem a bit like falling in love, at
least in the sense that they don't come along very often and cannot be produced at will. But I have shared feminist ideas, reading, projects, and debates with many other groups and individual colleagues over the years.
These relationships have been important because they have felt quite different from more conventional academic spaces. Within them, some understandings can be taken for granted, and one doesn't need to defend and
legitimate feminist principles and assumptions. We can and do question
our core ideas, as critics might, but this activity feels quite different when
undertaken with sympathetic colleagues. Within such groups, we give lots
of encouragement, we deal with emotional issues alongside intellectual ones,
and we find nothing strange or suspect in that agenda. Finally, we have
energy, fun, and, usually, a lot of laughter. Sometimes I feel that male colleagues are a bit jealous of these relationships (those who know about them,
at least), and I can see why they might feel that way.

## Getting In

I chose to study sociology during a period of contracting opportunities for academic work; we were warned, on that hopeful first day of graduate school, that many of us would have difficulty finding jobs. Thus, for nine years—from 1978, when I entered graduate school, until 1987, when I was hired as an assistant professor at Syracuse University—I had a keen sense of the possibility that I would never find stable employment as a sociologist. After completing my degree in 1984, I searched for a permanent job for three years, scrambling to find work and moving every year. During one difficult year in Boston, I supported myself with part-time teaching: a more than full-time schedule for less than half-time pay. I was quietly enraged for much of that year; the most difficult job was managing those emotions and considering how long I could persist in such a life. It was then that I met Tracy Paget, who never held a permanent teaching post. During much of our time together, she supported her scholarly work as many artists support their creative projects: by enduring periods of temporary clerical work so that she could also have periods of uninterrupted writing. She didn't often tell about this strategy while she was alive; it didn't sound very "professional." But I think she wouldn't mind that I divulge the secret here. I think she would agree that it is important to speak about such women and their work. Challenging disciplinary tradition leaves many innovative scholars outside the institutions of scholarship and personally vulnerable. I believe that the discipline is impoverished by their absence.

One of the things that feminism has provided for me is an analysis of the evaluative and gatekeeping processes that structure these experiences. It has given me a way to think about some of the difficult moments in my professional life. I have learned to think long and hard about audiences for my writing, and I have learned to evaluate the gatekeepers: when my work is judged, I ask who is judging it and on what terms. When I hear, "But that's not sociology," I have learned to say (or at least think), "Maybe not yet."

The character of the theory I deployed during my training can be seen in an episode of graduate student activism. During 1982–1983, I began to work, with Patty Passuth, Lisa Jones, and other graduate students at Northwestern, on something we called "the gender project": a survey of graduate student experiences in our department, which we hoped would help us to understand the frustrations so many of us were feeling. We gathered data on attrition from the graduate program, interviewed all of the students in residence, and wrote an article-sized report for distribution to the department.[15] Although the attrition data were incomplete, it seemed that during the decade we had studied, women had been more likely than men to drop out of the program, especially at the dissertation stage. Introducing the document, we wrote:

> In a survey of all students, we found subtle differences in the ways that male and female students described their interactions with faculty members. Relative to men, women tended to feel more marginal to the department, and believed they were taken less seriously. They reported receiving less help and encouragement than men, were more pessimistic about their chances for employment, and their expectations were more likely than men's to have dropped since entering the program. A substantial number of women blamed themselves for the situations they described, reporting that their own work was marginal to the field, or that their experience in the program was "unusual" in some respect.[16]

In fine multimethod fashion, we presented tables and quotations from respondents to illustrate a pattern of "benign neglect" of women students. Although unwilling to "point with certainty" to causes, we suggested several factors that might explain these problems: the structural reality of a predominantly male faculty, documented differences in the interactional styles of men and women and the differential responses these styles elicit from others, and the incomplete acceptance of women's concerns within the discipline. Echoing "The Missing Feminist Revolution"[17]—which must have been circulating at the time, though I don't think we had read it—we concluded:

> Another possible cause for the differential experience of men and women students is that by following their own concerns—an approach to research encouraged by this department—female students are more likely than men to be working on non-traditional topics or approaching traditional topics in original ways. Thus, they may have more difficulty formulating their ideas, and faculty may have a harder time understanding them or seeing the significance of their work.
>
> The research literature which incorporates women's perspectives into sociology—developed over the past 20 years—has been integrated into "mainstream" courses only to a limited extent. Researchers have found that after taking women's studies courses, female students report feeling more included in academic disciplines, more serious about themselves as scholars and more assertive about their studies. Thus,

more active efforts to incorporate new knowledge especially relevant
to women may help to combat female students' feelings of marginality.[18]

I have quoted at some length from this document because I think it
illustrates how I used feminist analysis at that time to construct and sustain
a sense of opposition to business as usual in graduate training. It also displays the construction of our activism within the boundaries of the institution and shows how the goal of "getting in" to the profession shaped the
substance and form of our resistance. As I look back at this document, I am
struck by its heartfelt but measured concern and by our earnestly "professional" tone. Our confidence in the effectiveness of "the facts," presented
well, suggests a considerable measure of political naïveté, as well as the
kind of comfort we felt within the program in spite of our complaints. And
the carefully suppressed anger in the document points to the extent to which
we had already accepted a powerful professional discipline.

I learned several lessons from my involvement in this project. I learned,
in the end, that researching injustice carries the seeds of cooptation: though
it provoked much discussion, our report resulted mostly in calls for further
research. I also learned, however, that speaking out about these problems
could bring women together. We were surprised when women faculty in
the department expressed gratitude that we had raised these issues. And
the intense work of writing the report together was a powerful and energizing experience of collective analysis. For a while at least, our report constructed a lively solidarity among women in the department. Finally, I learned
that my personal skills could be used to stir up some trouble within an
institution and that stirring up trouble felt like a very good thing to do.

I have suggested that feminism was for me a theory that made immediate and personal sense. I do not mean to suggest that the kind of analysis
just described exhausts the meanings of feminism or provides a full account; any adequate feminism must also fit for other women, most of whom
are in situations quite different from those of sociology graduate students.
In addition, my location as a woman intersects with other privileges and
oppressions shaping my experience. It is for this reason that I have tried to
display my middle-class, academic background in my telling of this story. I
have wanted to give a sense for the particular kind of gendered life I have
led and how it has shaped both my feminism and my career. (I learned
several kinds of lessons, for example, from observation of my father's work
life, including the following: that academic work could be profoundly satisfying; that an academic can chart her own course in many ways; that institutional politics requires particular kinds of entrepreneurship; and,

perhaps most important, that the academy is no paradise.[19] I also learned a style of demeanor and discourse so that the kinds of talk required in institutional settings feel relatively familiar. I wanted to resist adopting wholesale my father's consuming absorption in work, which sometimes felt distancing to me as a child—I remember the often closed and inviolable door to his study—but that has been more difficult than I expected.)

My feminism has provided a perspective that sustains a useful, restrained resistance to some aspects of business as usual, while continuing other aspects of this "business" with a vengeance. It seems important to acknowledge these limits, but I want to resist the view that this version of feminism can serve only to support the advancement of privileged middle-class academics. As I analyzed my own marginality, I could readily see that there were similar obstacles for other underrepresented groups and that I would need to use my theory reflexively to analyze my own blindnesses and exclusions. My personal sense of oppression has, I think, helped me not only to hear but also to feel, with some urgency, the complaints of those excluded on bases other than gender. When students complain about my courses, I do not want to reply that I hadn't thought about lesbians (for example), that I couldn't find any material on women of color (for example), or that surely one class on women with disabilities (for example) is enough. These lame excuses sound far too familiar. And I am convinced—because I have worked so hard to convince those who resisted my feminist complaints—that really working to change the way I think will enliven my work and move us all forward.

## And Now...

Through the early years of my career, I've been motivated and sustained by a sense of resistance to disciplinary traditions that has bordered on hostility. Feminism has provided pathways (or lifelines) out of the discipline. I have read feminist works outside of sociology, and I often find that they are more productive of the insights I need than the writings of other sociologists. I do not mean that I ignore or dismiss feminist work in sociology but that I have been interested in the challenge of getting out of the discipline, and then back in, exiting and reentering with transformative ideas.

Now that I feel reasonably well established in the discipline, I find, tellingly, that I am more interested in sociology. I want to know more about the history of the discipline, and I feel more interested (in both senses) in its future. One can certainly read this shift as a simple economic response to a change in my situation; I would not discount this reading entirely. But

I think this reaction to acceptance also signals the implicit messages about "ownership" of the discipline that are sent when some groups are virtually excluded from participation and hints at the costs to the profession of these kinds of exclusions.

Feminism has led me to questions about the disciplinary context within which I struggle to construct meaningful work. In the process of "becoming a sociologist," I have come to feel that I need to understand how sociology works, as a discipline, to include and exclude topics and perspectives, to advance and coopt projects of inquiry, to resist and tame transformative agendas. I want to understand what it means to adopt a "discipline": how a discipline produces a discourse that enables some projects and rules others out of bounds. One aspect of a recent project (on the work of dietitians and nutritionists) involves an exploration of the force of "disciplinarity."[20] In pursuing this research, I have been interviewing professional women who are in positions similar to mine and whose career stories and concerns with work often mirror mine. We work inside the structures of institutional power but not at their centers, and this kind of position, as "marginal insider," gives rise to characteristic troubles and ambivalences. My aim is to make visible the sticky web of disciplinarity and professionalism within which they (and I) work. These interests arise, in part, from my own puzzles. They are also a product of new intellectual currents, including postmodern meditations on knowledge production and questions about the place of feminism within, among, and across disciplines. Thus, I still struggle with questions about locating myself as a feminist scholar.

In 1992, poised on the brink of tenure, I met the fifteen women and one man who had enrolled in my graduate seminar in feminist research. For the first class, I had chosen as our texts two poems: Kate Rushin's "Bridge Poem" and Marge Piercy's "Unlearning to Not Speak."[21] I had planned to read the poems aloud, and I had resolved to read with feeling. I was nervous, a bit hesitant, but the words carried me along, and my voice broke with feeling as I read. We all noticed, and that moment of emotion became a topic for discussion: why do we feel this way, and what does it mean? By the end of class, one student was ready to admit that she'd been dismayed at first to find poetry in a sociology classroom—so "soft" and womanish! Starting outside of the discipline, I think, had the effect I'd intended: we began to construct space for experimentation. About halfway through the semester, I noticed with surprise and some embarrassment that I was listening to students' presentations and worrying, "But is it sociology?" My feminism kept me quiet for the moment and gave them license to proceed.

Near the end of the course, however, I began to feel an urgent need to lecture and warn them, to point out the necessity of living within, as well as between, disciplines. "I want you to be bold, take risks, and make trouble," I told them. "But I also want you to be here, to *survive* in this institutional space. For that, you have to accept a discipline."

In spite of the comforts of the second generation, survival hasn't felt easy. Some days, it seems that the feminist revolution is still missing: my feminist courses attract mostly women students, and I often feel that I live my professional life in a parallel female world apart from the "main business" of my institution and profession. Some days, I notice how many of us are now at work, and I think the revolution may be sneaking up on us, arriving while we're busy with office hours, so that we hardly have time to notice. As I write this last sentence, I am conscious of my easy use of the word "us," and I worry: about my sense that I might be turning into one of "them" and my desire to construct a "we" that continues to press at the boundaries of disciplinary traditions. Almost all the time, I'm interested to see what will come next.

## Notes

Some of this material first appeared in my remarks at a panel discussion I organized jointly with Ruth Linden ("Works/Disciplines/Lives: Locating Ourselves as Feminists in Sociology," Annual Stone Symposium of the Society for the Study of Symbolic Interaction, University of California, San Francisco, February, 1991); our discussions then shaped some of these reflections. I am also grateful for the support provided through a 1993–1994 research leave granted by Syracuse University and an appointment that year as visiting scholar in the Women's Studies Program at Brandeis University.

1. I have borrowed this section's heading from Mirra Komarovsky, whose article "Cultural Contradictions and Sex Roles," *American Journal of Sociology* 52 (1946): 184–189, describes aspects of the situation I mean to evoke in this section, even though her analysis is based on data from an earlier generation.
2. What I remember, actually, is an extended argument about the logistics of a dual-career marriage; as I recall it, I was the only one willing to argue that a woman shouldn't necessarily follow her husband wherever he might go. Now as my partner and I struggle through our tenth year of a 300-mile separation, this memory has an uncomfortably ironic edge.
3. Her first article on the topic was Elizabeth Fennema, "Mathematics Learning and the Sexes: A Review," *Journal for Research in Mathematics Education* 5 (1974): 126–139. She went on to collaborate with Julia Sherman on a series of NSF-sponsored studies that examined differential participation and attitudes, and were widely quoted as interest in gender and mathematics grew. Her most recent thinking on the topic

is summarized in Elizabeth Fennema, "Mathematics, Gender, and Research," in Gila Hanna, ed., *Towards Gender Equity in Mathematics Education* (Dordrecht: Kluwer, 1996), pp. 9–26. Other Wisconsin faculty who were important for my developing outlook were Jack Kean, in whose language arts class I read Women on Words and Images, *Dick and Jane as Victims* (Princeton, N.J.: Women on Words and Images, 1972); and my adviser Thomas Popkewitz, who introduced me to sociology via Peter L. Berger and Thomas Luckmann, *The Social Construction of Reality* (Garden City, N.Y.: Doubleday, 1966).

4. This course, which provided the foundation for my understanding of women's studies as an academic field, was taught by literary scholars Susan Stanford Friedman and Susan Snaider Lanser.

5. See Ileen DeVault, *Sons and Daughters of Labor: Class and Clerical Work in Turn-of-the-century Pittsburgh* (Ithaca, N.Y.: Cornell University Press, 1990).

6. C. Wright Mills, *The Sociological Imagination* (New York: Oxford University Press, 1959).

7. Janet L. Abu-Lughod, "Engendering Knowledge: Women and the University" (Evanston, Ill.: Northwestern University Program on Women, 1981). Abu-Lughod was probably chosen to deliver this prestigious annual lecture because she had just published a book on North African cities. She surprised the faculty selection committee, she believes, when she used the occasion to address issues of women's status in the academy, which were being discussed by the newly formed Organization of Women Faculty at Northwestern. The group still exists there, and Arlene Daniels's decision to use the 1993–1994 lectureship to provide an update to Abu-Lughod's lecture illustrates the kind of collaborative activism I learned from them.

8. I relied heavily on the following: Ann Oakley, *The Sociology of Housework* (New York: Pantheon Books, 1974); Catherine White Berheide, Sarah Fenstermaker Berk, and Richard A. Berk, "Household Work in the Suburbs: The Job and Its Participants," *Pacific Sociological Review* 19 (1976): 491–517; Richard A. Berk and Sarah Fenstermaker Berk, *Labor and Leisure at Home: Content and Organization of the Household Day* (Beverly Hills, Calif.: Sage, 1979). There was also an earlier study by Helena Z. Lopata, *Occupation: Housewife* (New York: Oxford University Press, 1971), which took "housewives," rather than "housework," as the topic but also took their activity seriously as work. And there was an emerging Marxist literature on domestic labor.

9. Eventually the dissertation became a book: Marjorie L. DeVault, *Feeding the Family: The Social Organization of Caring as Gendered Work* (Chicago: University of Chicago Press, 1991).

10. Arlene Kaplan Daniels, *Invisible Careers: Women Civic Leaders from the Volunteer World* (Chicago: University of Chicago Press, 1988).

11. Arlene Kaplan Daniels, "Invisible Work," *Social Problems* 34 (1987): 403–415.

12. I use the term "acceptable" with Ruddick's analysis of "maternal thinking" in mind. See Sara Ruddick, "Maternal Thinking," *Feminist Studies* 6 (1980): 342–367; and Sara Ruddick, *Maternal Thinking: Toward a Politics of Peace* (Boston: Beacon Press, 1989). Ruddick points out that one of the demands of mothering is to produce a child "acceptable" to the society—a demand that sometimes conflicts with a mother's own values.

13. Arlene Kaplan Daniels, "When We Were All Boys Together: Graduate School in the

Fifties and Beyond," in Kathryn P. Meadow Orlans and Ruth A. Wallace, *Gender and the Academic Experience: Berkeley Women Sociologists* (Lincoln: University of Nebraska Press, 1994), pp. 27–43.

14. Shulamit Reinharz, "Teaching the History of Women in Sociology: Or Dorothy Swaine Thomas, Wasn't She the Woman Married to William I.?" *American Sociologist* 20 (1989): 87–94. See also the historical material in Shulamit Reinharz, *Feminist Methods in Social Research* (New York: Oxford University Press, 1992). For an account of Tracy's cancer experience in light of her writing on medical error, see Marianne A. Paget, *A Complex Sorrow: Reflections on Cancer and an Abbreviated Life,* ed. Marjorie L. DeVault (Philadelphia: Temple University Press, 1993).

15. Marjorie DeVault, Lisa Jones, and Patty Passuth, "Gender Differences in Graduate Students' Experiences" (Paper prepared as a project of the Graduate Student Association, Department of Sociology, Northwestern University, Evanston, Illinois, May 1983).

16. Ibid., p. 1.

17. Judith Stacey and Barrie Thorne, "The Missing Feminist Revolution in Sociology," *Social Problems* 32 (1985): 301–316.

18. DeVault et al., "Gender Differences," p. 33.

19. Cf. the accounts of academics from working-class backgrounds in Jake Ryan and Charles Shackrey, *Strangers in Paradise: Academics from the Working Class* (Boston: South End Press, 1984).

20. Marjorie L. DeVault, "Between Science and Food: Nutrition Professionals in the Health-Care Hierarchy," in Jennie J. Kronenfeld, ed., *Research on the Sociology of Health Care* (Greenwich, Conn.: JAI Press, 1995), pp. 287–312; Marjorie L. DeVault, "Ethnicity and Expertise: Racial-ethnic Knowledge in Sociological Research," *Gender and Society* 9 (1995): 612–631.

21. "The Bridge Poem" appears in Cherríe Moraga and Gloria Anzaldúa, eds., *This Bridge Called My Back: Writings by Radical Women of Color* (Watertown, Mass.: Persephone Press, 1981), pp. xxi–xxii; "Unlearning to Not Speak" comes from Marge Piercy, *To Be of Use* (Garden City, N.Y.: Doubleday, 1973), p. 38.

# About the Authors

JOAN ACKER, professor emerita of sociology, University of Oregon, is the author of *Doing Comparable Worth: Gender, Class, and Pay Equity* (1989), *Developing a Feminist Sociology* (forthcoming), and many articles on women and social class, stratification, organizations, and work. In 1989 she received the Jessie Bernard Award, and in 1993 she received the American Sociological Association Career of Distinguished Scholarship Award.

R. W. CONNELL is professor of education at the University of Sydney, Australia. He has been professor of sociology at University of California, Santa Cruz, and has held visiting positions in other North American universities. He is author or coauthor of *Masculinities* (1995), *Gender and Power* (1987), *Schools and Social Justice* (1993), and *Making the Difference* (1982), and he has been involved in labor, peace, and progressive politics for about thirty years without ever convincingly learning to sing.

DESLEY DEACON is associate professor of American studies and sociology at the University of Texas, Austin. She is the author of *Elsie Clews Parsons: Inventing Modern Life* (1997) and "Bringing Social Science Back Home: Theory and Practice in the Life and Work of Elsie Clews Parsons," in Helene Silverberg, ed., *Social Science Engendered* (1997). She is now working on a book about trauma and feminist science, based on the life of Katharine Dexter McCormick, the woman who financed the development of the contraceptive pill.

MARJORIE L. DEVAULT is associate professor of sociology and a member of the Women's Studies Program at Syracuse University. She is the author of *Feeding the Family: The Social Organization of Caring as Gendered Work* (1991) and the editor of Marianne A. Paget, *A Complex Sorrow: Reflections on Cancer and an Abbreviated Life* (1993). Her current projects focus on feminist methodology, gender dynamics of professional work, and constructionist approaches to family.

BONNIE THORNTON DILL is professor of women's studies and affiliate professor of sociology at the University of Maryland, College Park. She researches African-American women, work, and family and is currently studying the coping and survival strategies of low-income single mothers in several rural southern communities. She was the founding director of the Center for Research on Women at the University of Memphis from 1982 until 1988. Her books include *Women of Color in U.S. Society* (coedited with Maxine Baca Zinn, 1994) and *Across the Boundaries of Race and Class: Work and Family Among Black Female Domestic Servants* (1994).

SARAH FENSTERMAKER is professor of sociology and women's studies at the University of California, Santa Barbara. She has published widely in the areas of gender, work, and domestic violence and is perhaps best known for her book *The Gender Factory: The Allocation of Work in American Households* (1985). She has recently coedited (with Ann Goetting) *Individual Voices, Collective Visions: Fifty Years of Women in Sociology* (1995). Her current work focuses on the theoretical articulation of race, gender, and class in women's work.

EVELYN NAKANO GLENN is professor of women's studies and ethnic studies at the University of California, Berkeley. Her interests center on women's work, the political economy of households, and the intersection of race and gender. She has written extensively on a variety of topics within these broad areas, including racial/ethnic women's labor, paid domestic work, impacts of changing technology on clerical labor processes, gender and immigration, and the social constructions of mothering. She is the author of *Issei, Nisei, Warbride* (1986) and coeditor (with Grace Chang and Linda Forcey) of *Mothering: Ideology, Experience, and Agency* (1994). Her current research focuses on raced and gendered constructions of labor and citizenship in three regions of the United States.

ELIZABETH HIGGINBOTHAM is professor of sociology in the Center for Research on Women and the Department of Sociology and Social Work at the University of Memphis. Her work has appeared in *Gender & Society, Women's Studies Quarterly*, other journals, and many edited collections. Her research projects have focused on how race, class, and gender impact the lives of women, particularly mobility issues for black women and for black and white professional and managerial women in the Memphis area. She is completing a book entitled *Too Much to Ask: The Cost of Black Female Success.*

SUSAN KRIEGER teaches in the Program in Feminist Studies at Stanford University and is the author of *Hip Capitalism* (1979), *The Mirror Dance: Identity in a Women's Community* (1983), *Social Science and the Self: Personal Essays on an Art Form* (1991), and *The Family Silver: Essays on Relationships among Women* (1996).

BARBARA LASLETT is professor of sociology at the University of Minnesota and was editor of *Signs* (with Ruth-Ellen B. Joeres) between 1990 and 1995. She has coedited several collections of *Signs* readings, including *Rethinking the Political: Gender, Resistance, and the State* (1995), *Gender and Scientific Authority* (1996), and *The Second Signs Reader* (1996). Her research and writing have focused primarily on the historical sociology of the family and of American sociology. She edited *Contemporary Sociology* between 1983 and 1986 and is past president of the Social Science History Association. She is currently working on a collaborative project (with Mary Jo Maynes and Jennifer Pierce) on the uses of personal narratives in the social sciences.

JUDITH STACEY is Streisand Professor of Contemporary Gender Studies and professor of sociology at the University of Southern California. She has written extensively on the politics of family change and feminist knowledge. Her publications include *In the Name of the Family: Rethinking Family Values in the Postmodern Age* (1996) and *Brave New Families: Stories of Domestic Upheaval in Late Twentieth Century America* (1990).

BARRIE THORNE is professor of sociology and women's studies at the University of California, Berkeley. She is the author of *Gender Play: Girls and Boys in School* (1993) and coeditor (with Marilyn Yalom) of *Rethinking the Family: Some Feminist Questions* (1990) and *Language, Gender, and Society* (1983). She is currently working on a comparative ethnographic study of childhoods in California communities that vary in social class, race, and ethnic composition and in histories of immigration.

LYNN WEBER is director of women's studies and professor of sociology at the University of South Carolina. She served as director of the Center for Research on Women at the University of Memphis from 1988 to 1994 and associate director from 1982 to 1988. At the University of Memphis, she worked with Elizabeth Higginbotham on a project exploring the background and current status of black and white professional and managerial women. They have produced several publications from this work. She is also coauthor (with Reeve Vanneman) of *The American Perception of Class* (1987). She is currently writing a book on the intersections of race, class, gender, and sexuality.

# Index